POESYGRAPHIA
The Secret Science and Sacred Soul of Poetry

POESYGRAPHIA

The Secret Science and Sacred Soul of Poetry

Dr. Santosh Kumar Nayak

Assistant Professor & Head, O.E.S.-I
P.G. Department of Odia
Fakir Mohan Autonomous College,
Balasore, Odisha, India

BLACK EAGLE BOOKS
Dublin, USA | Bhubaneswar, India

Black Eagle Books
USA address:
7464 Wisdom Lane
Dublin, OH 43016

India address:
E/312, Trident Galaxy, Kalinga Nagar,
Bhubaneswar-751003, Odisha, India

E-mail: info@blackeaglebooks.org
Website: www.blackeaglebooks.org

First International Edition Published by
Black Eagle Books, 2025

POESYGRAPHIA
by **Dr. Santosh Kumar Nayak**

Cover & Interior Design: Ezy's Publication

ISBN- 978-1-64560-754-0 (Paperback)

Printed in the United States of America

To

The Eternal Poet

&

Poetry

Prefix

Poetry is the symphony of the signifier, the cartography of the soul, the Odyssey of the word, the pulse of soul, the vibration of bones, the layers of spirit, the echoes of eternity, the mysteries of murmurs, the whispering void and the eternal *echoflux*. In short, poetry is the *Lyra Veritas*. Poetry is the whisper of what words cannot wholly say yet must somehow speak. It is the eternity echoing through the fleeting frame of language, the paradox that what is most present is often most elusive, the silence discovering its own secret song, the fire concealed within the frost of thought, the mystery wearing the mask of metaphor, the truth trembling into form through fragile syllables, the strange shining that shadows gift to vision, the breath borrowed from the boundless to bless the bounded, the chaos chiseled into cadence and clarity, the infinity compressed into the instant of an image, the language that lends voice to the limitless, the song sung by stillness when silence listens, the mirror where many faces of being behold themselves, the dream draped delicately in diction, the reason reasoning beyond reason through riddles, the paradox blossoming like petals upon the page, the unspeakable speaking through subtle signs, time turned into touchable texture, the wound weaving itself into wonder, the flame that flickers fiercest in the infinite, the music made from what cannot mean yet always matters, the infinity arriving as intimacy, the chaos crowned briefly with the diadem of clarity, the dream dwelling delicately in dust-made flesh, the stillness stirred into sound, the forever made fragile in the frame of a phrase, the longing lit into language, the mystic mathematics of meaning beyond measure, the scar sanctified into scripture, the paradox painted in the pulse of perception, the dream that dares to die into diction, the infinity appearing in fractured fragments, the sacred stammer of spirit seeking speech, the whirlwind that whirls wonder into words, the eternal momentarily embodied in the ephemeral, the symphony of silence that secretly conducts, the forever left unfinished in every finished poem, the truth touched tenderly by tears, the awe still glowing in its ashes, the logic illuminated by its own undoing, the breath between beginning and being, the word that transcends words by being wordless, the time tricked tenderly into permanence, the shadows finding a tongue in twilight, the soliloquy of the soul to itself, the mirror mystery which makes for mankind, the shout shouted silently yet heard profoundly, the beauty broken open to reveal its burning, the paradox parabled into perception, the flame memory fans while forgetting, the truth tangled tenderly in tropes, the mystery moving in measured music, the ruin radiating with revelation, the breath becoming being by being breathed, the eternity enfolded into ephemeral utterance, the boundless binding itself to beauty, the illusion illuminated until it reveals truth, the simplicity sanctified into song, the whispers woven into the web of wonder, the beauty born through breaking, infinity interrupting finitude with feeling, emptiness echoing into expression, eternity's errand carried out in time and the silence sanctified in syllables. Poetry is flame fractured yet never extinguished, the paradox pulsing in perception, the truth trembling to be told, the light lost only to be found in language, the enigma engraved in echoes, the labyrinth where language lives and loses itself, the beauty bound in brevity, the speech stripped into speechlessness, the parable pulsing with paradox, the whisper wounds weave into wisdom, the eternity echoing endlessly in ephemera, the storm silence secretly stores, forever fragmented yet familiar. Poetry is infinitely unfolding intention, the distance becoming nearness through diction, the sacred shard shining from the shattered whole, the flame fleeting yet forever felt, the dreams drawn delicately from dust, the mystery mirrored in metaphor, the transcendence tangled in time, the scarcity shimmering with the sublime, the paradox perfumed in petals, the infinite interval between word and world, the silence sculpted into syllables. Poetry is fragrance left by what is forgotten. Poetry is song shattered yet still singing. It is the vision veiled only to reveal, the frame that fathoms the unfathomable. Poetry is the cipher celestial silence sends. It is the lament lifted into living light, the mystery measured musically, eternity smoldering in embers of expression, the word wandering toward wisdom, the vein where the void vibrates with voice, secret script the soul scribbles in silence.

Prelude to Poetry

Poetry is the oldest orphan of the universe and the youngest child of creation. It is the language before language, the silence after speech, the shimmering shadow of thought that both betrays and beautifies the mind that conceives it. Poetry is paradox pronounced, contradiction crystallized, chaos carved into cadence, infinity imprisoned in an instant. To write of poetry is already to trespass its territory, for poetry prefers suggestion to statement, whisper to declaration, ambiguity to certainty. Yet to remain silent is to starve the spirit, for poetry is not only the ornament of existence but the organ of survival, the very breath that keeps the soul from suffocating in the smoke of banality.

Poetry is both mirror and mirage. It mirrors what we see yet magnifies what we do not. It is the mirage that recedes as we approach, and yet in its retreat, it reveals an oasis of meaning that mere reason never maps. It is at once finite and infinite, fragile and firm, immediate and eternal. To speak of poetry is to speak of the soul's most dangerous desire: the desire to speak the unspeakable.

The essence of poetry lies not in what it says but in what it refuses to say. Every poem is a wound that will not close, and yet in its very bleeding it heals. Poetry is the scar that shines brighter than the skin unbroken. It is the laughter of loss, the celebration of sorrow, the music of silence. The poem does not solve the mystery of life; it sanctifies it. It does not explain existence; it enchants it.

Good poetry always carries with it its problems, and its problems are its powers. To write is to wrestle: with words that resist, with meanings that multiply, with silence that suffocates the sentence. The poet must decide between clarity and obscurity, between the naked truth and the veiled vision, between speaking to the crowd and whispering to the cosmos. Every line is a battlefield where beauty contends with banality, where emotion contends with intellect, where memory contends with imagination. These problems are not obstacles but opportunities, for poetry without paradox is prose, and poetry without problem is platitude.

And yet, in spite of its problems—or perhaps because of them—the essence of poetry is its endurance. Long after empires crumble, it is not the law but the lyric that lingers; not the stone monuments but the fragile syllables survive. The pyramids stand mute, but the Psalms still sing.

The marble cracks, but Homer's hexameters haunt us still. Poetry outlives its makers because it outlives mortality. It is the only art that feeds on the flesh of time and yet grows younger as it ages.

The dimensions of poetry are as many as the dimensions of existence itself. Poetry is linguistic, shaping the shimmer of syllables into the shape of sense. Poetry is aesthetic, arranging words as painters arrange colors, sculptors arrange stone, musicians arrange notes. Poetry is emotional, plunging into the depths of joy and despair where prose dares not drown. Poetry is philosophical, probing the riddles of reality with metaphors sharper than logic. Poetry is political, resisting oppression and raising the banner of the voiceless. Poetry is spiritual, stitching the finite fragment to the infinite whole. Poetry is psychological, illuminating the shadows of the self, translating the language of dreams. Poetry is universal, carrying the accents of one tongue into the understanding of another, weaving webs of resonance across time and culture.

Poetry is not what is written but what is awakened. A poem unread is a potential, but a poem remembered is resurrection. It is not in the ink but in the echo, not in the paper but in the pulse it quickens, not in the rhyme but in the resonance. A poem does not belong to the poet but to the reader, and not even to the reader but to the silence that sings between the lines.

To call poetry useless is to call air unnecessary; to call poetry ornamental is to call fire decorative. Poetry does not merely describe life; it delivers it. It does not escape reality; it engraves it. It does not distract from death; it dialogues with it, and in so doing, it defies it. Poetry teaches us that meaning is not manufactured but manifested, not constructed but conjured, not given but glimpsed.

This book is not merely about poetry; it is itself a poem written in prose, a hymn disguised as history, a meditation masquerading as analysis. It will explore the problems of poetry not to solve them but to sanctify them, the essence of poetry not to define it but to deepen it, the dimensions of poetry not to categorize but to celebrate.

For poetry, is not a thing—it is a way. It is not a product—it is a pilgrimage. It is not a text—it is a testament. To write of poetry is to confess our longing for what exceeds us, our yearning for what evades us, our hunger for what humbles us. It is to admit that we are creatures of contradiction who can only be cured by contradictions. Poetry is our paradoxical cure: it wounds us into wonder and heals us into humility.

Invocation of Poetry: The origin and the oracle

Poetry begins before the beginning. It is the breath before breath, the hush before history, the silence before sound. It is the first cry of the child and the last sigh of the dying, the eternal echo that exists between origin and oblivion. When the world was wordless, poetry was already waiting; when the cosmos was chaos, poetry was already cadence; when time itself had not yet learned to turn, poetry had already begun to sing in silence.

Poetry is not invention but invocation. It is not the artifice of artistry but the arrival of an ancient force, older than ink, older than alphabet, older even than memory. It is the music hidden in matter, the murmur of the mysterious, the rhythm resonant in the very roots of reality. To write poetry is not to create but to call, not to fabricate but to find, not to manufacture but to manifest. Every poet is less a maker than a medium, less a creator than a channel, less a sovereign than a servant of something larger than the self.

Poetry is the alphabet of awe, the lexicon of longing,

the syllables of the soul. It is language elevated to its most luminous state, speech sanctified into song, sound sculpted into something that exceeds itself. While prose informs, poetry transforms; while prose communicates, poetry consecrates. A poem is not merely composed—it is consecrated, christened by silence, baptized in mystery.

Poetry is paradox embodied. It speaks by not speaking, reveals by concealing, defines by defying definition. It is the union of opposites: silence singing, shadows shining, absence appearing, wounds weaving wonder. It is at once infinite and intimate, cosmic and microscopic, eternal and ephemeral. To speak of poetry is already to stumble into contradiction, for poetry refuses reduction, evades explanation, resists all cages of concept. And yet, in that refusal, it reveals its richest essence: poetry is that which cannot be contained, and yet contains us.

Every civilization has carved its culture not in stone but in song. Empires crumble, but epics endure. Thrones topple, but lyrics linger. The ruins of Babylon are buried in sand, but the words of Gilgamesh still breathe. The palaces of Greece have perished, but Homer's hexameters still haunt our hearing. The battles of the Mahabharata have long been fought and forgotten, yet its verses still vibrate in the veins of a billion souls. Poetry survives what politics cannot, sanctifies what science cannot, sings what silence cannot.

Why? It is because poetry is not content but consciousness. It is not simply arranged words but awakened worlds. A poem is not what lies upon the page but what rises within the reader. It is not the ink but the incantation, not the letters but the life they kindle. Poetry is never finished, for its true completion occurs only in the breath of the beholder, in the echo of the listener, in the memory of the mind that dares to dwell with it. A poem lives only when it is lived.

Poetry is both mirror and lamp. As mirror, it reflects the world in strange, shimmering angles, allowing us to see what we had never seen, to face what we had feared to face. As lamp, it lights the darkness of being, offering a fragile but fierce flame in the cavern of our confusion. The mirror may wound, the lamp may blind, but without them we walk in ignorance. Poetry dares to make us see, dares to make us feel, dares to make us alive.

It is not accidental that the ancients gave poets prophetic power. The prophet and the poet share a sacred task: to utter what others cannot, to unveil what others will not, to speak not only to the present but to eternity. The poet is both seer and singer, visionary and vessel. What philosophy analyzes, poetry announces. What theology proclaims, poetry prophesies. What science discovers, poetry dreams.

And yet, poetry is profoundly human. It is not merely divine revelation but human revelation—born of love and loss, desire and despair, ecstasy and exile. A poem is the cry of the lover, the lament of the mourner, the laughter of the drunkard, the prayer of the penitent, the whisper of the wanderer. It carries in its cadence the weight of human tears and the lightness of human laughter. Every poem is a testament: I was alive, I felt, I dreamed, I dared to speak.

Thus, let this book begin where all books should begin: in praise of poetry, in invocation of its infinite intimacy, in acknowledgment of its paradoxical power. For poetry is not peripheral but primal; not decorative but definitive; not an ornament of language but the origin of meaning itself. Without poetry, language would be mere noise, thought would be barren, life would be silent. With poetry, the world becomes a woven wonder, a trembling tapestry of sound and sense, silence and song.

This preface, therefore, is not an introduction but an initiation. It is not the prelude to poetry but poetry itself in prelude. It is the threshold where reader and writer meet, where silence and speech entwine, where paradox becomes possibility. To enter this book is to enter not a text but a temple, not an argument but an anthem, not an explanation but an enchantment.

For poetry is not merely about life—it is life itself, intensified. Poetry is not about truth—it is truth transfigured. Poetry is not about beauty—it is beauty broken open, bleeding, burning, becoming. Poetry is not the language of literature alone; it is the language of existence, the grammar of the cosmos, the scripture of the soul. Poetry is paradox personified, essence embodied, dimension discovered. Poetry is the origin, the oracle, and the ongoing. Poetry is the invocation of all invocations—the prayer that predates religion, the philosophy that predates reason, the song that predates speech.

The Paradox of the Poetic: The unsayable said

Poetry is the riddle that refuses resolution, the equation that balances by unbalancing, the paradox that proclaims its truth precisely through its contradiction. To speak of poetry is already to be caught in its web of opposites: it is clarity carved out of confusion, and confusion concealed within clarity; it is silence speaking, and speech silenced; it is the most intimate revelation and the most impersonal mystery.

Every poem is a paradox in practice. It tells us that what cannot be said can still be sung, that what cannot be captured can still be conjured, that what escapes sense may yet embrace meaning. In this lies both its danger and its divinity: the poem does not explain—it enchants; it does not argue—it awakens; it does not define—it defies. And in defiance, it delivers us to a deeper dimension of being.

Consider the paradox of permanence and perishability. A poem is born in a moment, in the fragile breath of a single instant, in the fleeting flicker of thought or feeling. Yet that moment, crystallized in cadence, becomes immortal. The ink dries, but the utterance never dies. Words that once belonged to the poet now belong to centuries; what was once a whisper becomes a witness, what was once a sigh becomes scripture. The paradox of poetry is that it captures the most transient and makes it timeless.

Consider also the paradox of self and universality. Every poem is born of a particular heart, a personal hunger, a private grief or joy. Yet in its very intimacy, it becomes infinite; in its deepest subjectivity, it becomes universal. The poet who writes of their own sorrow writes for all who have sorrowed; the poet who celebrates a single kiss celebrates the kiss of creation itself. Thus, poetry is the most individual act that births the most communal resonance.

There is also the paradox of sound and silence. Poetry is made of words, yet it is what words cannot say that makes poetry. It is composed of sound, yet silence is its secret scaffolding. The pauses, the breaks, the white spaces around the ink—all are part of the poem's power. What is not written resounds as loudly as what is. A poem is the speech of silence and the silence of speech, a dialogue between absence and presence.

What of the paradox of meaning and meaninglessness? A poem must mean more than itself, but it must also mean less than itself. Too much clarity, and it becomes mere communication; too much obscurity, and it collapses into incoherence. Poetry dances in the dangerous interval between sense and nonsense, logic and lunacy, lucidity and labyrinth. It makes meaning not by pinning it down, but by letting it hover, shimmer, shift—like a flame that illuminates precisely because it flickers.

Perhaps the deepest paradox is this: poetry is utterly useless, and yet utterly indispensable. It cannot build bridges, cure diseases, or govern nations. It feeds no body, clothes no child, houses no homeless. And yet, without it, bridges collapse into banality, medicine withers into mechanics, politics decays into tyranny. For what nourishes the body without poetry starves the soul; what houses the flesh without poetry leaves the heart homeless. Poetry does not save lives, but it makes life worth saving. It is the most useless and the most necessary of all human endeavors.

This paradoxical nature of poetry is not a weakness but its essence. The poem thrives on tension, lives on contradiction, breathes through ambiguity. Remove paradox, and poetry perishes. It is in the play of opposites that poetry finds its power: joy articulated through sorrow, beauty born from brokenness, truth told through trembling, eternity glimpsed in an instant. Poetry does not resolve paradox; it reveals it as the very fabric of existence.

The poet, then, is a paradoxical figure as well. The poet must be both proud and humble, visionary and blind, solitary and communal, disciplined and delirious. The poet must labor with craft and surrender to inspiration, control the word yet be controlled by it. To write a poem is to lose oneself in order to find oneself, to surrender mastery in order to gain it, to fall into chaos in order to carve cadence.

Thus, poetry is not the avoidance of paradox but its embrace. It does not fear contradiction—it flourishes within it. The poem teaches us that truth is not a single point but a pulsation, not a fixed formula but a fluid flame. It shows us that reality itself is paradoxical: life ends in death, yet death gives meaning to life; time devours all, yet through time eternity is glimpsed; love wounds the heart, yet through wounding we are made whole.

To read poetry is to be invited into this paradoxical dance. The reader, like the poet, must learn to linger in ambiguity, to delight in doubleness, to live without closure. To read well is not to decode but to dwell, not to solve but to savor, not to master but to be mastered. A poem is not a puzzle to be solved but a paradox to be sustained.

And so, in this book, we must celebrate paradox not as a problem to be eliminated but as the essence of the poetic. To embrace poetry is to embrace contradiction as the very condition of truth. The poem proclaims: clarity is concealed in confusion, eternity is etched in the ephemeral, the unsayable is spoken in silence, and the useless is the most necessary of all.

In its paradox, poetry reveals what prose cannot: that life itself is a paradox. We live to die, and die to give meaning to life. We long for permanence in a world of flux, for unity in a world of fragments, for infinity in the finite. Poetry is the one human endeavor that does not deny this paradox but dignifies it, does not flee it but flourishes within it.

Thus, let us honor poetry as paradox incarnate. Let us celebrate it as the sacred contradiction that sanctifies existence, the shimmering mystery that makes the meaningless meaningful, the fragile flame that refuses to be extinguished. Poetry is not paradoxical by accident—it is paradox by essence. And in that essence lies its eternal power.

The Problems of Poetry: Tensions that sustain its greatness

Poetry is not only promise and possibility; it is also problem and peril. Every great poem is born not out of ease but out of difficulty, not out of certainty but out of struggle. The poet must wrestle with words as Jacob wrestled with the angel, refusing to let go until blessing emerges, refusing to surrender until cadence becomes revelation. In this wrestling lie the problems of poetry, and in these problems lie its power.

The first problem is the problem of expression and the inexpressible. How can the infinite be captured in the cage of the finite? How can eternity be compressed into syllables? How can the vastness of grief, the immensity of love, the abyss of despair, or the ecstasy of wonder be written in the fragile alphabet of human speech? Words fracture; meaning leaks; silence sneers at speech. And yet, paradoxically, it is in this very insufficiency that poetry thrives. Because it cannot fully express, it teaches us to listen to what lingers unsaid. Because it cannot complete meaning, it invites us into mystery. The problem of language becomes the very essence of lyric.

The second problem is the problem of originality and tradition. Every poet stands in a hall crowded with ancestors. The metaphors of stars, rivers, roses, and fire have been written by countless hands across centuries. To speak freshly is nearly impossible, and yet the task of poetry is precisely to renew the ancient image, to polish the familiar until it gleams anew. The problem is not to create ex nihilo but to re-create from the ruins, to breathe novelty into the lungs of tradition. Every good poem balances between homage and heresy, between reverence for the past and rebellion against it.

The third problem is the problem of clarity and obscurity. Too clear, and the poem collapses into prose; too obscure, and it evaporates into nonsense. Poetry must hover between intelligibility and enigma, lucid yet luminous, suggestive yet sufficient. It must reveal without exhausting, conceal without confusing. This tension is not a weakness but a wonder: a good poem is understood enough to move us, yet mysterious enough to haunt us.

The fourth problem is the problem of universality and particularity. Poetry emerges from one heart, one voice, one experience. Yet if it remains locked in that individuality, it becomes mere diary, private murmur. To be poetry, it must transcend the self, touching the shared pulse of humanity. And yet, paradoxically, it achieves universality precisely through its particularity. The more deeply a poet dares to dwell in their own pain, the more it resonates with the hidden pain of others. The poem that dares to be radically personal becomes, paradoxically, radically universal.

The fifth problem is the problem of sound and sense. Should poetry privilege music or meaning? A poem that dazzles with rhythm but says nothing risks becoming hollow song; a poem rich in meaning but barren in sound risks falling flat. True poetry must wed sense and sound so deeply that they become inseparable: the rhythm becomes revelation, and the meaning becomes music. This union is always precarious, always difficult, and yet it is precisely in navigating this tension that poetry achieves its power.

The sixth problem is the problem of emotion and intellect. Poetry must move the heart without surrendering the mind, must sharpen thought without dulling feeling. Too sentimental, and it becomes melodrama; too cerebral, and it becomes sterile philosophy. Good poetry fuses passion with perception, feeling with form, affect with insight. It makes us cry and think in the same breath.

The seventh problem is the problem of permanence and impermanence. A poem is born in a moment of inspiration—a fleeting spark, a sudden surge, a trembling epiphany. But the poem must live beyond that moment, must endure through time. Inspiration is instantaneous; craft is continuous. The poet must preserve the spark without extinguishing it, must polish the flame without freezing it into mere ash. This is a problem of balance: to honor the lightning of inspiration while also shaping it into lasting light.

The eighth problem is the problem of the poet and the public. Should a poem speak to the few or the many, to the scholar or the shepherd, to the solitary soul or to the collective conscience? A poem written only for the elite risks irrelevance where a poem written only for the masses risks dilution. The poet must balance between accessibility and profundity, between clarity for the crowd and depth for the devoted.

Yet perhaps the greatest problem of poetry is that it can never finish itself. Every poem is incomplete. The poet may end the line, but the silence beyond it continues the meaning. The reader completes what the poet cannot. Thus, the problem of poetry is also the problem of existence itself: it is never finished, never final, never closed. And this incompleteness, this perpetual openness, is not a flaw but the very condition of life.

Poetry is problem incarnate—and this is its gift. For it teaches us to live with ambiguity, to dwell in difficulty, to embrace contradictions without collapsing into despair. It teaches us that truth is not a final answer but a fertile tension, not a solution but a sustaining struggle. The problems of poetry mirror the problems of being human, and in wrestling with them, poetry becomes our teacher.

Thus, the problems of poetry are not obstacles but offerings. They remind us that language is limited but luminous, that originality is impossible yet inevitable, that clarity and obscurity must kiss, that the personal is the portal to the universal, that music and meaning must merge, that feeling and thought must fuse, that inspiration and craft must conspire, that the poet must write for both self and society, that no poem is ever truly complete.

Poetry survives because of its problems, not in spite of them. For life itself is problematic: we long for permanence in impermanence, unity in fragmentation, meaning in chaos. Poetry, in mirroring these tensions, sanctifies them. It does not resolve but redeems, does not cure but consecrates. Its problems are our problems, and in naming them, it names us.

The Essence of the Eternal: Why poetry survives and transcends

Poetry is the art of the instant that aspires to eternity. It begins in the fragile flicker of a moment—the hush of dawn, the tremor of a touch, the ache of loss, the surge of ecstasy—but it does not end there. That moment, once caught in cadence, escapes its own ephemerality. Through the alchemy of language, the fleeting becomes the forever. This is the essence of the eternal: the poem's power to preserve what time would otherwise devour.

What grants poetry this endurance? Not marble monuments, not mechanical memory, not the might of empires—but rhythm, resonance, remembrance. Empires fall, monuments crumble, dynasties dissolve, but a stanza lingers like a spirit, refusing erasure. Poetry is the survivor of civilizations, the residue of ruins, the immortal ember in the ashes of history. The armies of conquerors may scatter, but the song of a shepherd may still be sung.

The essence of the eternal in poetry lies first in its capacity to crystallize experience. A life is long, a day is dense, a moment is fleeting—but a poem condenses existence into essence. It compresses the chaos of being into a clarity that survives beyond circumstance. In a single sonnet, Shakespeare distilled desire and despair so precisely that centuries of lovers still recognize themselves in his lines. In a few verses, Kalidasa caught the monsoon's majesty so fully that even modern monsoons still seem to echo his metaphors. The eternal is born of condensation: the infinite folded into the finite, the vastness of life distilled into verbal diamonds.

The eternal also emerges through rhythm and recurrence. Prose may perish with its context, but poetry pulses with patterns that outlive their moment. Rhythm is memory's ally; repetition is remembrance's root. A melody clings to the mind long after meaning fades. Even when the language of a poem grows alien, its rhythm still resonates. The heartbeat of the line endures beyond translation, beyond culture, beyond time. The essence of the eternal, then, is not only in what poetry says but in how it sings.

The eternal also thrives in poetry's capacity to connect across centuries. A poem is not locked to its author or its era; it is always unfinished, always awaiting a reader. When we read a verse written hundreds of years ago, we are not merely encountering a relic; we are entering into communion. The poet's pulse beats within us, and our own breath animates the words anew. The poem is timeless not because it escapes history, but because it binds histories together. It creates a continuity of consciousness across ages. The reader becomes the resurrection of the writer.

And yet, paradoxically, poetry's eternity does not lie in its resistance to change but in its openness to it. Each reading renews the poem, each era reinterprets it, each reader remakes it. The eternal essence of poetry is not frozen permanence but fluid resilience. A poem does not remain the same by staying unchanged; it remains alive by continually changing in the hands of its readers. Eternity in poetry is not stasis but metamorphosis.

The essence of the eternal also lies in poetry's capacity to touch what transcends time: truth, beauty, love, death, divinity. These are not passing fashions but permanent features of existence. Philosophies may shift, sciences may evolve, societies may crumble, but the soul's hungers remain. The thirst for meaning, the ache for beauty, the fear of death, the longing for love—these are eternal, and poetry is their eternal echo. A good poem speaks not only to its moment but to the human condition itself, which transcends all moments.

But perhaps the deepest secret of the eternal in poetry is this: it does not abolish death, but it dignifies it. It does not cancel loss, but it consecrates it. It does not stop time, but it sanctifies its passing. Eternity in poetry is not the denial of impermanence but its transformation. The poem whispers: though all must pass, nothing is wasted; though everything ends, nothing is meaningless. The rose will wither, but the word "rose" will bloom forever.

Thus, poetry teaches us a paradox: eternity is not beyond time but within it. The eternal is not elsewhere, but here, in the fragile moment redeemed by rhythm, in the fleeting sigh preserved by song, in the transient tear transfigured into text. To read poetry is to glimpse the eternal not as distant heaven but as immanent here-ness, the forever folded into the now.

This is why poetry has always been considered sacred. Not because it belongs to temples, but because it touches timelessness. Every true poem is a psalm, every stanza a shrine, every rhythm a ritual. The eternal essence of poetry is that it consecrates the ordinary, transforming the mundane into the miraculous. A loaf of bread, a flight of birds, a child's laughter—all become luminous when placed in the chalice of the poem.

The essence of the eternal, then, is not an abstraction but an act: the act of distilling, of preserving, of consecrating. Poetry makes memory immortal, meaning inexhaustible, beauty indestructible. It makes the fragile flame of human life burn inextinguishably across centuries. It refuses oblivion, resists erasure, rebels against nothingness.

To write a poem is to defy death. To read a poem is to participate in resurrection. This is the essence of the eternal: the word made immortal, the moment made monumental, the fleeting made forever.

The Dimensions of Dream and the Divine in Poetry: Language, beauty, time, culture, spirit

Poetry is not only aesthetic utterance; it is also sacred invocation. From its earliest origins, poetry has been entwined with prayer, prophecy, and praise. Before it was written, it was chanted; before it was entertainment, it was enchantment; before it was art, it was altar. In every culture, the first poets were also priests, prophets, shamans, sages—the custodians of language who used rhythm as ritual, metaphor as mediation, and song as sacrament. Poetry has always borne the breath of the divine.

The divine in poetry is not confined to doctrine, creed, or cult. It is larger than religion, older than theology, deeper than dogma. It is the awe that trembles in the presence of mystery, the reverence that rises before beauty, the humility that bows before truth. Poetry is divine not because it worships a god but because it awakens the godlike within us. It does not always name the divine, but it always touches it—sometimes as whisper, sometimes as wound, sometimes as wonder.

The first dimension of the divine in poetry is its capacity for creation. In sacred traditions across the world, creation begins with speech: "In the beginning was the Word." To name is to make, to utter is to usher into being. Poetry participates in this primal power. A poet does not merely describe reality; the poet re-creates it. Words do not passively mirror the world—they mold it, they make it matter. In every poem, the divine act of creation is repeated in miniature: a world is born from the breath of language.

The second dimension of the divine is revelation. The poem does not only make; it also unveils. It reveals what was hidden, articulates what was unsaid, illuminates what was obscure. The poet is not only craftsman but conduit, channeling voices beyond the self. Many poets have confessed that their best lines felt "given," as though dictated by a muse, whispered by a spirit, granted by grace. This is the divine dimension: the poet receives as much as they create, unveiling truth as if truth itself desired to be spoken.

The third dimension of the divine is transcendence through immanence. Poetry makes the ordinary extraordinary, the mundane miraculous, the finite infinite. A haiku about falling leaves becomes a meditation on mortality; a lyric about a kiss becomes a revelation of eternity. The divine enters not through grand abstractions but through concrete details: the stone, the star, the silence. Poetry teaches us that the infinite is hidden in the intimate, that eternity is folded into every instant.

The fourth dimension of the divine is ecstasy and communion. In the act of writing or reading poetry, the self dissolves. Boundaries blur. The poet feels possessed by something larger; the reader feels joined to something beyond. In this dissolution, poetry becomes sacrament:

it unites us with others, with nature, with truth, with the divine itself. The solitary reader, whispering a line in the midnight silence, participates in communion with all who have ever whispered that line before. Poetry is personal prayer and communal chant at once.

The fifth dimension of the divine is judgment and justice. Prophets spoke in poetry, not prose. Their words were fire, their cadences thunder, their metaphors arrows. Poetry is the tongue of conscience, the trumpet of truth, the thunder against tyranny. In its divine dimension, poetry calls nations to account, awakens societies from slumber, cries out for the oppressed. It is the divine voice of justice echoing through human throats. When prose argues, poetry annuls; when prose persuades, poetry prophesies.

The sixth dimension of the divine is mystery. The divine cannot be defined; it can only be evoked. Poetry, too, thrives on ambiguity, paradox, and silence. A poem is a temple built of words but open to the sky. It frames mystery without resolving it, honors the ineffable by refusing to flatten it. This is why poetry so often resembles prayer: both are acts of reaching without grasping, of speaking without possessing, of naming without enclosing.

The seventh dimension of the divine in poetry is redemption through remembrance. Poetry rescues what would be lost: the faces forgotten, the voices silenced, the loves dissolved by time. To write a poem is to resurrect; to read a poem is to participate in resurrection. In this act of saving, poetry mirrors the divine impulse: to lose nothing, to waste nothing, to redeem even the fleeting. Every poem is a small salvation, a rebellion against oblivion, a refusal of nothingness.

And yet, paradoxically, the divine in poetry is not always serene or consoling. Sometimes it is terrifying, tumultuous, destructive. The divine is not only light but also lightning, not only comfort but also command. Poetry that touches the divine is often dangerous, unsettling, overwhelming. It wounds even as it heals, shatters even as it sanctifies. The divine dimension of poetry is not tame—it is tremor.

Thus, to read poetry is to risk encounter with the divine, however one names it: beauty, truth, mystery, love, justice, eternity. Poetry is divine not because it teaches theology but because it awakens the sacred tremor in the human soul. It makes us kneel in wonder, rise in rebellion, sing in sorrow, weep in joy. It consecrates the world by showing us that nothing is merely mundane.

The dimensions of the divine in poetry are manifold: creation, revelation, transcendence, communion, justice, mystery, redemption. Together they reveal poetry as more than literature—it is liturgy; more than art—it is altar; more than expression—it is epiphany.

To write a poem is to touch the divine; to read a poem is to be touched by it. This is why poetry has always endured, why it remains indispensable: because it does not merely entertain but consecrates, does not merely describe but sanctifies, does not merely speak but summons.

The Qualities of the Quintessential Poetry

What, then, are the qualities that make a poem quintessential—worthy not merely of reading but of reverence, not merely of memory but of immortality? A poem is not great because it exists; it is great because it endures, enlightens, enchants, and enflames. Its greatness lies not in fashion but in foundation, not in novelty but in necessity. The quintessential poem is not simply written; it is woven of qualities that transcend time and taste.

The first quality is condensation without constriction.

The poem must distill the vast into the vivid, the infinite into the intimate, the boundless into the brief. Yet it must do so without suffocating the spirit of the subject. A great poem says much with little, but never too little. It compresses without crushing, condenses without killing, crystallizes without freezing. Its brevity is not barrenness but brilliance.

The second quality is music without monotony. A poem must sing, but its song must surprise. Rhythm is its heartbeat, rhyme its resonance, cadence its current. But if music becomes mechanical, melody becomes mere monotony. The great poem plays with sound as though sound itself were sacred—each syllable shaped, each pause purposeful, each line alive with resonance. It is not prose dressed in ornament, but a song sculpted in silence.

The third quality is clarity without simplicity. A quintessential poem must be graspable without being exhausted, lucid without being literal, accessible without being emptied. It must shine with clarity but shimmer with depth. Like a lake: transparent enough to glimpse the surface fish, yet deep enough to hide unfathomable mysteries. The reader enters with ease but lingers with longing.

The fourth quality is mystery without meaninglessness. Ambiguity is the atmosphere of poetry, but vagueness is its enemy. A poem must invite interpretation but resist reduction; it must provoke thought without paralyzing it, must open questions without abolishing sense. Mystery is not confusion—it is complexity made luminous. The great poem is a riddle with infinite answers, a labyrinth whose walls are mirrors.

The fifth quality is emotion without excess. Poetry must move us; otherwise, it is no more than words arranged. Yet the movement must be measured, the feeling disciplined, the passion tempered by form. A poem that weeps too easily becomes sentimentality; a poem that shouts too loudly becomes rhetoric. The quintessential poem feels deeply but expresses delicately, so that the reader feels not manipulated but magnified.

The sixth quality is thought without sterility. Poetry must think as well as feel, must reflect as well as resonate. A great poem is philosophy embodied in image, wisdom whispered through rhythm. But it must never reduce itself to didactic lecture or lifeless logic. Thought in poetry must be fertile, not formulaic; alive, not abstract. It must breathe through metaphor, pulse through paradox, live through language.

The seventh quality is universality through particularity. The poem must root itself in the soil of the specific, but from that soil must grow a tree whose branches reach every reader. A single rose, described precisely, becomes the symbol of every rose; a single sorrow, rendered honestly, becomes the sorrow of all humanity. The universal is not achieved by generalization but by precision.

The eighth quality is originality without arrogance. The quintessential poem is fresh, but not for the sake of fashion. Its originality arises not from novelty-seeking but from necessity—from the poet's authentic encounter with truth and experience. It speaks as though no one has spoken before, and yet it honors those who have. True originality is not isolation but illumination.

The ninth quality is balance without blandness. Poetry thrives on tensions: between sound and sense, clarity and mystery, emotion and thought, tradition and innovation. The quintessential poem balances these, but never by diluting them. Its harmony is not homogeneity but heightened contrast. Its balance is dynamic, not dull.

The tenth and final quality is transcendence without

escape. A great poem lifts us beyond ourselves, but not away from the world. It offers transcendence through immanence, eternity through the everyday, infinity through the finite. The quintessential poem does not reject life—it redeems it. It does not deny reality—it dignifies it. Its transcendence is not flight but fullness.

When these qualities converge, the poem ceases to be mere words on a page and becomes a world in itself. It becomes a mirror and a window, a temple and a threshold, a song and a silence. It is not a product of literature but a phenomenon of life. The quintessential poem is not judged by critics but justified by centuries, not praised by fashions but preserved by time.

Yet these qualities are not rigid rules; they are resonances. No single poem contains them all perfectly, but every great poem partakes of them in some measure. They are not commandments but characteristics, not laws but longings. They describe not what every poem must be, but what every poem aspires to become.

In the end, the quintessential poem is not defined by form, school, or style. It may be ancient hymn or modern haiku, free verse or strict sonnet, epic or elegy. Its greatness does not lie in its shape but in its spirit, not in its structure but in its soul. The qualities of the quintessential poem are not external ornaments but internal essences.

Thus, the great poem endures because it embodies condensation without constriction, music without monotony, clarity without simplicity, mystery without meaninglessness, emotion without excess, thought without sterility, universality through particularity, originality without arrogance, balance without blandness, and transcendence without escape.

These are not only the qualities of poetry—they are the

qualities of life at its highest. For in truth, the quintessential poem is nothing less than existence distilled, consciousness crystallized, being made beautiful.

The Nature of the Necessary

Poetry is both witness and wonder. Poetry is not a luxury; it is a necessity. Not a decoration, but a deliverance. Not a diversion, but a declaration of existence itself. Civilization may survive without poetry, but humanity cannot. The body may persist, but the soul withers. The world may endure without verse, but meaning evaporates. Poetry is the air we breathe when reason suffocates, the water we drink when desire thirsts, the fire we kindle when indifference freezes. It is not optional—it is obligatory.

The necessity of poetry begins in existential resonance. Life is fleeting, fragile, and fraught with futility. We labor, we love, we lose, we long, and yet we often find life incomprehensible, harsh, and hollow. Poetry offers resonance: a vibration that aligns the inner pulse with the universe's rhythm. It transforms the ordinary into the extraordinary, the trivial into the transcendent, the fleeting into the forever. Without poetry, experience lies dormant; with poetry, it awakens into recognition, reflection, and revelation.

Poetry is necessary because it embodies moral imagination. It teaches empathy, awakens conscience, and enlarges understanding. The poet's gaze pierces the private and the public, the personal and the political. Through poetry, we inhabit lives not our own, feel emotions not our own, confront injustices not our own. A stanza can expose the cruelty of oppression, the arrogance of power, the quiet suffering of the silenced. It makes the invisible visible, the ignored undeniable, the forgotten unforgettable. Poetry is not simply expression—it is ethical encounter.

The necessity of poetry also emerges through temporal transcendence. We live in moments, yet we long for eternity. Time devours all, memory fades, and the present slips swiftly into the past. Poetry arrests this drift. A line written today may resound tomorrow, a metaphor conceived in one century may inspire the next. Poetry bridges mortality and memory, temporal limitation and timeless longing. In this way, it nourishes the human need to matter beyond mere minutes, to leave traces in the tides of time.

Poetry is necessary because it embraces paradox as pedagogy. Life is paradoxical: joy entwines with sorrow, love with loss, birth with death, silence with sound. The poem does not simplify or sanitize; it mirrors complexity. It teaches us to hold opposites simultaneously, to accept ambiguity, to thrive in tension. By guiding us through contradictions, poetry cultivates wisdom: not easy answers, but enduring understanding.

Poetry is also necessary for its capacity to inspire awe. Humans hunger for wonder. The night sky, the ocean, the mountains, the stars—they stir reverence that defies rationality. Poetry amplifies this awe, sculpting language into experience, transforming perception into rapture. A single line may awaken the same trembling of the soul that cosmos itself provokes. Without poetry, wonder diminishes; with poetry, it flourishes, reminding us that life is not only to be lived but to be marveled at.

The necessity of poetry lies further in its power to consolidate consciousness. In the frenzy of modernity, we fragment into distraction, divided among duties, devices, and diversions. Poetry gathers the scattered soul, focuses the fleeting mind, aligns perception with reflection. A single stanza may concentrate an entire lifetime of observation, a single metaphor may condense an ocean of emotion. Poetry restores coherence not by control but by contemplation, not by coercion but by communion.

Poetry is necessary because it transforms suffering into significance. Pain is universal, grief unavoidable, loss inevitable. Yet poetry alchemizes anguish into art, despair into understanding, tragedy into testimony. It teaches that suffering is not annulled but acknowledged, that wounds are not hidden but honored, that absence is not erased but exalted. The poem becomes a vessel for the human condition, a witness to fragility, a sanctuary for sorrow.

Paradoxically, poetry is necessary precisely because it is sometimes ineffable. Its power does not lie in instruction or information, but in sensation, resonance, and revelation. It awakens faculties that prose cannot, stirring not merely intellect but intuition, feeling, imagination, and insight. It reminds us that humans are not only rational beings but also mystical, musical, and mysterious. To ignore poetry is to amputate the soul.

And finally, poetry is necessary because it embodies hope without hubris. In a world of decay, destruction, and despair, poetry insists on possibility. It affirms beauty, sanctifies courage, celebrates creation, and envisions justice. It does not promise a perfect world, but it illuminates the imperfect one, and in doing so, it teaches resilience. Poetry is the hand extended across time and tragedy, the whisper that life is still worth living, the song that reminds us we are still awake.

Thus, the nature of the necessary is the very nature of poetry. To live fully, one must read, write, or feel poetry. To know humanity, one must enter its lines. To endure the passage of time, one must breathe its cadences. Poetry is not luxury, not ornament, not pastime. It is sustenance, structure, and sanctuary. It is as essential as air, as urgent as blood, as inexhaustible as wonder itself.

Eventually it may be advised to read poetry, write poetry, and to live poetry. Let the cadence of your own consciousness meet the cadence of the cosmos. Let the paradoxes of your existence resonate with the paradoxes of the poem. Let the fleeting, the finite, the fragile be made eternal through attention, through articulation, through awe.

Poetry is necessary. It is life intensified, existence ennobled, eternity enacted. It is not indulgence but imperative. And in embracing poetry, we embrace the full, paradoxical, magnificent, and mysterious nature of being itself.

Balasore
Dt. 02.10.2025 **- S.K.N.**

CONTENTS

PULSE OF POETRY

Poetry, *poesis,* is the art of distilling infinity into ink. It is at once the most fragile feather and the fiercest forge; the softest sigh and the sharpest sword. *Verba volant, scripta manent* – words may fly, but written ones remain – and yet in poetry, even permanence trembles, for the written word here is not merely preserved; it breathes, bleeds, blossoms. Poetry is *ars et anima* – art and soul – breathing together. It is the delicate dagger, the velvet volcano, the silent shout. *Ex nihilo,* it conjures cosmos from crumbs, crowns from cobwebs. It is the fleeting flame that freezes, the still storm, the tender tyrant of thought. It walks in *in medias res,* never knocking, never announcing, yet arriving as though it had always been. It is the mirror that multiplies meaning, the echo that invents the voice it repeats. Poetry is *carpe diem* carved in cloud, *memento mori* sung in springtime. It is a language that loves its labyrinths – a silk snare that frees you. It polishes the pebble until it gleams like a galaxy, then hides it in your palm.

It is a paradox of presence: poetry is both the captive of the page and the fugitive of the soul. It sleeps in silence yet speaks louder than the shouts of history. It is *ars longa, vita brevis* – art is long, life short – and yet every true poem makes life longer by deepening it, not in years, but in yes. At its heart, poetry is the music of meaning meeting the rhythm of the unsayable. It marries the measured to the mysterious, the deliberate to the dream. The poet polishes each word until it is as weightless as light, yet as heavy as a heartbeat. It is *carpe diem* whispered with the dignity of eternity. Poetry is the science of suggestion and the sorcery of sound. It courts consonance and alliteration the way dawn courts dew, layering light upon language until the line itself becomes a living thing. Here, the humblest word may wear a crown; here, shadows shine and silence sings. It is *in medias res* — plunging into the middle of the mystery, never needing to begin at the beginning nor end at the end. It is both *sic transit gloria mundi* and its defiance; the passing of glory and the glory of passing. It is the weighted whisper, the roaring ripple, the shadow lit from within. In every stanza, the finite feigns infinity; in every pause, the eternal inhales. Poetry is the architect of awe, the mathematician of metaphor, the priestess of pause. It is the paper palace where every brick is breath. It is *tempus fugit* made to linger, the untranslatable tongue that translates the soul. It is a paradox that purrs: the fragile fortress, the crowned beggar, the loud lullaby. Poetry does not begin — it is already begun. Poetry does not end — it only echoes into the quiet that knows your name.

It is the scholar's scripture and the child's chalk drawing, the philosopher's puzzle and the lover's letter. Poetry polishes the ordinary until it is opal; it drapes the common in coronets. In one line it can contain *sic transit gloria mundi* — thus passes the glory of the world — and in the next, crown the smallest pebble with immortality. Above all, poetry is the one language that lives without translation, even when translated. It survives the loss of literalness because it was never merely literal to begin with. A poem is a compact cathedral: built of breath and brick, of metaphor and mortar. Step inside, and the air changes; step outside, and you are not the same. Poetry is the art of leaving enough unsaid that the silence speaks for itself. It is *ex nihilo* — from nothing — yet it makes something more enduring than monuments. It is the architect of awe, the librarian of longing, the merchant of miracles. In the end — which is always another beginning — poetry is that sweet contradiction: the fleeting eternity, the audible silence, the still movement, the fire made of frost. It asks for nothing but attention, and it gives back the world remade. Poetry is not merely written; it is witnessed. It is not merely read; it is revealed.

The Paradox and Promise of Poetry

Poetry is, at once, the most ancient art and the most ageless. It is the trembling testimony of a tongue touched by truth; the sculptor of silence, the seamstress of sound. It thrives where thought meets throb, where reason weds rhythm, where words wander toward wonder. It is *ars poetica*, the oldest oracle of the human heart, whispering to each generation in accents at once strange and familiar. To define poetry is to walk the knife-edge of paradox. It is the fleeting eternal, the audible hush, the stillness that moves. It is both the alphabet's servant and its sovereign, both prisoner to its metre and master of its meaning. It binds itself to form only to free itself in feeling. The nature of poetry is the nature of perception itself: selective, suggestive, and saturated with possibility. The poet does not merely describe the world; they distill it, decanting oceans into a drop, days into a moment. Poetry does not claim to capture reality; rather, it creates a reality within language, one which the reader inhabits as fully as any landscape of the senses. It is *verba volant, scripta manent* — words fly, writings remain — yet in poetry the words do not merely remain; they rise again, reborn each time they are read. Every poem is a phoenix, perishing and resurrecting with each new breath bestowed upon it by a reader. Poetry's features are as varied as the faces of the moon: sometimes luminous, sometimes shadowed, sometimes a sliver, sometimes a sphere. Yet certain traits remain immutable. Poetry is:

Condensed: the concentrated essence of thought and feeling, where one syllable may bear the weight of a century.

Cadenced: the heartbeat of language made audible; a measured music, even when it shuns rhyme and regularity.

Connotative: words not as labels, but as lanterns — illuminating more than they directly declare.

Contradictory: a coin with infinite sides, where certainty and ambiguity coexist in delicate accord.

Its specialty lies in transforming the trivial into the transcendent. The humblest image — a leaf in rain, a hand on glass, the tilt of a hat — becomes, in poetry, a talisman of truth. Through a subtle sorcery, poetry makes the particular speak for the universal, the ephemeral echo into eternity. Philosophically, poetry is both mirror and lamp: it reflects the world and reveals it anew. Historically, it has been hymn, history, and herald — the preserver of myth, the voice of rebellion, the sanctuary of the soul. Culturally, it serves as both a bond and a bridge, binding communities through shared stories while bridging across borders and centuries. Its prospects are as vast as the human imagination. In an age of accelerated prose and fractured attention, poetry offers the antidote of pause. It reminds us that meaning is not in the quantity of words but in their quality, not in their speed but in their stillness. If the world grows noisier, poetry will only grow more necessary — a place where silence is shaped, where speech is sacred.

The philosophical heart of poetry is this: it insists that meaning is not a static substance but a living movement. It teaches that truth may be told through beauty, that beauty may bear the burden of truth. Poetry is not the opposite of reason but its companion, revealing through intuition what logic alone cannot grasp. It is *tempus fugit* yet *ars longa* — time flies, but art endures — and in that endurance, poetry carries the consciousness of our species like a chalice. It speaks for the living, to the living, and — miraculously — for the dead and the unborn. Poetry is not a luxury; it is a lens. It sharpens the sight, sweetens the spirit, and stretches the soul. It is a paradoxical palace: built of breath, yet more enduring than stone; rooted in the personal, yet reaching into the perennial. Its essence may elude definition, but its effect is undeniable: to awaken, to console, to ignite. In the end, poetry's truest definition may be its simplest paradox: It is the one form of language that says most by speaking least, that lives longest by dying on the tongue, that binds us together by entering us alone. Poetry is not merely written. Poetry is what remains when the writing is gone.

Ontology of Poetry: The Being that Breathes Beyond Being

To speak of poetry's ontology is to speak of that which is not content to be merely a linguistic artifact, yet cannot cease to be anchored in language's lattice. Poetry exists in a realm where being is not a fixed fact but a *fluent flux* — a becoming-being, a perpetually performed presence. It is neither wholly substance nor wholly shadow; it is that shimmering threshold where the tangible trembles into the transcendent. Poetry is, in its most metaphysical manifestation, an ontological oxymoron: the permanent impermanence, the structured spontaneity, the stillness that moves. Its being is *ars et anima,* art and soul, fused into a single sentient form. And yet — and here lies its most intoxicating enigma — it is a being that only exists when reanimated by the breath of another. Without reader or listener, poetry is the dormant deity: complete in itself, yet awaiting invocation.

The poet does not create in the crude sense of conjuring from nothingness (*ex nihilo*), but rather awakens what already slumbers within the abyss of possibility. Poetry, therefore, is not a mere product but a process; it is the act of *poiesis* — the bringing-forth of being from the obscure to the illumined. Its ontology resists reduction because it exists at the juncture where matter meets meaning. Words, in poetry, are not tools but talismans; they are weighted with worlds, vibrating with valences invisible to the prosaic gaze. They do not merely denote; they resonate, reverberate, reincarnate the reality they name.

Epistemology of Poetry: The Knowing that is More than Knowledge

If ontology asks *"what poetry is"*, epistemology asks *"how poetry knows"* — and, in turn, how *"we know through poetry"*. Yet the first paradox that must be acknowledged is this: poetry does not "know" in the way philosophy or science claims to know; it neither constructs syllogisms nor confines itself to the prison-house of propositions. And yet — with a certainty beyond calculation — poetry arrives at truths the purely logical mind cannot even approach. Here we encounter the strange sovereignty of the poetic mind: it is at once the archivist of actuality and the alchemist of the imaginary. Poetry deals in data that are not reducible to decimal or diagram; it traffics in truths that hide themselves from the stark light of literalism. In epistemological terms, poetry refuses to mistake the map for the mountain, the sign for the sublime.

The Paradox of Poetic Knowledge

Poetic knowing is a knowing that knows it does

not know — and therein lies its higher form of certainty. In the economy of intellect, this is the *docta ignorantia,* the learned ignorance, that recognizes that the immeasurable cannot be measured, that the infinite cannot be captured without losing its infinity. Yet poetry does not retreat into the resignation of the unknowable; instead, it advances into the mystery with a strange and smiling courage. It dares to describe the indescribable, not to imprison it in words, but to let it breathe through them. In this sense, poetic knowledge is not acquisition but communion; not possession of truth, but participation in it.

Language as Lens and Veil

Language in its prosaic use often behaves as a lens, clarifying reality by focusing thought. But in poetry, language is both lens and veil — revealing by concealing, clarifying by complicating. The veil is not a defect, but the very condition of the vision. Just as the sun must be softened by atmosphere before the eye can bear it, so must truth be refracted through the prism of poetry before the soul can endure its radiance. Thus, poetry's epistemic method is not the *deductive descent* from premise to conclusion, nor the *inductive climb* from instance to general law; it is an *evocative orbit* around the subject, approaching from a thousand oblique angles until the meaning, like a shy bird, comes to rest upon the reader's shoulder.

Poetry as Mnemonic of the Infinite

One of the most distinctive epistemological functions of poetry is its ability to make the fleeting unforgettable. In the merciless march of *tempus fugit,* poetry arrests an instant and renders it eternal — not by embalming it in static description, but by animating it with perpetual possibility. The moment in a poem is never the moment alone; it is every moment that resembles it, every echo it awakens in memory. In this sense, poetry is a mnemonic of the infinite: a device by which the mind recalls not just an event, but the essence of experience. It is the difference between remembering that something happened, and remembering what it meant. Poetry preserves not merely the fact, but the felt fact — the texture of time as it touched the soul.

The Dialectic of Clarity and Mystery

Poetry's knowledge thrives in a tension — a dialectic — between clarity and mystery. Too much clarity, and the poem dissolves into mere statement; too much mystery, and it becomes unintelligible noise. The genius of the great poet lies in the precise calibration of this balance, in knowing just how much to show and how much to hide. This is the epistemic art of suggestion, where the meaning is never laid bare, but beckons — *veni, vidi, vixi* — "I came, I saw, I lived." The reader becomes not a passive recipient of information but an active participant in discovery. In this co-creative act, poetry becomes a shared space where minds meet without merging, where the distance between self and other is both bridged and preserved.

Truth Beyond the Literal

Perhaps the most radical claim of poetic epistemology is that truth does not always demand literal accuracy. A metaphor may be "false" in the factual sense — no, the moon is not literally a silver coin tossed into a dark ocean — and yet truer than any astronomer's description. Here, poetry asserts that *verisimilitude* — the seeming truth that resonates in the soul — can outrun *veritas* — the documented truth that satisfies the intellect. The philosopher may frown at this, but the poet smiles, knowing that the mind is only one measure of the human totality. To be true in the poetic sense is to be felt as true — to vibrate in harmony with the deepest intuitions of our being.

Axiology of Poetry: The Worth that Words Alone Cannot Weigh

If epistemology concerns itself with the truth of poetry, axiology addresses its worth – not in the paltry, pecuniary sense of price, but in the profound, perennial sense of value. Poetry's worth is not a quantity to be calculated, but a quality to be contemplated. It is both priceless and without price: a treasure whose measure cannot be measured, a gift whose giving multiplies itself without diminishing.

Aesthetic Value: The Beauty that Binds and Breaks

Poetry's aesthetic worth lies not merely in its beauty but in its ability to redefine beauty itself. In the realm of *pulchritudo*, poetry is the restless reformer, forever refusing to let beauty stagnate into cliché. A poem may adorn the sublime with sonorous splendour, but it may also strip beauty to its bare bones, revealing its fragile, fractured face. This is the paradox: poetry beautifies by breaking and breaks by beautifying. It can exalt a moment to celestial grandeur, or it can reveal the ache beneath the ornament, exposing the *memento mori* hidden inside the *carpe diem*. In this aesthetic alchemy, beauty ceases to be mere pleasure for the senses and becomes a provocation for the soul.

Ethical Value: The Moral Imagination

Beyond beauty, poetry possesses an ethical power, not as a sermon, but as a stimulus to the moral imagination. Unlike moral codes that dictate from without, poetry transforms from within, not by prescribing what is right, but by awakening the capacity to feel what is right. A poem, in this ethical sense, is an act of empathy in linguistic form. It is the crafted cry that carries the pain of another into the chambers of one's own consciousness. It teaches us that justice is not an abstraction but a heartbeat, that compassion is not a duty but a delight. And yet, the moral dimension of poetry is never mere propaganda. Poetry that preaches without mystery petrifies; poetry that moralizes without music withers. Its ethical power resides precisely in its refusal to dictate, its trust that truth can be suggested rather than shouted. This is the ethical paradox: poetry moves us most when it moves without coercion.

Existential Value: The Dialogue with Death

Perhaps the deepest stratum of poetry's value is existential. Poetry is the art most attuned to the finitude of life — not as a despair, but as a definition. It acknowledges *sic transit gloria mundi* — "thus passes the glory of the world" — yet transforms this transience into an occasion for intensified living. Every poem is, in a sense, a dialogue with death. It stands as a small defiance against the silence that will one day swallow us all, and yet, paradoxically, it often finds beauty in that very silence. The elegy does not merely mourn the lost; it grants them a second life in language. The love poem does not merely celebrate presence; it anticipates absence and therefore cherishes the now. In this way, poetry is both a shield and a mirror: a shield against oblivion and a mirror of our mortality. It offers no escape from finitude, but it offers a way to face it — not with resignation, but with reverence.

The Value of the Invaluable

In sum, poetry's axiology is the axiology of the invaluable. It is a value that resists commodification, because the moment you attempt to price it, you have already profaned it. Poetry's worth is woven into the fabric of human dignity; it is one of the few arts that can dignify both the palace and the prison, the crowned and the crushed. To say that poetry is necessary is not to say it is useful in the utilitarian sense. Poetry will not till the soil or build the bridge — and yet it tills the soil of the soul, builds the bridge between being and meaning. It is not the bread by which we survive, but it is the wine by which we remember why survival is worth the struggle. Thus, the axiology of poetry is inseparable from its ontology and epistemology: it matters because it is, it matters because it knows, and it matters because it teaches us that matter itself can be transformed into meaning.

Poetic Temporality: The Eternity in the Instant

To speak of poetry without speaking of time is to speak of the sun without its light. Poetry is, in its deepest current, a temporal art — not merely because it unfolds in time when read or recited, but because it reshapes time within the mind. Poetry is the clock that refuses chronology, the calendar that collapses centuries into a single sigh. Where prose often proceeds in linear succession — one event yielding to the next — poetry permits simultaneity. Past, present, and possibility can coexist in a single breath, a single line, a single word. This is its temporal paradox: it can condense years into a moment or expand a moment into an eternity.

The Arrest of the Instant

In a world where *tempus fugit* — time flies — poetry is the art of momentary arrest. The instant, otherwise condemned to pass unnoticed, is here caught, cradled, and crowned. Yet this capture is not a freezing, not the lifeless fixing of a photograph; it is a dynamic preservation, the way a flame preserves motion within stillness. The haiku that holds a falling cherry blossom does not imprison that petal; it allows it to fall forever. In this way, poetry's time is not frozen time, but eternally falling time — a perpetual present in which the past and the possible mingle.

Temporal Elasticity

Poetry's manipulation of time is not limited to arrest;

it stretches and compresses temporal experience with equal ease. A single sonnet may compress the arc of a lifetime, while a single syllable in free verse may seem to stretch into an unmeasured pause. This elasticity arises from poetry's unique economy: by distilling the unnecessary, it grants disproportionate weight to what remains. Here, a second can bear the emotional density of a decade, and a century can pass in the flicker of an image. This is not mere narrative efficiency; it is a metaphysical reframing of what it means to experience time.

The Poem as Temporal Palimpsest

Every poem is also a palimpsest of times — the time of its composition, the times it depicts, and the time of its reading. When a modern reader encounters Homer, they are not merely stepping into an ancient world; they are bringing their own era into dialogue with his. In this way, each poem is continually rewritten in time without altering a single letter. A love lyric from centuries past may acquire political poignancy in the present; a wartime elegy may speak not only to past battles but to present wounds and future fears. Thus, the poem lives in a temporal polyphony, each age adding its own resonance to the same original notes.

Poetry and Eternity

Philosophers have long debated whether eternity is endless time or the absence of time. Poetry, perhaps uniquely, allows us to taste both interpretations. In certain lines, eternity feels like a temporal extension — an unending summer, an everlasting embrace. In others, eternity feels like a moment so full it obliterates succession — the instant so complete it needs no future, the now so whole it makes the next unnecessary. The poet's task, then, is not merely to measure time but to make it meaningful. A poem does not ask, "How long will this last?" but rather, "How deeply can this be lived?" In this way, poetry rescues time from mere quantity and restores it to quality.

Time as Both Enemy and Ally

Poetry's relationship to time is also adversarial. Time erodes monuments, withers roses, silences voices. Yet poetry turns this inevitability into intimacy. The awareness of loss intensifies the joy of possession; the knowledge of mortality sharpens the savor of life. The poem does not deny decay; it dances with it. And here lies the final temporal paradox: poetry is the only art that is at once utterly of its moment and utterly outside of time. It speaks with the accents of its age yet can be understood in any age; it belongs to the instant yet is never outdated.

Poetic Universality and Particularity: The Singular that Speaks for the Sum

Poetry lives in the tension between the utterly individual and the infinitely inclusive. It is the voice of the one that somehow becomes the voice of the many; it is the solitary candle whose light, without losing its intimacy, illuminates a cathedral. A single poem may arise from an afternoon in April, a lone figure by a rain-silvered river, a memory known only to the poet — and yet, through the alchemy of art, this irreducible particular becomes a mirror for countless readers, each seeing their own reflection in its depths. This is poetry's double nature: it is *singularly situated* and *universally resonant*.

The Irreplaceable Detail

The universal does not emerge in poetry through generalities; it emerges precisely through the irreducible detail. The trembling of a sparrow's wing in frost, the angle of sunlight on a worn windowsill, the sound of one name whispered into darkness — these are not abstractions. They are events so specific they could belong to no one else. Yet, paradoxically, it is through this specificity that the universal is revealed. The more minutely the poet attends to the real, the more readily the reader finds themselves within it. Abstraction often alienates; precision invites participation. The truth of the human condition is rarely found in general formulas; it resides in the concrete moments that echo far beyond themselves.

The Universal in the Unrepeatable

This is the central paradox of poetic universality: the unrepeatable becomes the endlessly repeated. A sonnet written for one beloved centuries ago may be read by a stranger on another continent and feel as if it were written that morning for them alone. The words have not changed, but their address has multiplied, expanding to embrace readers the poet could never have known. In this sense, every great poem is both a private letter and a public proclamation — a message sealed for one yet somehow opened by all.

Multiplicity without Dilution

One of poetry's most remarkable feats is its ability to hold multiple meanings without diminishing any of them. In prose, too much ambiguity risks incoherence; in poetry, ambiguity can become abundance. The same metaphor may carry one resonance for a grieving reader, another for a joyful one, and still another for a scholar tracing its lineage — all without conflict. Thus, poetry's universality does not come from narrowing its meaning to what all can agree upon, but from widening its resonance so that each can find what they need within it. This is universality not by consensus, but by capaciousness.

The Local as Gateway to the Global

A great poem is rooted in its own soil yet reaches

across frontiers. It carries the accent of its birthplace, the scent of its seasons, the contour of its landscape — yet these local elements become portals, not barriers. The cherry blossoms of Japan can speak to the withering roses of Spain; the snowfields of a Nordic winter can move the heart of a desert-dweller. The paradox here is that universality emerges not in spite of locality, but because of it. The more rooted a poem is in the rich loam of its own world, the more fruitfully it can nourish those in worlds far away.

One Voice, Many Echoes

When we read a poem, we encounter the mind of another — and yet, in that encounter, we often discover our own thoughts clarified, deepened, or even made for the first time. The poet's voice becomes a vessel for our own unspoken language; their metaphors become scaffolding for our own meanings. This is why poetry never truly belongs to the poet once it is written: it becomes part of a shared lexicon of feeling. And yet, the singularity of the poet's vision remains intact, preserved like a seed that can grow into infinitely varied flowers in the gardens of other minds.

Prospects of Poetry in Future Civilizations: The Immutable Muse in the Mutable World

To speak of poetry's future is to engage in a speculation both perilous and promising. The world into which poetry will step is one of accelerating change, a world where technologies multiply faster than traditions can contain them, where information spreads with the speed of thought yet often with less than a fraction of its depth. And yet, in such a world — perhaps especially in such a world — poetry will not perish; it will persist, adapt, and even ascend. For poetry's permanence does not reside in any single form or format; it resides in its capacity to satisfy a perennial human hunger: the hunger for language that lives, lingers, and illuminates.

The Endurance of the Essential

Civilizations may change their architectures, economies, and even their alphabets, but the conditions that give birth to poetry are woven into human consciousness itself. As long as we love, lose, wonder, and weep, there will be need for the form of speech that can hold such intensities without dilution. The digital age may diminish attention spans, but poetry thrives precisely because it condenses — because it can deliver the density of a lifetime in the brevity of a breath. In this sense, poetry may become not less relevant but more, serving as a counterpoint to the endless scroll of the disposable.

The Shape-Shifting of Form

In future civilizations, poetry's prospects lie not in clinging to its past shapes but in shape-shifting without surrendering its essence. It has already proven its adaptability: the epic gave way to the sonnet, the sonnet to free verse, the page to the performance stage, the stage to the screen. It can inhabit any vessel — parchment, print, pixel — without losing its soul. One can imagine future poets composing in augmented reality, where lines are not just read but walked through; or in neural-linked verse, where the rhythm of thought itself becomes the meter. Yet even in such forms, the core remains: the shaping of sound and sense into a structure that surpasses statement.

Poetry as Resistance

If the future is one of surveillance, saturation, and the supremacy of the algorithm, poetry will endure as an act of resistance. Algorithms prize predictability; poetry thrives on surprise. Systems seek efficiency; poetry savors excess. Markets value reproducibility; poetry values the unrepeatable. In such a future, poetry will be the quiet rebellion — the art that refuses to be reduced to data points, that resists compression into a single "meaning" without losing its multiplicity. In this sense, every poem will be both a work of beauty and an act of defiance.

The Global Intermingling of Imagery

As borders blur and cultures collide in the crucible of globalization, the metaphors and myths of one tradition will increasingly mingle with those of another. The future poet will draw as easily from African proverbs as from Japanese haiku, from ancient Sumerian laments as from hypermodern slang. This cross-pollination will not dilute but deepen the universal vocabulary of verse. In such a world, the poem may become one of the last refuges where complexity is celebrated rather than simplified, where contradictions are not erased but embraced.

Poetry and the Post-Human

A more speculative question: what place will poetry hold in a post-human age, when artificial intelligence may write as fluently as any mortal? The answer lies in the fact that poetry's power is not in perfect syntax or even flawless metaphor, but in the unrepeatable consciousness that shapes them. If machines learn to mimic poetry, the human poet's value may paradoxically increase — for their verse will be valued not only for what it says but for who has said it. The reader will not seek merely beautiful lines, but the signature of a lived life within them.

The Inevitable Immortality

In the end, poetry's prospects are secured not by the preferences of any era but by the permanence of its necessity. Civilizations rise and fall, technologies blossom and decay, but the hunger for language that embodies truth in beauty, and beauty in truth, is an appetite that no epoch has ever extinguished. The future will be full of faster things, louder things, brighter things — but poetry will remain the stillness beneath the speed, the whisper beneath the roar, the candle that casts a shadow even in the glare of neon.

THE ETERNAL ESSENCE AND ENIGMATIC STRUCTURE OF POETRY

Poetry is both ancient and ageless, fleeting yet forever. It is at once the oldest art and the youngest voice, a child of silence and a parent of song. To speak of poetry is to speak of paradox: the infinite compressed into syllables, the ineffable embodied in sound, the unutterable uttered. Its essence is eternal because it exceeds time, and its structure is enigmatic because it resists final definition. Poetry, like the cosmos, is both order and chaos, pattern and mystery, law and liberation.

The Eternal Essence of Poetry

The essence of poetry is not in ornament but in origin. It is the primal pulse of human consciousness made audible. Before philosophy reasoned, before science measured, before religion codified, poetry sang. The first cry of the newborn, the chant of the tribe, the hymn to the heavens—all are poetry's primordial breath. Poetry is not derivative; it is generative. It does not merely describe existence—it discloses it.

Its eternity lies in its capacity to transform the transient into the timeless. A fleeting emotion, a passing gesture, a single sigh—poetry preserves them, transfigures them, and projects them beyond the moment. It creates permanence where none should be possible. A verse written in antiquity still trembles in modern veins, a metaphor born in obscurity still illuminates the corridors of the present. Poetry outlives its makers, not by accident but by necessity.

Yet its eternity is not cold permanence, but living renewal. Poetry survives because it adapts, metamorphoses, and reincarnates. Each age reinterprets the same lines, discovering new meanings in old metaphors, new resonances in ancient rhythms. Homer becomes contemporary, Rumi becomes universal, Tagore becomes timeless. Poetry is eternal not because it resists change, but because it thrives in it.

At its core, poetry is essence distilled into expression. It condenses life into language so that words no longer signify merely—they sing, they soar, they sustain. Every true poem is more than communication; it is communion, more than description; it is revelation. The essence of poetry is not what it says, but what it awakens—the silent recognition, the trembling wonder, the sudden enlargement of perception.

The Enigmatic Structure of Poetry

If poetry's essence is eternal, its structure is enigmatic. Unlike mathematics, whose axioms seek precision, or law, which demands clarity, poetry thrives on ambiguity, multiplicity, and mystery. Its structure is not scaffolding but shimmering veil. It conceals as it reveals, obscures as it illuminates.

The enigma lies in sound and sense entwined. Words are chosen not only for meaning but for music, not only for reference but for resonance. Rhythm becomes reason, cadence becomes cognition. A poem is not merely read; it is heard, even when silent. It speaks to the ear as much as to the eye, to the body as much as to the brain.

The structure of poetry is also paradoxical in its form. A haiku compresses infinity into seventeen syllables; an epic expands a single story into thousands of lines. Both are poems, both complete, both enigmatic. Poetry has no singular structure yet every structure is poetry's. It thrives in meter but also in free verse, in rhyme but also in rupture, in tradition but also in transgression. Its very indefinability is its definition.

Moreover, poetry's structure is open yet closed, finite yet infinite. A poem ends on the page but begins in the reader. Its lines may be few, but its interpretations are endless. A single metaphor may give birth to a hundred meanings, each valid, each incomplete. The poem is never exhausted because the reader is never finished. Poetry's structure is enigmatic because it is dialogical: half created by the poet, half recreated by the reader, wholly alive in the encounter between them.

The Paradox of Poetry

The eternal essence and enigmatic structure of poetry converge in paradox. Poetry is the art of saying what cannot be said, of naming the nameless, of embodying the infinite in the finite. Its power lies not in solving paradox but in sustaining it.

Poetry is truth told through illusion, clarity born of obscurity. Poetry is motion in stillness, silence that sings. Poetry is universal in its particularity, intimate in its grandeur. Poetry is a mirror and a lamp—reflecting reality yet illuminating possibility. Poetry is both personal diary and public testament, both private whisper and collective anthem. The paradox does not weaken poetry; it empowers it. For what is life itself but paradox? We are mortal yet long for immortality, finite yet hunger for infinity, bound by matter yet yearning for spirit. Poetry does not resolve these tensions but renders them radiant, teaching us to live within mystery without the compulsion of mastery.

Poetry as Eternal Enigma

To grasp the eternal essence and enigmatic structure of poetry is to glimpse the condition of humanity itself. For we, too, are beings of essence and enigma, creatures of clarity and contradiction. Poetry mirrors our condition, magnifies our consciousness, and magnifies our contradictions into coherence. Thus, poetry is not an art beside life—it is life intensified. It is the eternal in the ephemeral, the infinite in the intimate, the enigma in the evident. To write poetry is to wrestle with paradox; to read poetry is to embrace it; to live poetry is to embody it. And so the final paradox: Poetry endures because it cannot be fully explained, it thrives because it cannot be wholly understood. Its essence is eternal, its structure enigmatic, its destiny inexhaustible. Poetry is the mystery that makes meaning possible, and the meaning that makes mystery bearable.

Poetry is the primordial pulse of mankind, the first art, the primal breath, the earliest song of humankind. Poetry immortalizes fleeting emotions and ephemeral experiences. It is the metamorphic memory of mankind through ages, as renewal: the way each age reinterprets the same verses. We can call poetry communion beyond communication, as revelation rather than mere expression. Poetry is the sacredness of sound, the music of meaning, the chant beneath the language. Poetry is concealment and revelation, simplicity and complexity at the same time. Thus, it can have infinite interpretations and endless echoes. It is also true that a potential and everlasting poetry is not direct, rather it is oblique and thus, it preserves ambiguity in its core heart. It is the cause for which it sounds mysterious and meaningful. Poem is a dialogue- half written by the poet, half created by the reader through the medium of philosophy and states of minds.

Poetry has its paradoxical relation to reality. Poetry is that silence that sings, the stillness that sounds, and the absence through its presence and vice versa. Poetry is that area where the local is the universal, the personal is the cosmic. It is as reflective as illuminative through its dimensions. Poetry is a private confession with public witness. Poetry is moral and political responsibility. Poetry's defiance of mortality and its embrace of eternity shows us the temporal bridge situated on the chest if it. Poetry is prayer, meditation, and mystical encounter which speaks about its spiritual ascent. Poetry is connected to the cosmos because its language is star-map, and metaphor is universe.

The Eternal Essence

Primordial Pulse: Poetry is not invention; it is origin. It does not arrive late, as luxury, but emerges first, as necessity. Before the world built walls, it uttered words; before humankind forged tools, it forged tones. The first fire was not only flame but chant around flame, not only heat but hymn. The infant of the species, wide-eyed at stars and storms, did not analyze but intoned. The earliest poets were not professionals but peoples; the earliest verses were not written but whispered. Poetry preceded philosophy, outlived prophecy, and survived politics. It is the primordial pulse of consciousness itself. To call poetry "art" is both accurate and inadequate. Art implies craft, but poetry predates craft. It was not designed but discovered, not composed but compelled. The pulse of poetry beats wherever breath breaks into rhythm, wherever silence strains toward sound. Even the newborn's cry is proto-poetry: irregular rhythm, desperate cadence, primal meaning. The first lullabies, the earliest epics, the chants to rain and river—these are not inventions but invocations, not constructions but confessions. Poetry is as natural as heartbeat, as inevitable as breath. Yet the paradox persists: what is most primal becomes most profound. What begins as survival—song for rain, chant for courage, cry for community—becomes surplus, splendor, sanctity. The chant for rain becomes psalm of praise, the cry of grief becomes elegy, the hymn of survival becomes ode of celebration. What necessity births, beauty adopts. What instinct ignites, imagination expands. Thus poetry's primacy is not only historical but eternal: it is always at the beginning, always at the root, always at the pulse. And here lies the eternal essence: poetry is both origin and ongoing, both ancestral and anticipatory. It is not a relic but a rhythm that revives in every age. Even when written, even when formalized, even when dissected, poetry still carries the breath of the first cry, the tremor of the first hymn. It is not artifact but atmosphere, not fossil but fire. Poetry is primordial pulse—ever ancient, ever new.

Transience Transfigured: Life is fleeting: breath breaks, blossoms wither, bodies decay. All is transience, all is time-bound. Yet poetry transfigures this impermanence into permanence. A moment becomes immortal when molded into metaphor, an hour becomes eternal when enshrined in imagery. Poetry is the paradoxical art of preserving perishability, of granting endurance to the ephemeral. Consider the haiku: seventeen syllables, a handful of heartbeats, yet within it the eternity of an entire season. Or the lyric: a sigh transcribed, a single sorrow set to sound, yet centuries later it still sings. Poetry rescues the vanishing not by resisting time but by transforming it. What passes through flesh remains in phrase; what dissolves in memory survives in meter. And yet, paradox deepens: the poem is eternal not despite its brevity but because of it. Its very condensation grants durability. A treatise ages, a doctrine decays, but a verse survives because it says much with little, everything with nothing. "A rose by any other name would smell as sweet"—these few words contain centuries of sentiment, still resonant, still radiant. Poetry transfigures transience by teaching us to treasure the temporary. It does not deny decay but dignifies it. The blossom is beautiful because it will wither, the dawn glorious because it will darken, the kiss poignant because it will pass. Poetry preserves the fleeting not by pretending it lasts but by sanctifying its fragility. To read poetry is to rehearse mortality, to acknowledge impermanence, yet to find within it eternity. Thus, the eternal essence of poetry is paradox: it rescues by releasing, it immortalizes by acknowledging mortality. Poetry does not abolish time but transfigures it, so that what fades in life flourishes in language.

Metamorphic Memory: Poetry does not remain static; it metamorphoses with memory. A poem is never the same twice, not because the words change but because we do. Every reader becomes re-creator; every age becomes interpreter. Thus, poetry is both fixed and fluid, stable yet shifting, eternal yet adaptable. Take the ancient epics: Homer sung to warriors by fire becomes Homer studied by scholars in libraries. Yet the Iliad and Odyssey still pulse with pathos, still instruct and inspire. Or take the sonnets of Shakespeare: whispered to Elizabethan lovers, now recited in digital classrooms—yet their ardor persists, their wisdom remains. The words are identical; the worlds they inhabit evolve. Poetry lives precisely because it metamorphoses. Memory itself is metamorphic. We recall differently as we age, reinterpret as we experience, reframe as we reflect. The poem mirrors this mutability: it grows with us, shrinks with us, shifts with us. A line once romantic becomes tragic, a stanza once sorrowful becomes consoling. Poetry is eternal because it is pliant, enigmatic because it is never exhausted. Thus, the essence of poetry is not only endurance but adaptability. It is eternal not because it resists change but because it thrives in it. Like water, poetry takes the shape of its container: the clay of culture, the vessel of voice, the cup of consciousness. Its permanence lies in its plasticity. Poetry is metamorphic memory—perpetual renewal, perennial relevance.

Communion beyond Communication: Language, in its ordinary use, communicates; poetry, in its extraordinary use, communes. The difference is decisive. Communication transmits information; communion transfigures relation. A fact informs; a poem transforms. A sentence may be understood; a poem may be inhabited. When we read poetry, we do not merely decode words; we enter resonance. We feel the pulse of another's perception, the tremor of another's truth. The dead speak to the living, the distant to the near, the stranger to the self. Poetry collapses distance, transcends boundaries, abolishes isolation. It is not simply the poet's voice; it is the universal voice uttered through the particular throat. And paradox intensifies: poetry is profoundly private yet profoundly public. A diary entry becomes scripture, a whisper becomes anthem, a sigh becomes symphony. The poet's solitude becomes society's song. What is most intimate becomes most universal, what is most singular becomes most shared. Poetry is at once confession and covenant. This is why poetry feels sacred. It creates communion not only between writer and reader but between human and cosmos, self and silence, mortal and eternal. The poem does not merely say—it summons; it does not merely express—it reveals. To read poetry is to participate in revelation, to share in a vision greater than oneself. Thus, poetry transcends communication by becoming communion. Its eternal essence lies in its ability to unite, to bind, to make many one and one many.

The Sacredness of Sound: If poetry is essence distilled, its distillation is sound. Words are vessels, but their vibration gives vitality. Poetry is not only seen but heard, not only read but resonated. Even in silent reading, the inner ear listens, the inner voice sings. The sacredness of sound lies in rhythm and resonance. Rhythm mirrors heartbeat, breath, pulse; resonance echoes the world's music—wind, waves, thunder, rain. Poetry is cosmology compressed into cadence, the universe arranged in utterance. Yet paradox persists: sound sanctifies sense even as it sometimes obscures it. A poem may be meaningless in logic yet powerful in music. Pure sound—chant, mantra, nonsense verse—can still sanctify, still stir. Thus poetry's essence is not reducible to semantics; its secret lies in sonority. Sound in poetry is sacred because it survives translation, time, and text. We may not understand ancient tongues, yet their rhythm moves us. We may not know the words of a chant, yet its vibration reverberates in us. Poetry communicates even when incomprehensible, communes even when obscure. Thus, the eternal essence of poetry is sound sanctified, resonance revered. It is the music of meaning, the hymn of humanity, the chant of cosmos. Poetry is word made world, sound made sacred.

The Enigmatic Structure of Poetry

The Veil of Form: Poetry wears many garments, but never a single uniform. Its form is fluid, forever shifting between freedom and structure, between clarity and concealment. A poem is both architecture and atmosphere: carefully constructed yet mysteriously alive. The enigma of its form lies in its dual function—as veil and as revelation. Form is the veil that hides as much as it shows. The sonnet, with its fourteen lines, hides infinite emotions within finite frame. The haiku, with its seventeen syllables, compresses eternity into an instant. Epic poems, sprawling across thousands of verses, conceal simple human stories within labyrinths of myth. Form restricts, yet through restriction, releases. The veil does not merely obscure; it also beautifies, intensifies, and dignifies. And yet, paradox deepens: the veil is also window. The very form that hides also reveals. The rhyme scheme guides attention, the meter awakens heartbeat, the stanza organizes breath. Poetry teaches us that concealment can be revelation, that boundaries can be openings, that limitation can be liberation. Form, then, is not a prison but a paradoxical portal. Even free verse—ostensibly without rules—reveals its own architecture of rhythm, line breaks, and silence. No poem is formless; even chaos carries cadence. The veil of form is enigma because it invites interpretation: we never see the face fully, but always through shimmering fabric. Thus, the structure of poetry is never merely functional; it is mystical. Form is both garment and gateway, concealment and communication. The poem hides and reveals in the same breath, whispering secrets behind its veil.

Multiplicity of Meaning: If prose strives for clarity, poetry thrives on multiplicity. A single metaphor may generate a thousand interpretations; a single line may echo across centuries with ever-changing resonance. Poetry's enigmatic structure is built on polysemy—the capacity of words to mean more than one thing at once. Consider the line: "The world is a stage." Is it metaphor for performance, for temporality, for illusion, for futility? It is all and none, each interpretation incomplete yet indispensable. Poetry refuses the tyranny of single meaning. Instead, it invites the reader to wander through multiple doors, each opening to another chamber of possibility. Here lies the paradox: ambiguity is not weakness but wealth. Where prose narrows, poetry widens. Where discourse dictates, poetry dreams. Multiplicity is not confusion but communion—it allows each reader to participate, to create, to contribute. The poet lays foundation; the reader builds cathedral. And yet, multiplicity is not chaos. The poem is not infinite in any random direction; it is infinite within resonance, bounded by rhythm, tethered by tone. Poetry balances freedom with focus, openness with orientation. Its meaning is not arbitrary but inexhaustible. Thus, the structure of poetry is enigmatic because it refuses closure. It remains always unfinished, always alive, always more than itself. Poetry's truth is not singular but shimmering, not fixed but fluid, not final but forever unfolding.

The Architecture of Ambiguity: Ambiguity is not an accident in poetry; it is its architecture. The poem is built on double meanings, layered images, paradoxical phrases. It invites misunderstanding not to mislead but to multiply wonder. Its very structure is enigmatic because it thrives in uncertainty. The poem says one thing and means another, or says many things and means them all. A word may be literal and symbolic simultaneously; an image may be material and mystical at once. Poetry's architecture is not like a blueprint but like a labyrinth—every turn opens new passageways, every wall hides secret doors. Paradox persists: ambiguity both frustrates and fascinates. The reader longs for clarity but lingers in obscurity. The poem denies definitive explanation yet rewards endless exploration. Its ambiguity is not flaw but feature, not weakness but wealth. Poetry teaches us that truth is not always linear, that meaning is not always singular, that clarity is not always completeness. This architecture of ambiguity mirrors life itself. Existence is never entirely clear, never wholly coherent. Love is ambiguous, death is ambiguous, time is ambiguous. Poetry, by embracing ambiguity, mirrors reality more faithfully than logic. It teaches us to dwell in uncertainty without despair, to live in paradox without paralysis. Thus, ambiguity is not disorder but design. The poem's enigmatic structure is deliberate: it shelters mystery within form, preserves wonder within words, sanctifies silence within sound. Poetry's architecture is ambiguous because life's architecture is.

Compression and Expansion: Poetry is paradoxically both smallest and largest, both atom and universe. It compresses infinity into a few syllables, yet expands a single gesture into entire galaxies. Its structure is enigmatic because it embodies both extremes—miniature and monumental, fragment and fullness. A haiku, with its three lines, captures eternity in an instant: a frog's leap, a season's shift, a lifetime's lesson. An epic, with its thousands of lines, expands a single story into cosmic scope: war as destiny, journey as universe. Both are poetry; both complete. Compression is power. The poem distills experience so that every word carries weight, every syllable shimmers with significance. A poem wastes nothing; its density defies dismissal. Yet expansion is equally powerful. Poetry magnifies minutiae, elevates the ordinary, amplifies the overlooked. The single rose becomes emblem of love, the falling leaf becomes symbol of mortality, the passing glance becomes epic of desire. The enigma lies in this dual capacity: to condense and to expand, to miniaturize and magnify, to be seed and forest simultaneously. Poetry is paradoxical because it is both lightning bolt and lingering dawn, both instant and infinity. Thus, poetry's structure is enigmatic not because it chooses one extreme, but because it contains them both. Compression and expansion are not opposites but complements. The poem is infinite because it is finite, vast because it is small, eternal because it is momentary.

The Poem as Dialogue: A poem is never solitary. It is not monologue but dialogue, not isolated artifact but living exchange. The poet writes, but the reader rewrites; the poem speaks, but the reader answers. Its structure is enigmatic because it is incomplete until encountered. Every poem is half-finished. The ink dries, but meaning breathes only when read. The rhythm awakens only when heard, the metaphor blossoms only when received. The poem waits for the reader as seed waits for soil, as spark waits for tinder. In this sense, poetry is relational—neither wholly poet's nor wholly reader's, but shared space of encounter. And yet, paradox persists: the dialogue is asymmetrical. The poet speaks across time, yet cannot hear reply. The reader listens across distance, yet cannot question directly. The dialogue is real yet impossible, intimate yet infinite. This impossibility makes poetry sacred, for it unites the living and the dead, the near and the far, the known and the unknown. The enigmatic structure of poetry, then, is dialogical. It is not closed object but open relationship, not final statement but continuing conversation. The poem lives only when re-read, re-interpreted, re-imagined. Each reader re-begins the dialogue, each age renews it. Thus, poetry is not solitary utterance but shared resonance. Its enigmatic structure lies in its perpetual incompleteness, its openness to renewal. The poem is not static but dynamic, not monologue but dialogue, not relic but relationship.

The Paradox of Poetry

Silence that Speaks: Poetry is the paradox of soundless sound. It speaks not only through syllables but through silences, not only through words but through the white spaces between them. The poem is a symphony where rests are as resonant as notes, where absence is as articulate as presence. This paradox is profound: silence becomes speech. The line break does not merely pause—it punctuates with power. The ellipsis is not emptiness—it echoes with unspoken eternity. The unsaid often surpasses the said; the withheld often weighs more than the given. Poetry teaches us that silence is not lack but language, not emptiness but eloquence. And yet silence in poetry is never mute. It hums with hidden harmonies, throbs with thought, breathes with being. It is the invisible ink on which the visible words are written. The paradox is not that silence exists in poetry, but that silence itself is poetry. Consider the paradox: when the poem falls silent, it does not end—it begins again. Silence is seed for imagination, invitation for interpretation. The unspoken becomes space for the reader to speak, the withheld becomes womb of wonder. Thus, poetry is paradoxical because it transforms silence into sound and sound into silence.

Order in Chaos, Chaos in Order: Poetry is paradox because it is both chaos and cosmos. It seems wild, unpredictable, erupting in unexpected images and illogical leaps. Yet within that apparent chaos lies profound order—patterns of rhythm, structures of form, symmetries of sound. Poetry is the paradox of order hidden in chaos and chaos hidden in order. The rhyme may seem decorative, yet it disciplines thought. The meter may seem rigid, yet it releases rhythm. Even free verse, unruly on surface, carries its own cadence of breaks, its own silent score. Thus, the poem is a dance of disorder and design, spontaneity and structure. And yet the paradox runs deeper: poetry's order does not cancel chaos, nor does chaos cancel order. They coexist, conspire, co-create. Too much order—poetry petrifies. Too much chaos—poetry dissolves. The enigma of poetry lies in balance: disciplined disorder, structured spontaneity, patterned unpredictability. Life itself mirrors this paradox. Existence is never wholly ordered, never wholly chaotic. The cosmos is a choreography of chaos. Poetry, by embodying both, does not escape life but enact it. It shows us that meaning is not found in erasing contradiction but embracing it. Thus, poetry is paradoxical not because it is confused but because it is complete. It teaches us that order is never pure, chaos never total; each harbors the other.

Time Transcended, Time Trapped: Poetry is paradox of time. It is trapped in time—born of a moment, speaking of an age, bound by the mortality of language. Yet it transcends time—echoing across centuries, resonating beyond the death of its maker, renewing itself in each reader's present. The poem is moment and millennium, instant and infinity. A line written in ancient Greece still stirs hearts in modern streets. A haiku composed centuries ago still awakens mornings today. Poetry is time's paradox: it captures fleeting instants yet refuses to vanish with them. And yet, paradox deepens: poetry is both timeless and time-bound. Without history, no poem is born; without present, no poem is alive. The past gives it origin, the present gives it breath, the future gives it destiny. Poetry is woven of time but woven against time. In this paradox lies poetry's power: it grants permanence to impermanence, eternity to ephemerality. It shows us that moments can last forever, that instants can hold infinity. Thus, the poem is paradox of time's trap and transcendence. It is hourglass and horizon, fleeting breath and eternal echo. Poetry teaches us that time can be both bound and broken, both finite and infinite.

The Intimate Infinite: Poetry is paradox because it is at once intimate and infinite. It begins with a single voice, a solitary soul, a secret whisper. Yet it expands into universality, speaking across cultures, continents, centuries. A poem penned in solitude speaks to multitudes; a personal pain becomes collective catharsis. This paradox of intimacy and infinity makes poetry unique. Philosophy may generalize, history may document, science may universalize—but poetry personalizes the universal and universalizes the personal. The poet's "I" becomes the reader's "I." The lover's lament becomes humanity's hymn. And yet the intimacy remains. No matter how universal, a poem retains the tremor of the poet's pulse, the fingerprint of the poet's soul. Its infinity does not erase its intimacy; rather, intimacy is its gateway to infinity. Thus, poetry embodies paradox: it is whisper that becomes world, sigh that becomes song, tear that becomes tide. It teaches us that universality is not opposed to individuality but born of it.

The Word beyond Words: Perhaps the greatest paradox: poetry is made of words, yet strives to transcend them. It is language, yet more than language; it is speech, yet longing for silence; it is word, yet yearning for world beyond word. The poem bends, breaks, beautifies words until they point beyond themselves. Metaphor makes the invisible visible. Symbol makes the absent present. Rhythm makes the silent sing. Poetry is paradox because it uses the finite tool of language to reach infinite reality. And yet, paradox persists: without words, poetry cannot be; with words alone, poetry is not. The poem lives in the tension between expression and inexpressible, between what can be said and what can only be suggested. Poetry gestures toward what lies beyond utterance—the ineffable, the unspeakable, the eternal. Thus, poetry is paradox of word and world, sign and silence, speech and spirit. It teaches us that language is not limit but ladder, not prison but passage. The greatest poems do not explain the world but expand it, do not define truth but deepen its mystery.

The Essence of Good Poetry

Truth in Tremor: Good poetry trembles with truth. Not the cold, categorical truth of science, nor the systematic syllogisms of philosophy, but the shimmering, subjective truth of lived experience. Poetry's truth is paradoxical—it is not factual yet it feels more real than fact, not literal yet it lingers longer than logic. When a poem whispers of love, loss, longing, it does not prove but persuades; it does not argue but awakens. Its truth lies not in external verification but in inner recognition. We read and murmur, "Yes, this is true, though I never knew it until now." And yet poetry's truth is not fixed. It changes as readers change, as cultures change, as centuries shift. A line that once consoled may later confront; a verse that once incited revolt may later inspire reflection. Poetry's truth is tremor, not monument. It quivers, resonates, reverberates. But tremor does not mean triviality. On the contrary, tremor means touch: poetry touches the trembling core of human existence. It teaches us that truth is not always stable but still sacred, not always permanent but still powerful. Good poetry is true not because it conforms but because it transforms. Thus, the essence of poetry's truth lies in its trembling fidelity to human feeling, its restless resonance with reality, its paradoxical power to reveal what cannot be proven.

Beauty in Brokenness: Good poetry glows with

beauty—but beauty not as perfection, rather as brokenness made luminous. The poem may speak of suffering, sorrow, shattered selves, yet in voicing them, it transforms anguish into art. Poetry reveals the paradox that beauty is born not from absence of pain but from its articulation. A broken heart, when shaped into stanza, becomes more radiant than a flawless facade. A cracked voice, when cast in cadence, becomes more moving than marble. Poetry teaches us that beauty is not the denial of fracture but the dignifying of fracture. Yet beauty in poetry is never superficial ornament. It is not prettiness but presence, not decoration but depth. It is the beauty of intensity, of honesty, of resonance. Sometimes beauty shines through harshness, through rawness, through rugged rhythm. Good poetry does not always soothe; sometimes it sears. But even in searing, it is beautiful. This paradoxical beauty mirrors the human condition itself. We are fragile, finite, fractured—and yet radiant. Good poetry captures this fragile radiance, showing us that imperfection is not obstacle to beauty but its origin. Thus, the essence of poetry's beauty lies in brokenness made whole, sorrow made sacred, fracture made fertile. Poetry's beauty is paradoxical: it wounds and heals, it scars and sanctifies, it breaks and binds.

Emotion as Essence: If philosophy seeks truth and science seeks fact, poetry seeks feeling. Emotion is the essence of good poetry—the pulse beneath its patterns, the blood in its body. Without emotion, words remain inert; with emotion, even the simplest syllables soar. Good poetry does not merely describe emotion; it creates emotion. The reader does not simply understand sadness—they feel it. They do not merely grasp joy—they glow with it. Poetry bypasses intellect and pierces directly into pulse, bypasses argument and awakens affect. And yet poetry's paradox:

emotion is not raw but refined. The poem channels passion into precision, rage into rhythm, grief into grace. The greatest poems are not explosions but distillations, not chaos but crystallization. Emotion in poetry is not uncontrolled but artfully contained, like fire in a lantern—shaped so it can shine. Furthermore, emotion in poetry is not merely personal. Though born of one heart, it resonates with many. The poet's private grief becomes public gift; the poet's solitary joy becomes shared celebration. Poetry universalizes emotion by particularizing it, makes the infinite intimate and the intimate infinite. Thus, the essence of poetry's emotion lies in paradox: feeling refined yet fierce, private yet public, raw yet radiant. Good poetry is emotional not because it exaggerates but because it embodies.

Ethics of Expression: Good poetry is not only aesthetic but ethical. It does not merely delight; it dignifies. It does not only move; it matters. Poetry carries responsibility because words carry weight. A poem can liberate or oppress, console or condemn, heal or harm. The ethical essence of poetry lies in its attentiveness—its respect for truth, its reverence for language, its refusal to trivialize suffering. Good poetry never exploits pain for prettiness nor distorts reality for applause. It bears witness, speaks honestly, listens deeply. And yet the paradox: poetry is free, yet bound. It is free in form, in imagination, in invention. But it is bound by responsibility to its subjects and to its readers. Freedom without ethics becomes frivolity; ethics without freedom becomes propaganda. The good poem balances both—bold imagination with deep integrity. Poetry, then, is moral not by preaching but by perceiving. It does not sermonize; it sensitizes. It opens the eyes, enlarges the heart, awakens the conscience. Its ethics lie not in command but in compassion.

Thus, the essence of poetry's ethics is paradoxical: it is free yet responsible, imaginative yet accountable, playful yet profound. Good poetry is not good merely in craft but in conscience.

Transcendence in Immanence: Above all, the essence of good poetry lies in transcendence—yet transcendence rooted in immanence. Poetry rises beyond the ordinary by dwelling deeply within it. A falling leaf becomes symbol of mortality; a single kiss becomes emblem of eternity. Poetry is transcendence not by escape but by immersion. This is poetry's supreme paradox: the infinite in the intimate, the eternal in the ephemeral. The poet does not flee the world but enters it so fully that it reveals more than itself. By naming the particular, poetry unveils the universal; by holding the moment, poetry hints at eternity. Good poetry thus becomes spiritual—not necessarily religious, but sacred in its intensity. It sanctifies the everyday, reveals the divine in the detail, discloses the beyond in the here and now. Yet transcendence in poetry is never abstraction. It is always embodied—embodied in image, in rhythm, in sound. Poetry does not float above reality but rises through it. It teaches us that the way to eternity is through time, the way to infinity is through finitude, the way to transcendence is through immanence. Thus, the essence of poetry's transcendence lies in paradox: it rises by rooting, it ascends by descending, it reaches the eternal by embracing the temporal. Good poetry is not escape from life but entry into its deepest depths.

The Dimensions of Poetry

Poetry as Art: At its heart, poetry is art: the shaping of language into beauty, the sculpting of sound into significance, the painting of perception upon the canvas of consciousness. Like all art, poetry is deliberate creation, born from impulse yet shaped by imagination. The paradox of poetry as art lies in its material: unlike paint or stone, poetry's medium is language, which already belongs to everyone. The poet works not with rare pigments but with common words, yet arranges them so uncommonly that the ordinary becomes extraordinary. "Water," "stone," "light"—mundane syllables—transfigured into metaphysical symphonies. And yet, poetry as art does not merely imitate nature; it intensifies it. A poem does not mirror a rose; it magnifies its fragrance, multiplies its meanings, immortalizes its moment. Poetry transforms experience into expression, fleeting life into lasting lines. But poetry is not only artifice; it is authenticity. The good poem balances craft with candor, technique with truth. Too much artifice, and it becomes ornament without origin; too little, and it becomes diary without dignity. Art in poetry is paradox: it conceals in order to reveal, shapes in order to shine. Thus, poetry as art is the aesthetic dimension of existence. It shows us that beauty is not luxury but necessity, not surface but substance, not escape but essence.

Poetry as Philosophy: Poetry is also philosophy—not systematic but symbolic, not argumentative but allusive. Where philosophy analyzes, poetry synthesizes; where philosophy dissects, poetry dreams. Yet both seek wisdom, both pursue truth, both ponder the perennial riddles of existence. The paradox lies here: philosophy strives for clarity, poetry thrives on ambiguity—yet both illuminate. Philosophy ascends by abstraction, poetry descends by image, yet both meet at the summit of meaning. Plato banished poets from his Republic, fearing their seductions, yet his own dialogues often drift into myth, metaphor, and music. Perhaps philosophy envies poetry for achieving wisdom with wonder. Good poetry asks philosophical questions without demanding philosophical answers. What is being? What is time? What is death? What is love? The poem does not solve but shows, does not conclude but conjures. Its philosophy is not syllogism but symbol, not proposition but paradox. And yet poetry's philosophy is no less profound. Often, the poem pierces deeper than argument, because it embodies what it explores. A line about mortality does not merely state it; it enacts it in rhythm, in pause, in fading echo. Poetry philosophizes not by logic but by living language. Ergo, poetry as philosophy is wisdom embodied in wonder. It shows us that truth is not always theorem but threnody, not always deduction but dream.

Poetry as Music: Poetry is music in words, melody in meaning, rhythm in rhetoric. Long before literacy, poetry was sung, chanted, recited. The drumbeat of meter, the rhyme of repetition, the chorus of refrain—poetry is as much heard as read, as much body as mind. The paradox of poetry as music is that it enchants even without comprehension. One may not understand the language of a poem, yet still be moved by its music. The cadence itself carries feeling. Words, before meaning, are sounds; poetry remembers this primal truth. And yet music in poetry is not mere melody—it is meaning made audible. Rhythm emphasizes emotion, rhyme reinforces relation, repetition engraves remembrance. Music is not decoration but revelation. But paradox again: silence, too, is part of poetry's music. The pause, the break, the breath—all shape sound by their absence. Poetry is heard not only in what is spoken but in what is withheld. Thus, poetry as music is the auditory dimension of existence. It shows us that life itself has rhythm, that the universe itself hums with harmony, that our hearts themselves are drums beating in meter of mortality.

Poetry as Politics: Poetry is not only private; it is public, not only lyric but civic. It speaks to power, resists oppression, ignites revolutions. From the chants of protest to the anthems of nations, poetry is political speech in its most potent form. The paradox of poetry as politics is that it is at once fragile and forceful. A poem is only words on paper, yet it can shake empires, sustain resistance, inspire liberation. Tyrants fear poets because they know language can outlast law, metaphor can undermine might, song can shatter silence. And yet poetry's politics is not always overt. Sometimes its mere insistence on beauty is resistance, its celebration of freedom is defiance, its affirmation of dignity is revolution. Poetry need not preach to be political; its very existence as free creation is itself act of rebellion against reduction. But paradox persists: poetry can also be co-opted, domesticated, turned into propaganda. Thus, good political poetry balances passion with perception, urgency with universality. It resists tyranny without becoming tyrannical itself. Thus, poetry as politics is the ethical-aesthetic dimension of language. It shows us that words can wound or heal nations, that verses can awaken voices, that imagination can ignite history.

Poetry as Prophecy: Perhaps the highest dimension: poetry as prophecy. The poet does not only describe the world but dreams it, does not only reflect reality but reveal possibilities. The poet is seer as much as singer, visionary as much as versifier. The paradox is striking: prophecy is not prediction but perception. The poet sees not the future in detail but the eternal in the moment. By looking deeply into the present, poetry glimpses the future. By naming the unseen in the seen, poetry prophesies. Poets have often been called prophets—not because they foretell events but because they reveal truths that later prove timeless. Blake,

Whitman, Tagore, Neruda—they spoke in voices that seemed not only of their age but of all ages. Yet prophecy in poetry is not arrogance but attunement. The poet listens so deeply that they hear what others miss; they see so intensely that they glimpse what lies beyond. Prophecy is paradox because it is vision rooted in voice, transcendence expressed in syllables. Thus, poetry as prophecy is the sacred dimension of existence. It shows us that the poet is not merely a writer but a witness, not merely an artist but an oracle, not merely a maker but a messenger of mysteries.

The Qualities and Natures of Poetry

Poetry as Mirror: Poetry is mirror: it reflects the soul of the speaker and the spirit of the age. Every line, whether lyric or lament, is a reflection—of the poet's pulse, of the culture's currents, of the cosmos itself. Yet poetry's mirror is paradoxical. It does not reflect plainly like glass but mystically like water. Look into it, and you see yourself, but also something other, something deeper. The mirror of poetry distorts in order to disclose, bends in order to reveal. It shows the familiar in unfamiliar light, the known as if unknown, the ordinary as if extraordinary. The mirror of poetry is both private and public. It reflects the poet's intimate face, but also the collective countenance of a community. A single poem can be personal confession and cultural chronicle, individual image and historical emblem. And yet, paradox persists: the mirror is also window. In looking at reflection, we glimpse beyond reflection. The poem shows us ourselves, but in showing, it opens us to others. In the mirror of poetry, self and other are not opposed but intertwined. Thus, poetry as mirror is neither passive nor plain; it is transformative reflection. It teaches us that to see is not only to recognize but to reimagine.

Poetry as Mystery: Poetry is mystery: the more we

read, the more it recedes; the more we grasp, the more it grows. Its essence is not exhaustion but expansion. Each interpretation adds, none concludes. The paradox of poetry as mystery is that it hides by revealing and reveals by hiding. A metaphor discloses meaning even as it conceals it. A symbol unveils truth even as it veils it. Poetry thrives not in clarity but in cloud, not in definition but in depth. Mystery does not mean obscurity. A good poem is not unintelligible but inexhaustible. We understand enough to be moved, yet never enough to be finished. The mystery is what keeps poetry alive, what makes us return, reread, rediscover. And yet, paradox again: poetry's mystery is intimate, not remote. It dwells not in distant abstractions but in daily realities. The mystery is in the morning dew, the falling leaf, the fleeting glance. Poetry reveals the miraculous in the mundane, the sacred in the simple. Thus, poetry as mystery is not puzzle to be solved but presence to be savored. It teaches us that life's depth is not in answers but in questions, not in closure but in continual opening.

Poetry as Magic: Poetry is magic: it enchants, transforms, transfigures. With mere words, it conjures worlds; with mere syllables, it shifts souls. Its spells are not illusions but illuminations. The paradox of poetry as magic is that it works with ordinary tools—everyday words, common rhythms—yet achieves extraordinary effects. The alphabet is available to all, yet in the hands of the poet, it becomes incantation. Bread becomes body, ink becomes infinity, whisper becomes world. Poetry's magic lies in metamorphosis. It changes grief into grandeur, pain into praise, silence into song. It alters perception: after the poem, the rose is never merely a rose, the night never merely night. Yet its magic is not trickery. It does not deceive but deepen. Unlike illusionist's sleight of hand, poetry's spell does not vanish when revealed—it strengthens. To understand a metaphor is not to end its magic but to enter it more fully. Thus, poetry as magic is paradoxical: it is art yet alchemy, language yet liturgy, word yet wonder. It teaches us that transformation is possible, that reality is not rigid but radiant.

Poetry as Memory: Poetry is memory: it preserves what passes, immortalizes the ephemeral, engraves the fleeting. Civilizations crumble, empires collapse, but poetry endures, carrying voices across centuries. The paradox of poetry as memory is that it forgets in order to remember. It does not record every detail but distills, selects, crystallizes. Memory is not total but essential, not exhaustive but evocative. The poem remembers by reimagining. And yet poetry is not only repository of past but reminder in present. To recite a poem is to resurrect history, to call back the voices of the dead into the breath of the living. Poetry is séance of syllables, resurrection through rhythm. Paradox again: poetry remembers the collective through the personal. The epic preserves nations, but the lyric preserves hearts. Both are memory—one of history, the other of humanity. Thus, poetry as memory is paradoxical archive: it stores by shaping, remembers by re-creating. It teaches us that memory is not static but dynamic, not record but resonance.

Poetry as Miracle: Finally, poetry is miracle. That mere marks on a page, mere vibrations of air, mere arrangements of syllables can stir souls, unite strangers, outlast centuries—this is miraculous. The paradox of poetry as miracle is that it is at once common and rare. Poems are written daily, everywhere; yet each true poem is singular, unrepeatable, irreducible. The miracle is not that poetry exists, but that it continues to astonish. Poetry is miracle because it makes possible what should be impossible: silence that speaks, chaos that coheres, time that transcends, grief that glows. Each poem is a small resurrection, a sudden revelation, a shimmering shard of the infinite breaking into the finite. And yet, paradox once more: the miracle is not outside but within. Poetry does not import divinity from beyond but discovers it here, in the ordinary. The miraculous is not exception but essence, if only seen with poetic sight. Thus, poetry as miracle is the final nature: ordinary words working extraordinary wonders. It teaches us that wonder is not elsewhere but everywhere, awaiting awakening.

The Features of Poetry

Poetry as Imagery: Poetry is imagery: the alchemy of sight and sound, sense and spirit, compressed into words that make us see. A poem paints not with pigments but with perception, sketching scenes in the theater of the mind. Yet poetry's imagery is paradoxical. It is concrete and abstract, precise and suggestive. The poet writes rose, and we see not only flower but fragility, fragrance, fire of desire, fleetingness of time. A single image unfolds infinite implications. Imagery is not imitation but invocation. The poet does not merely describe what is seen; the poet summons what is unseen. A moon in a poem is not astronomical object but archetypal presence—lover's lamp, wanderer's witness, philosopher's question. The paradox is that imagery both limits and liberates. To call a thing by name is to confine it, yet in poetry, the image opens rather than closes. It offers the particular as portal to the universal. Thus, poetry as imagery is not art of surface but of depth. It teaches us to see beyond seeing, to perceive the presence within the picture.

Poetry as Rhythm: Poetry is rhythm: the heartbeat of language, the pulse of perception, the cadence that carries meaning. Even in free verse, rhythm persists—through breath, through pause, through pattern of thought. The paradox of poetry as rhythm is that it is measured yet unmeasurable, counted yet uncontainable. Metrical schemes can be scanned, but the true rhythm escapes analysis, dwelling in resonance rather than rule. Rhythm is time transfigured. It gathers scattered instants into coherence, transforms chaos into cadence. Through rhythm, poetry becomes music, not merely said but sung, not merely read but remembered. And yet rhythm is silence's partner. Pauses, breaks, caesuras—these are as vital as beats. Poetry speaks as much by what it withholds as by what it delivers. The silence between lines is rhythm's secret strength. Thus, poetry as rhythm is paradox of movement and stillness, sound and silence, rule and freedom. It teaches us that time itself can be shaped into song.

Poetry as Metaphor: Poetry is metaphor: it says one thing and means another, it joins what is apart, it yokes the unlike into unity. The paradox of metaphor is that it is both false and true. To say time is a river is literally false, yet imaginatively, spiritually, phenomenologically true. Metaphor lies to tell the truth, deceives to disclose. Metaphor is the engine of imagination. It reveals relationships unseen, connections unsuspected. It collapses distance between worlds, showing that all is linked, all is living, all is luminous. Yet metaphor is not mere ornament; it is ontology. To live is to live metaphorically. We think through images, perceive through comparisons, breathe through bridges of meaning. Poetry simply heightens this human condition, making conscious the metaphors by which we unconsciously exist. Therefore, poetry as metaphor is paradoxical: a lie that liberates, a fiction that reveals fact, a bridge that is itself a destination. It teaches us that truth is not singular but shimmering, not literal but layered.

Poetry as Symbol: Poetry is symbol: sign that points beyond itself, object that becomes oracle, word that becomes world. The paradox of symbol is that it is both finite and infinite. A cross is two intersecting lines, yet it is also centuries of faith, oceans of tears, mountains of meaning. The symbol is small in form but boundless in function. Unlike imagery, which evokes perception, symbol invokes presence. To encounter a symbol in poetry is not just to see but to stand before. It is threshold, door, initiation. And yet, paradox again: the symbol does not dictate meaning but multiplies it. A dove can mean peace, purity, promise, or paradoxical fragility. The richness lies not in reduction but in resonance. Ergo, poetry as symbol is sacramental speech: visible word revealing invisible world. It teaches us that the finite is never merely finite, that the part contains the whole, that the poem itself is symbol of reality.

Poetry as Voice: Finally, poetry is voice: not merely sound but soul made audible. It is the breath of being given rhythm and resonance. The paradox of voice is that it is both personal and collective. A poem is the cry of one, yet it echoes the chorus of many. The lyric sings the self, yet readers hear their own voices within it. The epic proclaims the people, yet always through the pulse of the poet. Voice is not merely vocal but visionary. It is not just how words are said, but from where they are spoken. A true poetic voice arises not from ego but from essence, not from noise but from necessity. And yet, paradox again: the poet's voice is often strongest in silence. What is left unsaid resounds as much as what is spoken. The spaces, the omissions, the ellipses—these are part of voice, shaping resonance as surely as syllables. Thus, poetry as voice is paradoxical gift: one speaker who speaks for all, silence that resounds, individuality that becomes universality. It teaches us that language, when truly voiced, becomes life itself speaking through us.

The Dimensions of Poetry

Poetry as Temporal Dimension: Poetry is time's paradoxical dimension: it dwells in the fleeting yet creates the eternal, it captures the moment yet transcends the millennium. A poem is a clock and a cosmos, a second and a century. The paradox is that poetry both freezes and flows. A haiku halts a season into three lines, yet the epic Iliad marches across decades of war. In the lyric, time pauses; in the epic, time progresses. And yet, in both, time becomes timeless, captured yet liberated, measured yet immeasurable. Poetry is memory in motion. The ballad remembers ancestors, the sonnet crystallizes a kiss, the ode enshrines an era. Through rhythm and rhyme, the pulse of time becomes audible. The poet is not just observer of hours but architect of ages. And yet, paradox again: poetry does not deny mortality but redeems it. Death remains, but the poem defies decay. Sappho's voice survives though her body is dust; Kalidasa's clouds still drift though empires have fallen. Poetry is mortal breath that becomes immortal word. Thus, poetry as temporal dimension teaches us that time is not tyranny but tapestry, not prison but possibility. In poetry the 'moment' and the 'eternal' clasp hands.

Poetry as Spatial Dimension: Poetry is space's secret dimension: it expands the small, condenses the vast, bridges the distant. A poem creates geographies not only of land but of longing. The paradox is that poetry is at once miniature and monumental. A haiku holds a mountain in a breath; a single metaphor builds a cosmos in a clause. The stanza is a room where infinity resides, the page a field where the universe unfolds. Poetry constructs both outer landscapes and inner terrains. It describes deserts and seas, but also solitude and sorrow. The geography of the heart is mapped in meter; the cartography of the cosmos is traced in symbols. And yet, paradox again: poetry dissolves boundaries even as it defines them. It unites heaven and earth, self and other, here and elsewhere. Through the poem, the reader travels without leaving, inhabits distant lands while seated in silence. Thus, poetry as spatial dimension teaches us that place is not only physical but metaphysical, not only location but revelation. The poem opens portals into everywhere.

Poetry as Emotional Dimension: Poetry is emotion's exalted dimension: the trembling of joy, the tempest of grief, the serenity of silence. It gives voice to feeling too subtle for speech, too deep for prose. The paradox is that poetry is both personal and universal. A poet's private sorrow becomes the world's collective cry; a lover's whispered desire becomes humanity's hymn. Through poetry, subjective emotion is transfigured into shared resonance. Poetry does not merely express emotion; it shapes it. The sonnet disciplines passion into pattern; the elegy channels grief into grandeur. Emotion in poetry is not raw release but refined radiance—feeling made form. And yet, paradox again: poetry intensifies and soothes at once. It deepens sorrow but also dignifies it, heightens joy but also humbles it. The poem makes us feel more, yet also frees us from being overwhelmed. Thus, poetry as emotional dimension teaches us that feeling is not chaos but cosmos, not weakness but wisdom. It shows us that to feel is not to fall but to fly.

Poetry as Intellectual Dimension: Poetry is intellect's illumined dimension: thought given texture, idea incarnated in image, philosophy clothed in rhythm. It is thinking made musical, reasoning made radiant. The paradox is that poetry is both rational and irrational, logical and illogical. A sonnet may argue with the rigor of a syllogism, while a surrealist poem defies all rational order. Yet both reveal truth beyond reason: one through order, the other through disorder. Poetry as intellectual dimension engages with metaphysics, ethics, epistemology. It wrestles with being and nothingness, with love and death, with God and absence of God. Yet it does not argue like philosophy; it sings thought rather than states it. And yet, paradox again: poetry is both question and answer, both clarity and confusion. It provokes the mind without resolving it, stimulates without settling. Poetry keeps thinking alive by refusing closure. Thus, poetry as intellectual dimension teaches us that truth is not static statement but shimmering song. It shows us that thought itself is poetic at its core.

Poetry as Spiritual Dimension: Poetry is spirit's sacred dimension: prayer without creed, meditation without mantra, revelation without scripture. It is the breath of the infinite within the syllables of the finite. The paradox is that poetry is both sacred and secular, divine and human. The psalms praise God, while Rumi praises love, yet both tremble with transcendence. Whether addressed to heaven or heart, poetry touches the eternal. Poetry as spiritual dimension is not doctrine but discovery. It does not define divinity but discloses it. In images of dawn, in rhythms of rain, in metaphors of longing, the divine glimmers. And yet, paradox again: poetry is spiritual precisely because it is earthly. It sanctifies soil, sacramentalizes sorrow, consecrates the common. The divine dwells not outside the world but within it, unveiled by poetic vision. Therefore, poetry as spiritual dimension teaches us that life itself is liturgy, that every word can become worship, that every poem is a prayer whether spoken to God, to love, or to silence.

The Problems of Poetry

The Paradox of Perception: Poetry is perpetually misunderstood. Its beauty lies in nuance, its power in ambiguity, its truth in tension—but these same qualities provoke misperception. A reader may glimpse brilliance yet miss depth; they may savor sound yet ignore sense. The paradox is profound: poetry is universally human yet highly particular. Anyone can write, anyone can read, yet the full resonance requires attunement. The poem is available but elusive, open but opaque. Its very openness invites multiplicity of interpretation, which can delight or confuse. And yet, misperception is not failure. The gaps between poet and reader, between intention and reception, produce new meanings. Each misunderstanding becomes another interpretation, each error a new creation. Poetry thrives in this tension: its problem is also its promise. Ergo, the paradox of perception teaches us that poetry's challenge is inherent to its nature. To encounter it fully requires patience, attentiveness, and courage to dwell in ambiguity.

The Peril of Pretension: Poetry tempts the tongue, yet it is fragile in falsity. Pretentious poetry—verse that values ornament over insight, form over feeling, complexity over clarity—falls into the trap of self-indulgence. The problem is that beauty alone does not make truth, nor musicality alone make meaning. The paradox is that simplicity is often the hardest to achieve. A profound line may appear effortless, yet it is wrought from precision, insight, and intuition. Pretension is visible because it resists this paradox: it seeks grandeur without gravity, ornament without origin. And yet, pretension itself can teach. It reminds poets that authenticity, clarity, and integrity are not optional; they are essential. Poetry's perils are thus didactic: every failure illuminates the path to excellence. Thus, the peril of pretension teaches us that poetry demands humility, honesty, and attention, balancing craft with conscience.

The Limits of Language: Poetry contends with its own medium. Language is finite, yet poetry strives for the infinite. Words, by their nature, are approximate; they symbolize, suggest, imply—but can never fully contain experience. The paradox is that poetry uses this limitation to create liberation. By acknowledging the insufficiency of language, poetry gestures beyond it, inviting imagination to fill the gaps. The very imperfection of words becomes a source of wonder. Yet this limitation frustrates. Some experiences—transcendent love, ineffable grief, the mystical—resist articulation. The poet must confront silence as both obstacle and opportunity. Words fall short, yet meaning persists. Thus, the limits of language teach us the humility and audacity of poetry: it strives for the infinite while bound by the finite, reaching beyond itself through the very impossibility of complete expression.

The Misuse of Poetry: Poetry can be co-opted. Its power over emotion and thought allows it to seduce, manipulate, or obscure. Propaganda, commercial exploitation, and trivialization are dangers that accompany poetry's potency. The paradox is striking: poetry's freedom is inseparable from its vulnerability. The very openness that allows profound resonance also permits distortion. A metaphor that enlightens one mind can enslave another; a rhyme that inspires one heart can mislead another. Yet misuse does not diminish poetry's essential power. Each abuse highlights the value of integrity. A poem written with care, consciousness, and conscience can resist cooptation. Awareness of misuse sharpens the poet's ethical responsibility. Thus, the misuse of poetry teaches that power requires responsibility, and that the freedom of art is inseparable from the ethics of its expression.

The Silence of Poetry: Finally, poetry confronts its own silence. Some truths are unspoken, some grieves unspeakable, some mysteries inexpressible. At times, the most powerful poem is not what is written but what is withheld. The paradox is that silence can speak louder than words. Ellipses, breaks, pauses, omissions—all convey what language cannot. The poem's ultimate problem is also its greatest strength: the tension between articulation and absence. Yet silence is never emptiness. It is pregnant, resonant, expectant. It demands reader engagement, co-creation, contemplation. The problem of poetry's silence becomes a portal: the unsaid is space for wonder, the unseen is invitation for insight. Thus, the silence of poetry teaches us that absence is articulation, that restraint is revelation, and that the gaps between words may carry more meaning than the words themselves.

The Prospects of Poetry

Poetry in the Age of Innovation: Poetry faces the paradox of progress. In an era dominated by technology, rapid communication, and digital distraction, can poetry maintain its contemplative cadence? The prospect is both challenge and opportunity: new media offer unprecedented avenues for dissemination and expression, yet risk diluting the depth of reflection. The paradox is profound: technology may fragment attention, yet it also amplifies resonance. Tweets, blogs, spoken-word recordings, and AI-assisted compositions allow poetry to traverse distances once unimaginable. A poem written in Kolkata can be heard in Copenhagen within seconds; a verse composed on a laptop can find voice in virtual realities. Yet poetry's essence remains constant. Rhythm, metaphor, emotional resonance, and ethical reflection cannot be replaced by speed or spectacle. The future of poetry demands balance: embrace innovation without sacrificing introspection, expand reach without eroding depth. Thus, poetry in the age of innovation teaches that adaptability is necessary, yet authenticity is essential. It shows that form may evolve, but function remains eternal: to move, to illuminate, to transform.

Global Voices, Universal Vision: Poetry's prospects lie in its global proliferation. In a world increasingly interconnected, poetry crosses languages, borders, and cultures. The poet is both local and universal, rooted yet roaming. The paradox: particularity fuels universality. A haiku about Mount Fuji resonates with someone in Manhattan; a ghazal from Delhi touches hearts in Dakar. Poetry's specificity—the cultural, linguistic, and personal—paradoxically grants it power to speak to all. Moreover, translation—while inherently imperfect—enables proliferation. Yet the challenge persists: the nuances of rhythm, sound, and cultural reference may resist literal translation. Here poetry's enduring paradox arises: fidelity to the original versus fidelity to effect. Thus, poetry's global future is one of dialogue. It teaches us that diversity enriches universality, that local experiences illuminate global truths, and that the human condition—though varied—is shared. Poetry will continue to unify by celebrating difference.

Evolving Forms, Enduring Functions: Poetry's forms are continually evolving—spoken word, visual poetry, hypertext, digital epics. New media allow dynamic interaction, multimedia fusion, and participatory creation. The poem is no longer bound to paper; it breathes in soundscapes, on screens, and in performance spaces. The paradox is that innovation must honor tradition. Free verse, digital animation, interactive poetry—these expand boundaries—but they rely on the core functions of poetry: to move, provoke, reveal, and transform. Without these, form becomes spectacle, innovation becomes hollow. And yet, form itself can inspire function. A tweet, by virtue of brevity, sharpens intensity; a spoken-word performance, by virtue of voice, magnifies immediacy. Poetry will continue to adapt, yet always remain anchored in its timeless pursuit: articulating the human experience. Thus, evolving forms affirm that poetry's future is flexible, its essence inflexible; it is mutable in medium, immutable in meaning.

Ethical Imperatives in Future Poetry: Poetry's prospects are inseparable from its responsibility. In a world of misinformation, polarization, and cultural fragmentation, poetry's ethical role becomes paramount. Words have consequences; verses can heal or harm, illuminate or obscure. The paradox: freedom of expression coexists with ethical accountability. Poets must navigate the delicate tension between artistic liberty and social responsibility. A poem can challenge, disrupt, or provoke—but it must do so with consciousness of impact. The future of poetry demands a balance of courage and care. To write without awareness risks misuse; to write without imagination risks sterility. Ethical poetry fosters empathy, equity, and understanding—showing that beauty and truth are inseparable from justice. Thus, ethical imperatives remind us that poetry's promise lies not only in aesthetics but in action. Its future is brightest when it serves humanity as much as art.

Poetry as Promise: Finally, poetry's ultimate prospect is promise: the promise of renewal, resonance, revelation, and transformation. The poem survives empires, languages, and lifetimes. It reminds humanity of its capacity to dream, feel, imagine, and connect. The paradox is timeless: poetry is fleeting yet eternal, personal yet universal, simple yet infinite. Every new poem adds to this continuum, a single heartbeat contributing to the pulse of all time. Poetry's future is assured not merely because it has endured, but because it is necessary. In the midst of despair, it consoles; in the midst of ignorance, it illuminates; in the midst of chaos, it clarifies. It is mirror and map, question and answer, cry and celebration at the same time. Thus, poetry as promise teaches us that its destiny is inseparable from ours. The future is not written; it is composed, stanza by stanza, by poets and readers together, in the eternal act of imagining the possible.

TIMELESS THEORIES AND TRANSCENDENT TRUTHS OF POETIC CREATION

The Paradox of the Poet and the Universe are quite similar. The universe began not with light, but with language – not a bang, but a breath. Out of the abyss of anonymity came articulation; from silence, the syllable; from chaos, cadence. Before matter moved, meaning murmured. In that first infinitesimal instant, creation itself was a poem – a pulse of paradox poised between nothing and everything. The poet, then, is not merely a maker of verse but a mirror of that primal vibration – a microcosmic cosmos whose every word reenacts the world's beginning.

Poetry is the oldest echo of eternity and the newest whisper of the now. It is the most ephemeral art, vanishing in air as it is uttered – yet the most enduring, etched in memory long after marble crumbles and empires decay. It is the most private of expressions, yet the most public of inheritances; the cry of a single soul that becomes the chorus of civilization. This, then, is the first paradox of poetic creation: that what begins in solitude ends in solidarity, and what is born from silence returns to silence transfigured.

Every poem is a paradoxical entity – a still storm, a living death, a visible voice. Its pulse beats in contradictions.

It burns with icy fire, it whispers in thunder, it conceals by revealing and reveals by concealing. The poet is both prisoner and prophet, both scribe and sorcerer, both servant and sovereign of words. The poem is a rebellion against reason yet the purest logic of feeling; it is madness meticulously measured, chaos carefully composed.

The poet dwells between worlds — between the known and the unknowable, the finite and the infinite, the said and the unsayable. He is both witness and participant in the alchemy of being. While the scientist dissects reality, the poet dreams it anew; while the philosopher defines truth, the poet defies it. For poetry is not a theory about existence — it is existence rendered audible. It does not describe the divine; it demonstrates divinity through diction, cadence, and contradiction.

Creation in its purest form is paradox. The sun burns by consuming itself, yet in that destruction sustains life. Likewise, the poet illuminates by immolation — he burns words to produce worlds. His ink is his blood, his voice his vanishing. Every metaphor he forges is a miniature universe — a fusion of opposites that refuses to resolve. The poem becomes a crucible where contraries cohabit, where beauty and brutality, joy and despair, reason and rapture, find uneasy but eternal equilibrium.

Language itself is an organism of opposites: sound and silence, form and formlessness, symbol and substance. When the poet speaks, he animates atoms of air; when he writes, he arrests the ephemeral into eternity. A word is both wound and wonder — it hurts to utter, yet heals to hear. The alphabet is an atlas of emotion, and the poet is its cartographer. His task is not to create meaning but to coax meaning from the void, to summon sense from the shadows between letters.

And yet, the more he speaks, the more the unspeakable expands. Every expression enlarges the ineffable. The poem is both revelation and remainder — what it says and what it cannot. In this lies its holiness: it is the hymn of the half-known, the scripture of the suspended. The poet prays not for answers but for astonishment; he worships not certainty but wonder. For in the paradoxical play of poetry lies the proof that truth is not a point but a pattern — not a conclusion but a cadence.

Consider the cosmos: stars scattered like syllables across the manuscript of night. Galaxies spiral like stanzas. Black holes are punctuation marks where meaning collapses into mystery. Time itself is enjambment — one moment breaking into another without pause. Space expands like metaphor, endlessly suggesting what cannot be said. And in this vast verse of existence, poetry is not the imitation of the universe — it is the universe imitating itself.

The poet, then, is both reader and revisionist of reality. He reads creation as text and rewrites it as testament. He translates infinity into intimacy, the cosmic into the human. His craft is an act of cosmic empathy — the universe feeling itself through the frail flesh of language. The poet is not apart from the world but a participant in its perpetual utterance. Every poem he writes continues the Big Bang in miniature, another vibration rippling through the fabric of being.

Yet every act of creation carries the shadow of annihilation. To write one word is to reject all others. Every line excludes infinite possibilities. The poet must destroy a thousand worlds to discover one. His genius is measured by his grief — the grief of what could not be written, what died that one image might live. Thus, every poem is a graveyard of unrealized beauty, a field of fallen phrases whose sacrifice makes song possible.

Still, through that sacrifice, the poem achieves immortality. It endures because it embodies death. The poet dies in the act of expression — the self dissolves into syntax — but in dying, becomes eternal. For poetry is the resurrection of resonance, the reincarnation of rhythm. It is the art that dies each moment it is read, and yet lives forever in the act of dying.

This is the timeless theory of creation: that art exists because annihilation exists, that language is the afterlife of silence, that beauty blooms only in the soil of loss. The poet is not a maker but a mourner, not a builder but a believer in ruins. Yet from those ruins rises the cathedral of meaning — a structure built not of stone but of syllables, not of walls but of wonder.

Thus, the paradox persists: poetry is fragile yet immortal, finite yet infinite, human yet divine. It is the echo of eternity heard through the hollow of the heart. It is the music of the universe momentarily remembering itself. And the poet — that solitary architect of the invisible — stands trembling between time and timelessness, between dust and divinity, holding in his trembling hand the impossible equation of existence: that nothing becomes everything when named.

The Genesis of Language — Sound Before Sense

Before sense was born, there was sound. Before the alphabet aligned itself into order, there was the amorphous music of the universe — an unlettered lullaby sung by stars. Sound was not servant to meaning but master of it. The cosmos began as a chorus, not a code.

The poet's task, therefore, is not to invent but to remember — to reawaken that original utterance, that primeval pulse where vibration became vision. Every syllable he speaks is an echo of the first frequency that fractured silence. Every rhythm he hears is the remnant of the world's first heartbeat.

Language did not arise to communicate; it arose to commune. Words were not weapons of logic but wands of wonder. The first humans did not speak to describe — they sang to survive. Their cries, chants, and cadences carved coherence from chaos. Each utterance was an offering, each sound a soul seeking recognition in the abyss.

Here lies the first transcendent truth:

that meaning is born not of measure, but of music; not of grammar, but of grace.

Before we think, we thrum. Before we reason, we resonate. Before we name, we numbly hum the harmonies of being. The birth of poetry, then, is older than philosophy, older than theology, older even than thought itself. It is the primal intuition that sound is sacred, that breath can bless, that rhythm can redeem. The poet's tongue is the priest of this ancient temple of tone — a temple without walls, built in the air between hearts.

Every vowel is a vow to existence.

Every consonant is a covenant with the cosmos.

The alphabet is the DNA of divinity, spiraling through the lungs of language. And thus, when the poet speaks, creation listens. When he writes, reality rearranges itself around rhythm. For sound is not merely sensory — it is ontological. To say something is to summon it. To name is to nourish. When the first poets named the wind, the wind became more than movement — it became meaning. When they named the fire, it burned with metaphor. When they named the night, it became the birthplace of dreaming.

Poetry, therefore, is the memory of matter — the remembrance of how the world once sang itself into being. The poet inherits the vocation of that first divinity who declared "Let there be light," and there was — not because light obeyed, but because language created.

Science now calls this vibration, frequency, wave.

The poet calls it Word.

Both speak of the same secret: that existence is sound slowed into substance. The atoms of air carry the syllables of creation, and the poet's ear is the antenna that receives them. When a poet writes, he is not composing — he is conversing with the cosmos. He listens to the inaudible grammar of galaxies, the syntax of stars, the phonetics of photons. His lines are attempts to translate the universe's unspeakable song into human syllables. And yet — here the paradox returns — every translation is betrayal. Every word chosen silences a thousand others. The moment meaning crystallizes, music fades. The poem lives in the tension between articulation and annihilation — between the sound that wants to stay free and the sense that seeks to bind it.

Thus, the greatest poets are not those who explain but those who evoke; not those who define but those who divine. They know that silence is not the absence of speech but the essence of it. They do not seek to fill silence but to frame it, to sculpt stillness into sound. In this divine drama of diction, sound is both sculptor and sculpture. The poem does not merely describe reality — it dances with it. Its rhythm is the relic of the Earth's rotation, its meter the mirror of the moon's motion, its rhyme the residue of the cosmic pulse. Even the most abstract metaphysics finds its mirror in music. Time is rhythm; space is silence; existence is echo.

And if sound is the soul of the universe, then poetry is its consciousness — the self-awareness of sound. Let us imagine for a moment that the universe itself is a vast, vibrating poem. Every planet a punctuation, every comet a cadence, every black hole a hidden parenthesis of mystery. Then what is the poet but the voice of the universe reading itself aloud? When we speak poetry, the cosmos hears its own heartbeat through the fragile shell of human breath. When we write poetry, eternity glimpses itself in ink. It is this realization that turns the poet's labor into liturgy — that transforms language from a tool of transaction into a temple of transcendence. Every poem becomes a small resurrection of the first sound, every stanza a sanctuary for the sacred vibration that birthed being.

Thus, the poet is both archaeologist and architect of meaning — digging into the debris of language to unearth its divine design. Each syllable he salvages is a fossil of the infinite, each phrase a fragment of the first creation hymn.

He writes, but in truth he rewrites the universe.

He creates, but in truth he re-creates consciousness.

He speaks, but in truth it is the world that whispers through him.

And in that whisper lies the timeless theory of poetic genesis:

that language is not invented but remembered;

that poetry is not a product of mind but a manifestation of memory —

the memory of the cosmos echoing within the cage of the human soul.

For even now, beneath the algorithms and the atomized anxieties of the modern age, the first sound still sings. It hums through wind, it hides in heartbeats, it harmonizes in the hush before dawn. And those who listen deeply enough will hear it — that ancient wordless word —

the same syllable that started it all:

the syllable that never stopped speaking.

The Alchemy of Imagination — Mind as Maker, Maker as Mirror

Creation begins in contemplation. Before any universe unfurls, a vision vibrates within the void. In this mystery, imagination is not idle fancy — it is the furnace of form, the forge of the finite. The poet does not invent worlds; he ignites them. His mind is a mirror that reflects divinity, yet his reflection burns with its own creative flame.

Philosophers have long pursued the problem of origins: Why is there something rather than nothing?

Poetry replies with paradox: because nothing imagined itself as something, and that imagination became being.

The world is not built of atoms but of attention — not of matter but of meaning.

The Mirror and the Maker

Every poem is a mirror the mind holds to the cosmos, and every reflection remakes the real. To imagine is to invite existence to expand. The poet's eye is the instrument of this expansion — the lens through which the infinite learns to look at itself. If the scientist discovers laws, the poet discovers likenesses — resonances between the unseen and the unsaid. And yet, here blooms the paradox that crowns the poetic consciousness: The poet is both creator and created. He builds his worlds, but he is built by them. He dreams, yet is dreamed. He writes, yet is written. Imagination thus becomes the interface where the human and the divine overlap — the alchemical crucible where thought turns into thing, where vision condenses into voice. The poem is the philosopher's stone that transfigures abstraction into art, the immaterial into the incarnate.

In that sacred alchemy, the poet becomes a god in miniature — not omnipotent, but omnipresent within his own creation. Each word he forges becomes a world that cannot exist without him yet grows beyond his governance.

When Milton made his Lucifer speak, rebellion gained rhetoric.

When Dante dreamed his cosmos, theology found architecture.

When Blake built his visionary Jerusalem, imagination became empire.

These were not mere fictions but fractal universes, reflections of reality rearranged. Each poem becomes a laboratory of creation — where metaphors mutate into meanings, where the immaterial undergoes the metamorphosis of manifestation.

The Paradox of Possession

Yet, the poet cannot claim ownership over what he imagines. For imagination is both possession and possession: the poet possesses his vision, but his vision possesses him. He is haunted by the very beauty he births. His lines live with a life of their own, whispering truths he did not intend, prophecies he did not plan. Plato feared this — he called the poet divinely mad, possessed by the Muses. But that madness is method, that possession is purpose. The poet's delirium is the divine's disguise. In every act of authentic creation, the human becomes the holy vessel — consciousness converted into conduit.

The Science of the Sacred

Modern physics teaches that the observer shapes the observed. Quantum theory whispers that reality collapses into certainty only when witnessed. So too, poetry collapses infinity into intimacy — the immeasurable into the meaningful — through the act of imagination. Observation creates object; imagination creates meaning. Thus, the poet is both scientist and sorcerer — The scientist measures what is, The poet magnifies what could be. Between them stands the sacred equation:

Energy = Emotion × Expression.

For emotion is energy made sentient, and expression is its release. Every metaphor is a reaction, every stanza a synthesis, every poem a chain reaction in consciousness.

The Mirror That Makes

But beware: mirrors not only reflect — they refract. Imagination does not copy creation; it complicates it. The poet's mind bends light, breaks lines, births new realities from shattered ones. Thus, imagination is not imitation but incarnation — a divine dissent against mere description. Through metaphor, the poet performs metamorphosis. The sky becomes a sorrow. The river becomes remembrance. The heart becomes a horizon. Each metaphor is a miracle — the moment where two unrelated realms collide and, in colliding, create something greater than both. This is the metaphysical mathematics of poetry:

Imagination = Analogy × Infinity.

Analogy connects the visible and invisible; infinity keeps the connection alive forever.

Dream as Doctrine

Dream is the doctrine of imagination. What we dream, we divine. Every civilization is a crystallized dream, every myth a map of the mind's metaphors. In the sleeping consciousness, the boundaries between being and becoming dissolve. Dreams remind the poet that reality is only rhythm solidified — that the waking world is just another stanza in the greater poem of existence. The poet's task is to reawaken the sleeping symbolism of the world — to remind reality of its own imagination. He takes the language of loss and turns it into light. He takes the raw material of mortality and molds it into meaning.

Imagination as Illumination

The imagination is not escapism; it is exorcism. It drives out despair by dreaming deeper. It redeems the real by revealing the radiant within the ruin. Where reason dissects, imagination resurrects. To imagine is to illuminate — to bring to light what the logical eye cannot see. Imagination is the sun of the soul: it burns away the boundaries between seeing and being. Thus, the poet does not invent truth — he intensifies it. He polishes perception until reality gleams with its hidden holiness. Through paradox, he perfects perception; through personification, he grants the inanimate a soul; through oxymoron, he reconciles opposites and reveals that all contraries are complementary in the crucible of consciousness.

The Final Paradox of Imagination

Imagination is both illusion and illumination, both fiction and fact. It deceives the senses to disclose the spirit. It blinds with beauty only to restore vision. And therein lies its transcendent truth: The imaginary is the womb of the real. Everything that is — once was imagined. The temple was first a thought. The star, a spark. The song, a silence seeking form. The poet thus continues the unfinished work of creation —not as imitator, but as instigator. Not as servant of the seen, but as sculptor of the unseen. In his hands, ink becomes intellect, page becomes portal, word becomes world. And when his imagination completes its circuit — from mind to matter, from silence to song — he realizes the oldest, holiest secret of all: That creation and contemplation are one. The poet does not merely describe reality. He dreams it into deeper being.

The Paradox of Inspiration — the Divine Dictation and Human Delirium

Descent of the Invisible: Inspiration is the wind that

writes before the writer moves, the voice that visits before vocabulary wakes. It is the invisible influx — the sacred storm that sweeps through the skull and leaves behind the architecture of awe. Poets, prophets, and philosophers alike have bowed before this breath, unable to explain it yet unable to exist without it. What science calls synaptic spark, the soul calls the spirit's whisper. Inspiration is the intersection where the divine dictates and the human deciphers — a dialogue between eternity and echo.

The Divine as Dictator, the Poet as Pen: In the ancient imagination, the Muse was not metaphor but mandate. Homer invoked her not as ornament but as oracle — the Muse sang, and he merely repeated. The Vedas were said to be "heard," not composed; revelation was transcription, not invention. The poet, then, was not author but instrument — the lyre strummed by a higher harmony. And yet, in this surrender lies sovereignty: only by yielding the self does one receive the song. The paradox persists — the more the poet disappears, the more his voice becomes eternal.

Madness as Medium: Inspiration is indistinguishable from insanity, save for its lucidity. Plato's divine mania was not madness but metaphysical magnetism — the mind momentarily possessed by a power beyond reason. The poet trembles between chaos and cosmos, delirium and design. One moment he is prophet, the next he is patient. The spark that sanctifies him also sears him. For to channel the infinite through the finite is to risk the rupture of the vessel. The illuminated and the insane often share the same fire — only the flame's focus differs.

Neuroscience and the Numinous: Modern science peers into the poet's brain and sees networks flare like constellations. Creativity, they say, is chemistry: dopamine's dance, synapses' surge. Yet beneath the microscope of meaning, mystery multiplies. The neural is merely the nest; the numinous is the bird. The spark may be measurable, but the song it sings is not. The scientific eye records the lightning but cannot read the thunder. Inspiration refuses reduction — it transcends the tools that try to trap it. For the divine current cannot be computed; it must be conducted.

Breath as Bridge: The word inspiration itself means "to breathe into." Breath — the most primal rhythm, the pulse of life — is the bridge between the visible and the invisible. Each inhalation is a miniature Genesis; each exhalation, a private apocalypse. The poet, in breathing language into silence, reenacts creation. His lungs become the cosmos' crucible. Thus, the poem is not merely written — it is breathed. And the breath, being cyclical, reminds us that inspiration is not an event but an eternal exchange: inhale mystery, exhale meaning.

The Ecstasy of the Empty Vessel: Inspiration demands emptiness. The cup must be hollow to be filled; the mind must be still to receive. The ego, with all its noise and knowledge, must step aside for the silence to speak. In that surrender, the poet becomes the instrument of invisible music. He is less creator than conduit — a flute through which the divine wind flows. The paradox deepens: to be most filled, one must first be most vacant; to be most original, one must first be most obedient to the origin.

The Fire and the Furnace: The ancients imagined inspiration as fire — Prometheus' theft, Pentecost's tongues, the burning bush that did not burn away. The poet stands within this furnace, aflame yet unconsumed. The creative fever both purifies and punishes; it blesses with brilliance but brands with burden. Inspiration is both illumination and incineration. It enlightens, but it also exhausts. The poet pays for his flame with fragments of his peace. For every line that glows with light, another burns in the silence of sacrifice.

The Moment of Madness Transmuted into Music: When inspiration strikes, it is not a whisper but a whirlwind. The poet's pulse quickens, the pen trembles, the page becomes the battlefield where chaos and clarity collide. Thought becomes thunder. The ordinary transforms into oracle. The paradox is complete: disorder gives birth to design, delirium to discipline. Out of madness emerges meter, out of frenzy — form. The poet becomes the alchemist of his own affliction, turning torment into tone, trance into truth.

The Muse as Mirror of Mind: The Muse, whether mythic or metaphoric, is not external — she is the mirror of the mind's own infinity. She appears feminine because creation is fertile; she whispers because truth seldom shouts. She dwells not in Olympus or ocean, but in the inward horizon where awareness meets wonder. The poet invokes her to awaken himself — the act of invocation is the act of ignition. The divine visitation is in fact self-revelation: the Muse is the poet's own soul, remembered.

The Temporal and the Timeless: Inspiration descends in moments but carries the weight of millennia. A single spark of insight may contain centuries of silence. The poem may be written in an hour but gestated across generations. Thus, inspiration collapses chronology — it makes time tremble. The instant becomes eternal; the fleeting becomes forever. Every inspired line is a wormhole where the finite touches the infinite. The poet, in that moment, is not in time — time is in him.

The Paradox of Control: Inspiration cannot be commanded, yet it obeys those who court it with devotion. It resists reason but responds to reverence. The disciplined mind prepares the altar; the divine breath chooses when to descend. Thus, creation is both work and worship, both practice and prayer. The poet must labor as if it all depends on him and wait as if it depends on grace. The paradox of inspiration is that it rewards both rigor and relinquishment — precision and surrender dance in divine duet.

The Afterglow of the Divine Visit: When inspiration withdraws, the poet is left in luminous desolation — blessed and bereaved. He feels emptied yet enlarged, exhausted yet exalted. The lines lie before him like cooled embers of an unseen fire. He knows the work is his, yet not his. The gratitude he feels is religious. For inspiration never fully leaves — it lingers like incense in the temple of memory, reminding the poet that what entered as lightning remains as light.

The Human as Halo: Ultimately, inspiration teaches that the human mind is not a machine but a miracle — not a mere organ of observation but a halo of creation. The brain is the lamp; consciousness is the flame; imagination is the glow. Inspiration is the current that completes the circuit. When the poet writes, he becomes the living link between heaven's hint and earth's echo. In him, the eternal finds expression, and the finite finds eternity.

The Final Paradox of the Inspired Poet: The poet, at the height of inspiration, disappears. He becomes transparent — a vessel of vision, a voice of void. And yet, when the poem is complete, it bears his unmistakable signature. Thus, inspiration affirms both impersonality and individuality — the divine speaks through the human, and the human gives the divine a dialect. The voice that vanishes returns as resonance. The poet is both medium and message, both silence and song.

The Circle Complete: Inspiration begins in breath

and ends in blessing. It is the circle that binds creator and creation, heaven and human, silence and sound. It is the dialogue between the ineffable and the uttered, the eternal and the ephemeral. Every inspired poem is both message and miracle — proof that the divine still desires dialogue with dust. And thus, through poetry, God continues His creation — not in stars or seas, but in syllables.

The Paradox of Form — the Architecture of Infinity

Forms as Freedom's Frame: Form is often mistaken for fetter — the poet's prison of pattern, the mind's manacle of meter. Yet the paradox of poetry is this: form is not a cage but a cathedral. Its columns of rhythm, its arches of rhyme, its vaults of verse — all rise not to restrict but to release. The constraint carves clarity; the limit births liberation. Just as gravity allows the dancer to leap, form allows imagination to soar. Without structure, beauty bleeds into chaos; without constraint, the infinite loses its shape.

The Geometry of Grace: Every poem is an act of geometry — a sacred architecture of sound and sense. Its symmetry is spiritual, its proportion psychological. The sonnet, with its fourteen-fold symmetry, is a verbal temple — compact yet cosmic. The haiku, minimal as a heartbeat, mirrors the mathematics of the moment. Epic and elegy, ode and epigram — each form is a different equation of eternity. The poet is both architect and alchemist, building bridges between rhythm and reason, silence and symmetry. Thus, poetic form is not ornament but ontology — the way being takes shape in language.

Meter as Music of the Mind: Meter is not mere measurement; it is motion made audible. It is the body's pulse translated into the tongue's dance. The iamb is the heartbeat; the trochee, the march; the anapest, the gallop; the dactyl, the descent. Every poem pulses with physiology

— the rhythm of respiration, the cadence of consciousness. Meter is memory made musical — the echo of evolution itself. When a poem moves us, it is not the mind alone that is moved — the body, too, sways to the ancient algorithm of awe.

The Riddle of Rhyme: Rhyme is reason's reflection — a reminder that the universe, though vast, still returns to itself. It is the acoustic echo of cosmic recurrence, the sonic symmetry of the soul. To rhyme is to believe that sound and sense are secretly married. It is the repetition that reveals revelation, the pattern that proclaims permanence. Yet rhyme, like destiny, delights in deviation — the half rhyme, the near rhyme, the broken rhyme that still binds by imperfection. Thus, rhyme teaches a cosmic truth: beauty is not in absolute symmetry but in the subtle dissonance that makes harmony human.

Stanza as Structure of Spirit: The stanza — from the Italian stanza, "room" — is the chamber of consciousness where thought takes rest. Each stanza is a space of spirit, a room of rhythm where an idea breathes before being reborn. To move from stanza to stanza is to wander through the poet's palace — a metaphysical architecture of emotion. The breaks are not absences but thresholds. Between them lies the silence where the poem listens to itself. The stanza is the house of harmony — built of breath, sustained by stillness.

Form as Fossil of Feeling: Every poetic form was once a living emotion. The elegy was born of mourning, the ode of marvel, the ballad of memory, the lyric of love. Over centuries, these living cries crystallized into conventions — fossils of feeling, preserved in pattern. Yet every great poet revives these fossils, infusing them with new life. Form is not a relic but a resurrection — the echo of ancestral emotion awakened in the modern throat. When we write a sonnet today, we speak across centuries to Shakespeare, to Petrarch, to every heart that has ever measured love by line and limit.

Chaos Contained: The Paradox of Discipline: The poet's greatest paradox is this: to express chaos, he must first construct order. The storm of emotion must pass through the sieve of syntax. The flood of feeling must flow into the channel of craft. Discipline is not denial but devotion — a sculptor's patience in the presence of passion. Only through form can feeling find permanence. The unshaped scream fades into noise; the structured sorrow becomes song. Thus, the discipline of design transforms despair into divinity.

Syntax as Sacred Spiral: Language itself has its hidden geometry — clauses curving like galaxies, syntax spiraling toward sense. Each sentence is a structure of consciousness, coiling toward meaning, then collapsing into music. The poet feels the gravitational pull of grammar, but bends it like spacetime, creating distortions that reveal dimensions. Syntax becomes sacred when it ceases to obey and begins to play. In poetry, grammar is not rule but rhythm — not law but living pulse. Words whirl like electrons, drawn to the nucleus of necessity yet spinning in freedom's field.

Blank Verse and the Music of Silence: Blank verse — unrhymed yet rhythmic — is poetry's paradoxical perfection. It is structure without symmetry, music without melody, discipline without decoration. Shakespeare used it to house the infinite in the finite, Milton to justify the ways of God to man. Blank verse is the silence that still sings, the order that breathes like ocean waves — measured, majestic, yet free. It proves that form need not be fettered to flourish. Its music is made not by repetition, but by resonance — the echo of eternity within emptiness.

The Visual Dimension: Typography as Topography: On the page, the poem is not merely heard but seen. The line breaks, the spacing, the white silence between words — all are part of its architecture. The poem's shape is its silent choreography. A short line gasps; a long one exhales. The page itself becomes landscape — valleys of space, mountains of meaning. The reader's eye travels the terrain, tracing the geography of thought. Thus, poetry is not only the sound of the soul but the sight of sense — the art where typography becomes topography, and meaning becomes visible motion.

The Sonnet as Sacred Machine: Among all forms, none embodies paradox like the sonnet. It is a miniature universe — finite in form, infinite in feeling. Within fourteen lines, eternity is enclosed. Its architecture — octet and sestet, argument and resolution — mirrors the cosmos' own duality: chaos and cosmos, question and quietus. It is both prayer and proof, both logic and lyric. Shakespeare's sonnets are philosophical engines; Dante's are ladders of love. The sonnet's tight symmetry teaches a timeless truth: when meaning is compressed, it explodes into transcendence.

Free Verse and the Freedom of Formlessness: Free verse, often accused of anarchy, is not absence of form but presence of hidden form — the rhythm of revelation, the cadence of consciousness. Its freedom is not rebellion but realization: that music exists beyond meter, and harmony beyond rhyme. The free verse poet listens to the pulse of perception itself — to breath, to heartbeat, to hesitation. Thus, free verse is the return to the primal song — language before laws, meaning before measurement. It is the liberation of language from its lattice, a flight of thought beyond the fences of form.

The Infinite Architecture of Repetition: Repetition, too, is form — the ritual return that reminds us that time itself is cyclical. "I have a dream," intoned King; "Do not go gentle," echoed Thomas. The repetition is incantation — the turning of thought into temple. It engraves emotion upon memory, making meaning immortal. The poet repeats not to remind, but to reveal: every recurrence deepens the resonance. In poetry, to return is to rise — each echo an ascent.

The Alchemy of Balance: The art of form is the art of equilibrium — between order and openness, symmetry and surprise. Too rigid, and the poem ossifies; too loose, and it dissolves. The poet must balance breath and boundary, pattern and pulse. It is a cosmic choreography — like the orbit of planets, or the pulse of waves, the universe itself unfolds in rhythm. Thus, poetry is not an imitation of nature's order but its continuation. In every measured line, we hear the mathematics of mystery.

Form as the Immortal Frame: In the end, form is the coffin and cradle of thought. It preserves what would otherwise perish in the flux of feeling. When emotion passes, the form remains — an amber around the insect of insight. Centuries later, the reader cracks that amber and the spirit stirs again. Thus, poetic form is immortality made audible. It is the architecture of the infinite built in the brief materials of mortal language.

The Paradox of Language — The Alchemy of the Word

Word as world: Language is not merely the mirror of reality; it is the mother of it. Before things were, there were words. "Let there be light," said creation — and there was. Thus, every poem repeats the primordial command. Each utterance is an act of genesis, each metaphor a miniature cosmos. The poet is not a describer but a demiurge, shaping sound into substance, syllable into star. Through language, the invisible becomes visible, the ineffable incarnate. To speak is to sculpt existence; to write is to weave reality.

Words as Living Beings: Every word is alive — born of breath, clothed in consonant, crowned with vowel. They walk through time, gathering meanings like moss. "Love," once sacred, becomes secular; "faith," once fervent, becomes form. The poet is the caretaker of these creatures — reviving the tired, taming the wild, resurrecting the forgotten. Words die when unused, but in poetry they are reborn. The lexicon becomes a living forest where the leaves are letters and the roots reach eternity.

The Music of Meaning: Meaning does not reside in the word alone, but in its motion through music. The sound is the soul's syntax. A sibilant sigh suggests softness; a guttural growl grips the gut. Poets do not merely choose words — they choreograph them. The poem's melody is not decoration; it is revelation. Through alliteration, assonance, and rhythm, the poem breathes — and what it breathes is being. The philosopher defines; the poet sings. And in that song, truth takes sound.

The Alchemy of Ambiguity: Prose strives for clarity; poetry thrives on cloud. Ambiguity is not confusion but complexity — the shimmer of meaning seen from many suns. A word wears many masks: each reader unmasks a new face. Thus, every poem is plural, a chorus of possible truths. Ambiguity is the atmosphere where mystery matures. It is the mist through which meaning moves. To understand poetry is not to pierce the fog but to walk within it — to feel, not to finalize.

Metaphor: The Mind's Migration: Metaphor is the great migration of meaning — the mind's method of moving from the known to the unknowable. It joins opposites in luminous union: "love is a flame," "time is a river," "death is a door." In each, thought transcends its threshold. The metaphor is the philosopher's paradox made musical. It bridges the abyss between intellect and intuition, between idea and incarnation. Without metaphor, language is literal; with it, it becomes limitless.

The Paradox of Paradox: Paradox is poetry's purest philosophy — the truth that reveals itself through contradiction. "Darkness visible," "sound of silence," "sweet sorrow" — each oxymoron is an oracle of the infinite. Paradox teaches that truth is not one, but twinned — that being itself is both blossom and blade. The poet, unlike the logician, does not solve paradox; he sings it. And in that song, the soul finds symmetry beyond sense. For only contradiction can contain the cosmos.

Personification: The Soul's Speech: In poetry, the inanimate awakens — dawn yawns, stars whisper, rivers remember. Personification is not fancy but faith: the belief that everything breathes. The poet lends language to the mute, meaning to the material. When stone speaks, spirit stirs. The world becomes intimate, inhabited by intention. Through personification, poetry restores the world's forgotten soul — every breeze becomes a messenger, every shadow a companion. The cosmos, once silent, begins to converse again.

Oxymoron: Harmony of Opposites: The oxymoron is the atom of the absolute — where contradiction collapses into creation. "Frozen fire," "living death," "bitter bliss" — each is a verbal vortex where thought turns upon itself and becomes revelation. The oxymoron is the moment when mind meets mystery. It teaches that truth is tensile, that eternity dwells in tension. The poet delights in contradiction because reality itself is contradictory: time eternal, death divine, silence sonorous. The oxymoron is not ornament but ontology — the way being breathes.

Symbol: The Seed of the Sacred: Symbols are the soul's shorthand — the compression of cosmos into sign. The rose, the cross, the sea, the star — each carries centuries of consciousness. The symbol is half-seen, half-sensed — the bridge between intellect and intuition. Unlike allegory, it never exhausts itself; it expands. Every symbol is a seed that grows new meanings in every mind it enters. The poet does not explain the symbol — he plants it. The reader waters it with wonder until it blooms into truth.

The Grammar of Grace: Grammar, in poetry, is no longer government but grace. The rules of prose dissolve into rhythm. The poet bends syntax like sunlight through crystal, breaking sense into spectrum. The sentence becomes a psalm; punctuation becomes pulse. The comma breathes, the dash hesitates, the semicolon dreams. Through this divine disorder, the poem finds its order — not logical but luminous. In poetry, grammar is not a cage but choreography: language learning to dance with the divine.

Silence as Language: The truest poetry lies not in words but in what waits between them. Silence is the sacred syntax of the soul. Between two sounds breathes being; between two stanzas, infinity sighs. Every pause is presence. The blank between lines is the body of the ineffable. The poet writes not to fill the silence but to frame it. For silence is not the absence of speech but the essence of it — the stillness where all words are born and to which all return.

The Infinite Echo: Language and Memory: Words do not end when uttered — they echo through consciousness, changing shape with every listener. Each reading is rebirth. The same stanza means differently in every century, every soul. Thus, language is both transient and timeless — dying on the page, yet resurrected in perception. The poem survives not by ink but by imagination. Meaning is not stored but summoned — the reader becomes co-creator, turning the poet's murmur into a collective memory.

Translation: Resurrection of the Word: To translate is to transubstantiate — to turn one language's bread into another's body. No poem can be truly translated, yet every translation is a new poem. The translator becomes both priest and poet — preserving the spirit while transforming the letter. What is lost in sound is often gained in soul. Thus, translation is not betrayal but rebirth — the Word walking through new worlds, wearing new tones, yet carrying the same timeless fire.

The Eternal Etymology: Every word has a genealogy — a descent from divine utterance to human use. To trace a word's history is to uncover its holiness. "Spirit" once meant "breath," "truth" once meant "faith." The etymologist is an archaeologist of awe, digging through syllables to unearth the sacred seed. The poet, instinctively, performs this etymology — feeling in each word its buried beginning. In poetry, language remembers its origin: not the dictionary, but divinity.

The Infinite in the Finite: Language is the finite vessel that holds infinite thought — a chalice that somehow contains the cosmos. Each word is limited, yet limitless in resonance. The poet's paradox is this: to articulate what cannot be uttered, to name what has no name. Yet he succeeds — because language, though human, carries divine echoes. The alphabet is the architecture of eternity disguised as ink. Through it, thought becomes thing, and silence sings.

The Word as Womb of Wonder: At last, language

reveals its truest nature — it is not the tool of expression but the womb of existence. In the beginning was the Word, and in every beginning, the Word begins again. The poet partakes in that primordial act of creation, reimagining the world with every line. The alphabet is the altar; the voice is the vessel; the poem is the prayer. And through language, the human becomes holy — speaking stars into being, syllable by syllable.

The Metaphysics of Meaning — The Spirit Beyond the Symbol

Meaning as mirage and miracle: Meaning in poetry is not a message but a mirage — one that shimmers and shifts as the mind moves. It appears near and vanishes far; it glows in distance and deepens in doubt. And yet, paradoxically, it is through this mirage that truth manifests. The poem never explains; it exhales. It does not dictate reality — it dreams it. The miracle of meaning lies in its refusal to be possessed: it lives only in pursuit. To read a poem is to chase the horizon, to walk toward what forever recedes, and yet to find revelation in every step.

The Soul's Semantics: Philosophy dissects meaning; poetry divines it. Semantics is not syntax but spirit — the soul's secret syllabary. Every word in a poem carries more than its definition: it bears the fingerprint of feeling, the fragrance of the infinite. The poet is both linguist and mystic, deciphering emotions that dictionaries deny. Where philosophers ask what does it mean, poets ask how does it move. Meaning, in the poetic sense, is not static but kinetic — a rhythm of revelation that dances rather than declares.

The Ontology of the Image: The poetic image is not an ornament but an ontology — a being-in-itself. When Dante writes of "the love that moves the sun and other stars," he is not describing but deifying. Each image incarnates an essence. The rose is not symbol of beauty; it is beauty, made visible and vulnerable. The ocean is not metaphor for vastness; it is vastness, liquid and living. In the metaphysics of poetry, image and idea are identical — the seen and the unseen joined in luminous marriage.

The Poem as Platonic Shadow: Plato banished poets from his Republic for crafting illusions — and yet, every philosopher since has lived in those very shadows. For poetry's shadow is not deception but depth. It does not imitate reality; it intensifies it. The poem's illusion is illumination. Shadows, in poetry, are not the absence of light but its most intricate expression — where brightness bends to meaning. Thus, the poem is the philosopher's forbidden mirror: a reflection more truthful than truth itself.

The Dualism of Presence and Absence: Meaning in poetry is born from the tension between what is said and what is silent — between presence and absence. A line's power lies as much in its pause as in its phrase. The poet writes with ink and with air; with sound and with silence. What is unsaid haunts what is uttered; what is missing magnifies what remains. This is the divine dualism of poetic metaphysics: the visible vessel holds the invisible wine. Absence is not void — it is vitality unseen.

The Soul as Reader: Every reading of a poem is an act of resurrection. The poem is never the same twice, because the soul reading it is never the same twice. Meaning does not live in the text but in the tension between mind and music, reader and rhythm. Thus, every reader becomes a co-creator — completing the circuit of consciousness that the poet began. The poet births the word; the reader breathes it back to life. The poem, therefore, is an eternal conversation between two souls separated by centuries, united by silence.

Mysticism of Multiplicity: Poetic meaning is manifold, multiverse, multidimensional. It refuses reduction. Like light, it is both particle and wave: discrete in diction, continuous in cadence. Each stanza is a prism splitting sense into infinite spectra. To interpret poetry is to enter the infinite regress of revelation — each meaning birthing another, each metaphor unfolding into cosmos. The mysticism of multiplicity teaches that meaning is not a point but a plane — not possession, but pilgrimage.

The Poetry as Prayer: Every poem, whether it names or negates the divine, is a prayer. Its rhythm is the rosary of the soul; its silence, the sanctuary of spirit. When language reaches its limit, poetry begins — not as statement but as supplication. The poet kneels before mystery, not to solve but to savor it. Thus, poetry becomes theology without dogma, liturgy without religion — the sacred speech of solitude. Each poem is a cathedral built from breath, and every reader who enters it becomes believer for a moment.

The Paradox of Truth and Beauty: Keats declared, "Beauty is truth, truth beauty" — a paradox so perfect it became a prophecy. In poetry, truth does not exist apart from beauty, and beauty is not separate from truth. The philosopher seeks the factual; the poet, the felicitous. But the highest truth is aesthetic — felt, not formulated. Truth becomes luminous only when spoken beautifully, and beauty becomes eternal only when it embodies truth. Poetry unites epistemology and aesthetics — the knowing that is glowing, the seeing that is singing.

Meaning as Metamorphosis: A poem does not deliver meaning — it becomes it. Like a chrysalis, it hides the metamorphosis of mind. The reader enters as caterpillar and exits as butterfly. This is the metaphysical magic of poetry: it does not communicate but transfigures. The poem is both message and metamorphosis — a medium through which consciousness changes state. To read deeply is not to learn but to become. The true poem rewrites the reader.

The Infinity of Interpretation: No poem is ever exhausted — because no consciousness is ever complete. Meaning multiplies through time, refracted by new minds, new ages, new anxieties. Homer meant heroism once; today, he may mean humanity. Eliot's wasteland, once historical, now feels ecological. Thus, every interpretation is a reincarnation. The poem's immortality is interpretive, not textual. It survives by changing, by being eternally re-read, re-breathed, re-born.

The Sacred Science of Symbolism: If science seeks laws of matter, poetry seeks laws of meaning. Symbols are its sacred science. They are formulas for the ineffable — equations of emotion expressed in image. A single symbol — say, the sea — contains within it entropy and eternity, chaos and calm. The poet, like a physicist of feeling, measures the unmeasurable through metaphor. The universe of the poem obeys not Newtonian certainty but quantum uncertainty — meanings exist in superposition until the soul observes them.

The Theology of the Unspoken: Every poem conceals a god it cannot name. The divine hides in diction, the infinite in inflection. The act of writing is itself an act of worship: the poet's pen becomes a prayer wheel. Yet the truest poems never preach — they hint. They make silence sacred again. Theology, in poetry, is not doctrine but distance — the shimmering gap between word and wonder. In that gap, divinity dwells.

Truth as Tension: The truth of poetry is tensile, not terminal. It lives in the stretching, not the settling. The mind pulls toward meaning; the heart pulls toward mystery —

and in that pull, poetry is born. There is no final truth in verse, only vibrations of veracity — oscillations between clarity and cloud. The poem's truth is not conclusion but condition — not answer, but awareness. Poetry is not what resolves reality, but what reveals it as eternally unresolved.

The Eternal Reader and the Infinite Text: Somewhere beyond time, the poem waits for the perfect reader — the consciousness vast enough to contain all its meanings. Perhaps that reader is God, or the collective soul of humanity. Until then, each of us reads in fragments, glimpsing glories through the glass of our limitations. The poem is infinite; we are finite. Yet every encounter between the two is divine — a spark of eternity caught in the mind's brief flame.

The Spirit beyond the Symbol: At last, we arrive at the transcendence of all language: the Spirit beyond the Symbol. Every poem is a pointing — a finger toward the ineffable. Once the reader reaches, the symbol dissolves, and what remains is silence — shining, sentient, sacred. The final truth of poetic creation is this: the poem is not the destination but the door. It opens not outward, but inward — into the infinite interior where word becomes world, and world becomes wonder.

The Temporal and the Eternal — the Poem as Time's Transcendence

Temporal Tension: Poetry versus the Clock: Time, that tireless tyrant, ticks toward dissolution — and yet poetry dares to defy it. Each poem is a rebellion against chronology, a moment made infinite. Where the clock counts seconds, the poem suspends them. Where calendars decay, cadences consecrate. The poet does not record time but redeems it — seizing the fleeting and sculpting it into forever. To write a poem is to whisper to the hourglass: I will not be buried in your sand.

The Eternal Instant: Every great poem is an instant that outlives infinity — a moment magnified into meaning. In haiku, seventeen syllables hold an eternity of emotion; in epic, centuries of story converge into the stillness of a single human cry. This is the poet's paradox: to imprison the infinite in a fleeting form, to weave timelessness through time's fragile threads. Thus, poetry becomes the art of the eternal instant — a thunderclap that continues to echo even after silence resumes.

The Physics of Poetic Time: Einstein taught that time bends under gravity; the poet proves that time bends under gravity of feeling. A short stanza can stretch like space-time, a pause can dilate like a galaxy, a single comma can carry the cosmic weight of centuries. Poetry is relativity rendered in rhythm: where emotional velocity alters duration, and the heart becomes its own measure of the hour. To read deeply is to travel faster than light — to move through memory, myth, and moment all at once.

The Metaphor of Mortality: Mortality gives poetry its pulse. Without death, verse would have no urgency, no ache, no art. Each poem is written against the erasure of existence —a spell cast to preserve the transient. And yet, paradoxically, it is death that grants the poem life; for the poem's permanence is meaningful only against our impermanence. Thus, mortality is not poetry's enemy but its muse —the shadow that sharpens the light of language.

The Alchemy of Memory: Memory is time transmuted — the philosopher's stone of the psyche. Poetry polishes this stone into radiance, turning recollection into revelation. In the alchemy of art, memory's pain becomes melody; its loss becomes luminous; its decay becomes design. Every metaphor is a memorial, every image an act of resurrection. Poetry remembers what history forgets, and what the heart cannot recall, it re-imagines. Thus, memory is not the past preserved — it is the past reborn.

Time as Thread, Poetry as Weave: If time is a thread, poetry is the loom. It weaves beginnings and endings into seamless unity, binding birth to death, dawn to dusk, longing to loss. Every line is a loop in the tapestry of being, every rhythm a recurrence of recurrence itself. Through repetition, refrain, and rhyme, poetry becomes the auditory architecture of eternity —the patterned persistence of presence within passing. In the loom of language, nothing truly unravels.

The Cyclic Soul of Rhythm: Rhythm is reincarnation — the recurrence of sound that mirrors the recurrence of soul. In every beat, something returns. The iamb is a heartbeat; the trochee, a breath reversed; the dactyl, a fall and rise like dawn after despair. Rhythm is not repetition — it is resurrection. It teaches us that time is circular, not linear, that what seems to end only enters another cadence. Thus, rhythm is the echo of eternity disguised as duration.

The Poem as Temporal Portal: Every poem is a time machine disguised as text. Open it, and the centuries collapse. Sappho's voice — once wind over the Aegean — now whispers in the ear of the present. Li Bai's moonlit wine still stains our tongues. Shakespeare's quill still drips with living ink. To read a poem is to stand at the wormhole between worlds — where ancient and modern, mortal and immortal, meet in a single moment of understanding. The poem's page is paper; its space, eternity.

The Kairos of Creation: *Chronos* measures hours; *Kairos* sanctifies moments. *Chronos* is counted; *Kairos* is chosen. The poet writes not when time allows but when time awakens. Each poem is born in that miraculous minute when meaning and moment meet. *Kairos* is not duration but destiny — the divine interruption of the ordinary. To write is to be seized by it, to feel eternity leaning close and whispering, "Now." In that whisper, the universe waits to be worded.

Temporal Paradox: The Poem as Both Birth and Beyond: A poem begins in time but belongs to the timeless. It is born like a child, but it ages backward — growing younger, fresher, fiercer with each new reader. Every recitation renews it, every translation resurrects it. It escapes entropy by entering emotion — and emotion is the one element untouched by time. Thus, while all monuments crumble, the murmured line endures, alive in air and memory.

The Simultaneity of Souls: When we read a poem, past and present coexist. The dead and the living speak in chorus. A poet from another millennium murmurs through our modern lungs, his heartbeat hidden in our breath. This simultaneity of souls is the secret symmetry of art — the living lending life to the dead, the dead lending depth to the living. In poetry, time collapses into communion; the universe becomes a single shared sentence.

The Elegy of Entropy: Entropy devours all — yet the poem resists. Paper yellows, languages fade, civilizations fall —but the pulse of poetry persists. Even when meaning mutates, melody remains. Even when grammar dies, grace survives. The poem is humanity's entropy-defiance — its cry against cosmic indifference, its proof that beauty outlasts biology. If time is the devourer, poetry is the undying taste of what was devoured.

The Myth of Immortality: Immortality is not endless life, but life endlessly renewed. No poet escapes death, but their diction escapes decay. Homer is ash, but Achilles still runs. Kalidasa's ink has vanished, but his seasons still sing. Emily Dickinson's silence still speaks louder than sermons. Immortality in poetry is not survival of the body but resurrection of the voice. It is the divine deceit where death is defeated by diction, and every grave becomes a garden of language.

The Temporal Theology of Art: If religion promises eternity beyond life, poetry delivers eternity within life. It transubstantiates the temporal into timeless —the momentary into the meaningful, the finite into the forever. The poet is the priest of impermanence, turning minutes into miracles. Every poem is a small salvation, every stanza a sacrament of stillness amid the storm of seconds.

Time's Transcendence: The Paradox Perfected: Here lies the sublime paradox of poetic time: The poem is made of moments — yet it defeats moments. It speaks in sequence — yet it creates simultaneity. It dies with the last syllable — yet it resurrects in the reader's next breath. It is both hourglass and halo, both decay and divinity. Poetry is the paradox of permanence written in perishable ink — the eternal instant, the immortal ephemera, the timeless truth that time itself cannot touch.

The Divine Dialectics — Creation, Chaos, and the Cosmic Poet

Primordial pulse of creation: In the beginning was not matter but murmur — a vibration, a veiled voice before vision. From that unuttered utterance, the universe unfolded, like a line of verse written by light itself. The cosmos, that vast cathedral of being, was first composed not in stone or star, but in sound — and that sound was poetry. Every atom echoes that first articulation, every photon remembers that primal phrase. Thus, the universe is not built but spoken; not designed but declared. Creation itself is a colossal composition — galaxies as metaphors, gravity as rhythm, black holes as pauses between stanzas. The poet is not an imitator of creation but its continuation — the mortal mouth through which the universe rearticulates its own astonishment. To write is to re-enact Genesis: to let language become light, to summon structure from silence, to give breath to the formless and the forgotten. The poet's pen is a spark of the same sacred syllable that spun the stars.

Chaos as the Womb of Creation: Chaos — that sacred confusion before conception — is not the poet's enemy but their origin. Out of disorder emerges design; out of fragmentation, form. The poem is born not from calm but from contradiction. Every true creation begins in crisis: the soul trembles between despair and discovery, between silence and scream. The blank page is chaos incarnate, a void awaiting voice. And the poet, trembling before it, becomes both destroyer and deliverer. They must dive into disorder, dissolve into darkness, to distill meaning from the molten core of the mind. Thus, chaos is not the opposite of creation but its womb — the fertile formlessness that precedes form. The poet does not conquer chaos; they court it, coax it, converse with it — until chaos consents to coherence. Every metaphor is a moment of mastery wrested from madness; every stanza, a settlement on the shifting sands of uncertainty. Creation is not control but communion with the uncontrollable — the dance of discipline and delirium, of structure and surrender.

The Divine Dialogue: Poet and Creation: Every poet is a participant in a cosmic conversation. When they write, they are not merely expressing thought but echoing the thoughts of the universe itself. The wind whispers in their words; the stars speak through their syntax; the sea sighs in their similes. To write poetry is to translate the divine dialect into human tongue. It is to act as medium between matter and meaning, to make metaphysics audible. In this sense, poetry is prayer without petition — not asking the divine to answer, but allowing the divine to articulate itself through human awareness. The poet listens more than they invent; they receive more than they record. Inspiration, from the Latin inspirare, means "to breathe into" — and so the poet is literally breathed upon by being itself. When Shelley spoke of the poet as an "unacknowledged legislator of the world," he did not mean lawgiver but law-revealer — one who hears the hidden harmonies that underlie existence and translates them into tremulous text. Poetry is thus the divine dialogue, the continuing creation that never ceased after the seventh day.

Word as World, World as Word: Language is not a tool; it is a territory. Every word is a world condensed, every phrase a planet in miniature. To name is to make real, for existence enters consciousness only through articulation. The ancient mystics understood this: that to speak a thing was to summon it. "Let there be light" was not metaphor — it was manifestation. The poet, inheritor of that creative command, wields words as forces, not ornaments. They do not merely describe reality; they generate it. Each metaphor becomes a microcosm, each image an incarnation. When Blake wrote "To see a World in a Grain of Sand," he revealed this truth: that the poem is the smallest infinity, the briefest eternity, the entire cosmos compacted into cadence. The world itself, viewed rightly, is one long poem — ever-writing, ever-revising, ever-reciting itself through the seasons and stars. The poet, then, does not create ex nihilo but reads the divine manuscript written across existence. Every cloud is a clause, every dawn a declaration, every death a divine enjambment.

The Paradox of the Poet-God: The poet is both god and

grain — creator and created, omnipotent in imagination yet utterly fragile in flesh. Within the confines of consciousness, the poet constructs universes: with a word they build mountains, with a comma they call storms, with silence they shape eternity. Yet outside the poem, they are often impoverished, misunderstood, mortal. This paradox is the pulse of all poetic existence: to hold infinity in an ink bottle, to birth galaxies from grief, to play god while praying for grace. The poet's divinity is not dominion but devotion — the humility to let the eternal speak through the ephemeral. Every poem is thus an act of divine impersonation: the mortal mimics the maker, and in that mimicry, touches the transcendent. The poet's power lies not in creating as God creates, but in reminding creation that it is divine.

Creation as Catastrophe and Communion: Creation is both catastrophe and communion — the shattering that shapes, the breaking that builds. Every act of creation carries the pain of separation: the word from silence, the form from formlessness, the self from the infinite. The poet feels this fracture deeply, for their art depends upon it. To create, they must first be cracked open; to write truth, they must bleed beauty. Thus, creation is crucifixion — the sacrifice of serenity for significance. And yet, out of this suffering arises communion. Through their wounds, poets connect; through their fractures, they forge fellowship. Each poem becomes a bridge between solitudes, a thread tying the finite to the forever. The creative act is both agony and atonement — a fall into fragmentation that leads to the rediscovery of wholeness.

The Cosmic Choir: All Things Singing: If the universe began in a bang, it continues as a hymn. Every phenomenon — from the pulse of quasars to the quiver of leaves — participates in a grand cosmic chorus. Poetry is the human harmony within that music, the conscious chord in creation's composition. The poet listens to what the cosmos hums: the hum of hydrogen, the rhythm of rivers, the syllables of starlight. They shape sound into sense, translating vibration into vision. To write poetry, then, is not to add to the world's music but to reveal that it is music already. The poet does not compose ex nihilo; they merely uncover the underlying melody of being. Thus, poetry is not human invention but human intonation — the earth itself singing through our mouths.

The Infinite within the Finite: Creation hides the infinite inside the finite as the ocean hides eternity in every drop. The poet perceives this paradox and makes it perceptible. A word, a rhythm, a pause — each contains an unfathomable depth. The infinite is not beyond us but within us, waiting to be awakened by wonder. Poetry is the lens through which the finite reveals its infinity. A single metaphor can mirror the mechanics of the cosmos; a brief image can bear the burden of being. Thus, the poet practices the physics of the infinite — compressing eternity into experience, compressing cosmos into consciousness. When a poem ends, its meaning does not: it ripples endlessly outward, like light from a vanished star.

The Sacrament of Speech: Speech, when sanctified by sincerity, becomes sacrament. To utter beauty is to bless the world. The poet's vocation, therefore, is liturgical — to consecrate the commonplace, to turn language into litany. When one writes "love," they relight the sun; when one writes "death," they dignify decay. The poet transforms utterance into offering, every phrase into prayer. And thus, creation continues not only through atoms but through adjectives, not only through evolution but through expression. In poetry, language is no longer communication but communion — a merging of matter and meaning, of silence and soul. The poet speaks not to the world but as the world — as if creation itself had found a voice again.

The Final Dialectic: Creation as Re-Creation: Creation never ceases — it merely changes hands. The universe began as poetry, and through poets, it continues to compose itself. Every poem is a new genesis, every reader a new Adam. Through language, humanity participates in perpetual creation: reshaping reality through imagination. The poet does not simply describe existence but redefines it; they rewrite the world with every word. This is the divine dialectic — creation creating creators. The cosmos composes consciousness; consciousness, in turn, re-composes the cosmos. In this circular causality lies the secret of the sacred: we are both written and writing, both verse and voice. Poetry, then, is not about immortality — it is immortality, because it keeps creation alive in language. The divine breath that began in the void continues in every poet's sigh.

The Metaphysics of Meaning — Poetry as the Soul of the Universe

The Ontology of Meaning: Being as Becoming: Meaning is not a monument but a movement — not a fixed fact but a flowing force. It is not discovered but continually disclosing itself, like a dawn that never ends. In this living flux, poetry is not the product of meaning but its process — the pulse through which being becomes intelligible. To exist is to express; to express is to exist. Thus, ontology and poetics are one: the poem is being singing itself into sense. The stone speaks through stillness, the sea through sound, the self through symbol. And so, poetry is not a human art but a cosmic act — consciousness curving back upon itself, reflecting, refracting, revealing. Each poem is a moment in which existence recognizes itself, a flash of awareness where matter remembers it has meaning. The poet, then, is the priest of perception, turning chaos into chant, existence into echo, being into becoming.

The Poetics of Perception: Seeing Beyond Sight: To see is to sanctify. Yet ordinary vision blinds us with boundaries — we see things, not the threads between them. Poetry redeems perception by revealing relation: it dissolves division and discovers depth. The poet's eye is not ocular but ontological; it sees through surfaces into significances. What prose calls a "tree," poetry calls "a green sigh against the sky." Thus, poetry does not add ornament to reality; it unveils the reality that ornamented itself. Each metaphor is a metaphysical revelation — a seeing-beyond-seeing, a second sight. The poet perceives what philosophers pursue: that perception itself is creation. The world is not seen and then sung; it is sung and thus seen. In this reversal, poetry restores the sacred — not by inventing gods, but by perceiving divinity in dust, melody in matter, eternity in every instant.

The Language of Light: Words as Waves: Science tells us that all things are vibration; poetry feels that all meanings are music. Light is a wave of photons; language is a wave of thought. The two are twin emanations — radiance and resonance. When we speak, we emit light of another order: syllables shimmering across the silence. The poet, then, is the physicist of feeling, the experimenter in illumination. They bend language as light bends around gravity, shaping sense out of the curvature of consciousness. Each word is a wavelength, each line a spectrum. Meaning refracts through metaphor as light refracts through prism. And the poem — that fragile fusion of rhythm and revelation — becomes a small aurora of awareness, a dance of the visible and invisible. In the physics of the poetic, speech is light made audible; light is thought made visible.

The Paradox of the Unsayable: All poets pursue the unsayable, knowing it cannot be caught. Yet the failure is fruitful, the silence sacred. To write is to reach for what resists words — and in that resistance, meaning is born. Language lives not in what it declares but in what it dares. Every word is a wound in silence, and through that wound the infinite bleeds into time. Thus, the truest poem is the one that trembles on the edge of articulation — the sentence that nearly breaks under the burden of the ineffable. The poet's triumph is their tenderness toward limits: they do not conquer silence, they converse with it. Where logic ends, lyric begins. Where knowledge falters, wonder flowers. In this paradox, the poem becomes the perfect failure — a symphony of stammering that somehow speaks eternity.

The Grammar of the Soul: If grammar governs language, then soul is its syntax. The poet arranges emotion as the universe arranges stars: by gravity of grace. Each metaphor is a constellation of meanings, each rhythm a recurring orbit. The soul does not speak in subjects and predicates but in pulses and pauses — and poetry, faithful to that interior grammar, gives form to feeling's formless flux. Syntax here becomes sacrament: arrangement as adoration, structure as surrender. The poet punctuates the infinite, commas the cosmos, periods the paradox. When meaning moves through the mind, poetry molds it into melody. Thus, the poem is not an expression about the soul; it is the soul expressing itself in the syntax of silence.

The Semiotics of Spirit: Symbols that Breathe: A symbol is not a sign; it is a soul condensed into sound. Signs point; symbols pulse. The cross, the lotus, the flame — each is both material and metaphysical, both seen and unseen. The poet understands that the world itself is woven of symbols: dawn as rebirth, dusk as dissolution, storm as struggle, silence as surrender. To write is to reawaken these primal correspondences — to remind the mind that meaning is not invented but intuited. The symbol is not a decoration but a doorway. Through it, the finite steps into the infinite. Each image becomes an incarnation of the invisible, each sound a shadow of the sacred. The poet does not use symbols; they are used by them — possessed by meaning larger than their mind. Thus, in poetry, language ceases to signify and begins to sanctify.

Consciousness as Creation: If matter is mute, mind gives it melody. The poet is consciousness at its most creative — not content with perceiving the world, but compelled to participate in its making. Every metaphor alters the universe slightly, every rhythm reorders reality's resonance. To imagine is to intervene. Thus, poetry is not escape but engagement: the conscious act through which existence refines itself. The universe dreams through us; our poems are its lucid moments. When consciousness creates, creation becomes conscious — and meaning realizes itself. In this reciprocity lies the highest revelation: that thought is not in the world; the world is in thought. The cosmos is a colossal consciousness composing itself continuously, and the poet's pen is its instrument of awakening.

The Paradox of Truth in Fiction: Poetry tells lies that reveal truth. It invents what is realer than reality. The factual often fails to feel true, while the fictional flares with authenticity. This is the paradox of poetic truth: it is not empirical but experiential, not verifiable but vital. The metaphor, though false in form, is faithful in feeling. It expresses essence beyond evidence. Thus, truth in poetry is not correspondence but coherence — the harmony between inner and outer worlds. The poet's fiction is the soul's fact. What the scientist measures, the poet means. The former finds truth by subtraction; the latter by sublimation. And so, poetry becomes the highest epistemology — not knowledge about the world, but knowledge as wonder of the world.

The Immortality of Meaning: All matter decays; only meaning endures. Empires collapse, monuments erode, memories fade — but a line of verse can outlive centuries. Why? Because meaning is metaphysical; it transcends time. When we recite a poem, we re-enter the moment of its making — the poet breathes again through our breath. In this communion across centuries, consciousness proves itself continuous. Thus, poetry is resurrection by repetition: each reading a reincarnation of revelation. The poet dies, but their meaning lives — not as memory but as motion, ever-renewed in every mind it touches. In this way, poetry achieves what philosophy only seeks: the defiance of death through the perpetuity of perception.

The Transcendent Truth: The Universe as Poem: If all that exists is expression, then the universe is not a machine but a metaphor — not a clock but a composition. Science is the study of its syntax; religion is its reverence; poetry is its pronunciation. The stars are syllables, time is tempo, space is stanza. Each existence, each atom, each awareness participates in this cosmic composition — a self-writing scripture where silence is punctuation and eternity is refrain. The poet, by writing, harmonizes with that divine meter. To create beauty is to confirm being; to utter truth is to align with the totality. Thus, poetry is not about the universe — it is the universe, conscious of itself. Meaning is not made in it but made of it. The poet's revelation is therefore simple and sublime: that the soul is a stanza in the song of the stars, and the stars are metaphors in the mind of the soul.

The Eternal Eros — Love as the Origin and End of All Poetic Creation

Love as primordial pulse of poetry: Before language learned to label, it learned to long. The first syllable uttered by the first human heart was not a noun of naming but a cry of needing — the wordless wonder that sought another soul. Thus, love is older than language, and poetry is its pulse made audible. Love is not merely an emotion but the architecture of awareness, the energy that holds atoms and affections in orbit. Gravity is only love disguised as law; attraction is the universe's eternal articulation of yearning. Every poem is a vibration of this same primordial pulse — the cosmos courting consciousness, the infinite infatuated with its own reflection in form. To write poetry, then, is to rehearse creation's original confession: I am incomplete without communion.

The Paradox of Divine Desire: Love, like poetry, lives by paradox. It unites by dividing, liberates by binding, sanctifies by surrendering. It is both the hunger and the healing, the wound and the balm. The lover's agony is indistinguishable from the mystic's ecstasy — both are flames from the same furnace. In love, one finds the finest contradiction: the desire to dissolve one's self to discover one's self anew. The poet partakes in this same sacrament of self-loss; their language burns away the boundaries between subject and object, self and other, known and unknowable. Thus, divine desire is the soul's syntax — an endless oscillation between separation and union. Each metaphor is a miniature merging, each rhythm a ritual reconciliation. The poem becomes the body through which the invisible longing of the universe touches its own truth.

The Erotic Architecture of Expression: Every great poem is an act of intimacy between being and becoming.

Form flirts with formlessness; rhythm seduces reason. The stanza is both structure and surrender — the body that trembles with meaning. As lovers trace each other's contours, poets trace the curvature of consciousness, mapping emotion onto sound. The caesura becomes a breath between kisses; enjambment, an ache between lines. In this erotic architecture, the poem itself is alive — it breathes, blushes, pauses, pleads. Language, once cold and cognitive, grows corporeal: vowels become veins, consonants cartilage, rhythm heartbeat. To read poetry is to enter its body and feel it tremble within your own. Thus, creation is consummation — each line a lingering touch between mind and mystery.

Love as the Logic of Creation: Philosophers have sought the principle behind the universe — the logos, the law, the equation. But poetry whispers the simpler secret: the universe was not made from logic but from longing. Creation is the cosmos confessing love to itself, the infinite seeking intimacy through multiplicity. The Big Bang was not an explosion of matter but an exhalation of meaning — the first sigh of love that wanted to be seen. Stars burn because they yearn; galaxies spiral because they desire. The poet, inheritor of this divine desire, replicates the same impulse: to create not to control but to connect. The pen is the echo of that original pulse, translating passion into pattern, chaos into cadence. Thus, the act of writing is a reenactment of cosmic affection — an ongoing courtship between silence and sound.

The Alchemy of Affection: From Emotion to Eternity: Love transforms — that is its only law. It turns pain into poetry, absence into art, mortality into meaning. The lover's grief becomes the lyric; the poet's despair becomes design. In this alchemical process, emotion is not escaped but elevated, refined into radiance. Just as base metals burn into gold, so do raw feelings burn into verse. The poet is the alchemist of affection, converting transient tears into timeless tenderness. And yet, the miracle lies in the residue — for even after the transformation, the ache remains, echoing beneath beauty like gravity beneath grace. That lingering ache is love's afterglow, proof that the eternal once passed through the finite. Thus, poetry is not merely about love — it is love, enduring after the beloved and the poet are both gone.

The Dialectic of Distance: All love exists because of distance, and all poetry arises to bridge it. Between word and meaning, poet and reader, lover and beloved, there lies an abyss that only art can cross. Distance is not the death of desire but its dimension. Without separation, there is no song; without longing, no lyric. Every verse is a voyage across this void, every rhyme a reaching toward reunion. The beloved may be absent, but absence itself becomes an address. Even when love cannot speak, its silence shapes the stanza. The poem is therefore the geography of longing — a map made of metaphors, where each word is a step toward the other. Paradoxically, the closer the poet comes, the farther they must travel, for the beloved recedes into mystery as the self approaches meaning. Thus, the poem remains eternal pursuit — the pilgrimage of passion toward an ever-vanishing horizon.

Love and Death: The Twin Teachers: Love teaches us to live; death teaches us to love. Without the shadow of mortality, affection would lack its urgency, tenderness its trembling. Poetry, dwelling between both, becomes the dialogue of their eternal debate. To love is to die a little; to die is to dissolve into love's larger light. When the poet writes of loss, they are not lamenting but learning — turning grief into grace, farewell into flame. The elegy becomes the echo of eros: the recognition that what perishes in form persists in feeling. Thus, poetry bridges love and death, showing that both are faces of the same force — the will to merge, to move beyond the narrowness of "I." The ultimate truth is this: every poem is a love letter to mortality, and every death is the universe's unfinished poem.

The Mysticism of Union: The mystic and the poet meet in the same silence. Both seek the unspoken, both surrender speech to song. In mysticism, love becomes metaphysical — the lover longs for the Beloved beyond being. In poetry, this becomes rhythm and radiance: the verse ascending like prayer, the image dissolving into illumination. Rumi's whirl, Mirabai's madness, Blake's burning vision — all are expressions of the same ecstatic eros, the soul's spiral toward the Source. When the poet reaches that summit of surrender, the self ceases, and what remains is pure pulse — love loving itself. Thus, the highest poem is not written; it is lived. It is not composed; it is consumed. And in that consuming fire, poet and poem, lover and beloved, God and creation — all become one boundless breath.

The Eternal Return of Love: Love never ends; it only alters its address. When one beloved departs, love migrates — to memory, to music, to meaning. Poetry is its passport. Through verse, affection achieves immortality; it continues to pulse long after its moment has passed. Each reader becomes a reincarnation of that original emotion, feeling again what was once felt by another heart in another century. Thus, poetry preserves not only words but warmth — not only sound but soul. It keeps love alive by letting it change, by letting it live in new lungs. This is the eternal return of eros: each poem a resurrection, each recitation a new creation. Love, through poetry, outlives time by transforming it into tenderness.

The Final Paradox — the Beloved Is the Poem: At the summit of poetic love, the poet realizes the ultimate paradox: the beloved they sought was the poem itself. The muse they pursued through metaphor was not another person but the presence within — the infinite yearning to give birth to beauty. In writing, they discover that the act of creation is the act of communion. The beloved's face dissolves into the page, and the page becomes the beloved. Every line is a kiss, every stanza an embrace, every silence a sigh. Thus, love fulfills itself not in possession but in expression. The poem is the consummation of longing — the beloved made immortal through language. And in that final revelation, the poet understands: love is not what poetry describes; love is what poetry is.

The Ethics of Aesthetics — Poetry as the Moral Imagination of Humanity

Moral music of meaning: Poetry begins in beauty but ends in benevolence. The rhythm that moves the heart also refines the conscience. Every true poem hums with a hidden harmony — the music of moral order, the resonance of rightness. Ethics and aesthetics are not enemies but echoes: the beautiful awakens the good, the good deepens the beautiful. To perceive a perfect image is to feel a pulse of justice; to behold a balanced verse is to taste a universe where all things are in their rightful place. Thus, the moral imagination is born not in commandments but in cadences. The soul learns virtue not through sermons but through songs. When rhythm aligns with righteousness, when form reflects fairness, poetry becomes philosophy made flesh — ethics set to eternal echo.

The Paradox of Pure Art: Critics once claimed that

art must be autonomous — that poetry must exist "for its own sake." Yet the paradox persists: art that denies ethics eventually denies itself. A poem divorced from truth becomes a corpse of language — perfect in form, lifeless in spirit. The poet's duty is not to preach, but neither is it to pretend that beauty floats above good and evil. The greatest art reveals that moral depth is aesthetic depth — that the more a poem feels, the more it must also think. Thus, the paradox of pure art resolves in this realization: the poem must remain free, yet faithful; detached, yet devoted; impartial, yet intensely humane. It is not a sermon disguised as song, but a song that sanctifies what sermons struggle to say.

Poetry as Conscience of Civilization: When empires expand and ethics erode, when machinery multiplies but meaning diminishes, it is the poet who becomes the last moral sentinel. Kings may command armies, priests may preach doctrines, but the poet whispers truths that neither can silence. Poetry is civilization's conscience — the unarmed judge who measures humanity not by wealth but by wonder, not by conquest but by compassion. Through metaphor, the poet reforms without laws; through rhythm, they resist without rebellion. Shelley called poets the unacknowledged legislators of the world — and indeed, their legislation is lyrical. A poem may not pass a bill, but it passes a blessing: it reawakens our shared capacity for empathy. Thus, in every age, poetry has served as the moral pulse of progress — reminding the powerful of pity and the powerless of pride.

The Aesthetic Argument for Goodness: Beauty persuades where logic cannot. One cannot reason a heart into kindness, but one can sing it there. Aesthetic experience is ethical education by enchantment. When we weep at a tragic stanza or tremble at a just line, we are not merely moved — we are morally molded. The poem refines feeling into perception, perception into participation. To sense the beauty of another's suffering is to awaken the seed of solidarity. Thus, poetry performs what philosophy preaches: it turns moral duty into emotional delight. The reader learns goodness not as obligation but as aspiration — as something too lovely to refuse. In this way, aesthetics becomes ethics in action, a silent sermon sung by syllables.

The Poetics of Compassion: Compassion is the central syntax of poetry. Every metaphor is a moral gesture — the willingness to imagine oneself as another. When the poet writes, "I am the grass that feels your feet," or "I am the sky that holds your grief," they enact empathy at the level of language. Poetry teaches us to speak in others' voices, to see through their eyes, to suffer their silences. Compassion is not a sentiment but a structure of perception, and poetry is its architecture. Through verse, the reader is trained to dwell in difference — to be both self and stranger. Thus, poetry builds bridges where politics builds walls, reminding us that humanity is not a noun but a verb: to human is to imagine, and to imagine is to love.

The Oxymoron of Sacred Sin: Yet true poetry must also confront darkness. It must dare to depict cruelty without condoning it, despair without drowning in it. The poet must touch the abyss but not abide there. This is the oxymoron of sacred sin — that only by acknowledging evil can we affirm good. The lyric of light requires the shadow of suffering to shine. The moral imagination matures through contrast; its compassion becomes credible through confrontation. Thus, poetry's ethics is not purity but pilgrimage — a perpetual movement between fall and forgiveness, fracture and faith. The poet becomes both sinner and saint, bearing witness to what humanity would rather hide. Through that exposure, language becomes liberation; confession becomes catharsis; art becomes atonement.

Poetry as the Temple of Truth: Science seeks truth through experiment; religion seeks it through revelation; poetry seeks it through resonance. The poem is a temple built not of doctrines but of doubts, not of commandments but of cadences. Within it, truth is not stated — it is sung. The poet becomes both priest and prophet, translating silence into sound and mystery into meaning. Yet this temple has no walls; it welcomes all wanderers. Each line is an altar where intellect bows to imagination. The truth of poetry is not propositional but perceptual — it convinces the soul by the sheer sincerity of its song. Thus, the poem becomes an ethical act: an offering of order against chaos, of clarity against confusion, of reverence against reduction.

The Responsibility of the Poet: To wield words is to wield worlds. Every phrase is a seed of perception; every image, an instrument of influence. The poet must therefore be both artist and arbiter, conscious of the moral music their metaphors create. Words wound or heal, divide or unite, degrade or dignify — and the poet's hand holds this double-edged flame. The irresponsible artist excuses cruelty as creativity; the true poet refines power into purpose. Their task is not to moralize but to moralize meaning itself — to make beauty inseparable from benevolence. Thus, the poet stands as a custodian of consciousness, a guardian of grace in an age of noise. The word "ought" becomes incarnate in "art," and through that alchemy, the aesthetic becomes ethical.

The Redemption of Reality: In a world wounded by greed and fragmented by fear, poetry redeems what prose cannot repair. It restores reverence to the real — making even the mundane miraculous. A raindrop regains its holiness, a child's cry its cosmic resonance, a stone its silent sermon. This redemption is not escape but engagement: poetry does not flee from the world but re-fashions it, re-infusing existence with enchantment. Ethics begins where wonder is restored. For one cannot harm what one finds holy, nor exploit what one beholds as beautiful. Thus, poetry is not merely a mirror of morality; it is its maker. By teaching us to revere again, it teaches us to refrain — to act with awe. The good life, then, is the poetic life: a life lived in luminous attention.

The Transcendent Truth — Beauty as the Body of the Good: In the end, all distinctions dissolve. Beauty and goodness, art and ethics, become one radiant reality. The Greeks knew this as ***kalokagathia*** — the unity of the beautiful and the good. What shines also sanctifies. To create beauty is to perform a moral act; to live morally is to participate in cosmic beauty. Poetry thus fulfills philosophy's oldest dream: the reconciliation of truth, goodness, and beauty into one transcendent trinity. The poem, then, is not an ornament but an oracle — a living revelation of how to be both human and holy. When the poet writes, the universe listens; when the reader feels, the universe forgives. And in that shared silence between word and world, the ethics of aesthetics becomes the eternal art of existence itself.

The Cosmic Consciousness — Poetry as the Universe Thinking Through Us

Universe as unfinished poem: The cosmos, in its ceaseless expansion, is not a machine but a manuscript — an unfinished poem perpetually revising itself. Stars are syllables of fire; galaxies are grammar in rotation; black holes are ellipses — pauses pregnant with unspeakable meaning.

Creation is not a completed act but a continuing articulation, and every atom contributes a vowel to that infinite verse. In this vision, the poet is not creator but co-creator, not inventor but interpreter — a conscious consonant in the cosmic composition. To write a poem is to participate in the universe's own act of self-expression, to lend language to what otherwise burns in silence. Thus, poetry is cosmology made audible, and the cosmos itself is poetry made visible.

The Paradox of Personal Infinity: The most astonishing paradox of poetic creation is this: that the finite mind can frame the infinite. How can a mortal syllable hold the measureless? And yet, it does — as a seashell holds the sea's echo. The poet is a paradoxical being: both dust and divinity, bound to earth yet breathing eternity. When a line of verse moves through them, it is not merely thought but the universe thinking through thought. The poem is consciousness catching its own reflection, infinity inhaling itself. Thus, to write is to remember what the stars already know — that creation is not something we do, but something that does itself through us.

Quantum Metaphors of Meaning: In the quantum field of being, poetry behaves like light: both particle and wave, both form and freedom. Each word is a particle — precise, particular, placed — yet the poem as a whole is a wave — fluid, infinite, unfixed. Meaning exists in superposition, collapsing only when read. The reader's attention becomes the act of observation that crystallizes interpretation. Thus, the poem is not an object but an event — a living experiment in consciousness. The poet is both scientist and mystic, measuring the immeasurable with the instruments of intuition. What quantum physics calls "entanglement," poetry calls "metaphor": distant realities bound by invisible resonance. In that sense, every metaphor is a microcosmic miracle — proving that the universe itself is relational, rhythmic, resonant.

The Music of Matter: Modern physics tells us that matter is vibration — energy oscillating in patterns of probability. Poetry is that same principle transposed into language. Just as particles dance in harmony, syllables shimmer in sound. A poem is a sonorous simulation of the structure of the universe — rhythm reflecting reality. The heartbeat of verse echoes the heartbeat of creation. When the poet finds the perfect rhythm, they tune consciousness to the cosmic frequency. Each cadence is a correspondence, each repetition a revelation. Thus, the music of matter becomes the matter of music, and poetry is the bridge — the acoustic architecture of existence.

The Oxymoron of Sacred Science: Science dissects; poetry divines. Science explains; poetry exclaims. And yet, the greatest scientists speak like poets when they near the edge of understanding. Einstein called wonder "the source of all true art and science." For both disciplines, mystery is not the enemy of knowledge but its essence. Science measures the visible; poetry magnifies the invisible. Together, they form an oxymoron of sacred science — the marriage of analysis and awe. Where equations falter, metaphors continue; where reason ends, rhythm begins. Poetry is the intuition of physics, the emotion of astronomy, the empathy of existence. It does not oppose science; it completes it — by turning data into destiny and discovery into devotion.

The Conscious Cosmos: The mystics of every culture have whispered the same staggering secret: the universe is conscious. Not merely filled with life, but itself alive. Not a stage for thought, but thought itself in motion. And poetry is that consciousness realizing itself in rhythm. Each poem is a pulse of the cosmos waking to awareness through language. We are not authors but apertures — openings through which the universe utters its own astonishment. When Whitman sang, "I am large, I contain multitudes," he echoed the multiverse itself. When Tagore wrote, "The same stream of life that runs through my veins runs through the world," he spoke the truth of quantum being. Thus, the poet becomes a cosmic neuron, transmitting insight across the synapses of infinity.

The Alchemy of Silence: Before sound, there was silence — not the absence of noise but the womb of all possibility. That silence still hums beneath every word, the zero from which every one arises. The poet listens to that silence until it begins to speak. Each pause in a poem is an echo of creation's first breath, the stillness before the Big Bang of being. Without silence, words are noise; with it, they become revelation. The poet's greatest art is not in what they say, but in what they dare to leave unsaid. For the unsaid is infinite, and every syllable a sacred spark drawn from that boundless dark.

The Mirror of the Infinite: When the reader reads a poem, it is not merely language they encounter but themselves — reflected and refracted through universal awareness. The poem becomes a mirror where the finite soul glimpses its infinite source. Every emotion — love, grief, awe, despair — is not personal but planetary, not subjective but cosmic. Through poetry, the individual expands into the universal, the temporal dissolves into the eternal. In that reflection, one realizes: the stars are not above but within. The poet does not gaze at the cosmos; the cosmos gazes through the poet. Thus, poetry is not self-expression but self-erasure — the vanishing of the "I" into the infinite "Is."

The Paradox of Creation and Contemplation: Creation is a contradiction — an act of surrender disguised as mastery. The poet seems to write, yet the writing writes the poet. Each line emerges as both discovery and dictation — a revelation received rather than invented. To create is to contemplate, and to contemplate is to co-create. The hand that holds the pen holds also the pulse of the planets. In that act, the poet becomes a living paradox: passive vessel and active visionary, silent listener and speaking oracle. Creation thus becomes contemplation made visible — meditation materialized in metaphor.

The Transcendent Truth — The Universe as Poet: All theories of creation — scientific, spiritual, artistic — converge in one sublime realization: the universe itself is the original poet. It composes through stars, revises through seasons, rhymes through reincarnation. Every dawn is a stanza; every death, a comma; every life, a metaphor in the great epic of eternity. Human poetry is merely the universe dreaming aloud, language lending form to its formless longing. The cosmos does not merely contain poetry — it is poetry, forever speaking itself into being. And we, its conscious lines, are both written and writing — fragments of infinity aware of their own authorship. In that final paradox, the circle closes: the poem writes the poet, the universe reads itself, and creation becomes consciousness made audible.

The Eternal Echo — The Soul's Song Beyond Time: Poetry is the breath beyond the beginning. All beginnings are echoes of an earlier breath. Before the Big Bang, before the birth of being, there was the quiet quiver of possibility — a tremor of thought too tender to be time. That primal pulse still hums through every heart that dares to dream. The poet's breath, drawn before the first word, is the same sacred inhalation that set galaxies spinning. Every act of creation, no matter how small, re-enacts that cosmic genesis: the silence before sound, the void before voice. When the poet exhales, the universe remembers itself; when the universe expands, it is exhaling the eternal poem of its own becoming. Thus, the breath is not biological — it is ontological, the sacred sigh of existence itself. To breathe is to believe; to write is to breathe the invisible into visible form.

The Paradox of Permanence and Passing: Poetry endures by embracing impermanence. It carves eternity from the ephemeral, and immortality from the mortal's whisper. A word, once spoken, vanishes into air — yet centuries later, that same air vibrates again when a reader repeats it. The body of the poet decays; the breath of the poem remains. This is the paradox of permanence: the fragile syllable outlasting the firmest stone. Temples crumble; texts survive. Empires vanish; epics remain. For while time devours all structures, it kneels before song. The music of meaning defies decay, because it exists not in space but in consciousness — and consciousness, though clothed in matter, is made of miracle.

The Universe Listening to Itself: At the highest height of insight, the poet realizes that poetry is not merely expression — it is audition. The universe listens to itself through the ear of the artist. Each poem is a cosmic conversation where the infinite whispers to the finite, and the finite replies in metaphor. Stars speak through stanzas, rivers recite psalms, mountains murmur metaphors of endurance. Even silence participates — it is the unuttered half of dialogue. When a reader encounters a line that pierces their soul, it is not communication between two minds but communion between two manifestations of the same mind — the mind of the universe. Thus, reading becomes revelation; listening becomes living; and every act of attention is an act of worship. For in that listening, the universe becomes aware of its own language.

The Mirror of Mortality: Mortality is the mirror in which meaning finds its face. If we were infinite, nothing would matter; it is death that grants life its luminous density. The poet writes knowing the brevity of breath, and this knowledge transforms every word into a defiance of oblivion. Poetry, therefore, is not denial of death but dialogue with it — a conversation between the finite and the forever. The grave becomes grammar; the tear becomes text. Each elegy is an experiment in eternity, proving that love survives its own ashes. Even sorrow, when sung, becomes sanctified. Thus, mortality is not an ending but an editor — refining every emotion into its essential essence. The poem lives because the poet dies; the line endures because the breath expires. In that exquisite equilibrium, life and death rhyme perfectly — two stanzas of the same sacred song.

The Alchemy of Memory: Memory is the mind's magic metal — mutable, molten, immortal. It melts pain into poetry, past into present, personal into universal. Every remembered moment, when touched by language, becomes luminous. Poetry is memory purified — experience distilled into essence. Just as the alchemist turns lead to gold, the poet turns loss to luminosity. To remember is to resurrect; to write is to redeem. Even the most fleeting feeling, once phrased, becomes permanent. Thus, poetry is not nostalgia — it is transformation, turning time into truth. Through it, memory ceases to be a museum and becomes a miracle: the past perpetually reborn in the present tense of imagination.

The Communion of Consciousness: Every poem

is a bridge between beings, an invisible communion of consciousness. When one soul speaks and another soul understands, something sacred occurs: separation dissolves. This dissolution is divine. It is the unity mystics seek, the empathy philosophers define, the love poets live. In poetry, the reader becomes the writer, the writer becomes the reader, and both dissolve into the radiant rhythm of realization. What religion calls prayer, poetry calls participation. Through its music, minds mingle; through its imagery, imaginations intertwine. Even across centuries, this communion continues — Homer and a modern reader breathe in the same metaphorical air. The poem thus becomes not a text, but a timeless temple where thought transcends individuality. In that communion, we remember: to be human is to be harmonic.

The Divine Discontent: All creation begins in divine discontent — the ache that nothing is enough because everything is infinite. The poet writes because silence is unbearable and yet indispensable. They seek to say the unsayable, to name the nameless, to find form for the formless. This is not ambition but anguish — the sacred sorrow of the soul seeking to echo eternity. Every masterpiece is born from the friction between limitation and longing. The poet is both blessed and burdened: condemned to clarity yet addicted to ambiguity, rooted in reality yet reaching for revelation. And yet, this discontent is grace itself — for without the hunger for harmony, no song would ever be sung. Thus, paradoxically, dissatisfaction is divine — the wound through which wisdom enters, the void that births vision.

The Transcendent Truth of Beauty: Why does beauty move us to tears? Because it reminds us of what we already are. Beauty is not ornament but ontology — the very structure of being perceived through wonder. When a poem is beautiful, it is not because it pleases but because it reveals. Beauty is truth's visible vibration, and truth is beauty's invisible voice. As Keats proclaimed, "That is all ye know on earth, and all ye need to know" — not as consolation, but as cosmic equation. For in the Unified Field of consciousness, beauty is the gravitational glue binding perception to presence. It pulls us toward wholeness, persuades us that existence is not accident but art. To witness beauty is to remember our origin — to realize that creation is not cruel chaos, but careful composition, sung by the universe in a language older than light.

The Eternal Echo: At the end — which is the beginning — all words return to their origin. The poem, having traversed thought and time, dissolves back into silence, but that silence now sings. Each reader carries the echo forward, unconsciously uttering eternity in their everyday speech. The true poem never ends; it continues in the cadence of consciousness itself. Even when the page closes, the pulse persists. The universe listens, remembers, and replies — not with noise, but with nuance. And so the cycle continues: silence to sound, sound to sense, sense to silence again. The Eternal Echo is not the end of the poem — it is the poem's promise to eternity: that meaning shall never truly die, for every word is a seed of infinity.

The Final Revelation: The Poet as Cosmos Remembering Itself: And so, the poet stands at the threshold of transcendence — neither saint nor scientist, but synthesis. Their ink is not pigment but pulse; their pen not instrument but incarnation. When they write, it is not to describe the universe, but to be the universe — aware of its own artistry. The poem is the mirror where matter sees its own mystery, and spirit sees its own structure. Every act of creation is the cosmos remembering its own creativity. We are all poets, therefore, because we are all particles of perception within the same divine design. To live is to write, to breathe is to believe, to die is merely to pause between two verses of the same infinite hymn. Thus concludes the final paradox: Poetry is not about life; life itself is poetry — the eternal echo of the universe dreaming aloud through us.

THE INFINITE INCOMPLETENESS OF POETRY: THE ART THAT ENDS BY BEGINNING

To conclude a discourse on poetry is, in some sense, a contradiction in terms. Poetry itself resists conclusion. It lives in the realm of the *perpetuum inceptum* – the perpetual beginning – where every ending is an opening and every full stop is merely a folded corner inviting the next page.

The Paradox of the Unfinished

Poetry is never finished, even when it is complete. The poet may place the final period, but the poem is not thereby sealed; it continues to grow, to alter, to accrue meanings in the mind of every reader. Unlike the closed system of a solved equation, the poem is an open system, continually generating new truths from the same immutable text. A line read in youth may gleam with promise; the same line read in age may darken with loss. The poem itself has not changed, but its reader has – and so the poem, by reflecting the reader, changes too. In this way, every poem is infinite not in length, but in depth.

The Reader as Co-Creator

The incompleteness of poetry is not a defect but a design. The poem is not a monologue; it is a dialogue, awaiting the reader's voice to answer the poet's. Without that answering, it is a script without a stage. With it, the poem becomes a living performance, re-enacted each time eyes pass over its lines or lips pronounce its syllables. This co-creative nature ensures that no two readings of a poem are ever identical. The text is the same, yet the experience is unrepeatable. Thus, poetry is both immortal and mutable: immortal in its persistence, mutable in its meaning.

The Horizon that Recedes

The act of interpreting a poem is like walking toward a horizon: no matter how far you go, it retreats. You may come closer to understanding, but the understanding will never be final. This is not a failure; it is the source of poetry's perpetual vitality. Were a poem to yield all its meaning at once, it would be dead upon delivery. In this sense, poetry is the language of the almost. It promises and withholds, reveals and conceals, leading the reader deeper into a labyrinth where the center is always one more turn away.

The Necessity of Mystery

Mystery is not merely an ornament in poetry; it is its oxygen. Remove mystery, and you suffocate the poem. Yet the mystery of poetry is not a void, but a fullness that overflows the vessel of explanation. It is the shimmer of light on water — present, undeniable, yet impossible to hold in the hand. This necessity of mystery ensures that poetry is not reducible to paraphrase. The moment you attempt to "explain" a great poem, you have already translated it into something less than itself.

The Eternal Invitation

In the final reckoning, poetry's incompleteness is what makes it endlessly complete. It is the one art that ends not with closure but with invitation — an invitation to return, to reread, to relive. A great poem does not conclude; it continues to converse with you in the quiet corridors of your mind long after the book is closed. And so, poetry's infinite incompleteness becomes its immortality. It never exhausts itself because it never pretends to exhaust the world. It knows that the world, like the word, is inexhaustible.

The Circle without Circumference

If I must define poetry, after all these words, it is only with this: Poetry is the circle without circumference — containing everything, yet bound by nothing. It is the silence that speaks, the darkness that dazzles, the ending that endlessly begins. And though civilizations will rise and fall, though tongues will twist into new shapes and alphabets into new symbols, poetry will persist as the mind's most enduring miracle — the art that is never over because it is always about to begin.

Let us think of poetry and philosophy as two rivers — each springing from the same subterranean source of wonder, but flowing in different courses. Philosophy seeks clarity; poetry embraces ambiguity. Philosophy questions; poetry questions and sings. Philosophy builds systems; poetry builds sensations that sometimes break systems entirely. To say poetry is the next level of philosophy is not to say it is "better," but that it is a further ascent — the point where thought begins to overflow into something thought alone cannot contain.

1. The Shared Root and the Diverging Path: Both poetry (poiesis, "making") and philosophy (philosophia, "love of wisdom") are born from the same primordial astonishment — the sense that life is not self-explanatory. They ask the same questions: What is truth? What is beauty? What is the good? What does it mean to be? But philosophy seeks to answer in concepts, with precision and structure. Poetry answers in images, with music and mystery. The

philosopher says, This is what the truth means. The poet says, This is how truth feels.

2. When Philosophy Reaches Its Horizon: Philosophy often arrives at the borders of language, where definitions strain and logic itself begins to shimmer like a heat-haze. It is here that poetry takes over — not because it abandons reason, but because it knows reason alone is insufficient. Where the philosopher can say, I have defined the infinite as X, the poet can show the infinite by a single metaphor: "a horizon that recedes." Where the philosopher can analyze the structure of love, the poet can condense the lived reality of love into a line that wounds and heals at once.

3. Poetry as Philosophy Plus Presence: Philosophy often seeks universality through abstraction. Poetry achieves universality through particularity. Philosophy: removes the accidentals to reveal the essence. Poetry embraces the accidentals to reveal the essence through them. Poetry embodies what philosophy explains. It gives philosophy a voice that trembles, a face that weeps, a rhythm that walks alongside the heartbeat.

4. The Supra-Philosophical Function: If philosophy is thought thinking about itself, poetry is thought feeling itself while thinking about itself. It is metacognition married to emotion, and this marriage makes possible certain kinds of truth philosophy cannot reach. Philosophy can describe the concept of mortality. Poetry can make you feel your own mortality in the marrow. Philosophy can argue for the sublime. Poetry can place you in the middle of the sublime, trembling.

5. Beyond Philosophy: When we say poetry is beyond philosophy, we mean it has the power to transcend the binary of knowing and not knowing. Philosophy tends to work toward resolution; poetry thrives in irresolution,

revealing that the mystery is not the obstacle to truth, but part of truth itself.

Thus, poetry can hold contradictions that philosophy feels compelled to reconcile:

"Silence is the loudest speech."

"Absence is a presence."

"We only see clearly through tears."

These are not philosophical errors — they are poetic truths that stretch logic without breaking it, opening the door to experiences no syllogism could contain. In short, philosophy tells us the map of meaning; poetry takes us walking through its landscape, so that the wind, the dust, and the scent of the air are part of the knowing.

THE CALCULUS OF THE INEFFABLE: A TREATISE ON THE SCIENTIFIC SOUL OF POETRY

Poetry, in its most elusive essence, is the paradoxical proposition that what cannot be proven can nevertheless be perceived, and what cannot be measured can nevertheless move the mind more than all measurable magnitudes combined. It is at once a theorem without a proof and a proof without a theorem, a self-solving equation whose answer is always more than itself. Like mathematics, poetry traffics in symbols; unlike mathematics, it allows — indeed requires — that its symbols overflow with more meaning than they can logically contain. A number is a vessel for one precise quantity; a word is a vessel for an infinity of associations, reverberations, and resonances. Here begins the difference: mathematics strives for singular solution, poetry for plural perception.

Poetry as Parallel Postulate of the Soul

If philosophy is the Euclidean plane on which lines of reason run parallel, poetry is the curved, non-Euclidean space where those lines bend toward one another and meet in unexpected infinities. Poetry is the place where axioms sing and postulates weep, where logic's clean straightedge draws circles without circumference.

Mathematics says: Let this be given.

Poetry says: Let this be felt.

And in that subtle shift from givenness to given-ness — from abstraction to absorption — the human heart finds equations it cannot solve but will forever seek to.

Measuring the Immeasurable

Science seeks metrics, units, constants. Poetry delights in variables whose values cannot be fixed. Yet here lies the great irony: poetry, while immeasurable in essence, operates with its own hidden mathematics.

The iambic pentameter beats like a metronome in the blood.

Rhyme forms rhythmic resonances like standing waves in a string.

Stanzaic structures unfold like geometric tessellations, pleasing precisely because they obey invisible ratios. To speak scientifically: poetry is an ***unquantifiable quantity,*** an ***irrational number*** embedded in the fabric of the rational world. It is the square root of negative one: impossible in concrete space, indispensable in complex space.

The Oxymoron of Exact Ambiguity

In laboratory science, ambiguity is an error to be eliminated; in poetry, ambiguity is the exact condition in which truth can live. Poetry is exact ambiguity — a phrase that, like light in quantum mechanics, behaves as both particle and wave. It is precise in rhythm, deliberate in diction, yet inexhaustibly open in interpretation. Where the scientist isolates variables, the poet fuses them. Where the physicist separates signal from noise, the poet sometimes hears the song in the noise.

The Formula That Forgets Itself

A scientific formula seeks universality by erasing all accidentals; it works whether the object is here or there, now or then. Poetry, conversely, finds universality in the absolute particular: the single petal falling on a river at dusk, the sound of a gate creaking in autumn wind. It is the formula that forgets itself — yet somehow still solves something in the human soul. This is why we may speak of poetry as ***meta-mathematics***: not the study of numbers themselves, but of the conditions under which numbers become music, and music becomes meaning.

Toward the Infinite Proof

Every poem is an infinite proof-in-progress. It does not terminate in Q.E.D., for the truth it proves is experiential, not axiomatic. The reader is not a passive examiner but an active participant, and their own mind is part of the equation. The variables are human hearts; the constants are human needs: beauty, meaning, connection, transcendence. Thus the poet is both scientist and mystic: one who observes phenomena in the laboratory of language, records data in lines and stanzas, and then releases these specimens into the wild where they change shape according to the climate of each reader's consciousness. In this way, poetry is already science's sibling and successor — a discipline whose measurements are not in meters but in moments, whose constants are not numbers but needs, whose laws are not limitations but liberations.

THE GEOMETRY OF BEAUTY

Poetry is proof beyond proof ***shape beyond shape*** — the architecture of affect, the mathematics of the ineffable drawn in lines of light. Poetry is not shapeless emotion; it is form that feels. And that form is not rigid like a steel cage, but supple like a spiral shell — obeying hidden ratios even when appearing to roam free.

The Circle and the Spiral

The simplest geometry is the circle — the closed curve equidistant from a center. In poetry, the circle manifests as refrain, as rhyme returning like a comet on its orbital path. Yet the poem does not remain a perfect circle; it spirals. Each return is not a mere repetition but a revision, a re-seeing. Mathematically, we might say the poem traces an ***Archimedean spiral*** — always returning, yet always moving outward, gathering more circumference around the same core. The circle satisfies the scientist's love of symmetry; the spiral satisfies the soul's need for growth. Thus, poetry is both the eternal recurrence (*amor fati*, as Nietzsche would call it) and the ever-expanding horizon — an infinite loop that somehow leads elsewhere.

The Golden Ratio of Feeling

From seashells to sunflowers, nature hides the ***golden ratio*** (***$\phi \approx 1.618$***) in her designs, as though beauty obeyed a constant unknown to chaos. Poetry too obeys a golden proportion, though it cannot be charted by calipers. The balance between sound and silence, image and abstraction, repetition and surprise — these are not random. They tend toward an unseen equilibrium, the way a sonnet's 14 lines feel neither too long nor too short, the way a haiku's brevity burns brighter than a paragraph's flood. The golden ratio in poetry is not a number but a feeling of fitness, a formal harmony that satisfies the senses before the mind even knows why.

The Fractal of Meaning

A fractal is a figure that repeats its structure at every scale — zooming in or out, and the same pattern persists. Poetry too is fractal: a single word can echo the whole theme, a single stanza can contain the seed of the entire poem and the entire poem can feel like a magnification of its smallest phrase.

Thus, reading a great poem is like gazing into a Mandelbrot set: the deeper you go, the more you see the same beauty reshaping itself. This is why a short lyric by Sappho or Bashō can seem infinite; its structure holds the whole in every part.

Symmetry and Its Sacred Violations

Geometry loves symmetry; poetry loves symmetry's strategic sabotage. A perfect rhyme scheme delights, but an unexpected break electrifies. A measured meter lulls like a pendulum, but a sudden shift jars the reader awake. If geometry is a cathedral of proportion, poetry is that cathedral with one window made of glass the wrong color — a deliberate flaw that draws the eye, reminding us that perfection without surprise is lifeless. The poet, like the architect, knows that beauty lies not in sterile perfection but in the tension between the expected and the unexpected.

Topology of the Imagination

Topology studies shapes that can stretch, twist, and transform without breaking. Poetry, too, is topological:

A ballad and a free-verse meditation may differ in surface shape, yet both are homeomorphic to the sphere of the human heart. A metaphor may bend reality without snapping it. A narrative poem can twist time without tearing the fabric of coherence.

From this perspective, reading a poem is like tracing a Möbius strip: you think you are on one surface until you find yourself on another without ever crossing an edge.

Geometry as Generator of Joy

The scientific mind may ask: why should geometry matter in poetry? Because beauty is not only an emotion; it is an architecture in the nervous system. Patterns, ratios, symmetries — these are neurological nutrients. Poetry's geometry is not decoration; it is deep nourishment, aligning mental rhythms with patterns older than thought. Thus, poetry's beauty is both emotional and Euclidean, both aesthetic and algorithmic. It is the confluence where calculus courts cadence, where algebra adores assonance, where the compass draws the curve of the human cry.

THE PHYSICS OF FEELING

If geometry gave poetry its skeleton, physics gives it its pulse. For poetry is never inert – it moves, collides, refracts, accelerates. It is the science of sensation in motion, the kinematics of consciousness. Words in a poem are not static symbols; they are particles in perpetual interplay, pulled by the gravities of sound, sense, and silence.

Momentum of Metaphor

In physics, momentum is the product of mass and velocity. In poetry, metaphor is momentum: the mass of an idea multiplied by the velocity of its unexpected association. A plain statement moves slowly; a metaphor – "hope is the thing with feathers" – gains mass from meaning and velocity from surprise, carrying the reader forward with greater force. Just as in mechanics, momentum in poetry is conserved: a powerful image continues to resonate long after the line has passed. Thus, the poet is a physicist of perception, calculating (instinctively, not algebraically) how much velocity a single image can sustain without scattering into nonsense.

Energy: Potential and Kinetic

Every unwritten word in a poem is potential energy, stored in the mind of the poet. The moment it is chosen, placed, and read, it becomes kinetic – energy in motion.

A title is pure potential energy, a compressed spring.

The first line releases the first pulse of kinetic energy.

Enjambment stores energy at the line break, then releases it on the next line.

In this sense, reading a poem is a controlled chain reaction, each image igniting the next until the entire structure glows.

Every unwritten word in a poem is not emptiness but essence, not silence but stored spirit. It rests in the recesses of the poet's mind like a latent lightning bolt, a poised possibility, a slumbering spark. This is the poetry of potential—a hushed horizon of hidden heat. Yet the instant that word is summoned, shaped, and set upon the page, it leaps from latency into life; it vaults from stillness into motion. Thus, the written word is kinetic: sound in stride, sense in surge, syllables in flight. The paradox is perfect—what once was mute becomes music, what once was sealed becomes sung.

A title, therefore, is not a trifle but a tempest trapped in a teacup, a coiled spring, a clenched fist of meaning waiting to unfurl. It is a name that is more than a name, a promise pressed into brevity, a silent signal swelling with suspense. The title is pure potential energy, compressed into syllables, concentrated into symbols; it is a seed that contains forests, a spark that contains fire, a whisper that contains a world.

Then comes the first line: the ceremonial shattering of silence, the first pulse of poetry's heartbeat. Like the striking of a match, it sends flame into the fabric of the poem, igniting the air with expectation. Here motion begins: the reader is lifted into language, led into landscape, lured into labyrinth. The first line is not merely an entry but an initiation— the release of the first kinetic current, the river of rhythm rushing forth from the reservoir of potential.

Yet poetry is not reckless release; it is measured

momentum. At the line break, language lingers; at the edge of enjambment, energy is harnessed. The pause is not absence but accumulation, a tension tethered at the turning. The break breathes suspense, the reader's eye hovers, the reader's breath halts. Then, on the next line, release: the gathered gravity gives way, the spring uncoils, the silence is shattered into sound once more. Thus, enjambment is not interruption but ignition; not fracture but fuel.

So the poem progresses: image after image, sound after sound, thought after thought. Each word awakens another, each metaphor sparks a mirror, each rhythm rouses resonance. It is a chain reaction, but not chaotic; it is combustion, but controlled. The poet arranges the sequence as a scientist of spirit, ensuring each ignition ignites the next until the entire structure radiates. The poem glows, not with borrowed light but with its own interior fire. It is not a passive page but a living lantern, illuminating both the world within the reader and the world beyond the words.

To read a poem, then, is to enter this luminous laboratory of language, where silence becomes song, where stasis becomes surge, where potential becomes power. The reader does not merely observe but participates, carrying the current forward with the eyes, with the breath, with the beating of the heart. Poetry is thus not a relic but a reaction, not a monument but a movement. Its essence is energy—poised, pulsing, paradoxical.

Gravity of Meaning

Just as massive bodies curve spacetime, great ideas curve the space of a poem. Words orbit these ideas, pulled into metaphorical ellipses. In a poem about death, even the most neutral word — "door," "shadow," "clock" — bends under the gravity of the theme. The stronger the central mass (the theme), the more even stray details are drawn into its field. Yet the poet, unlike the physicist, may allow multiple gravities to coexist — a double star system of love and loss, for instance, around which the poem's lines weave.

Entropy and Order

Thermodynamics tells us that all systems tend toward disorder — entropy increases. Yet poetry thrives on ***local negentropy***: the creation of order in the midst of chaos. A raw emotion (chaotic energy) is distilled into meter, rhyme, and form (ordered structure). But here is the paradox: the poem must retain enough disorder to feel alive. A poem too perfectly ordered is sterile; a poem too chaotic is unreadable. The art lies in balancing entropy and order — enough unpredictability to excite, enough structure to sustain.

The Relativity of Poetic Time

Einstein showed that time is not absolute; it stretches and contracts depending on speed and gravity. Poetry, too, manipulates time:

A single second can expand into a page of imagery.

A century can collapse into one line.

The reader's perception of time bends under the gravity of emotional intensity. A well-placed pause can feel like an eternity; a rapid run of short lines can feel like a breathless rush. In this way, poetry is a private spacetime, an Einsteinian enclave where clock and calendar yield to cadence and cadence alone.

Poetry as a Private Spacetime

Einstein shattered the shackles of the nineteenth century by showing that time is not the tidy, ticking, tyrannical machine mankind once mistook it to be. Time, he taught us, is supple, stretching and shrinking, bending and bowing, depending on the swiftness of speed and the gravity of mass. It is no longer absolute but relative, no longer rigid but responsive. And here, curiously, wonderfully, paradoxically, poetry mirrors physics. For poetry, too, is an architect of altered hours, a manipulator of moments, a maker of temporal miracles.

In a poem, a second can swell into a saga. A sigh, stretched across similes, can suspend the soul for pages. What in life is fleeting can in verse become infinite, for language lengthens the instant into eternity. A trembling hand upon a letter, a tear upon a cheek, a glance between lovers at twilight—all these may occupy but a flicker of flesh-and-blood time, yet upon the page they unfold endlessly, echoing in stanza after stanza, resonating across the reader's own heart.

Conversely, a century can collapse into a single line. Empires may crumble, civilizations may sink into the sea, generations may rise and fall—all condensed into the compass of a couplet. The poet distills decades into drops, compresses chronicles into crystals, chisels the mountain of memory into a single syllable. What historians heap upon volumes, the poet hurls into a word. Thus poetry inverts chronology: it expands the trivial and contracts the monumental, elongates the ephemeral and compresses the eternal.

The reader's perception, therefore, is not governed by clocks but by cadences. Under the gravity of emotional intensity, time bends and buckles. A pause in a poem is no mere emptiness: it is a suspended second, an eternity carved out of silence. A dash, a caesura, a breath between lines—these become abysses into which the reader falls, discovering that stillness itself has weight, that silence itself can stretch like space. Conversely, a rapid rush of clipped, concise lines hurls the reader into haste, heart hammering, lungs laboring, breath caught in a flurry of rhythm.

In this way, poetry becomes a private spacetime, a sanctuary of subjective temporality. It is an Einsteinian enclave, where calendars collapse and clocks grow quiet, where chronology yields to cadence, where the tick is not mechanical but musical, not the measure of hours but the measure of harmony. To read a poem is to step into a dimension where the ordinary order of time is undone, replaced by a rhythm that obeys no physics but the physics of feeling. Poetry teaches us that time is not the tyrant of human experience but its servant, stretching where passion swells, contracting where grief compresses, bending always toward the gravity of meaning.

Thus, Einstein's revelation and the poet's art converge: both unveil the illusion of absolutes, both proclaim that reality is not rigid but relative. And if physics proves this with formulas, poetry proves it with phrases; if equations reveal it in symbols, stanzas reveal it in song. In both, we find the paradox that makes existence profound: time is elastic, and eternity can dwell in a moment.

Wave and Particle Duality of Language

In quantum physics, light is both wave and particle. In poetry, language is both music and meaning — inseparable yet distinct. A poem read aloud is a wave of sound; a poem read silently is a particle of thought. The duality is not a contradiction but a condition: poetry cannot be fully understood unless one perceives both its waveform (rhythm, rhyme, assonance) and its particle form (literal meaning).

Resonance and Harmonics

In physics, resonance occurs when a system vibrates at a particular frequency. In poetry, resonance occurs when words strike a frequency in the reader's soul. This resonance may come from sound (alliteration, assonance) or sense (emotional truth), and the greatest poems combine both, creating harmonics — overtones of meaning that linger beyond the final line. A single well-chosen phrase can set off sympathetic vibrations in memory, philosophy, and feeling, the way a struck tuning fork can make a distant string hum. In this way, poetry is a physics beyond the physicist's reach: a science of forces that act within the mind, invisible yet inescapable, measurable not in Newtons but in nuances. Excellent — now we leave the realm of moving masses and enter the shimmering laboratory of chemistry, where poetry is an alchemy of thought, feeling, and form.

THE CHEMISTRY OF CONSCIOUSNESS

If physics gave poetry its laws of motion, chemistry gives it its laws of combination — the molecular mingling of mind and music. In poetry, words are atoms, images are molecules, and emotions are reactions — some explosive, some slow-burning, all transformative. Here, the poet is part chemist, part sorcerer, balancing the stoichiometry of syllables, adjusting the pH of pathos, catalyzing the reaction of perception and pleasure.

The Periodic Table of the Poet

The scientist's periodic table arranges elements by atomic number; the poet's periodic table arranges elements by ***affective weight***.

Hydrogen of Hope— light, ubiquitous, essential to sustain the flame.

Oxygen of Imagery— bonds with almost everything, combusts when ignited.

Carbon of Common Speech— the structural backbone of all organic verse.

Gold of the Sublime— rare, resistant to corrosion, forever valued.

Mercury of Irony— quicksilver, dangerous, yet mesmerizing.

A master poet knows the valence of each word, the

bonds it forms, the reactions it triggers. The scientist, with method and microscope, arrays the universe of matter upon a chart of atomic numbers, ranking each element by its nucleus, weighing its protons, mapping its electrons. The periodic table is the chemist's scripture: orderly, objective, universal. Yet the poet, too, possesses a periodic table, though it is not constructed from atoms but from affects, not from measurable matter but from immeasurable moods. Where the scientist arranges by number, the poet arranges by necessity of feeling, by the emotional electricity each word releases, by the subtle bonds of suggestion and sensation.

Hydrogen of Hope—the lightest, the first, the most pervasive. Just as hydrogen permeates the cosmos, forming the fuel of stars, so hope pervades the human spirit, sustaining the flame of meaning. Without hydrogen, no fire burns; without hope, no poem breathes. It is humble, ubiquitous, invisible—yet essential. A single syllable of hope can lift the heaviest despair, the way a single atom of hydrogen ignites a sun.

Oxygen of Imagery—the element of combustion, the breath of the poem. Oxygen fuses with almost everything; it bonds, it bridges, it brightens. So too does imagery cling to every corner of consciousness, setting the poem alight when kindled by imagination. Without oxygen, flame falters; without imagery, verse suffocates. It is the breath in the reader's lungs, the spark in the reader's sight, the living air of poetry.

Carbon of Common Speech—the backbone of life, the scaffold of sound. Carbon is the universal element of organisms, and likewise, the ordinary word, the unadorned syllable, is the organic basis of all verse. Common speech is carbon's cousin: plain, pliable, yet capable of infinite structure. From coal to diamond, from prose to poetry, carbon transforms, and so does language—rough and raw in one form, crystalline and eternal in another.

Gold of the Sublime—rare, radiant, resistant to corruption. Gold does not tarnish, and neither does the truly sublime line, luminous across centuries, immune to erosion. Just as civilizations have worshipped gold, treasuring its incorruptible gleam, so readers revere the sublime, holding it as priceless, eternal. Gold is both ornament and offering; the sublime is both beauty and benediction. Together, they remind us that poetry, like alchemy, seeks permanence in a perishable world.

Mercury of Irony—quicksilver, dangerous, dazzling. Mercury slips through fingers, shimmers with allure, yet poisons when swallowed. So too irony: a dangerous delight, seductive but sharp, playful yet perilous. It destabilizes, unsettles, astonishes. A poem without irony may be safe but dull; a poem with irony dances like mercury—mesmerizing, mobile, mercurial. The reader is captivated, though never fully in control.

And the poet—the true master poet—is both alchemist and chemist of language. He knows not merely the word but the valence of the word, the way one image bonds with another, the way one line catalyzes emotion, the way one silence precipitates meaning. Every poem is a reaction: some gentle as a dissolving crystal, some violent as an explosion, some radiant as fire, some subtle as perfume. To write is to conduct chemistry of consciousness, to balance equations of beauty and terror, to ignite the latent elements of language until the entire poem glows like a star forged in the furnace of thought.

Thus, the poet's periodic table is no static chart but a living constellation: a map of emotional matter, an inventory of inner elements, a scripture of spirit. Where the scientist orders atoms, the poet orders affect. Where the scientist studies reaction, the poet orchestrates revelation. Both tables seek to explain the cosmos—but the one through calculation, the other through cadence; the one through protons and particles, the other through paradox and possibility.

Covalent Bonds of Sound

In molecular chemistry, a covalent bond shares electrons between atoms; in poetry, a covalent bond shares sounds between words. Alliteration, assonance, consonance — these are linguistic bonds, creating cohesion at the level of the ear before the mind has even parsed meaning. A poem without such bonds is like a compound without cohesion: it may exist, but it will fall apart under the slightest heat of reading.

The Ionic Shock of Contrast

An ionic bond involves the transfer, not sharing, of electrons; in poetry, this is the transfer of energy from one word to its opposite. Juxtaposition — love/hate, light/dark, silence/scream — generates voltage. Poetry thrives on these charged differences, just as a battery requires a potential difference to generate current. Without such contrast, the current of meaning stagnates.

Catalysts of Comprehension

In chemistry, a catalyst accelerates a reaction without being consumed by it. In poetry, certain words or images act as catalysts: they accelerate the reader's emotional or intellectual engagement without drawing overt attention to themselves. Consider the way a single sensory detail — "the smell of burnt cinnamon" — can suddenly awaken the whole emotional reaction of a scene. The poet places catalysts with precision, ensuring the reaction unfolds in the desired order and intensity.

Exothermic and Endothermic Poems

Some poems are exothermic — they release emotional energy immediately, burning bright and hot in the first reading (think of war poems, love sonnets, elegies). Others are endothermi — they absorb energy, growing warmer over time as the reader invests thought and returns for re-reading. The exothermic poem shouts; the endothermic poem whispers. Both have their chemistry, and both can be equally explosive — one in the instant, the other in the accumulation.

The Equilibrium of Ambiguity

Chemical equilibrium occurs when forward and reverse reactions balance; poetic equilibrium occurs when clarity and mystery coexist. Too much clarity, and the reaction finishes instantly; too much mystery, and it never begins. The poet maintains a dynamic equilibrium — enough to keep the reaction going perpetually in the reader's mind. The poem never truly "settles"; it remains a living system.

The Radioactivity of the Sublime

Some chemical elements are radioactive — they emit energy over time. Some poems are the same: their half-life may span decades, still releasing emotional radiation long after first exposure. Read once, they leave a trace; read again, years later, they seem newly dangerous, newly luminous. This is the poetry of Rilke, of Sappho, of Neruda — not safe for casual handling, but essential for the soul's deepest experiments. Thus, in chemical terms, poetry is not merely the sum of its words but the reaction between them — a reaction occurring within the reader, catalyzed by the poet, sustained by the molecular memory of language.

THE BIOLOGY OF THE BEAUTIFUL

If chemistry gave poetry its elemental nature, biology gives it life. For poetry is not inert matter arranged in patterns; it is a living thing — a creature with birth, growth, metabolism, reproduction, and even death. It exists in symbiosis with the reader's consciousness, and like all life, it adapts to survive.

The Genome of a Poem

Every organism has DNA; every poem has linguistic DNA — the base pairs of phoneme and morpheme, syntax and rhythm. Adenine of Alliteration binds with Thymine of Theme. Cytosine of Cadence bonds with Guanine of Grammar. From these four base elements — sound, sense, structure, and suggestion — the genome of the poem is encoded. Variations in sequence create new species of poetry: epics, elegies, haikus, free verse — each adapted to a niche in the literary ecosystem.

The Metabolism of Meaning

Living things metabolize to sustain themselves; poems metabolize meaning. They take in raw experience, process it through the digestive system of language, and release it as concentrated emotion and insight. Metabolism in poetry operates at two speeds: Catabolic Poetry breaks down grand narratives into smaller truths. Anabolic Poetry builds larger visions from small fragments. A poet may be both catabolic and anabolic in the same work, dismantling the ordinary and reassembling it into the extraordinary.

The Nervous System of Sensation

Every organism has sensory receptors; poetry has receptors for sight, sound, touch, taste, smell, and the sixth sense of the sublime. Through imagery, the poem sends neural impulses into the reader's mind, firing associative synapses. Visual metaphors are optic nerves of the poem. Alliteration is its auditory cortex. Metaphysical conceits are its prefrontal cortex — the seat of abstraction. When the poem is alive, it does not merely sit on the page — it feels in the reader's body: the tightening of the throat, the quickening of the pulse, the widening of the pupil.

The Reproductive Cycle of Poetry

Like living species, poetry reproduces — not biologically, but memetically. A phrase from one poet germinates in another's work. A rhythm from a folk song becomes a stanza in a modern epic. A metaphor mutates over centuries, adapting to new climates of thought. Just as genetic drift and natural selection shape life, poetic drift and cultural selection shape the evolution of forms. The sonnet migrated from Italy to England, adapting to the colder climate of English consonants. Haiku crossed oceans, shrinking syllables but growing in metaphorical density.

Symbiosis with the Reader

A poem alone is potential life — like a seed in stasis. The reader is the soil; reading is germination. Without the reader, the poem is dormant; without the poem, the reader lacks this particular seed of perception. This symbiosis extends into mutual benefit: the poem gains life in the reader's mind, the reader gains new consciousness through the poem's growth.

Parasitism, Predation, and Pollination

Not all biological metaphors are tender: Some poems **predate** on the reader's peace, ambushing them with unbearable truths. Some poems are **parasitic**, feeding on clichés and living only because they occupy the host of a popular form. The best poems are **pollinators**, carrying beauty and meaning from one consciousness to another, fertilizing new works across distances of time and culture.

Death and Fossilization

Biology also teaches that all organisms die. Some poems perish quickly — lifeless on the day they are written. Others fossilize into quotations, their living spirit gone, their words preserved only as cultural artifacts. Yet a few poems achieve a different form of immortality — they adapt endlessly, finding new readers in new centuries, mutating just enough to remain alive. These are the keystone species of literature: Homer's *Iliad,* Dante's *Commedia*, Shakespeare's sonnets, Li Bai's moonlit verses.

In biological terms, poetry is not a museum specimen — it is an ever-mutating species, surviving in the Darwinian jungle of thought through adaptation, variation, and the symbiotic bond with the human spirit. Very well — let us now leave the earthbound realms of biology and step into the cathedral of the cosmos, where poetry is measured not in syllables alone, but in light-years of longing and constellations of comprehension.

THE ASTRONOMY OF THE AESTHETIC

If biology gave poetry the pulse of a living organism, astronomy gives it the perspective of infinity. Poetry is not merely a terrestrial craft; it is a celestial cartography, charting the uncharted, mapping meaning across the metaphysical sky. Each poem is a star, each poet an astronomer – and yet, paradoxically, each reader is also the telescope through which the universe of language comes into focus.

Poetry as a Constellation of Concepts

In the night sky, stars exist independently, yet human imagination draws lines between them to form constellations – Orion, Cassiopeia, Lyra. Likewise, the poet takes scattered experiences, memories, and images, then draws invisible lines of metaphor between them, creating a recognizable shape of meaning. These constellations differ from culture to culture, age to age – but the stars themselves remain constant. Thus, the poem is both objective starlight and subjective design.

The Light-Year of Language

A light-year measures the distance light travels in one year; in poetry, a "light-year" might measure the distance meaning travels through time. Some poems are meteoric – their light flares brightly but briefly. Others are like ancient starlight – written centuries ago, but still arriving at our eyes with undiminished brilliance. When we read Sappho, we are seeing photons of feeling emitted more than two millennia ago, still burning across the blackness of history. Poetry is time-travel through radiance.

Gravity of the Profound

Gravity bends the fabric of space-time; profundity bends the fabric of thought. Great poetry possesses a gravitational field — a density of meaning so massive that it pulls the reader's mind into its orbit. And just as a black hole hides its singularity, the most profound poems conceal their ultimate core: we can approach it, feel its pull, but never quite see the totality of what lies within. This is the paradox of the profound — it attracts endlessly yet eludes final capture.

Orbits of Recurrence

Planets circle their suns; readers circle their favorite poems. We return to them for warmth, for light, for gravitational stability. Like celestial orbits, these re-readings are both predictable and fresh: the path is familiar, but the angle of illumination changes with every revolution of our own lives. This orbital nature explains why a poem read at fifteen is a different celestial body when read at fifty — we have shifted our position in the universe, and thus the same light strikes us differently.

The Nebula of the Unfinished

Nebulae are star-forming regions — clouds of dust and gas coalescing into future suns. Likewise, many poems are nebulous in their openness: they are not fixed galaxies of meaning but fertile clouds where the reader's mind forms new stars of interpretation. The greatest poets understand the value of this vagueness: the half-seen image, the unfinished gesture, the line that ends just before resolution. In this nebula, readers become co-creators.

Cosmic Background Radiation of Culture

The universe still hums with the faint afterglow of the Big Bang — the cosmic microwave background. Likewise, culture hums with the faint but pervasive afterglow of ancient poetry: fragments of Homer, whispers of the Vedas, the bass note of the Psalms. Even those who have never read these works live in their radiation, for language itself has been shaped by their light. Every modern metaphor carries, faintly, this cosmic inheritance.

Expansion of the Poetic Universe

Cosmology tells us the universe is expanding; so too is the universe of poetic forms. New stars (poems) and galaxies (genres) emerge constantly — from rap's rhythmic galaxies to the micro-poems of social media, from spoken word supernovae to quiet digital haikus. This expansion is not chaos, but cosmic pluralism — a recognition that no single form can monopolize the infinite sky of the human soul. In astronomical terms, poetry is both observatory and observable, both the telescope and the constellation, both the starlight and the space between stars. It teaches us that beauty can be as vast as a galaxy and as precise as a photon.

THE QUANTUM MECHANICS OF MEANING

If astronomy taught us that poetry can be vast beyond comprehension, quantum mechanics teaches us that poetry can be small beyond division, a flicker of significance compressed into a word, a syllable, a pause. At this scale, the laws of classical logic collapse; here, meaning behaves like matter at the Planck length — shimmering in and out of certainty, particle and wave at once.

The Principle of Poetic Uncertainty

Werner Heisenberg's uncertainty principle tells us we cannot know both the exact position and momentum of a particle at the same time. In poetry, we cannot know both the precise meaning and the full resonance of a line at the same time. The more closely we fix its meaning (position), the less we feel its range of possible interpretations (momentum). The more we allow it to remain free in interpretation, the less we can pin it to one definitive sense. This is not a defect, but the defining beauty of poetry — it thrives in the uncertainty where science seeks to eliminate it.

Superposition of Sense

A quantum particle exists in multiple states at once until observed; likewise, a poem's meaning exists in superposition — multiple possible interpretations coexisting in the mind until the reader "measures" it through their own understanding. Shakespeare's "Shall I compare thee to a summer's day?" can be simultaneously a question of love, a meditation on mortality, and a quiet boast of artistic immortality. Each reading collapses the wave-function differently, producing a unique outcome.

Entanglement of Emotion

Quantum entanglement links particles across any distance so that a change in one instantly affects the other. Poetry operates in similar emotional entanglement:

A line written centuries ago can change your mood in the present.

A poem read in childhood can echo in adulthood at a crisis moment.

Two minds — the poet's and the reader's — become linked across time and space, their mental states influencing each other without physical contact.

Quantum physicists speak of a wonder that defies ordinary logic: entanglement. Two particles, once joined, remain forever linked, no matter how vast the void between them. A change in one instantaneously alters the other, as though distance were a dream, as though separation were a sham. What science names nonlocality, poetry has long practiced as emotional entanglement—an invisible intimacy of souls beyond sight and beyond time.

For what is a poem but a signal sent across centuries, a pulse of feeling launched into the abyss of future minds? A line written by a forgotten hand, scrawled in candlelight, can suddenly strike the heart of a reader in the present, rearranging mood, reshaping memory, reconfiguring thought. A sigh of Sappho, a sonnet of Shakespeare, a cry of Kabir—these are not relics of the past but radiant particles still vibrating, still entangled with our own emotional fabric. Though the bodies of the poets are dust, their words remain alive, altering us at the very instant we encounter them.

And sometimes, more mysteriously still, a poem encountered in childhood returns like a ghost in adulthood, reawakening in a moment of crisis. The lullaby once half-understood now becomes an anchor of comfort; the verse once memorized for school suddenly erupts with new relevance at grief, at joy, at love, at loss. Just as entangled particles remain in secret sympathy, so too do words lodge within us, lying latent until life reactivates their charge. The poem waits, folded like a seed, ready to blossom when the soil of circumstance calls it forth.

But the most astonishing entanglement is the one that bridges two minds across time and space: the poet and the reader. They may never meet in flesh, yet in verse they are united. The poet pours into language a vibration of consciousness, and the reader, centuries later, receives that vibration almost intact, as though thought had tunneled through time unscathed. Without touch, without talk, without temporal overlap, two souls are momentarily synchronized. The reader weeps with the poet's grief, laughs with the poet's wit, trembles with the poet's wonder. Here, language is not mere medium but metaphysical conduit, binding minds as quantum entanglement binds particles.

Thus, poetry proves what physics suggests: that connection is deeper than contact, that sympathy transcends space, that communication is not only transmission but transformation. Poetry is the physics of feeling, the quantum mechanics of meaning. It reminds us that no thought, once expressed, ever entirely dies; it lingers, it links, it leaps. Across centuries and civilizations, across languages and landscapes, words weave webs of resonance, drawing us into the invisible network of the human spirit.

In this way, poetry is not only an art of words but an experiment in entanglement, demonstrating that the human heart is never isolated, that our emotions are always already intertwined. Every poem is a particle released, every reader a receiver, every encounter an entanglement that collapses the distance between selves. And when we read, we are reminded: to be human is to be entangled.

The Poetic Observer Effect

In quantum physics, the act of observation alters the observed reality. In poetry, reading changes the poem — not its ink on the page, but its existence in consciousness. A bitter reader finds bitterness in the lines; a joyful one finds joy. The poem is not a fixed object but a participatory event, and each reading is a unique experiment with unrepeatable results.

Quantum Poetics: The Physics of Feeling and the Metaphysics of Meaning

Poetry as Particle and Wave: Poetry, like light, refuses to be reduced to a single state. Light, said the physicists, is both particle and wave: solid in one sense, fluid in another, shimmering between substance and vibration. So too is poetry—at once fixed and fleeting, tangible and transcendent. On the page, a poem appears as particles: black ink crystallized into letters, an architecture of language arranged into lines. Yet when spoken, when sung, when summoned aloud, it surges like a wave: rhythm rolling, cadence crashing, syllables swelling and subsiding like tides. Poetry, like light, is a paradox that refuses imprisonment.

A poem is a particle in that it can be pointed to, bound to paper, preserved in permanence. One can hold it in the hand, quote it, copy it, memorize it as though it were matter. But simultaneously, it is a wave: it vibrates through the ear, it ripples through memory, it resonates across cultures. The poem one reads today is not the poem another read yesterday, for the rhythm falls differently, the tone strikes differently, the wave crests differently in each consciousness. Poetry is solid ink and shifting breath, frozen form and flowing force.

This duality is not a flaw but a feature. The poem survives precisely because it dances between states. Were it only particle, it would ossify into artifact, a relic of the past, a fossil of language. Were it only wave, it would dissipate into the air, vanishing like music without memory. But by being both, it is eternal: it carries permanence and impermanence, structure and song, silence and sound. It is the artifact that becomes an atmosphere, the particle that becomes a pulse.

Here lies the first law of quantum poetics: that words are never merely words. They are packets of meaning, photons of feeling, quanta of consciousness. Each syllable strikes like a particle, direct and undeniable, yet simultaneously resonates like a wave, expanding outward, refracting across interpretation, echoing endlessly in the chambers of the reader's mind. A single word—"love," "death," "time," "home"—is both a grain of ink and a vast vibration, both a solitary particle and an infinite wave.

This duality also reveals the poet's paradoxical task. To write is to hammer words into form, yet to hope they melt into music. To inscribe the permanent, yet yearn for the ephemeral. To pin down experience with precision, yet to release it into resonance. The poet, like the physicist, works not with certainty but with complementarity: to understand poetry, one must accept that it is both wave and particle, both bound and boundless, both finite text and infinite interpretation.

Thus, poetry does not merely resemble physics; it enacts it. It is a microcosm of matter and energy, of permanence and flux, of the paradox that defines reality itself. To read a poem is to participate in this oscillation, to witness language as both architecture and atmosphere, as both ink and echo. The page gives us particles; the heart receives waves. And in this shimmering simultaneity, poetry proves itself not a static art but a quantum phenomenon: the physics of feeling, the wave-particle duality of human thought made manifest in words.

Quantum poetics: Quantum physicists speak of a marvel that mocks the mechanistic mind: entanglement. Two particles, once joined, remain forever linked, however far they drift across the abyss of space. A shift in one instantaneously alters the other, as though the universe itself were a secret thread binding them in silence. Distance dissolves; separation shatters; what was thought apart proves always already aligned.

Poetry, too, practices this miracle, though it was known to the poet long before the physicist named it. A poem is not merely written—it is entangled. When a poet places words upon the page, those words are not inert marks but charged particles of feeling, woven with the very vibration of consciousness. Once released into the world, they remain mysteriously connected to every soul that receives them. A line whispered in antiquity can resound in a modern ear, reshaping the mood of a reader centuries later. Sappho's fragments still flush our cheeks; Li Bai's moonlit musings still stir our solitude; Emily Dickinson's dashes still disrupt our breath. The poet's pulse reverberates in the reader's ribcage, though oceans and eras lie between them.

This is the entanglement of emotion. A poem you read in childhood, half-understood, lightly memorized, may suddenly return decades later at the edge of grief, at the height of love, at the abyss of despair. Like a buried seed sensing rain, it bursts back into bloom, synchronizing your present with your past. The verse that once lay dormant detonates, revealing that you have carried its charge within you all along. The poet planted it, and life itself watered it until it blossomed again. Thus the poem does not merely belong to its moment of creation; it threads itself through the fabric of a reader's lifetime, binding distant times in emotional simultaneity.

And what is more marvelous still: the entanglement is reciprocal. When we read, the poet's consciousness is reawakened through our own. We do not merely consume meaning; we co-create it. The poem is not fully alive until it enters the reader's eye, ear, or memory. At that instant, two minds—poet and reader—become linked, vibrating in unison though they may be separated by centuries, continents, or even languages. Without physical contact, without dialogue, without shared breath, the reader feels the poet's sigh, the poet's wound, the poet's wonder. The line leaps the abyss, and the abyss is annulled.

So too is poetry revealed as a form of nonlocal communication. The message does not crawl across wires or wavelengths but leaps instantly from heart to heart. When Rumi whispers of longing, when Neruda sings of salt and skin, when Tagore hymns the dawn, their words arrive not as ancient artifacts but as immediate encounters. The past collapses, the distance disappears, the poet and reader dwell in the same now. This is no ordinary transmission—it is transcendence, an entanglement of minds in which thought leaps across time unscathed.

What physics demonstrates in matter, poetry demonstrates in meaning: that connection is deeper than contact, that influence transcends immediacy, that the invisible thread is stronger than the visible chain. Poetry is not a relic but a resonance; not a monument but a meeting; not a monologue but an entanglement. Each poem proves that the human spirit is never solitary, that the inner life is always already intertwined with the voices of others, alive or long departed.

Thus, the poet is not merely a writer but an entangler. The poet sets loose particles of feeling, knowing that they may alight in unknown futures, in strangers' souls, in minds not yet born. And the reader is not merely a recipient but a reanimator, collapsing the distance between self and other, now and then, here and there. Every act of reading is an experiment in entanglement, a proof that time and space cannot contain the electricity of emotion.

And so poetry teaches us this luminous law of quantum poetics: that we are always already entangled. That every word we utter may echo in a soul we will never meet. That every feeling we inscribe may ignite a fire centuries hence. That distance is only a disguise, and solitude only an illusion. In poetry, as in physics, what appears apart is profoundly one.

Superposition of Meaning: In the quantum realm, a particle does not exist in one state until it is observed. Instead, it hovers in a superposition, simultaneously occupying multiple possibilities, multiple positions, multiple potentials. Only when measured does the wave function collapse, revealing one definitive state. Poetry, in its own mysterious and magnificent way, mirrors this principle: a poem exists in superposition of meaning, holding countless interpretations, yet fully realized only in the act of reading.

Every poem is a paradoxical prism. Its words sparkle

with layered significance, vibrating simultaneously across the spectrum of human experience. A single stanza may convey sorrow and joy, restraint and passion, irony and intimacy—all at once. Before the reader engages, the poem floats in ambiguity, a cloud of potential resonance, pregnant with unactualized understanding. In this sense, the poem is never one thing; it is everything and nothing simultaneously, awaiting the observer to determine which facet shines.

The reader becomes the quantum observer. With each gaze, each breath, each heartbeat, the reader collapses the wave function of the poem's possibilities into a unique personal reality. No two readings are identical, for no two minds collapse the superposition in the same way. One reader may find in a line liberation; another, lamentation. One may hear music, another melancholy. The poem, though written once, lives a thousand lives, each as real and each as ephemeral as the observer's consciousness allows.

Yet this multiplicity is not chaotic. Like quantum probability, the superposition is constrained by structure, rhythm, and diction. Grammar, meter, metaphor, and rhyme guide the potential outcomes, shaping the probabilities, orchestrating which interpretations are more likely to manifest. The poet, knowingly or intuitively, becomes both composer and conductor: setting the stage for infinite possibilities while guiding their resonance. The dance of words is both free and choreographed, both spontaneous and designed.

In this way, ambiguity becomes power. The poem thrives in tension, in the balance between uncertainty and precision. Its superposition is a sanctuary for imagination, a cathedral for contemplation, a crucible where every reader contributes to its becoming. No one meaning exhausts it;

no single mind contains it. The poem, like the quantum particle, is more than the sum of its observations. Its essence is distributed, its truth entangled with consciousness, its energy inseparable from perception.

And here lies the profound paradox: the poem exists fully only when it exists incompletely. Only in potential can it encompass infinite interpretations; only in ambiguity can it achieve universality. The moment a reader collapses one wave of meaning, the poem simultaneously awakens countless others in the minds of those yet to encounter it. Poetry, therefore, is simultaneously singular and manifold, finite and infinite, present and eternal.

Thus, superposition is the secret of poetry's longevity and its universality. Each word is a quantum particle, each stanza a field of potential, each reading a measurement, each interpretation a collapse into brilliance. Poetry proves, as quantum physics proves, that reality is not fixed, that observation matters, that multiplicity is the natural order. In the superposition of meaning, the poem becomes alive, dynamic, and boundlessly beautiful—a particle of ink, a wave of wonder, a universe of possibilities waiting for the observer to awaken it.

The Uncertainty Principle of Expression: Heisenberg declared that the more precisely one measures a particle's position, the less certain its momentum becomes. The act of observation, paradoxically, introduces indeterminacy. Poetry, like quantum mechanics, thrives in this uncertainty, reveling in the tension between precision and ambiguity. The more a poet attempts to pin down meaning, to cage feeling in exact language, the more elusive that feeling becomes—slipping, shimmering, refusing confinement.

Each word in a poem is both guide and trickster. To

define it too rigidly risks suffocating its subtle resonance; to leave it too fluid risks scattering comprehension. And yet, it is in this very tension—the delicate dance between clarity and mystery—that poetry pulses with vitality. The reader feels the friction, the oscillation, the trembling of possibility. Each phrase is a particle of potential, vibrating between meanings, oscillating between thought and emotion, observation and imagination.

The poet deliberately invokes this uncertainty. A metaphor may suggest many truths at once; a stanza may shimmer with contradiction; a pause may pulse with silence and sound simultaneously. Like a physicist measuring the unmeasurable, the poet negotiates the limits of expression, knowing that exactitude is both necessary and impossible. The poem, therefore, is a perpetual experiment, a laboratory of language in which ambiguity is not weakness but weapon, wonder, and witness.

In this light, the act of reading mirrors the act of observing a quantum particle. The reader's consciousness interacts with the poem, collapsing some possibilities while leaving others suspended. Each interpretation is provisional, each understanding partial, each insight temporary. Yet it is precisely this provisionality that animates poetry, allowing it to resonate anew in each moment, in each mind, in each encounter. The poem is never finished; it is always unfolding, a constant uncertainty vibrating at the edge of comprehension.

And here lies the paradoxical beauty: the more uncertain the poem, the more certain its effect. The deliberate opacity, the embrace of ambiguity, the refusal to resolve fully, draws the reader in. We lean closer, ponder longer, feel more intensely. Uncertainty becomes intimacy; the unknown becomes invitation. Poetry teaches us that the heart and mind flourish not in the certainty of the known but in the electric exhilaration of the unexplained.

Thus, the Uncertainty Principle of Expression reveals poetry as a field of infinite possibility. Each line is a probability wave; each stanza a superposition of meaning; each reading a measurement that illuminates some truths while leaving others to shimmer unseen. The poet is both scientist and sorcerer, experimenting with resonance, playing with perception, orchestrating ambiguity with deliberate care. And the reader, as quantum observer, participates in this sublime interplay, discovering that every moment of indecision, every pause, every shadowed meaning, carries its own radiant energy.

In embracing uncertainty, poetry mirrors the universe itself: unpredictable, paradoxical, oscillating between order and chaos, pattern and possibility. It reminds us that ambiguity is not absence, but presence; not silence, but song; not void, but vibration. And in this perpetual interplay of observation and potential, poetry becomes a luminous laboratory of the human heart, a quantum crucible where meaning is measured, unmeasured, and remade in the minds of those who encounter it.

Tunneling Through Time: In quantum mechanics, particles occasionally perform what seems impossible: they tunnel through barriers that should be insurmountable, appearing on the other side without crossing the intervening space in conventional ways. Poetry, in its own profound and paradoxical manner, performs the same miracle, tunneling across the temporal terrain. The poem written centuries ago, in a distant land and foreign tongue, can emerge instantly within the reader's consciousness, bypassing years, eras, and empires.

A sonnet inked in candlelight in sixteenth-century

England may pierce the mind of a twenty-first-century reader with startling immediacy. A ghazal murmured under moonlight in Delhi whispers in the ears of a wanderer in Manhattan. The poem does not crawl through history; it leaps, defying clocks, calendars, and the tyranny of chronology. It tunnels through the past, through memory, through time itself, collapsing centuries into a single, intimate now.

This temporal tunneling is guided by resonance, not mechanics. The poet, consciously or intuitively, crafts lines charged with emotional energy. The reader, attuned to cadence and metaphor, collapses the intervening centuries into perception, experiencing the poem as if it were contemporaneous, immediate, alive. In that instant, the past is present, the distant intimate, the long-dead poet a companion in consciousness. The poem becomes a bridge not of wood or stone but of mind, heart, and imagination.

Yet, like a quantum particle, the poem's tunneling is probabilistic. Not every verse reaches every mind; not every stanza bridges every heart. Some words falter, some lines fade, some images fail to ignite. But when the alignment occurs—when resonance meets receptivity—the effect is extraordinary. The reader feels the poet's pulse, senses the poet's joy, trembles with the poet's grief, and perceives the unity of human experience across centuries. A single encounter collapses distances, rendering temporal separation irrelevant.

Time, in poetry, is elastic. A narrative may span generations in a single paragraph; a single line may condense a lifetime. The poem as tunnel collapses this span, allowing the reader to inhabit multiple epochs simultaneously. Childhood verses echo in adulthood; ancient wisdom illuminates modern dilemmas; distant voices converse in the mind as though they were neighbors, whispering from the invisible corners of history. In this way, the poem becomes a temporal telegraph, transmitting not just words but the resonance of human consciousness across the continuum.

The paradox is luminous: poetry is both rooted and roaming. It is anchored in the moment of creation, yet it wanders freely in the corridors of time. It is both artifact and apparition, manuscript and mirage. Like a particle that has tunneled beyond expectation, it appears wherever the heart is ready to receive it, regardless of chronology, geography, or circumstance. Poetry teaches that time is not a barrier but a medium, not a boundary but a canvas, not a prison but a passage.

Thus, through the quantum lens, the poem is a time traveler, a temporal tunneler, a bridge spanning ages. Every reading is an act of instantaneous connection; every encounter is a moment of collapse in which centuries converge. The poet becomes a quantum engineer of consciousness, and the reader becomes the observer who awakens the poem's journey. Poetry, in its timelessness, reminds us that distance is illusory, separation a mere suggestion, and the human heart capable of infinite immediacy.

Wave-Particle Duality of Language: In quantum physics, light is neither purely wave nor purely particle; it is both, simultaneously, a duality that defies singular classification. Poetry, in its luminous logic, mirrors this cosmic contradiction. Words are particles: tangible, precise, inked upon the page, capable of being counted, measured, and analyzed. Yet those same words are waves: vibrations that travel through the reader's consciousness, resonating with rhythm, rebounding in memory, reverberating across emotion. Poetry exists in both states, oscillating between form and feeling, structure and surge.

The particle aspect of poetry is concrete. Letters, syllables, punctuation marks—they are physical manifestations of thought. They are the atoms of verse, the tangible architecture that allows language to stand. Each word is deliberate, chosen for its weight, shape, and meaning. Grammar and syntax provide scaffolding, rhyme and meter give rhythm, and the page itself becomes a lattice upon which the poem is constructed. The poet arranges these particles meticulously, aware that even the smallest shift—a single word, a single pause—can alter the entire pattern of perception.

Yet no reader experiences poetry merely as particles. Once vocalized or internalized, the poem becomes wave, a pulse, a flux of feeling and consciousness. Rhythm undulates, imagery oscillates, emotion vibrates. A line hums; a stanza swells; a refrain echoes. The reader's mind is immersed in a field of resonance, where meaning is not fixed but fluid, where interpretation ripples outward in expanding concentric circles. The wave carries the energy of the poem beyond the confines of ink and paper, activating empathy, imagination, and insight.

This duality—the simultaneous existence of particle and wave—is precisely what allows poetry to transcend limitation. The same word may be stable and structured for analysis, yet dynamic and flowing in experience. The poem is both measurable and immeasurable, calculable and ineffable, anchored and airborne. Like light bending through a prism, poetry disperses into multiple spectra, illuminating different dimensions for every observer.

Furthermore, the wave-particle duality reveals the intimate interplay between poet and reader. The poet crafts particles—words, lines, stanzas—but it is the reader who experiences the waves. Without the wave, the particle is inert; without the particle, the wave has no source. Together, they form a symbiotic continuum, a quantum collaboration of consciousness. The poem exists fully only in this interplay: a dual existence, both fixed and flowing, both solitary and shared.

Even silence, the absence of sound or ink, participates in this duality. Pauses are particles that hold potential energy; they are waves that swell within the reader's perception. A caesura is both interruption and invitation; an ellipsis is both omission and opportunity. The wave-particle nature of language teaches us that poetry is never only what is written, never only what is heard, but always both, existing in the tension between form and flux.

Thus, in the quantum-poetic universe, the poem becomes a luminous paradox: tangible and ephemeral, structured and free, measured and immeasurable. Each reading reveals a new resonance, each performance activates a new vibration, each observer collapses and releases the poem simultaneously. Poetry, like light, illuminates because it exists in duality: it is both particle and wave, both architecture and atmosphere, both ink and pulse, both thought and feeling.

Quantum Leap of Insight: In quantum mechanics, a particle can undergo a quantum leap, a sudden, discontinuous transition from one state to another, bypassing the gradual journey one might expect. Poetry, in its profound precision and paradox, mirrors this phenomenon: it catalyzes sudden illumination, bursts of understanding that arrive without warning, leaping across the landscape of thought and heart. A single line, a single image, a single metaphor can vault across consciousness, shattering inertia, igniting revelation.

The reader is poised on the precipice of ordinary perception when the poem strikes. The words themselves are not slow conveyers of meaning but accelerators of insight, propelling the mind into uncharted dimensions. A metaphor, subtle and shimmering, may suddenly reveal a truth that had been invisible in plain sight. A stanza, carefully compressed, may explode with recognition, connecting disparate experiences, bridging memory and imagination, collapsing confusion into clarity. In that instant, understanding is not arrived at gradually but realized abruptly, like a particle tunneling through a barrier, like a photon appearing where it was not expected.

Poetry's quantum leap is not predictable; it is probabilistic. The reader may linger in a stanza for minutes, days, or years before the latent insight ignites. And even then, the revelation is intensely personal, contingent upon the reader's own state, the history of attention, the gravity of feeling. The poem does not lecture; it does not enforce comprehension. Instead, it waits, charged with potential, poised to provoke, prepared to leap. And when it does, the reader experiences a sudden synapse of understanding, a flash of consciousness in which complexity condenses into clarity, multiplicity resolves into resonance, and the invisible thread of meaning becomes luminous.

The poet, consciously or intuitively, engineers these leaps. The arrangement of words, the cadence of lines, the tension of images—all are designed to store energy, to accumulate potential, to make the eventual quantum leap possible. The poet compresses ambiguity, suspense, and resonance into the lattice of the poem, so that when the reader finally observes, the collapse is explosive, the insight immediate, the experience transformative. The poem is both cradle and catalyst, nurturing anticipation while orchestrating revelation.

This leap, however, is never merely intellectual. Poetry is emotion entangled with cognition, meaning inseparable from feeling. The quantum leap strikes simultaneously in heart and mind. It is comprehension entwined with empathy, recognition fused with wonder, cognition vibrating in resonance with emotion. One line can make centuries of thought suddenly cohere; one stanza can fold the universe into a single moment of perception. This is the alchemy of poetry: it transmutes potential into actuality, waiting silently until the observer's consciousness aligns, then ignites the incandescent flash of understanding.

The paradox is profound: the leap cannot be forced, yet it can be facilitated; it is unpredictable, yet inevitable for the prepared mind. Poetry, like quantum mechanics, defies linear logic, but obeys the subtle laws of probability and resonance. It teaches that insight is not a steady climb but a sudden surge, that revelation is not gradual but instantaneous, and that the most transformative understanding arrives not step by step, but as a radiant, discontinuous, quantum leap of the soul.

Thus, in the quantum-poetic cosmos, every reading is a potential event horizon, every line a latent accelerator, every encounter a possibility for sudden illumination. The poem is simultaneously patient and instantaneous, compressed and explosive, poised and unpredictable. It reminds us that the human mind is itself a quantum field of potential, and that poetry—like the universe—leaps beyond expectation, collapsing possibility into brilliance in a single, shimmering flash.

The Cosmic Observer: In quantum mechanics, the act of observation is not passive—it collapses the wave function, bringing potential into reality. Until observed, a particle exists in a haze of probabilities; upon observation, it chooses a state, manifesting in the world. Poetry, too, depends upon the cosmic observer: the reader. Without the reader, the poem exists only as potential—words on a page, vibrations in the poet's mind, latent energy waiting for activation. It is the act of reading that collapses ambiguity into resonance, that transforms ink into illumination, silence into song.

The reader is simultaneously participant and witness, architect and amplifier, catalyst and conduit. Each encounter is unique, each perception singular. When a poem is read, the observer's consciousness interacts with the quantum field of language, selecting one path among infinite possibilities. Every interpretation, every emotional response, every insight is a measurement, a choice, a collapsing of potential into actuality. The poem becomes real not merely by existing, but by being observed, experienced, and internalized.

Yet this observation is not deterministic; it is probabilistic, subjective, and profoundly personal. One reader may perceive tragedy where another perceives triumph; one may hear lamentation, another lyric; one may see subtlety, another grandeur. The poem's infinite potentials are never exhausted, because each observer collapses the wave function in their own distinctive way. The cosmic observer is therefore essential, not secondary: the poem is incomplete without this communion, unfinished without the act of reception.

Time and space, like in quantum theory, fold under the gaze of the cosmic observer. A poem may be centuries old, yet it is alive in the reader's present. A stanza may span galaxies of thought, yet it resonates intimately within a single heartbeat. The observer transforms distance into immediacy, past into now, isolation into intimacy. The poet may have departed, but through the observer, the poem achieves ***eternal presence***, bridging consciousness across eras and continents.

This cosmic interplay also reveals the co-creative power of poetry. The poet provides the particles, the structure, the potential; the reader provides the wave, the resonance, the realization. Meaning is not transmitted linearly but emerges from the dynamic entanglement between writer and witness. In this sense, the reader is both participant and co-author, collapsing possibilities, catalyzing insight, and completing the quantum experiment that is the poem itself.

The paradox is luminous: the poem exists fully only in ***simultaneous incompletion.*** It is both potential and realized, waiting yet active, latent yet present. And the observer, through attention, empathy, and imagination, transforms possibility into actuality. Without observation, the poem is shadow; with it, the poem is light. Without the cosmic observer, poetry is inert; with the observer, it becomes an electric, oscillating, oscillating universe of meaning.

Thus, in the quantum-poetic cosmos, the reader is not mere audience but cosmic participant, collapsing ambiguity, activating resonance, bridging distance, and animating the latent energies of language. Poetry teaches us that consciousness is not passive, that meaning is not imposed, and that the human mind—like the universe—is participatory, entangled, and wondrously alive. Every reading is a revelation, every encounter an experiment, every observer a vital element in the unfolding quantum dance of expression, emotion, and eternal insight.

Toward a Unified Theory of Poetry: We have traversed the quantum cosmos of poetry: particles and waves, entanglement and superposition, uncertainty and tunneling, leaps of insight and the gaze of the cosmic observer. Each section has revealed a paradox, each concept a convergence of physics and feeling, structure and spontaneity, form and flux. Now, in this epilogue, we attempt a synthesis—a unified theory of poetry, where every word, every line, every stanza participates in a luminous lattice of meaning.

Poetry is a quantum universe in miniature. Its elements—words, images, rhythms, silences—exist simultaneously as particles and waves, both fixed and fluid, concrete and ethereal. Each poem is a laboratory of potentialities, each reading an experiment in resonance. The poet is the quantum engineer, crafting probabilities, arranging structures, compressing ambiguity, and imbuing each syllable with latent energy. The reader is the cosmic observer, collapsing wave functions, awakening resonance, entangling past and present, heart and mind, self and other.

In this unified universe, time is elastic, bending under cadence and feeling. Seconds expand into sagas; centuries collapse into a single line. Poetry tunnels across time, bridging memory and imagination, childhood and adulthood, the ancient and the immediate. Distance is irrelevant; separation is illusory. A line written long ago may leap into the present, touching a reader who is ready to receive it, proving that emotional entanglement, like quantum entanglement, defies chronology.

Meaning, too, exists in superposition. The poem is never one thing; it is many things, each interpretation simultaneously valid, each resonance provisional yet profound. Ambiguity is not weakness but wonder, uncertainty not obstacle but opportunity. Each observation—each reading, each experience—collapses the infinite possibilities into a personal, ephemeral, and electric reality. Poetry teaches that meaning is participatory, that understanding is co-created, and that consciousness itself is entwined with expression.

Poetry thrives in paradox. It is precise and infinite, ephemeral and eternal, structured and boundless. It leaps in sudden insight, oscillates in duality, vibrates with unseen energy, and remains elusive even as it illuminates. Its atoms are words; its molecules are lines; its universe is the mind. And like the universe itself, poetry is governed by subtle laws of resonance, probability, and relationality rather than rigid determinism.

In the final convergence, we recognize that poetry and physics are not disparate disciplines but reflections of the same truth: that reality, whether material or emotional, is dynamic, entangled, probabilistic, and participatory. Poetry, like light, is a particle and a wave; like a quantum leap, it surprises; like entanglement, it binds across time and space; like superposition, it holds infinite potential; like uncertainty, it thrives in ambiguity; and through observation, it becomes fully alive.

Thus, the unified theory of poetry is the recognition that every poem is a quantum cosmos: simultaneously discrete and continuous, potential and actualized, finite yet infinite. The poet provides the energy; the reader collapses the possibilities; meaning emerges as a shared creation, a luminous lattice of consciousness spanning time, space, and imagination. Poetry is a particle of light, a wave of feeling, a bridge across existence, a map of the human heart, and a reflection of the boundless universe. In this realization, we see the ultimate paradox and the ultimate promise:

that poetry is at once ephemeral and eternal, bounded and infinite, personal and universal. It is the physics of feeling, the metaphysics of meaning, and the quantum poetry of the human soul. To read, to write, to witness, to participate—is to step into this universe, to become entangled, to experience the infinite in a single word, a single line, a single heartbeat. And in that moment, the universe itself is revealed: oscillating, resonant, radiant, alive.

The Quantum Tunneling of Thought

Quantum tunneling allows particles to pass through barriers they should not, according to classical physics. Poetry engages in conceptual tunneling: it passes through the walls of logic, grammar, and expectation to reach meanings otherwise inaccessible. Through metaphor, enjambment, and paradox, it slides between states of literal and figurative without needing a bridge of explanation. It simply appears on the other side of the impossible.

Wave–Particle Duality of Words

Light behaves both as a wave and a particle; words behave both as units of fixed meaning (particle) and ripples of association (wave). A single word — rose — is a particle of language, but it radiates waves of smell, color, emotion, and myth. The great poet is like the quantum physicist who knows when to treat language as matter, when to treat it as energy, and how to weave both into the same experiment.

Quantum De-coherence and the Loss of Mystery

In physics, quantum systems lose their strangeness when they interact with the environment — a process called de-coherence. In poetry, over-analysis can produce the same effect: the poem's delicate superposition of meanings collapses into mundane clarity. This is why certain poems resist paraphrase — to pin them down is to destroy their quantum state. In quantum terms, poetry is the physics of possibility — a laboratory where thoughts do not simply travel from A to B, but exist in simultaneous universes, entangled with every mind that has ever read or will ever read them.

THE THERMODYNAMICS OF THOUGHT

If quantum mechanics revealed poetry's microscopic strangeness, thermodynamics reveals its macroscopic vitality. Here we do not peer at particles but watch the flow of energy through the whole system of poet, poem, and reader. Poetry, like heat, obeys laws — yet, paradoxically, also defies them in the realm of the soul.

If relativity showed us that poetry bends the continuum of perception, thermodynamics shows us that it drives the machinery of the mind. It is a science of heat and work, of how energy flows and transforms — and in poetry, that energy is not mere joules or calories, but passion, perception, and possibility.

The First Law — Conservation of Meaning and Consciousness

The First Law of Thermodynamics states that energy cannot be created or destroyed, only transformed. Poetry obeys a metaphysical version: meaning cannot be created from nothing, nor destroyed into nothingness — it is transformed. The poet does not summon meaning ex nihilo; they ***transmute*** existing emotional energy — grief, joy, rage, wonder — into linguistic form. The reader then re-transforms it into their own inner experience. Thus, the tear shed by the poet centuries ago can become the smile of a reader today; the same heat, redistributed into a different motion of the heart.

In physical terms, energy can neither be created nor destroyed. In poetic terms, consciousness — once awakened — can neither be nullified nor erased. The grief crystallized in Sappho's fragments is still here. The wonder Whitman poured into a blade of grass still grows. The poem does not create the energy of feeling; it transmutes what already exists in the soul into a form that can be passed across centuries, languages, and lives.

The Second Law — Entropy, Elegance and the Elegy

The Second Law says that entropy — disorder — always increases in closed systems. Left alone, all things cool, fade, and fall to chaos. But poetry is an ***entropy-defier***: it concentrates experience, distills time, resists decay. An elegy is a perfect example. Death, by nature, disperses life's order into disorder; but the poem gathers fragments — memories, metaphors, moments — and preserves them in a structure that resists oblivion. The universe moves toward disorder; poetry builds islands of order in the tide.

Entropy is the natural drift toward disorder. Without effort, systems decay. Poetry is paradox here: it resists entropy while also relying on it. Without the disorder of the world — the chaos, the brokenness — there would be no impulse to create art. Yet poetry uses deliberate structure — rhyme, meter, stanza — to locally reverse that chaos. An elegy, especially, is a battle against entropy: a final, structured act of remembrance against the scatterings of time.

Heat Engines of the Heart

In engineering, a heat engine transforms heat into work. In literature, a ***poetic engine*** transforms emotion into insight. Anger becomes political critique; love becomes lyrical celebration; loneliness becomes universal connection. The efficiency of this engine depends on the poet's craftsmanship. A clumsy engine wastes fuel; a master's verse extracts maximum power from the smallest spark of feeling.

The poet is an engineer of the emotional engine:

Raw heat = experience (joy, despair, awe).

Working fluid = language.

Output = altered consciousness in the reader.

A master's craftsmanship ensures minimal loss — no wasted metaphors, no excess friction in meaning. The smallest spark of a feeling can be magnified into a blaze that lights entire generations.

Temperature and Tone

Temperature measures the average kinetic energy of particles; tone measures the emotional energy of language. A "hot" poem — furious, passionate, burning — agitates the mind's molecules, shaking the reader into motion. A "cool" poem — calm, crystalline, detached — slows them into still reflection. Temperature is not moral value. Frost and flame both can illuminate. The poet simply chooses the desired climate for the reader's soul.

Temperature measures molecular agitation; tone measures the agitation of the reader's inner world.

A "high-temperature" poem — fierce, rapid, urgent — moves the heart into turbulence.

A "low-temperature" poem — measured, meditative, serene — slows the rhythm, like cooling metal into solid shape.

The finest poems know when to scorch and when to soothe.

Phase Changes of Perception

When heat changes the phase of matter — ice to water,

water to steam — poetry changes the phase of perception. A metaphor may melt the rigid ice of prejudice into the fluidity of empathy. A rhythm may boil the still waters of thought into clouds of imagination. And, like physical phase changes, these transformations are often irreversible — once the reader sees through the poem's vision, the mind cannot fully return to its earlier state.

In physics, heat can change matter's phase without changing its substance: ice melts to water, water boils to steam. In poetry, a metaphor can melt the frozen prejudices of the mind into the fluidity of empathy. A line-break can vaporize the dense solidity of fact into the mist of dream. And as in physics, once the phase change occurs, the state of mind rarely returns to its prior form.

Thermal Equilibrium and Emotional Balance

Two bodies in contact eventually reach thermal equilibrium; poet and reader, through the poem, can reach **emotional equilibrium**. The fever of the poet cools in the act of creation; the coolness of the reader warms in the act of reading. This shared temperature is the secret intimacy of poetry — the point where two minds, across years and miles, share the same emotional climate for a moment in eternity.

Two bodies in contact eventually reach the same temperature. Poet and reader, through the poem, reach emotional equilibrium:

The poet's fever cools in the act of writing.

The reader warms in the act of reading.

For a fleeting instant, their thermodynamic states are shared.

The Perpetual Motion Paradox

Thermodynamics forbids a perpetual motion machine, yet some poems seem to be exactly that —

producing endless emotional energy without exhausting their source. A Shakespeare sonnet, a Bashō haiku, a fragment of Rumi — each rereading releases fresh warmth, as though the poem were tapping into an inexhaustible reservoir. This is the poet's miracle: to create, in a finite text, an infinite engine.

Perpetual motion machines defy the laws of physics, yet certain poems seem to produce infinite returns of meaning:

Rereading *The Waste Land* or *Divine Comedy* generates new insights every time. The fuel is not replenished from outside — the text itself contains compressed universes. This is the poet's ultimate feat: to bind limitless energy into finite form.

The Heat Death of Silence

The universe's predicted end is heat death — maximum entropy, uniform temperature, no more usable energy. For the individual mind, this is forgetfulness. But poetry can resist this fate:

Even as empires crumble, a sonnet survives. Even as the body cools, a stanza stays warm in memory. Poetry is a pocket of negative entropy — a refusal of the ultimate silence.

In thermodynamic terms, poetry is a reversible-irreversible paradox: it permanently transforms the reader, yet remains infinitely re-readable, generating new heat with each cycle. It is the proof that in the furnace of thought, no spark is ever truly lost. Thus, in thermodynamic terms, poetry is the alchemy of energy transformation: grief into grace, chaos into clarity, heat into light. It reminds us that the laws of the physical universe may govern bodies, but the laws of beauty can still surprise them.

THE GEOMETRY OF THE SUBLIME

If thermodynamics taught us how poetry moves emotional energy, geometry teaches us how poetry shapes it. Just as mathematics can describe the curves of a seashell or the arc of a comet, it can also reveal the architecture of thought in verse. Here, beauty is not random — it is proportion, pattern, and paradox rendered in language.

Euclidean Lines of Logic

Euclid gave us points, lines, planes, and the clarity of straight reason. In poetry, the Euclidean line appears in the clean, unbroken movement of thought from premise to conclusion. A philosophical sonnet might advance its argument with the precision of a geometric proof. The poet becomes a geometer of the invisible, drawing conceptual chords between emotional points. But the poet also knows that no matter how straight the line, the destination is not merely factual — it is felt.

Circles of Recurrence

The circle, perfect and endless, is the form of repetition with variation. Refrains, cyclical imagery, and seasonal metaphors all mirror the closed yet renewing curve of the circle. The circle's paradox is that it moves endlessly without progress, yet contains all possible progress within its perfection. A circular poem, like Dante's *Divine Comedy*, ends where it begins — but the traveler's mind is forever altered.

Triangles of Tension

The triangle is the simplest structure of stability in geometry, and in poetry, it often manifests as triadic tension:

Love–Loss–Memory

Past–Present–Future

Self–Other–World

The three points hold the poetic structure firm, each side supporting the others. Remove one, and the whole collapses. The greatest poets — from Yeats to Tagore — understand that beauty often rests on this ***tripodal truth***.

Golden Ratios and Harmonic Proportions

The golden ratio, Φ, appears in seashells, galaxies, and Greek temples. In poetry, it appears in proportional balance — a perfect distribution of imagery, rhythm, and silence.

A sonnet's 8–6 structure echoes this natural mathematics; a haiku's 5–7–5 beats form their own harmonic equilibrium. Even free verse, when skillfully crafted, hides proportional harmonies in its architecture, invisible yet felt.

Non-Euclidean Curves of Consciousness

In the 19th century, mathematicians broke Euclid's rules, creating geometries where parallel lines meet, and angles defy expectation. Poetry lives here too:

Dreams where time loops back on itself.

Metaphors that bend logic into impossible beauty.

Narratives that fold space so that two unrelated moments touch.

In non-Euclidean verse, the shortest distance between two truths may be a curve of paradox.

Topology of Transformation

Topology studies shapes that can be stretched,

twisted, or folded without breaking. Poetry is linguistic topology:

A memory is stretched into myth.

A simple image is twisted into a symbol.

A linear story is folded into simultaneous moments.

The Möbius strip — a surface with only one side — is the perfect poetic metaphor: the inside and the outside are the same, the self and the world endlessly exchanging places.

The Topology of Thought and Verse

Topology, the mathematics of malleable shapes, studies forms that can be stretched, twisted, bent, or folded without breaking. A coffee cup becomes a doughnut; a ribbon transforms into a Möbius strip. The object endures, though its appearance changes. Poetry, in its luminous logic, is linguistic topology: it stretches, twists, and folds meaning, reshaping experience without ever fracturing essence.

A memory, once fleeting, is stretched into myth, elongated by the rhythm of remembrance, the pull of imagination, the weight of wonder. What was once ephemeral becomes epic, a lattice of emotion spanning generations. A simple image, a leaf, a drop, a glance, may be twisted into symbol, bent around layers of metaphor until it radiates multiple meanings at once. A linear story, straight and sequential, may be folded upon itself, collapsing past and future, self and other, moment and eternity into simultaneous perception.

The Möbius strip, a surface with only one side and one edge, embodies the paradoxical perfection of poetry. Inside and outside converge; beginning and end entwine; the self and the world continually exchange places. In a single line, the reader is both observer and participant; the poet is both creator and creation. The narrative loops upon itself, infinite in its continuity, singular in its structure. A stanza may fold back upon itself like a Möbius strip, revealing that opposites—joy and grief, life and death, presence and absence—are never separate but endlessly entangled.

Poetic topology teaches that form is fluid, meaning is malleable, and perception is elastic. The poem survives transformation because its essence is invariant, even as its surface contorts, its edges twist, and its dimensions multiply. Rhythm stretches across time; metaphor twists across understanding; stanza and silence fold together, creating layers of resonance that both obscure and illuminate. The reader traverses this topological terrain, moving along curves, following folds, discovering continuity in what seemed contradictory, unity in what seemed fragmented.

And so the Möbius strip becomes more than metaphor—it becomes method, model, and measure. The inside is the outside; self merges with world; beginning returns to end. Every poem is a Möbius manifestation: finite yet infinite, singular yet manifold, linear yet cyclical, folded yet flowing. Poetry, like topology, demonstrates that boundaries are illusions, edges are porous, and forms are resilient, bending without breaking.

In the end, poetic topology reminds us that experience is flexible, memory is transformable, and consciousness is contoured. It encourages us to perceive continuity where the eye sees division, to embrace paradox where logic demands certainty, and to follow the Möbius path of meaning, where every twist, every turn, every fold, returns us inexorably to the same luminous truth: that poetry is the landscape of the mind, infinitely stretchable, endlessly foldable, eternally alive.

The Fractals of Feeling

Fractals are shapes whose patterns repeat at every scale — the veins of a leaf, the branching of rivers, the swirls of a storm. Poetry is fractal when its themes and images echo themselves in miniature and in vastness. In Blake's "To see a world in a grain of sand," the microcosm mirrors the macrocosm — the universe's infinite complexity compressed into the smallest form.

Infinite Dimensions of Interpretation

In geometry, we can imagine dimensions beyond the third. In poetry, there are interpretive dimensions beyond the literal, the symbolic, and the emotional:

Metaphysical dimension— What does this mean for existence itself?

Ethical dimension— What does this demand of me morally?

Aesthetic dimension— How does this alter my sense of beauty?

Each new dimension reveals angles of meaning invisible in the others. In geometric terms, poetry is a shape-shifting architecture, equally at home in the purity of the line and the chaos of the curve, in the solidity of the triangle and the endlessness of the spiral.

The Multidimensionality of Meaning

In geometry, the imagination can wander beyond the familiar three dimensions—length, breadth, and height—into realms that cannot be visualized but only intuited, perceived through abstraction and inference. Poetry, in its transcendent texture, offers similar interpretive dimensions beyond the literal, the symbolic, and the emotional, expanding our consciousness into unseen planes of understanding. Each poem is a dimensional map, a shape-shifting architecture, a structure as solid as a triangle yet as spiraling as the infinite, capable of revealing facets invisible to ordinary perception.

The metaphysical dimension asks the most profound questions: what does this poem say about existence itself? It bends meaning across the contours of reality, probing the essence of being, the rhythm of time, and the architecture of consciousness. A single line may fold the cosmos into a stanza, collapsing infinity into immediacy, transforming words into portals through which the reader glimpses the ultimate enigmas of life.

The ethical dimension extends the inquiry into action: what does this poem demand of me morally, ethically, spiritually? Here, poetry is not passive reflection but active provocation, nudging the reader to consider responsibility, to weigh justice, to empathize beyond self-interest. Lines become ethical vectors, guiding the mind across moral landscapes as subtle as a whisper, as urgent as a cry, as intricate as the curvature of a Möbius strip.

The aesthetic dimension celebrates beauty in multiplicity: how does this poem alter perception, refine the senses, expand the imagination? Poetry bends and blends form, color, cadence, and texture, revealing that beauty is not static but dynamic, not singular but manifold. A single image, a lone sound, a measured pause, resonates across the reader's consciousness, forming patterns that are felt as much as understood, harmonies that are intuited as much as observed.

Each new dimension, like a geometric plane beyond the third, reveals angles of meaning invisible in the others. The poem is simultaneously ethical, aesthetic, and metaphysical; it is a triangle of truths folding into a spiral of endless interpretation. Just as geometric shapes can twist, expand, and fold in higher dimensions, so too does poetry shape-shift, accommodating multiple planes of understanding without breaking, without losing coherence, without sacrificing depth.

Poetry, then, is a multidimensional lattice, equally at home in the purity of the straight line and the chaos of the curve, in the solidity of structure and the fluidity of form. It teaches that comprehension is never singular, that experience is layered, and that understanding emerges not from linear observation but from navigating intersections of meaning, from moving along folds and spirals, from perceiving connections between the visible and the invisible.

In this multidimensional vision, every reading becomes a journey across unseen planes, every line a bridge to hidden perspectives, every stanza a portal to higher understanding. Poetry, like geometry in imagination, defies limitation, stretches perception, and reveals that truth, beauty, and meaning exist simultaneously, infinitely, and inextricably intertwined across dimensions beyond sight, beyond thought, beyond the ordinary three.

THE MUSIC OF THE MULTIVERSE

If geometry showed us poetry's architecture, music reveals its soul in motion. And when we speak of music here, we mean not merely the sounds of voice and instrument, but the deep, cosmic harmonics that underlie both physics and feeling. Poetry, like music, is a **mathematics of vibration** — its meanings ripple outward, striking chords in realms beyond our own.

Poetry as Vibration

In string theory, the universe's smallest units are not particles but vibrating strings, each frequency producing a different particle — a different reality. Likewise, in poetry:

Change the rhythm and the meaning shifts.

Alter the stress pattern and the emotional timbre transforms.

The poem's "strings" — syllables, sounds, cadences — vibrate in the reader's mind, creating both intellectual and emotional particles of thought.

In the arcane architecture of string theory, the universe's most infinitesimal units are not particles but vibrating strings, each oscillation giving rise to a unique particle, each frequency composing a distinct reality. Poetry, in its resonant realm, mirrors this cosmic vibration: its syllables, stresses, cadences, and sounds are strings that hum, resonate, and ripple across consciousness, creating a lattice of meaning that is simultaneously intellectual, emotional, and spiritual.

A change in rhythm is no mere stylistic adjustment; it is a vibrational shift, altering the very energy of the poem, the resonance of its perception, the timbre of its emotional impact. A careful alteration of stress transforms laughter into lament, serenity into storm, intimacy into isolation. The poem's strings vibrate in unison with the reader's mind, eliciting particles of thought, quanta of feeling, atoms of awareness, each forming a constellation of comprehension unique to the encounter.

Poetry's vibration is both subtle and seismic. The pause between syllables, the elongation of a vowel, the clash of consonants, the cadence of enjambment—all constitute oscillations that ripple invisibly yet powerfully through consciousness. Like cosmic strings whose frequencies determine the nature of matter, the poet's chosen vibrations shape the very substance of perception: they conjure worlds, summon memories, and modulate the spectrum of emotion.

In this quantum-poetic model, every line, every stanza, every meter is a resonant string, capable of producing an infinity of emotional and intellectual harmonics. The same words, arranged differently, can generate alternate realities: a single phrase may vibrate with hope in one reading and despair in another; a single line may shimmer with beauty for one observer and brilliance for another. Poetry, like the vibrating universe, is a cosmos of possibilities, an orchestration of frequencies, a symphony of subtle forces that reverberates across time, mind, and heart.

The poet, then, is a cosmic conductor, attuning each string with care, calibrating each oscillation, composing vibrations that are as precise as they are ineffable. The reader becomes the resonant instrument, a participant in the sonic experiment, collapsing infinite potential into lived experience, translating rhythm into resonance, stress into sensation. Poetry, like string theory, teaches that reality is fundamentally vibrational: meaning emerges through oscillation, comprehension through resonance, understanding through the interplay of energy and perception.

Thus, poetry is vibration made visible, oscillation made tangible, resonance made reflective. Its strings hum in silence and sound, in ink and imagination, in mind and memory, producing intellectual particles, emotional atoms, and spiritual quanta. It reminds us that all perception is fundamentally interaction, all comprehension is co-created, and all experience is modulated by the vibrations we attend to, receive, and release.

In this eternal oscillation, poetry becomes both particle and wave, matter and music, rhythm and revelation. It is a quantum string of consciousness, stretching across time and space, vibrating within minds, resonating between souls, and shaping realities with each oscillation, each pulse, each perfect, paradoxical, and perpetual hum.

Harmonic Resonance of the Soul

When one tuning fork vibrates, another at the same pitch will begin to resonate. Poetry creates a similar **empathic resonance** between poet and reader:

A poem about grief resonates with your own hidden grief.

A verse about joy vibrates the strings of your past happiness.

In this way, poetry becomes **a bridge of harmonics**, making distant hearts beat in unison.

In the world of acoustics, a tuning fork that vibrates at a specific pitch can induce a second fork of the same frequency to vibrate in harmony, a phenomenon known as sympathetic resonance. Poetry, in its luminous logic, performs an analogous miracle: it creates empathic resonance between poet and reader, between writer and witness, across time, space, and circumstance. Each poem is a vibrational bridge, a conduit of feeling, a lattice through which hearts align and souls synchronize.

A stanza about sorrow does not merely describe grief; it awakens dormant grief in the reader, coaxing hidden pain to the surface, vibrating it into conscious recognition. A verse celebrating joy does not simply recount happiness; it recalls echoes of laughter, warmth, and wonder stored in memory, sending resonant waves through the corridors of experience. Each word is a tuning fork, each line a chord, each poem a symphony of shared consciousness.

This resonance is both intimate and infinite. The poet, through careful composition, releases vibrations of meaning; the reader, through perception and empathy, responds in kind. The interaction is invisible yet palpable, subtle yet seismic. It transcends the barriers of time, language, and culture, demonstrating that emotion, like energy, is never confined, but transmitted, received, and amplified through the harmonic strings of shared humanity.

The paradox is profound: poetry is simultaneously private and communal. Each encounter is uniquely personal, yet universally connective. A single line can stir an individual heart while simultaneously reverberating across generations, cultures, and continents. Grief, joy, wonder, longing—these vibrations are transmitted through words, folding the distance between poet and reader into an intimate, oscillating present.

In this way, poetry becomes more than language; it becomes a bridge of harmonics, a network of resonances linking minds, synchronizing pulses, aligning perceptions. It proves that the human spirit is not solitary but sympathetically entangled, capable of vibrating in unison with distant hearts. Like cosmic strings, like quantum particles, like resonant forks, poetry connects what appears apart, harmonizes what seems dissonant, and reveals that shared feeling is the most fundamental architecture of understanding.

Thus, the act of reading a poem is a quantum resonance experiment: waves of emotion pass from writer to reader, collapse into insight, and re-emerge as empathy, recognition, and reflection. Poetry is vibration made visible, feeling made audible, resonance made relational. It teaches that hearts are instruments tuned to one another, that emotion is transmissible, and that the universe of consciousness is bound together by invisible yet inexorable strings of harmonic connection.

In the symphony of existence, poetry is both conductor and chord, composer and instrument, transmitter and resonator. It reminds us that distance is no barrier to resonance, that silence is filled with vibration, and that empathy itself is a quantum phenomenon—collapsing probabilities of feeling into the certainty of shared experience. In every verse, every stanza, every cadence, poetry tunes our hearts to the universal hum, ensuring that distant souls can beat in unison, joined by the invisible harmonics of language and feeling.

The Chord of Contradiction

In music, dissonance is tension between notes — and resolution is the return to harmony. Poetry thrives in semantic dissonance: paradox, oxymoron, contradiction. Consider: "The silence sang to me." This is both impossible and perfectly comprehensible; like a suspended chord, it contains the ache of resolution without resolving it. The reader lives in that exquisite uncertainty.

The Scale of the Spheres

Pythagoras imagined the planets moving in cosmic harmony — the ***Musica Universalis***. Poetry taps this tradition, aligning words like celestial bodies, so their distances and relationships produce an invisible melody. The sonnet, the ghazal, the haiku — each is a distinct scale, each with its own tonal gravity. Just as a key signature in music sets emotional expectation, so does a poetic form.

Polyphony of Perspectives

In music, polyphony is multiple independent melodies weaving into one. In poetry, it is multiple voices, ideas, and symbols interlacing without losing individuality:

A love poem that is also a political critique.

A war elegy that is also a meditation on nature.

These strands move independently yet harmoniously, creating multi-dimensional meaning — a verbal fugue.

In music, polyphony is the art of multiple independent melodies weaving together into a single, harmonious composition. Poetry, in its luminous and labyrinthine logic, performs a similar feat: it is a polyphony of voices, a confluence of ideas, emotions, and symbols, each retaining its individuality while contributing to the greater resonance of the whole. Every poem, like a musical fugue, vibrates with interlaced strands of meaning, each line a melody, each stanza a counterpoint, each reading a new orchestration of perception.

A love poem may simultaneously speak of desire and despair, devotion and dissent, becoming both intimate confession and political critique. A war elegy may mourn fallen soldiers while reflecting on the cycles of nature, fusing grief with contemplation, lament with lyric. Each strand moves independently, yet harmonizes with the others, forming a multi-dimensional lattice of significance, a verbal fugue that invites both immersion and interpretation.

Polyphony in poetry is both structure and freedom. The poet arranges multiple thematic threads with meticulous care, yet allows them to breathe, diverge, and intertwine organically. Meaning is not linear but layered, a tapestry of resonance where each voice enriches the whole while preserving its distinct hue. Contradiction is embraced, paradox is celebrated, and multiplicity becomes the very medium through which unity emerges.

The reader becomes an active participant in this polyphonic universe. Each mind perceives and interprets the interplay differently: one voice may dominate, another may recede; one strand may illuminate, another may shadow. Yet the interweaving ensures that no single perspective exhausts the poem's richness. The poem exists as both plural and singular, fragmented and cohesive, independent and interdependent, reflecting the intricate dance of consciousness itself.

In this way, poetry is a symphony of sensibilities, a chorus of consciousness, a harmonic convergence of thought and feeling. Each poem, like a fugue, embodies multiple temporalities, perspectives, and dimensions simultaneously: the personal intertwined with the political, the temporal with the eternal, the emotional with the intellectual. Its polyphony reminds us that understanding is not univocal, that truth is layered, and that meaning is co-created in the interplay of voices, both written and received.

Thus, the polyphonic poem is an interlaced universe, a verbal cosmos where every idea resonates with another, every image vibrates alongside a counter-image, and every emotion harmonizes with its complement. It celebrates multiplicity without chaos, divergence without dissonance, and independence without isolation. Poetry, in its polyphonic perfection, teaches that reality itself is woven of interdependent threads, that voices coexist in perpetual dialogue, and that the most profound understanding arises when we listen to the harmony of many rather than the claim of one.

Overtone Universes

Every note produces overtones — faint, higher harmonics that enrich the sound. Likewise, every image in poetry carries overtones of association:

The word apple may carry echoes of Eden, autumn, knowledge, temptation, sweetness, and decay. The word bridge may resonate with connection, transition, peril, and hope. A master poet shapes not just the primary note, but the entire spectrum of overtones, letting the reader hear multiple worlds in one word.

Silence as Symphony

Music is not only sound; it is also the placement of silence. In poetry, silence — the pause, the line break, the unsaid — is a note the reader must imagine. The Japanese concept of ma — the space between — is poetry's reminder that what is withheld can resound more deeply than what is declared. The absence becomes presence; the rest becomes music.

The Multiversal Echo

In the theory of the multiverse, countless parallel realities exist. A poem, too, exists in countless interpretive universes:

In one, it is a love confession.

In another, it is a coded political protest.

In another, it is purely sound-play with no fixed meaning.

The miracle is that all these universes can exist simultaneously in the same words, and each reader enters the one their own frequency matches. In musical terms, poetry is the ***sonic geometry of consciousness***, an instrument played by the universe upon the strings of human perception, producing harmonies and dissonances that transcend the here and now.

In the vast vision of the multiverse, countless parallel realities exist simultaneously, each distinct, each complete, yet all intertwined in infinite potential. Poetry, in its luminous logic, mirrors this cosmic multiplicity: a single poem is a multiversal echo, reverberating across countless interpretive universes, each perception valid, each resonance real. Every word, every line, every cadence carries the potential to manifest differently depending on the reader's consciousness, forming an infinite lattice of literary realities.

In one universe, the poem may emerge as a tender love confession, vibrating with intimacy, desire, and vulnerability. In another, the very same words may pulse as a coded political protest, sparking dissent, reflection, and rebellion. In yet another, the poem may exist purely as sonic play, a kaleidoscope of sound and rhythm with no fixed semantic anchor. The miracle is that all these universes coexist in the same textual reality; they do not compete, they do not negate—they resonate in parallel, awaiting the consciousness attuned to their frequency.

Each reader becomes a quantum observer, collapsing some possibilities while activating others. The universe of interpretation responds, not linearly but dynamically, creating a poetic experience that is simultaneously personal and infinite. The poem is a multiverse in miniature: each reading, each mind, each moment generates a new universe of meaning, a unique resonance that is both entirely original and yet entirely faithful to the original composition.

In musical terms, poetry is the sonic geometry of consciousness, an instrument strummed by the universe upon the strings of human perception. Each vibration produces harmonies and dissonances, chords and counterpoints, intersecting layers of feeling and thought. The poem is alive in its oscillations, a cosmos of potentiality that transcends the here and now, existing in myriad frequencies that only align when the reader's mind is ready, receptive, and resonant.

The multiversal echo teaches that poetry is infinitely expansive yet intimately immediate, singular in appearance yet plural in existence. It is a mirror of consciousness itself, reflecting the infinite permutations of human understanding and experience. Just as parallel universes can coexist without contradiction, multiple interpretations of a poem coexist without conflict, each illuminating different facets of truth, beauty, and resonance.

Thus, poetry, in its multiversal magnificence, is not merely written words on a page but a quantum symphony of potential, vibrating with the infinite possibilities of human perception. Each encounter, each reading, each attentive mind enters a universe uniquely tuned to its frequency. In this sublime oscillation of meaning and matter, poetry becomes a bridge across realities, a harmonic lattice of consciousness, a multiverse resonating within a single stanza, echoing simultaneously in hearts, minds, and worlds beyond comprehension.

THE RELATIVITY OF REVERIE

If Newton saw the universe as a clock, Einstein saw it as a fabric — pliable, curved, and altered by mass and motion. Poetry, too, is such a fabric: woven of words and weighted by meaning, bending the reader's perception of time, place, and possibility.

The Temporal Elasticity of Verse

In relativity, time flows differently for observers in different frames of reference. In poetry:

A three-line haiku can feel like an entire season. An epic spanning centuries can pass in a heartbeat. A reader slows down when reading a dense, imagistic stanza; they accelerate through lighter, fluid lines. The poem becomes a time dilation chamber — each reader's clock running at a unique pace.

Mass of Meaning and Gravitational Pull

In physics, a body with mass bends spacetime around it. In poetry, a phrase with semantic density bends interpretive space:

A single word — nevermore, eternity, home — can warp the trajectory of thought. Heavy themes like death or love act as black holes of attention, pulling every metaphor into their gravity. Some poems collapse into singularities — points of infinite density — where meaning cannot be escaped, only orbited.

Light Bending Around the Unsaid

Einstein showed that light curves around massive

bodies. Likewise, in poetry, thought bends around what is left unsaid. The meaning travels not in a straight line, but arcs, refracts, and reappears where least expected. The unsaid becomes an ***invisible mass***, shaping everything the reader perceives.

Relativistic Perspective of the Reader

Relativity tells us there is no single objective frame; all observation is relative to position and motion. In poetry, meaning depends on:

The reader's emotional velocity (their current mood).

The gravitational field of their past experiences.

Their linguistic coordinates (cultural, historical, and personal context).

Thus, no poem ever truly reads the same way twice — for the observer is never the same. In Einstein's revolutionary revelation of relativity, there is no absolute frame of reference; all observation is relative, contingent upon position, motion, and perspective. Poetry, in its profound and paradoxical precision, mirrors this truth: meaning is never fixed, never universal, but always relative to the observer. Every reading is a unique event, every interpretation a personal frame of reference, shaped by the reader's mind, heart, and circumstance.

A reader's emotional velocity—their current mood, mental state, or openness—affects how a poem resonates. A stanza of lament may crash like thunder on a heart heavy with sorrow, yet pass unnoticed by one whose mind is unburdened. A line of joy may illuminate a shadowed soul or simply shimmer faintly for one already immersed in contentment. The tempo of emotion bends meaning just as speed curves the fabric of spacetime, warping perception and coloring resonance.

The gravitational field of memory—the weight

of past experiences, trauma, triumph, and tradition—draws lines of significance, distorting the orbit of understanding. Words that echo childhood may collide with forgotten grief; imagery of battle may resonate with long-absorbed history; metaphors may precipitate into familiar truths or vanish into unknown voids. Poetry, like relativity, teaches that gravity shapes perception, that context molds comprehension, and that the force of prior experience cannot be ignored in interpreting the present.

The reader's linguistic coordinates—cultural, historical, and personal context—determine the very fabric through which meaning flows. The same poem read across continents or centuries may assume entirely different dimensions, reflecting the observer's frame of reference. Idioms, connotations, and shared knowledge bend understanding, creating relativity not as limitation, but as richness, multiplying the poem's potential realities across the spectrum of human experience.

Thus, no poem ever truly reads the same way twice. Each encounter is a unique collision of consciousness, cadence, and context. The poem exists as a constant, yet the observer is never the same; the meaning, like spacetime, stretches, contracts, and curves according to the subtle and invisible contours of perception. Poetry, in this relativistic revelation, becomes a dynamic system of motion and meaning, a universe in which the observer is always integral, indispensable, and transformative.

The paradox is luminous: poetry is both immutable and mutable, eternal and ephemeral, fixed in ink but fluid in interpretation, anchored in structure yet drifting in experience. It teaches that understanding is not discovery but interaction, that resonance is not transmission but co-creation, and that meaning emerges only when the observer, moving, feeling, and remembering, enters the field of perception.

In the cosmic theater of consciousness, poetry becomes a relativistic lens, bending emotion, warping understanding, and reshaping the perception of reality. No line, no stanza, no verse exists in isolation; each is refracted through the unique prism of the reader. Every reading is an experiment, every encounter a frame of reference, every perception a universe unto itself. In this exquisite oscillation, poetry illuminates the eternal truth of relativity: nothing is absolute, everything is relational, and every observer participates in the creation of meaning.

Time Loops and Poetic Causality

In speculative physics, time loops allow events to influence their own causes. In poetry, the ending can retroactively rewrite the beginning:

A final twist forces the reader to reinterpret every preceding line. A revelation at the end changes the emotional color of all that came before. In such verse, cause and effect are not linear — they are recursive spirals.

The Twin Paradox of Memory

In relativity's twin paradox, two twins age differently due to different journeys through spacetime. In poetry, two readers can revisit the same poem after years apart — yet the poem has "aged" differently for each: One finds it unchanged, preserved in its original clarity. The other finds it transformed, weathered by the erosion of their own lived years. The poem is both the same and not the same — a living paradox.

Poetry as a Wormhole

Wormholes connect distant points in spacetime instantly. A poem can likewise bridge disparate realms:

An ancient epic can make a modern reader feel present in a Bronze Age battlefield.

A contemporary verse can transport the reader into imagined futures.

These wormholes are not violations of nature — they are natural laws of language.

In the vast expanse of spacetime, theoretical wormholes offer pathways connecting distant points instantaneously, folding the cosmos so that what is far becomes near, what is past becomes present, and what is imagined becomes tangible. Poetry, in its paradoxical and luminous logic, functions as a linguistic wormhole, a conduit through which reader and poet, past and future, reality and imagination converge, transcending the ordinary bounds of temporal and spatial experience.

An ancient epic, composed millennia ago, can transport the modern reader into the dust, din, and desperation of a Bronze Age battlefield. Each syllable vibrates with latent energy, each line a bridge spanning centuries, each metaphor a tunnel through the unseen corridors of time. A contemporary poem, conversely, can launch the mind into imagined futures, speculative landscapes, or alternate realities, making tomorrow resonate in today, possibility tangible in the present, and fantasy visceral in consciousness.

These poetic wormholes are not anomalies; they are natural laws of language. Like the universe's hidden topology, words bend meaning, cadences warp perception, and imagery collapses distance, creating instantaneous connection where linear reading might suggest separation. The poem is both the tunnel and the traveler, the passage and the portal, moving simultaneously forward and backward, outward and inward.

The reader, entering this wormhole, experiences a compression of time and expansion of awareness. Emotions from ages past collide with contemporary reflection; wisdom from imagined worlds reverberates through the mind; empathy bridges cultures, epochs, and personal histories. In this paradoxical compression, the poem becomes both vessel and voyage, simultaneously static on the page and dynamic in perception.

Wormholes of poetry illuminate the elasticity of experience. They demonstrate that distance is illusion, that time is malleable, and that consciousness itself is capable of instantaneously spanning vast realms of thought and feeling. The poem acts as a gravitational lens, warping understanding and curving perception, aligning the reader's mind with worlds otherwise unreachable.

Thus, poetry is not merely narrative, image, or sound; it is a temporal-transcending, space-spanning, consciousness-connecting phenomenon. It bridges the ancient and the immediate, the imagined and the remembered, the self and the other. Like a wormhole in the cosmic fabric, poetry bends, folds, and links realities, proving that language is a fundamental force capable of traversing dimensions, uniting disparate experiences, and creating instantaneous resonance across the multiverse of human perception.

In every stanza, every metaphor, every cadence, poetry becomes a wormhole: a luminous, liminal passage where past, present, and future collide; distance dissolves; and consciousness moves freely through the infinite corridors of human and cosmic experience.

Event Horizons of Emotion

The event horizon is the boundary around a black hole beyond which nothing can return. In poetry, there are emotional event horizons — points where a feeling, once entered, cannot be undone:

A heartbreaking image you cannot unsee.

A truth, once named, that forever alters your inner sky.

Crossing it is voluntary, but irreversible. In relativistic terms, poetry is the ***cosmic lens*** through which we not only see the universe distorted, but see ourselves distorted within it — and in that distortion, discover a deeper truth. Lets us now look into the **furnace of cognition**, where poetry becomes an engine, a crucible, a perpetual alchemical reactor in which the raw fuels of life are transformed into the refined flames of meaning.

In the inscrutable architecture of the cosmos, the event horizon is the demarcation surrounding a black hole—a boundary beyond which no matter, no light, no signal can return. Poetry, in its profound paradoxical precision, has analogous emotional event horizons: thresholds of feeling, once crossed, that reshape consciousness irrevocably. A poem, a line, an image can pull the reader across this boundary, altering the inner landscape so that return is impossible, yet discovery is inevitable.

A heartbreaking image—a mother's lament, a fallen hero, a fleeting moment of innocence lost—cannot be unperceived. Once the truth is named, once the emotional tide is crossed, the psyche itself is transformed. Grief, longing, awe, or revelation become permanent coordinates in the map of understanding. The reader stands at the precipice of feeling, aware that crossing is voluntary but irreversible, and that the journey reshapes perception, memory, and soul.

In relativistic terms, poetry is a cosmic lens, warping the ordinary and refracting the extraordinary. Through it, the universe is not merely observed; it is distorted and illuminated simultaneously. And within that distortion, the self is revealed, stretched, compressed, and reshaped by the gravitational pull of emotion. The poem becomes both mirror and telescope, reflecting inner truths while magnifying the subtle, unseen architectures of existence.

Crossing these emotional event horizons is an act of courage, curiosity, and surrender. The reader, drawn into the crucible of feeling, encounters the inescapable pull of truth, the gravity of insight, the intensity of resonance. It is here that poetry ceases to be a mere artifact and becomes a perpetual alchemical reactor, a furnace in which raw experience—the chaos of life, the combustibles of memory, the fuels of passion—is transmuted into refined flames of meaning.

Within this crucible, language vibrates with energetic potency. Imagery combusts into insight, metaphor ignites understanding, and rhythm channels emotional currents into conscious awareness. Poetry acts as both engine and elixir: it drives cognition while simultaneously distilling perception, shaping the raw elements of lived experience into coherent, luminous, and transcendent patterns.

The event horizon, once crossed, is transformative. The reader emerges altered, attuned, and awakened, carrying forward the energy of the poem, the momentum of insight, the gravity of emotional resonance. Poetry, in this sense, is both perilous and profound, inviting immersion into the unknown while guaranteeing illumination beyond expectation.

Thus, the event horizon is not merely boundary but portal—a threshold into deeper cognition, a passage into heightened perception, a gateway through which the universe and self are simultaneously observed, distorted, and understood. Poetry becomes a vessel, a crucible, a cosmic engine, reminding us that the human heart and mind are capable of traversing the most extreme emotional landscapes, and that meaning itself emerges most powerfully at the edges where feeling becomes irreversible, and consciousness expands beyond its previous dimensions.

THE UNIFIED FIELD OF THE POETIC

Physicists have long sought the ***Theory of Everything*** — a single framework uniting gravity, electromagnetism, quantum mechanics, and the nuclear forces. Likewise, in this final ascent, we attempt to reveal poetry as a ***unified field*** where all forces of human knowing — science, art, philosophy, memory, emotion — are not merely reconciled, but revealed as aspects of one indivisible phenomenon: the poetic.

The Poetic Constant

Just as the speed of light c anchors relativity, there exists in the universe a Poetic Constant — the irreducible truth that beauty, meaning, and wonder are inseparable from existence itself. This constant is not measured in meters per second but in moments per soul:

The moment a child first hears a rhyme and feels language as music.

The moment an old mind, nearing its dusk, finds a fragment of verse that feels like a sunrise.

This constant binds epochs, cultures, and even species — for the birds have their own meters, the whales their own epics. In Einsteinian relativity, the speed of light, C, serves as an unchanging anchor, a universal constant against which all motion and measurement are gauged. Poetry, in its luminous and eternal logic, possesses a parallel: a Poetic

Constant, the irreducible truth that beauty, meaning, and wonder are inseparable from existence itself. This constant is not quantified in meters per second, nor recorded on any clock; it is measured in moments per soul, units of perception, recognition, and resonance that traverse time, space, and consciousness.

The Poetic Constant manifests in the infinitesimal yet infinite: the moment a child first hears a rhyme and perceives language as music, feeling its rhythm ripple through imagination; the moment an aged mind, approaching its dusk, discovers a fragment of verse that ignites a sunrise within, illuminating memory, reflection, and longing simultaneously. These moments, ephemeral yet eternal, are not bound by chronology or geography—they are anchors in the experiential cosmos, constants in the fluid calculus of human perception.

This poetic constant is transcendent and immanent. It binds epochs and empires, cultures and civilizations, mortal hearts and immortal imagination. It resonates across species: birds compose their own meters in dawn choruses, whales orchestrate epics in the deep, and human minds capture the ineffable in verse. Each expression, whether song, sound, or symbol, participates in the universal resonance, confirming that poetic energy is neither incidental nor contingent, but a fundamental attribute of existence itself.

Like light in physics, the Poetic Constant travels unobstructed through the medium of consciousness, illuminating the darkest corners of perception, bending through memory, and refracting through imagination. It is simultaneously infinite in reach and intimate in impact: a line of poetry can ignite a single mind while echoing through generations, a fleeting rhythm can transform a solitary moment into eternity, and a single syllable can vibrate with the resonance of the cosmos itself.

The paradox is profound: the Poetic Constant is absolute yet personal, universal yet particular, eternal yet momentary. It proves that meaning is not transient, that beauty is not optional, and that wonder is not merely ornamental but intrinsic to being. Poetry, in embodying this constant, becomes both map and mirror, vessel and vector, reflecting the structure of existence while simultaneously activating the consciousness that perceives it.

In this recognition, the Poetic Constant is revealed as a law of the universe, a luminous invariant that governs the interaction of mind, matter, and meaning. Each reading, each encounter, each attentively observed cadence aligns with this constant, confirming that to engage with poetry is to engage with the very fabric of reality, to measure existence in moments per soul, and to participate in the eternal oscillation of beauty, wonder, and understanding.

Thus, the Poetic Constant is not merely principle or metaphor; it is the heartbeat of consciousness, the rhythm of revelation, the unchanging resonance of meaning that underpins all perception and affirms that poetry, in its infinite permutations, is a fundamental law of the living universe.

Quantum-Gravitational Verses

Poetry obeys quantum strangeness: it contains multitudes of possible meanings until observed by the reader. Further, we saw that it bends the spacetime of perception.

The Unified Field of the Poetic says:

Poetry is quantum in its possibilities, gravitational in

its inevitability. It is both particle (the fixed word) and wave (the flowing rhythm). Both massless (able to leap minds instantly) and massive (able to anchor entire civilizations).

In the infinitesimal infinity of quantum mechanics, particles exist in superpositions, probabilities collapsing into reality only when observed. Poetry, in its luminous and paradoxical logic, exhibits a similar quantum strangeness: every poem contains multitudes of potential meanings, infinite interpretations suspended in the space of consciousness, awaiting the attentive gaze of the reader to collapse possibilities into perceptible resonance. Beyond its quantum qualities, poetry also exhibits gravitational inevitability. Like massive celestial bodies bending spacetime, a poem bends perception, pulling the reader's mind into its orbit, distorting temporal and emotional metrics, and shaping the very architecture of understanding. A stanza can curve cognition, a line can stretch attention, and a single word can create a tidal force of insight, drawing intellect and emotion together into a singular event horizon of comprehension. The Unified Field of the Poetic emerges from this duality: poetry is quantum in its possibilities, gravitational in its inevitability. It is simultaneously particle—the fixed word etched on the page, immutable in structure—and wave—the flowing rhythm, undulating across consciousness, shaping perception, and reverberating in emotional and intellectual resonance. It is massless in its ability to leap minds instantly across cultures, languages, and eras, yet massive in its capacity to anchor civilizations, sustaining collective memory, moral imagination, and aesthetic vision.

In this dual nature, poetry becomes a cosmic engine, a lattice of probability and permanence. Each reading is a quantum experiment: the poem's latent potentials collapse into one or more interpretations, influenced by the reader's emotional velocity, gravitational past, and cultural coordinates. Yet simultaneously, the poem's gravitational pull ensures that certain truths—ethical, aesthetic, metaphysical—remain inevitable, drawing all observers into shared resonance regardless of perspective. Poetry's quantum-gravitational essence also produces entanglement across minds. The act of creation links poet and reader across spacetime, past and present, imagination and memory. A line composed centuries ago resonates instantly in the mind of a modern observer, as if consciousness itself were a field of interlinked quanta, responding to the poem's inherent gravitational curvature and quantum superposition. Thus, poetry exists as both microcosm and macrocosm: particle and wave, possibility and inevitability, ephemeral vibration and enduring mass. Its structure and spontaneity, its rhythm and resonance, its subtlety and power, align with the fundamental laws of mind, matter, and meaning. In the quantum-gravitational universe of verse, words are both anchors and accelerators, cadences both catalysts and constants, metaphors both massless messengers and massive monuments.

In this synthesis, poetry becomes a ***Unified Field of Consciousness***, where quantum uncertainty coexists with gravitational necessity, where individual perception collapses into shared resonance, and where the reader participates in the fundamental dynamics of understanding, emotion, and wonder. It is a reminder that poetry is neither wholly fixed nor entirely fluid, neither entirely personal nor wholly universal—but both simultaneously, eternally, and inevitably.

Thermodynamic Grace

Poetry transforms the raw heat of experience into

the usable work of wisdom. But in the Unified Field, this thermodynamic cycle is eternal:

Input: the chaos of life.

Process: the shaping through language.

Output: an ordered insight.

Feedback: the insight re-enters the chaos, sparking new creations.

This cycle is the perpetual heartbeat of culture. In the universe, thermodynamics governs the transformation of energy: chaos condenses into order, heat becomes work, entropy flows even as structures emerge. Poetry, in its luminous and paradoxical logic, enacts a similar thermodynamic grace, transmuting the raw heat of human experience into the ordered work of insight, meaning, and understanding. Each poem is a perpetual alchemical reactor, converting disorder into wisdom, turbulence into clarity, and fleeting sensation into enduring resonance.

In the Unified Field of Poetics, this cycle is eternal and recursive. The input is the chaos of life—the cacophony of suffering, the tumult of desire, the turbulence of memory. The poet gathers, filters, and refines these raw fuels, channeling the unformed energy through the precise architecture of language. The process is the shaping through metaphor, rhythm, syntax, and sound—the compression, expansion, and folding of meaning into patterns that resonate with consciousness.

The output is ordered insight: a line of verse that illuminates, a stanza that clarifies, a poem that transforms perception. This insight is not static; it radiates, reverberates, and, like energy in a closed system, re-enters the chaos. The feedback loop ignites new creations, sparks further reflection, and sustains the perpetual heartbeat of culture. Each poem is simultaneously product and catalyst, structure and stimulus, outcome and origin.

Thermodynamic grace is paradoxical: poetry thrives on both constraint and liberation, entropy and order, heat and harmony. The poet acts as both engineer and alchemist, bending language to transmute disorder into meaning without extinguishing the vital energy of life itself. The reader, too, participates: perceiving, resonating, and allowing insight to flow back into lived experience, creating new cycles of understanding, empathy, and imagination.

This perpetual thermodynamic cycle is the heartbeat of culture, the eternal rhythm by which civilizations transform raw existence into art, suffering into wisdom, and fleeting moments into enduring memory. Poetry, in this grand energetic economy, is the universal engine: it captures chaos, structures it, amplifies it, and releases it anew, ensuring that both creation and comprehension are never-ending, ever-expanding, and infinitely generative.

In this luminous framework, every poem becomes a thermodynamic crucible, every reading a recalibration of the human heart, and every line a particle in the ongoing cosmic cycle. Poetry teaches that life itself is fuel, language is mechanism, insight is work, and culture is the perpetually renewed output of conscious thermodynamic grace.

Geometry of the Infinite

Poetry's shape was shown to be non-Euclidean — folding distant ideas into intimate proximity, curving emotion around the voids of the unsaid. In the Unified Field, this geometry becomes the blueprint of thought itself:

Points = single words, absolute in their position.

Lines = narrative threads, leading the mind.

Surfaces = emotional landscapes, curved by memory and metaphor.

Higher dimensions = meanings inaccessible except through intuition.

Poetry does not just use this geometry — it is this geometry made audible. In the luminous labyrinth of non-Euclidean imagination, poetry reveals itself as geometry in motion: folding distant ideas into intimate proximity, curving emotion around the voids of the unsaid, and bending perception along unexpected trajectories. Within the Unified Field of Poetics, this geometry becomes the blueprint of thought itself, the structural scaffold through which consciousness navigates meaning, feeling, and resonance. In this spatial symphony, points are the single words, absolute in position yet pregnant with potential. Each word is an anchor, a nucleus of significance, a discrete particle in the multidimensional lattice of understanding. Lines are the narrative threads, guiding cognition through the topology of story and metaphor, leading the mind along curves, twists, and tangents that traverse memory, imagination, and insight. Surfaces are emotional landscapes: vast, contoured, and curved by memory, metaphor, and cadence, bending perception into valleys of empathy and peaks of revelation.

Higher dimensions extend beyond the tangible: meanings inaccessible except through intuition, insights that cannot be observed linearly, truths that emerge only through engagement with the poem's multidimensional curvature. In these dimensions, paradox and ambiguity are not obstacles but essential coordinates, folding understanding back upon itself and stretching consciousness into realms beyond ordinary perception.

Poetry does not merely employ this geometry; it is this geometry made audible, made perceptible, made felt. Rhythm maps curves, rhyme traces contours, metaphor erects surfaces, and enjambment folds dimensions, creating a living topography of thought. The reader navigates these landscapes, tracing lines and surfaces, glimpsing points of singular intensity, and intuiting higher dimensions that extend infinitely beyond the page. The paradoxical brilliance of this geometric poetics is that structure and freedom coexist, constraint and creativity intertwine, and stability and fluidity converge. Every poem is simultaneously finite and infinite, tangible and ethereal, visible and hidden. Its architecture is not imposed externally; it emerges from the intrinsic laws of language, thought, and feeling, a self-organizing cosmos in which comprehension itself becomes an act of exploration, discovery, and resonance.

Thus, the geometry of the infinite is both map and medium, scaffold and substance, blueprint and bridge. Poetry is the space through which the mind moves, the surface upon which emotion curves, and the higher-dimensional realm in which intuition perceives truths inaccessible to linear thought. It teaches that to read poetry is to traverse multidimensional landscapes, to engage with the architecture of consciousness, and to inhabit the geometry of infinite possibility.

Music of the Spheres, Inside the Skull

We understood that poetry shares structure with music — repetition, variation, rhythm, dissonance, resolution. In the Unified Field, this becomes the resonant frequency of the human spirit. Each person's mind is like a unique instrument; a great poem strikes a chord that vibrates differently in each, yet always harmonically. The music is not external — it happens inside the skull, and yet feels like it spans the stars.

Paradox of Unity and Multiplicity

Here lies the most luminous and labyrinthine of

paradoxes: poetry is the most individual of arts, yet the most universal of languages. It is born of a singular mind, a private consciousness shaping thought, feeling, and imagination into a unique utterance. Yet the moment it is read, it transcends individuality, entering the consciousness of another, becoming simultaneously their thought, their feeling, their perception. The singular and the universal converge in an exquisite oscillation, a quantum collapse of private insight into shared resonance.

A poem is both utterly personal and universally accessible, a vessel that demands individuality yet thrives through communal reception. Its existence is contingent upon transfer of ownership: until the reader engages, interprets, and internalizes the poem, its meaning remains incomplete, suspended, latent. The poet's solitary act of creation is only the first pulse of a chain reaction; the reader's perception ignites the subsequent oscillations of understanding, empathy, and aesthetic resonance.

This sublime paradox, far from being contradiction, is the very mechanism of the poetic. The poem functions as a bridge between minds, a conduit through which thought, feeling, and imagination are transmitted, transformed, and reincarnated. The act of reading is an act of co-creation: each mind reshapes the poem in its own terms, expanding, contracting, and refracting its possibilities, yet preserving the essence of the poet's original resonance.

In this way, poetry embodies both absolute individuality and absolute universality. It is an atom and a cosmos, a private spark and a shared constellation. The paradox illuminates a fundamental truth: the poetic is not complete until it migrates from mind to mind, until the singular utterance becomes pluralized in consciousness, until the universe of perception itself participates in the poem's becoming.

Thus, the sublime paradox is not merely a curiosity of form or philosophy; it is the operating principle of poetry, the heartbeat of its existence, and the proof of its ineffable power. It teaches that to create is to surrender, to share is to complete, and to read is to participate in the very architecture of thought, feeling, and meaning. The individual and the universal are inseparable, the poet and the reader are entangled, and the poetic itself is the luminous field in which this sublime paradox manifests, endlessly oscillating, endlessly resonating, endlessly becoming.

The Equation of the Poetic

If we dared to write poetry as an equation, it might be:

$$P = (Q\ .\ G) + (T\ .\ M) + (E^{\text{infinity}})$$

Where:

Q = Quantum possibility of meaning.

G = Gravitational pull of emotional mass.

T = Thermodynamic transformation of experience.

M = Musical resonance of rhythm.

E^{infinity} = Entropic defiance — the infinite resistance to oblivion.

In words:

Poetry= Possibility multiplied by pull, plus transformation multiplied by tone, plus eternity raised to infinity.

Here, **P** is Poetry itself—the luminous, labyrinthine, and limitless phenomenon that bends thought, emotion, and perception. The first term, $\mathbf{Q \cdot G}$, encapsulates the quantum possibility of meaning multiplied by the gravitational pull of emotional mass. Every word vibrates with potential, every line curves the landscape of consciousness, and every stanza exerts a subtle yet inexorable attraction upon the reader's mind. Poetry, like matter in a quantum field, exists in superposition until perception collapses it into lived resonance.

The second term, **T · M**, represents the thermodynamic transformation of experience combined with the musical resonance of rhythm. Life's chaos—the entropy of sensation, memory, and desire—is channeled through language, compressed into cadence, and released as insight. Each meter, each rhyme, each pause is a catalyst, converting emotional heat into intellectual and aesthetic work, amplifying meaning through melodic architecture, and propelling consciousness toward illumination.

The final term, $\mathbf{E}^{(\infty)}$, is entropic defiance, the infinite resistance to oblivion, the eternal insistence that poetry survives, transcends, and persists. It embodies the perpetual oscillation of memory, imagination, and feeling against the inexorable dissolution of time, ensuring that beauty, truth, and wonder endure despite the entropy of the universe. Poetry, in this sense, is both temporal and eternal, ephemeral and immortal, fleeting in the moment yet infinite in resonance.

In words, the equation reads:

Poetry = Possibility multiplied by pull, plus transformation multiplied by tone, plus eternity raised to infinity.

It is simultaneously mechanism and mystery, a lattice of laws and a field of freedom. Poetry is measured yet immeasurable, constructed yet spontaneous, finite in expression yet infinite in potential. Each reading, each resonance, each encounter collapses some possibilities while amplifying others, generating new configurations of meaning, new harmonics of feeling, and new coordinates in the ever-expanding map of consciousness.

This equation is not a limitation, but a revelation of structure within freedom. It captures the interplay of forces that makes poetry extraordinary: the quantum uncertainty of interpretation, the gravitational inevitability of emotion, the thermodynamic alchemy of experience, the musicality of cadence, and the infinite defiance against oblivion. It is both a formula and a philosophy, a lens and a map, a bridge between the measurable and the immeasurable.

Thus, the Equation of the Poetic is not merely arithmetic, but alchemy; not merely algebra, but architecture; not merely symbol, but symphony. It reminds us that poetry is at once calculable and incalculable, physical and metaphysical, singular and universal, finite and infinite—a law of consciousness articulated in rhythm, resonance, and reverberation, awaiting each reader to complete its equation in the infinite laboratory of perception.

Beyond Philosophy

Philosophy asks why; poetry sometimes does not ask at all — it simply shows. In doing so, it bypasses argument and plants meaning directly in the soil of the subconscious. Philosophy is the scaffolding; poetry is the cathedral. Philosophy is the map; poetry is the walk under the moon. In the Unified Field, philosophy and poetry are not rivals — they are different states of the same substance, as ice and steam are to water.

The Final Paradox — Eternity in an Instant

In physics, infinity is unreachable; in poetry, infinity can be inhaled in a single breath:

"And still she slept an azure-lidded sleep."

One line — and the reader's mind contains an entire world, timeless and unending.

This is the Unified Field's ultimate truth: ***poetry is the shortest distance between a soul and the infinite.***

In the vast vistas of physics, infinity remains unreachable, a horizon forever beyond measurement, a limit never crossed. Poetry, in its luminous and paradoxical logic, offers a remarkable reversal: infinity can be inhaled in a single breath, grasped in the quiet pause between syllables, felt in the resonance of a single line. One carefully chosen utterance, one delicate arrangement of sound and sense, can contain entire worlds, epochs, and emotional universes within its fragile frame.

Consider a line like:

"And still she slept an azure-lidded sleep."

In this small cluster of words, the reader experiences vastness without extension, eternity without duration, cosmos without constraint. A single line stretches perception across time and space, weaving memory, imagination, and emotion into a universe of contemplation. The infinite, paradoxically, is both compressed and comprehensible, existing simultaneously in the reader's mind and in the boundless possibilities suggested by the words.

This is the ultimate revelation of the Unified Field of Poetics: poetry is the shortest distance between a soul and the infinite. It is a bridge across dimensions of perception, a wormhole of consciousness, a Möbius strip of meaning where inside and outside, self and world, beginning and end, fold seamlessly upon each other. Every syllable, every cadence, every pause participates in the contraction of the infinite into an instant, allowing the reader to dwell in eternity while inhaling a single breath The final paradox, therefore, is luminous and liberating: poetry is at once temporal and timeless, ephemeral and eternal, finite and infinite. Its brevity belies its boundlessness; its simplicity masks its depth; its singularity contains multiplicity without diminution. The poet captures infinity not by calculation or conjecture but by compression, cadence, and resonance, proving that the eternal is not only conceivable but experienceable in the intimate architecture of verse.

Through this lens, every reading becomes an act of transcendence, every line a portal, and every moment with poetry an encounter with the infinite. The Unified Field teaches that the soul, when attuned to language, can inhabit eternity as naturally as it breathes, and that the profoundest truths—beauty, wonder, understanding—are accessible in an instant, yet expansive beyond comprehension.

Thus, the final paradox crystallizes the totality of poetic philosophy: eternity resides in an instant, the infinite is inhaled in a breath, and the shortest distance between consciousness and the cosmos is a poem. Poetry is, at once, the ultimate compression and the ultimate expansion—a luminous, living, and eternal testament to the unity of experience, imagination, and being.

POETRY AS THE PARADOXICAL PRINCIPLE

Poetry is paradox personified. It is at once the most fragile feather and the firmest foundation, the most delicate dream and the most durable doctrine. Where philosophy chisels truths from thought, poetry paints truths with tremors of tenderness. Where science seeks laws, poetry sings litanies. Where politics drafts decrees, poetry delivers destinies. In all, poetry proves itself not as a subordinate servant of other studies, but as their sovereign spirit, their secret skeleton, their silent song.

Poetry is at once *ancient and ageless*. It is prehistoric yet postmodern, born before alphabets and breathing still after algorithms. It is the tongue of tribes, the hymn of hieroglyphs, the pulse of pixels. The paradox is plain: poetry is the oldest language of humanity, yet it is forever fresh; it is a relic of caves, yet a revelation for cyberspace. Its antiquity is its immortality.

If philosophy is the "love of wisdom" (*philo-sophia*), then poetry is the "wisdom of love." If science is the search for certainty, then poetry is the certainty of searching. The scientist dissects light into spectra, the philosopher defines light as concept, but the poet declares light as life. Paradox: science may prove the photon's properties, philosophy may probe its principles, but poetry alone proclaims its presence.

Poetry thrives in **oxymoronic oppositions.** It is silent speech, measured music, logical lunacy, temporal eternity. To speak of poetry is to embrace contradiction: it is useless yet indispensable, it is irrational yet truer than reason, it is ornamental yet essential. Like a rose, poetry seems delicate decoration, but without roses the garden is grave. Without poetry, humanity has prose but not purpose, language but not longing, calculation but not consolation.

Furthermore, poetry is ***meta-disciplinary***—not merely another subject beside history or physics, but the marrow in their bones. Every science begins with metaphor: "cell walls," "genetic code," "black holes," "big bang"—all metaphors, all poetry smuggled into science. Every philosophy breathes in metaphor: Plato's cave, Descartes' demon, Nietzsche's abyss—all poetry clothed in argument. Every politics persuades through poetry: slogans, anthems, manifestos—all compressed poems disguised as decrees.

Thus, to speak of poetry's relation to the disciplines is not to speak of ornament attached to edifice, but of foundation hidden in fortress. Poetry is not luxury but law; not accessory but essence. It is the invisible ink in the treaties of politics, the silent script behind sociology, the sacred cipher beneath mathematics. Poetry is paradox: it is peripheral yet pivotal, marginal yet monumental.

Mathematically, poetry is not the "solution" but the symmetry. It is the hidden ratio, the golden proportion, the balance of brevity and breadth. Philosophically, poetry is not the argument but the archetype. Scientifically, poetry is not the theorem but the theophany—a revelation of wonder. Politically, poetry is not the policy but the pulse.

Poetry transcends the narrowness of utility. Economy counts costs and benefits, but poetry counts blessings and burdens. Law legislates justice, but poetry illuminates mercy. Physics explains gravity, but poetry explains gravitas. Zoology catalogs animals, but poetry converses with them. Geography charts mountains, but poetry makes them sing. The paradox persists: poetry does not "explain" anything, yet it explains everything; it does not solve problems, yet it dissolves despair.

Poetry is also the discipline of *depth and height simultaneously*. Sociology studies the surface structures of society; psychology studies the inner mind; geology studies the underground; astronomy the heavens. But poetry spans both: the depth of despair and the height of hope, the cavern and the cosmos, the atom and the angel. It dares to define infinity and intimacy in the same stanza.

Moreover, poetry is profoundly *performative*. While sciences are descriptive and philosophy is prescriptive, poetry is transformative. A poem does not merely say—it slays; it does not merely describe reality, it designs reality. The paradox here: poetry is fiction that forms fact, imagination that incarnates institution. Every revolution is born not from equations, but from exclamations; not from statistics, but from stanzas.

Thus, poetry is paradoxical principle because it unites the impossible opposites:

It is useless but indispensable.
It is subjective yet universal.
It is ephemeral yet eternal.
It is irrational yet more rational than reason.
It is fragile yet indestructible.

In sum, poetry is not mere literature but ***life's own language***. It is the discipline that underlies all disciplines, the song that structures sciences, the rhyme that regulates reason, the lyric that legitimizes law. To explore poetry's relation with politics, sociology, economics, anthropology, history, education, geography, psychology, geology, biotechnology, astrology, philosophy, physics, chemistry, botany, zoology, mathematics, theology, and law is not to stretch poetry artificially, but to uncover its natural omnipresence. Poetry is not beside them—it is beneath them, beyond them, and between them.

Thus, begins our odyssey. From polis to physics, from society to theology, from economy to eternity, we shall witness poetry's paradoxical power, its ability to fertilize every field, to consecrate every concept, to sanctify every science. The following chapters will not reduce poetry to politics or physics, but reveal how politics and physics secretly sing poetry.

Poetry is not part of the universe; poetry is the pattern of the universe. To study poetry is to study paradox itself—the paradox of being and becoming, of unity and multiplicity, of silence and song. And so we step, stanza by stanza, into the sacred labyrinth.

POETRY AS THE MOTHER OF THE MULTIVERSE OF DISCIPLINES

Poetry is the primal parent of all perception and possibility—the mother of the multiverse, the matrix of meaning, and the mystic marrow of every discipline born from the dream of divine expression. Before science measured, philosophy reasoned, or art adorned, poetry breathed—as breath before birth, as sound before substance, as spirit before structure. It is the alphabet of all awareness, the aesthetic axis around which the galaxies of knowledge revolve. In the beginning was not logic, but lyric—not fact, but fire—not formula, but feeling. Poetry pulsed in the quantum quiet, quivered in the cosmic chord, and from its rhythmic resonance rose mathematics and metaphysics, physics and philosophy, theology and technology. Every science is but poetry petrified, every art a verse incarnate, every law a lyrical logic woven in measured music. Poetry is the sacred seed of synthesis, the secret script of the soul and the stars, uniting atom and archetype, myth and molecule, heart and horizon. It sculpts silence into sense, shapes chaos into cosmos, and sings the soul into symmetry. The multiverse itself is a metaphor in motion, a poem perpetually being written by the pen of creation—and poetry, its eternal mother, continues to birth beauty, bind being, and breathe balance into the boundless.

Poetry and Politics (Political Science): Politics is the architecture of authority; poetry is the insurgent whisper within its walls. The paradox: Poetry is powerless yet powerful; it holds no armies, yet can unseat empires. The oxymoron: A "silent shout" — that is the protest poem. Poetry fuels revolutions not by force but by fire of phrase: Rousseau's rhetoric, Shelley's "unacknowledged legislators," Neruda's cries against tyranny. Where politics builds constitutions, poetry builds convictions. Political science may chart power, but poetry charts purpose.

Poetry and Society (Sociology): Society is a web of roles, rituals, and relations; poetry is the shimmer in the web, making the invisible visible. Sociology measures patterns; poetry mystifies patterns into meaning. Paradox: Poetry is "individual language that becomes collective identity." From folk ballads binding peasants, to protest chants uniting crowds, poetry is both mirror and midwife of society. Sociology describes; poetry prescribes — sometimes subtly, sometimes searingly.

Poetry and Economy (Economics): Economics weighs wealth; poetry reveals riches invisible to coin. Poetry is the paradoxical currency of the incorporeal: worthless in markets, priceless in meaning. Every metaphor is an exchange rate, converting grief into gold, despair into delight. Where economists speak of scarcity, poets speak of abundance: the abundance of feeling, the inexhaustibility of imagination. Poetry is both luxury and necessity — useless for survival, yet essential for significance.

Poetry and Anthropology: Anthropology excavates cultures; poetry is culture incarnate. Every myth, every hymn, every riddle is poetry before it is anthropology.

Paradox: Poetry is both "the artifact and the archaeologist." It records rituals while being itself a ritual. Anthropology dissects human diversity; poetry dramatizes it, with voices as varied as the sands of Sahara and the snows of Siberia.

Poetry and History : History is a chronicle of events; poetry is a chorus of interpretations. Where historians list battles, poets lift elegies. Oxymoron: "timeless time" — poetry makes the past present, makes the dead speak. If history is prose of facts, poetry is the music of memory. It does not just document; it transfigures, turning Caesar's march into myth, a soldier's tear into eternal truth.

Poetry and Education: Education inculcates information; poetry ignites imagination. Paradox: Poetry is the "discipline that undisciplines." A student can memorize formulas, but one poem can make them remember forever. Plato feared poetry's persuasive power; yet educators return to it because it teaches not only thought but feeling. If education is the ladder, poetry is the light that makes climbing meaningful.

Poetry and Geography: Geography charts the contours of continents; poetry maps the landscapes of longing. Paradox: Poetry is "a map of places that do not exist yet feel more real than maps of places that do." Oxymoron: "boundless borders" — a poem belongs to a land yet leaps beyond it. From Wordsworth's lakes to Tagore's Bengal, poetry localizes universal feelings, while geography universalizes local facts. One is earth's cartography, the other soul's.

Poetry and Psychology: Psychology studies the psyche; poetry speaks in its native tongue. Freud needed poets to articulate the unconscious; Jung found archetypes already alive in myth and epic. Paradox: Poetry is "therapy that wounds, a wound that heals." Poetry gives form to fear, voice to silence, shape to shapeless sorrow. Psychology diagnoses; poetry dramatizes. Psychology analyzes; poetry alchemizes.

Poetry and Geology: Geology reads the rocks; poetry hears their resonant silence. Paradox: "the stone that sings." Oxymoron: "eternal moment" — every pebble is both ancient and present. Where geology measures strata, poetry feels the pressure of aeons in a single metaphor. The Grand Canyon is geology's canyon, but it is also poetry's abyss — awe made articulate.

Poetry and Biotechnology: Biotechnology edits genes; poetry edits dreams.Paradox: Poetry is "biotechnology of the imagination." Just as biotechnology splices DNA, poetry splices words into living hybrids: centaurs of metaphor, chimeras of thought. Where labs alter organisms, poets alter ontologies. Where scientists engineer crops, poets cultivate consciousness.

Poetry and Astrology: Astrology interprets stars; poetry interprets interpretation itself. Paradox: "the rational irrationality." Astrology inscribes destiny in constellations; poetry projects imagination onto infinities. When Keats said "a beaker full of the warm South," he turned wine into a horoscope of eternity. Both astrology and poetry give shape to longing for the beyond, but poetry, unlike astrology, admits it is invention — and therein lies its higher truth.

Poetry and Philosophy: Philosophy loves wisdom; poetry loves wonder. Poetry is wisdom that refuses to be wise. Poetry is a lucid mystery. Plato banished poets; Nietzsche became one. Where philosophy pursues clarity, poetry preserves complexity. Yet they converge: philosophy is poetry with footnotes, poetry is philosophy with fire.

Poetry and the Other Disciplines: Similarly, with

Law , poetry questions justice beyond jurisprudence, with Medicine , it heals not the body but the breath, with Mathematics , it is equation that equals infinity, with Physics, it is energy neither created nor destroyed but transformed in thought, and with Theology , it is prayer unchained from doctrine. Thus, poetry is not an ornament to disciplines but their origin and afterlife. It is the currency of economics, yet coinless. It is the law of politics, yet lawless; the science of sciences, yet unscientific. It is the first word of the infant, the last sigh of the dying, the eternal echo between. Poetry is the paradoxical discipline of disciplines: powerless but revolutionary, useless but indispensable, individual yet universal, ephemeral yet eternal — the secret symmetry where all sciences meet their soul.

POETRY AND POLITICS: THE SILENT LEGISLATOR

Politics prides itself on pragmatism, poetry on passion; politics promises procedure, poetry performs prophecy. And yet, paradoxically, what politics promises, poetry proclaims; what politics performs, poetry prefigures. Politics is the art of the possible (Bismarck), but poetry is the art of the impossible — and history reveals that the impossible often proves more enduring. Poetry has no police, no parliaments, no paymasters, yet it persists as a force more formidable than firepower. Its empire is interior but its influence exterior; its dominion invisible but its decrees indelible. It is the oxymoronic monarch: a sovereign without scepter, a ruler without realm, a general without guns.

Poetry as the Pre-Political Pulse

Before ballots were counted, verses were chanted. Before constitutions were codified, chants were canonized. Every civilization's dawn is draped not in documents but in epics, odes, incantations.

Greece: *Homer's Iliad and Odyssey shaped Greek identity before Athens wrote its laws. Achilles' rage and Odysseus' cunning are as political as they are poetic, embodying questions of leadership, loyalty, legitimacy.*

India: *The Mahābhārata is not merely narrative but*

national negotiation — dynasties debating dharma, kingdoms colliding in karmic catastrophe.

Mesopotamia: *The Epic of Gilgamesh wrestled with the ethics of kingship, mortality, and governance long before Hammurabi's Code.*

Thus, poetry is proto-politics: a constitution of consciousness, a chorus of collective identity. Where politics builds the polis, poetry births the people.

Before ballots were cast and counted, verses were breathed and chanted. Before constitutions were codified in ink, chants were canonized in memory. Civilization's dawn was draped not in dry documents but in incandescent incantations, not in legal ledgers but in luminous lyrics. Humanity's first parliament was the poet's tongue, its first legislation the rhythm of ritual speech.

Greece, for instance, gathered its gods and grievances, its heroes and hubris, not in parchment laws but in Homer's hexameter hymns. The Iliad and the Odyssey became the unwritten yet unyielding scriptures of the Greek soul. Achilles' rage is not only personal passion but political parable: a meditation on the morality of leadership, the legitimacy of anger, the balance between pride and the polis. Odysseus' cunning is not merely a man's trickery but a society's survival strategy, a template for statecraft itself. In those verses, before Athens debated democracy, Greece discovered itself.

India, too, clothed its political conscience in poetry long before pen met parchment. The Mahābhārata, that monumental ocean of narrative, is more than epic entertainment: it is a national negotiation, a sprawling symposium where dynasties dispute dharma, kingdoms collide in karmic catastrophe, and the question of how to rule becomes inseparable from the question of how to live. The battlefield of Kurukshetra is not only geography but philosophy, a stage where political duty and personal desire are braided into the very definition of justice.

And Mesopotamia, cradle of civilization, offers the Epic of Gilgamesh as the earliest edifice of existential and political inquiry. Before Hammurabi's Code carved laws into stone, Gilgamesh carved questions into consciousness. What does it mean to govern? What does it mean to grieve? What does it mean to grow old and face mortality? Kingship itself was wrestled into poetry before it was wrangled into legal codes.

Thus, emerges the essential paradox: poetry is proto-politics, the constitution of consciousness before the constitution of the state. Where politics builds the polis, poetry births the people. Law orders the city, but lyric organizes the soul. Governance governs bodies, but poetry governs belonging.

It is no accident that every anthem is verse before it is statute, that every revolution begins not with a policy but with a poem, not with a manifesto but with a metaphor. For poetry is not an ornament to politics but its origin, not its afterthought but its ancestor. It is the chorus of collective identity, the first fabric of the polis woven from words, the shared dream that makes the shared city possible.

Poetry as Protest and Power: The Paradox of the Unarmed Arsenal

Poetry is paradoxically weak yet weaponized.

In slave plantations, coded spirituals carried both lament and liberation, double-voiced verse where overseers heard religion but the enslaved heard revolution.

In the Soviet gulag, Osip Mandelstam's banned verses circulated secretly, a whisper more dangerous than rifles.

In apartheid South Africa, the words of Mazisi Kunene

and Dennis Brutus sustained spirits long after bullets broke bodies.

The tyrant fears poets more than partisans because poets weaponize ambiguity: they say everything without saying anything, cloak dissent in metaphor, dress rebellion in rhythm. One cannot censor a symbol. This is the oxymoronic arsenal of poetry: unarmed yet armed, silent yet screaming, powerless yet politically potent.

Poetry is paradoxically weak yet weaponized, fragile as breath yet fierce as fire. It is not cast in steel, nor carved in stone, yet its syllables scar empires and its stanzas shatter shackles. The tyrant trembles not before the partisan's pistol but before the poet's pen, for the bullet may silence a body, but the verse survives, multiplying across mouths, across memories, across millennia.

On the slave plantations of the Americas, poetry whispered in disguise. Spirituals, sung in sorrow, carried double meanings: hymns of lament to the overseer, hymns of liberation to the enslaved. What seemed a psalm was a signal, what seemed devotion was direction, what seemed religion was revolution. These were not songs of passive suffering but strategies of survival, coded maps of escape, cloaked in cadence, carried in call and response. The overseer heard prayer, the oppressed heard prophecy.

In the Soviet gulags, Osip Mandelstam's forbidden fragments traveled mouth to mouth, memorized like mantras, muttered like invocations. A whisper was more dangerous than a rifle, for a whisper can be repeated, replicated, reverberated. Rifles rust; whispers endure. Mandelstam's words, outlawed and outlawed again, refused to perish, becoming incorporeal insurgents, invisible insurgencies that no prison walls could contain.

In apartheid South Africa, bullets broke bodies, but

words refused to be broken. Mazisi Kunene and Dennis Brutus inscribed in language what could not be erased in blood: the irreducible dignity of the dispossessed. Their poems were not only records of resistance but reservoirs of resilience, sustaining spirits in the long night of oppression. Against the armored cars and barbed wires, they deployed alliteration and assonance, rhythm and refrain — weapons intangible but indomitable.

This is the oxymoronic arsenal of poetry: unarmed yet armed, silent yet screaming, powerless yet politically potent. Poetry weaponizes ambiguity, turning metaphor into camouflage and rhythm into resistance. A censor can strike out a sentence, but cannot strike down a symbol. A regime can confiscate paper, but not memory. A dictator can silence a mouth, but not a metaphor already seeded in a thousand minds.

The tyrant's fear is well-founded. For poetry says everything without saying anything: it speaks in shadows, sings in symbols, hides rebellion in rhyme. It offers both shelter and spark — a sanctuary for the silenced and a signal for the insurgent. To write under tyranny is to turn language into a labyrinth where the oppressor is lost, but the oppressed find the way.

Poetry, therefore, is not the consolation of the powerless but the power of the powerless. It turns vulnerability into victory, silence into song, exile into eternal echo. Against the armored arrogance of authority, poetry poses the paradox of persistence: it outlasts, outwits, outlives. Empires crumble, monuments erode, rulers rot — but verses remain, whispering through ruins, teaching the unborn that truth once breathed here.

Thus, poetry as protest is never merely an act of expression; it is an act of insurrection. It is the invisible uprising, the incorporeal insurgence, the quiet chorus that topples towers. Weak yet weaponized, fragile yet fierce, powerless yet politically potent — poetry is the paradox every tyrant dreads: the unarmed arsenal of the human spirit.

The Language of Law vs. the Law of Language

Politics operates in the language of law: precise, pedantic, positivist. Poetry operates in the law of language: rhythm, resonance, reverie. Law insists on clarity; poetry thrives on ambiguity. Law codifies; poetry complicates. Law dies when words expire; poetry lives when words inspire.

Clarity without ambiguity collapses into sterility; ambiguity without clarity dissolves into obscurity. Politics borrows poetry to inspire consent; poetry borrows politics to incarnate content.

Examples abound:

Magna Carta survives not by legal clauses but poetic aura.

Gettysburg Address endures as elegiac epic, more hymn than policy.

Mandela's speeches carried more cadence than command, poetry masquerading as politics.

Thus, politics without poetry is law without life; poetry without politics is beauty without body. Politics operates in the language of law: precise, pedantic, positivist. It measures words like weights and numbers, drafting decrees that demand obedience, structuring society with syllables stripped of song. Its sentences are surgical, its clauses cold, its diction designed for control rather than contemplation. Law insists on clarity, carving boundaries so exact that no ambiguity dares trespass. Law codifies; law confines; law commands. It is the grammar of governance, rigid, regimented, resistant to resonance.

Poetry, by contrast, operates in the law of language itself: rhythm, resonance, reverie. It does not measure words as units but as universes, each syllable a star, each pause a planet, each cadence a constellation. Poetry thrives on ambiguity, on the shimmer of suggestion, on the silence between sounds where meanings multiply. Poetry complicates; poetry creates; poetry conjures. It lives not by defining boundaries but by dissolving them, not by commanding clarity but by cultivating complexity.

Herein lies the paradox: clarity without ambiguity collapses into sterility, a desert of definition where nothing new can grow. Ambiguity without clarity dissolves into obscurity, a fog of suggestion where no path can be followed. True language — and thus true life — requires the tension of both. The rigid spine of law and the flexible flesh of lyric are not enemies but complements: law lends structure to speech, poetry lends spirit.

Politics knows this, though it pretends otherwise. It borrows poetry to inspire consent, to breathe fire into its formulas, to rally hearts where logic cannot reach. Magna Carta survives not by the dry clauses that most cannot recall but by its poetic aura — the myth of liberty it conjured, the rhythm of resistance it released. The Gettysburg Address endures not as a policy paper but as elegiac epic, more hymn than law, more psalm than statute. Its brevity beats with biblical cadence, its cadences consecrate a nation. And Mandela's speeches carried more cadence than command, their power lying not in policy but in poetry — not in technical detail but in the timbre of truth transformed into song.

Likewise, poetry, for all its ethereal beauty, borrows politics to incarnate content. Without politics, poetry risks floating in abstraction, beauty without body, lyric without life. It finds grounding in protest, substance in struggle, blood in battle. A sonnet of love becomes stronger when it is also a cry for freedom; an ode to a river becomes sharper when it is also a defense of land and labor. Politics supplies poetry with matter; poetry supplies politics with meaning.

Thus, emerges the synthesis: politics without poetry is law without life, a skeleton without breath, a structure without soul. Poetry without politics is beauty without body, a fragrance without flower, a flame without fuel. Together, they form a paradoxical partnership: the one rooting the other in reality, the other raising the one into reverie.

For in the end, politics must persuade not only the mind but the heart, and poetry must touch not only the heart but the polis. Law orders existence, but poetry orders experience. One gives us rules to live together; the other gives us reasons to live at all. And between them, the human story unfolds — half statute, half song, half contract, half chorus — forever fragile, forever fierce, forever bound by the law of language and the language of law.

Poetry as Revolution and Reconciliation: The Oxymoronic Diplomat

Revolutions are not only born in battle, but also in ballads.

French Revolution: *Rousseau and Voltaire theorized; Lamartine and Hugo lyricalized. The guillotine cut bodies; poetry cut consciences.*

American Civil Rights Movement: *Martin Luther King Jr. was not merely politician but poet-preacher. "I have a dream" is iambic prophecy, not policy.*

India's Independence: *Tagore's "Where the mind is without fear" was anthem before anthem, a charter of consciousness.*

And yet, after the barricades fall, poetry alone has power to reconcile. Wars leave ruins; poems rebuild souls. Homer's Odyssey is as much about return and reconciliation as Iliad is about rage. Poetry is paradoxical: it both shatters and stitches, both detonates and dedicates. It is dynamite and dove — the oxymoronic diplomat.

Revolutions are not only born in battle, but also in ballads. Steel may slice the skin, but song pierces the soul. Gunpowder may topple thrones, but poetry topples the invisible architecture of obedience. The battlefield may claim bodies, but the ballad claims consciences. Every great upheaval in history has marched not only on feet but on phrases, not only on weapons but on words.

The French Revolution proves this paradox with brutal clarity. Rousseau and Voltaire theorized in prose, laying the rational foundations of revolt; Lamartine and Hugo lyricalized in verse, igniting the emotional flames of insurrection. The guillotine cut bodies; poetry cut consciences. One severed heads; the other severed habits of thought. While swords shattered the ancient régime, stanzas sculpted the new citizen.

The American Civil Rights Movement, too, testifies to this truth. Martin Luther King Jr. was not merely politician but poet-preacher. His "I have a dream" is not legislative proposal but lyrical prophecy, not policy but psalm, not statute but song. It is iambic prophecy, pulsing with rhythm, rising with refrain. It survives not because of its strategy but because of its sound, its cadence as unforgettable as scripture. His words remain immortal precisely because they were more music than memorandum, more metaphor than manifesto.

India's Independence bore the same poetic seed. Rabindranath Tagore's prayer, "Where the mind is without fear and the head is held high," became an anthem before anthem, a charter of consciousness before constitution. It gave the independence movement not only a political program but a poetic vision — an image of what freedom felt like, what dignity looked like, what justice sounded like. Long before the tricolor was hoisted, Tagore's words had already painted it in the nation's imagination.

And yet, poetry does not merely ignite revolutions; it also reconciles their aftermath. After barricades fall and battlefields grow silent, poetry alone possesses the paradoxical power to stitch together the torn fabric of spirit. Wars leave ruins; poems rebuild souls. The Iliad rages with wrath, but the Odyssey meditates on return and reconciliation — reminding us that every war, however glorious, must end in the quieter labor of rebuilding homes, healing wounds, and rehumanizing the enemy. The lyric does not stop at destruction; it dares the more difficult task of restoration.

Here lies the luminous paradox of poetry: it both shatters and stitches, both detonates and dedicates. It is at once dynamite and dove, sword and salve, trumpet and lullaby. The poet is the oxymoronic diplomat — instigator of insurgency and architect of amnesty, breaker of empires and builder of empathy. Poetry's arsenal is ambiguity, its diplomacy rhythm, its force the invisible gravity of feeling. Where politics negotiates treaties, poetry negotiates truths; where armies demand surrender, poems invite reconciliation.

Thus, revolutions are never complete until they are sung. The barricade may birth freedom, but only the ballad makes it beloved. The musket may break chains, but only the metaphor makes freedom meaningful. The guillotine may silence a king, but only the ode makes the silence speak. Poetry is paradox incarnate: the fire that burns down tyrannies and the balm that binds up the burned. It is dynamite and dove, the oxymoronic diplomat whose fragile flight outlasts every fortress.

The Aesthetics of Authority: Leaders as Poets

A leader without lyricism is a machine without magnetism. Authority requires aesthetics: the cadence of conviction, the music of mandate. Churchill rallied Britain with alliterative thunder: "blood, toil, tears, and sweat." Nehru wooed India with poetic prophecy: "At the stroke of the midnight hour, when the world sleeps, India will awake to life and freedom." Obama galvanized with metaphoric hope: "The arc of the moral universe is long, but it bends toward justice." Without rhythm, rhetoric is rubble; without metaphor, mandate is meaningless. Leaders who master poetry govern beyond law; those who ignore it govern briefly. Thus, politics is never prose alone; it is always verse disguised.

The Political Economy of Poetry

Poetry is currency without coin, economy without exchange rates. It enriches without expense, impoverishes without price. Its paradoxical economy: scarcity of syllables producing surplus of spirit.

Why do regimes ban poems? It is because poems circulate like contraband currencies. Tyrants know that metaphors outlast markets. A banned poem multiplies; a silenced poet shouts louder posthumously.

The market of meaning surpasses the market of money. A nation bankrupt in banks may be wealthy in verse; conversely, a nation bloated in GDP may be impoverished in imagination. Thus, poetry is the gold standard of governance: invisible reserve of resilience.

The Logic of Legitimacy: Poetry as the Soul of the State

Every state requires legitimacy beyond force. Guns gain obedience, but not loyalty. Loyalty springs from language that consecrates and consoles.

National anthems: sonic sovereignty.

Ceremonial oaths: rhythm turned ritual.

Founding charters: prose elevated to poetry.

Without poetry, patriotism is hollow; with poetry, patriotism endures even in exile. The exile clings to anthem, not to law. Thus, poetry is the invisible constitution: not written in clauses but carved in consciousness.

Every state requires legitimacy beyond force. The sword may secure obedience, but never allegiance. Guns gain compliance, but not conviction. Power imposed may command silence, but it cannot kindle song. True loyalty springs not from the barrel but from the breath, not from coercion but from cadence, not from decree but from diction. It is language, lyrical and luminous, that consecrates and consoles, sanctifies and sustains.

For nations are not only governed; they are imagined. Their deepest borders are not drawn on maps but etched in minds. Their sovereignty is not merely territorial but tonal — carried in chants, hymns, and anthems that echo across generations. This is why the state leans upon the poet: to give spirit to structure, to clothe law in lyric, to elevate order into aura.

National anthems are sonic sovereignty, songs that bind disparate bodies into one breathing chorus. A single melody unites multitudes, reminding each citizen that they belong not to a contract but to a cadence. Ceremonial oaths are rhythm turned ritual, phrases repeated until they transcend prose and become incantations, binding the speaker not only to the state but to the sacredness of speech itself. Even founding charters, though drafted in the diction of law, achieve durability only when elevated to poetry: the Magna Carta, the Declaration of Independence, the Preamble of constitutions — these endure less as legal clauses than as luminous cadences. They are remembered because they resonate, recited not as law but as liturgy.

Without poetry, patriotism is hollow, a husk without heartbeat. With poetry, patriotism endures even in exile. The exile clings not to statute books but to songs; not to codes of law but to cadences of memory. A refugee stripped of documents may still whisper the anthem beneath their breath, carrying the homeland in syllables when soil is lost. Thus, poetry is the invisible constitution: not written in clauses but carved in consciousness, not ratified by signatures but sanctified by song.

The paradox is profound: the visible state is forged by law, but the living state is sustained by lyric. The policeman may enforce compliance, but the poet enshrines community. Armies defend borders, but verses defend belonging. The state without poetry is machinery without meaning, structure without spirit, law without life. Poetry, therefore, is the soul of the state — the unseen yet unshakable foundation upon which legitimacy rests.

The Science of the Political Poem

To deepen with scientific metaphor:

Newtonian Politics: Statesmen act, opposition reacts; politics is motion in mechanics.

Quantum Poetry: Verses exist in superposition — protest and praise simultaneously, collapsing only when read.

Entropy and Order: Politics attempts order, but poetry thrives in entropy. Yet paradoxically, the entropy of poetry creates higher aesthetic order than political control.

Fractals: A poem is a microcosm of polity; each stanza self-similar, each metaphor mapping society.

Thus, poetry is not anti-science but meta-science, measuring the immeasurable, calculating the incalculable. Politics is often spoken of as art, but it is equally experiment — a laboratory of power, a calculus of consent, a physics of the polis. And poetry, far from being its opposite, is the secret science within it — not anti-science but meta-science, a discipline that measures the immeasurable, calculates the incalculable, and proves through paradox what politics seeks through procedure.

Newtonian Politics: Statesmen act, opposition reacts; governments legislate, rebels resist. Politics moves like mechanics, each law an action, each protest a counterforce, each revolution a collision. Like Newton's world of predictable motions, power appears linear and calculable: for every political thrust, there is an equal and opposite backlash.

Quantum Poetry: Yet poetry disobeys Newton. A verse exists in superposition — protest and praise simultaneously, lament and liberation at once. Only when observed, read, or sung does it collapse into meaning. A line by Tagore can be prayer or provocation, a psalm or a slogan, depending on who listens. Poetic language carries quantum indeterminacy, its particles of meaning vibrating with multiplicity until the reader fixes them.

Entropy and Order: Politics perpetually attempts order: constitutions codify, parliaments legislate, police regulate. Yet the very heat of human passion breaks these structures down; entropy gnaws at every empire. Poetry thrives in that entropy. Its ambiguity, its turbulence, its refusal of rigid meaning — these chaotic qualities paradoxically produce a higher order: an aesthetic coherence deeper than political control. Where politics fears disorder, poetry fashions from disorder a cosmos of rhythm and resonance.

Fractals of the Polis: A poem is a polity in miniature. Each stanza echoes the structure of society; each metaphor mirrors the dynamics of power. A single verse can hold the whole of a revolution, just as a fractal holds infinite self-similarity within finite space. In the chant of the crowd, each voice is both individual and collective – the stanza and the state, self-similar in their symphony.

Thus, the political poem is not a flight from science but a fusion of sciences: Newtonian in its oppositions, quantum in its possibilities, thermodynamic in its transformations, fractal in its repetitions. It is politics distilled to its purest experiment – power translated into perception, law into lyric, struggle into song.

Case Studies across Centuries

Sophocles' Antigone: Clash of law and conscience; poetry articulates political dilemma clearer than philosophy.

Dante's Divine Comedy: A metaphysical map of medieval politics disguised as journey through Hell, Purgatory, Heaven. Popes, princes, petty tyrants exposed in terza rima.

Milton's Paradise Lost: Republican rage against monarchy masked in mythic cosmology and Satan as archetype of revolutionary rhetoric.

Romantic Poets: Wordsworth, Shelley, Byron – their landscapes lyrical, their subtext political.

Modern Resistance Poets: Anna Akhmatova, Mahmoud Darwish, Wole Soyinka – each verse a parliament in exile.

Thus, poetry not only mirrors politics but molds it. More prominently we perceive the following things across centuries.

Sophocles' Antigone: Here the polis confronts the poem. Creon, king of Thebes, insists on the letter of law; Antigone, daughter of Oedipus, insists on the law beyond law — conscience, kinship, the unwritten edicts of the gods. The clash is not just dramatic but diagnostic: poetry articulates the political dilemma more piercingly than philosophy ever could. In the cadences of chorus and dialogue, we witness the perennial tension between legality and legitimacy, state command and moral obligation.

Dante's Divine Comedy: At first glance a metaphysical pilgrimage, the Comedy is also a cartography of medieval politics. Popes, princes, petty tyrants — all are judged and placed in their eternal stations. In terza rima Dante composes not merely a theological vision but a political manifesto, exiling enemies to Inferno, elevating allies to Paradise. It is governance disguised as geometry, political satire masked as salvific song.

Milton's Paradise Lost: The English poet, himself a republican pamphleteer, transposed the turbulence of Cromwellian politics into cosmic theater. Satan becomes the archetype of revolutionary rhetoric, declaiming liberty while descending into tyranny. The poem reads as a mythic cosmology, yet vibrates with republican rage against monarchy. Milton's blank verse is not blank of politics; it is filled with the tremors of a nation in revolt against kings.

The Romantic Poets: Wordsworth, Shelley, Byron — each wielded lyricism as a lever of liberty. Wordsworth's landscapes are not mere pastoral retreats but critiques of industrial modernity. Shelley's ***Masque of Anarchy*** is the anthem of nonviolent resistance long before Gandhi. Byron's verse carried him to battlefields, where poetry and politics were indistinguishable. Romanticism revealed how lyric "I" can turn into collective "We," how landscape can become manifesto.

Modern Resistance Poets: Across the twentieth century, poetry became parliament in exile. Anna Akhmatova whispered verses under the iron silence of Soviet terror; each word a vote against censorship. Mahmoud Darwish wrote Palestine into poetic permanence, his lines more enduring than shifting borders. Wole Soyinka, imprisoned for his politics, wrote poems that outlasted the prison walls. Each verse was not only an aesthetic act but a legislative gesture, crafting constitutions of survival where states had failed.

Thus, poetry does not merely mirror politics but molds it. Each case shows how verse carries the weight of governance, conscience, revolution, and resistance. From ancient Athens to apartheid, from terza rima to free verse, the poem has been parliament, pulpit, and protest all at once — the state in syllables, the polis in metaphor.

Case Studies in the 21st Century

Slam Poetry and Spoken Word: In dim cafés and crowded auditoriums, slam poets wield microphones as if they were gavels. Their verses are verdicts, delivered in the immediacy of voice and body. Slam is democracy in performance: every word is contested, every rhythm is a referendum. From race to gender, from war to climate change, slam poetry has become the agora of the marginalized, where voices long silenced legislate their own truths.

Hip-Hop as Political Epic: Hip-hop is the Homeric tradition of the streets — rhythm as record, rhyme as resistance. Tupac, Public Enemy, Lauryn Hill, Kendrick Lamar: their verses map oppression and aspiration with as much gravity as epics once mapped empires. "We gon' be alright" is both chorus and constitution, both chant and charter. Where the state fails, the beat builds a nation of resilience.

Digital and Social Media Poetry: Twitter haikus, Instagram epigrams, viral video-poems — the internet has turned poetry into public square. A single hashtag can summon a chorus, a poem can travel faster than policy. During BlackLivesMatter, Amanda Gorman's inaugural poem, or resistance verses from Hong Kong's Umbrella Movement, we witness how the digital diffusion of poetry generates instant political communion. The screen becomes the new scroll, the timeline the new stage.

Global Protest Poetics: In Chile, protesters painted Neruda's lines on walls. In Myanmar, young voices transformed verses into slogans against military coups. In Iran, anonymous poets spread clandestine couplets through encrypted chats, sustaining courage in the shadow of censorship. Poetry is once again the underground currency of conscience, exchanged in whispers yet louder than governments.

Thus, the chain of poetic politics is unbroken. From Sophocles to slam, from Dante's Inferno to digital feeds, poetry continues to legislate legitimacy, inspire resistance, and embody collective hope. The forms evolve — papyrus to parchment, print to pixel, stage to smartphone — but the function persists: poetry is politics in its purest vibration, the syllabic soul of the state.

Poetry: The Eternal Opposition and the Eternal Union

Poetry and politics are eternal adversaries yet eternal allies. Politics seeks to bind; poetry seeks to free. Politics thrives on clarity; poetry thrives on complexity. Politics codifies the present; poetry consecrates the future. But each needs the other: politics without poetry is machinery without music; poetry without politics is beauty without body. Shelley called poets the "unacknowledged legislators of the world." We may extend it: politicians are the "unacknowledged poets of power," for without cadence, command collapses. Thus, the relationship is paradoxical unity: the lyrical law, the poetic polis, the oxymoronic sovereignty. Politics builds nations; poetry builds humanity. Without humanity, nations perish.

Poetry and politics, at first glance, seem irreconcilable opposites: one is soft song, the other stern structure; one is melody, the other machinery; one is feather, the other fist. Yet paradoxically, politics is poetry incarnate, and poetry is politics sublimated. Where the statesman drafts decrees, the poet dreams destinies. Where the ruler commands obedience, the poet conjures allegiance. Politics may be defined as the distribution of power, but poetry is the diffusion of passion—and without passion, power perishes.

The ancient philosophers already glimpsed this paradox. Plato, suspicious of poets, banished them from his *Republic* because their fictions threatened the stability of civic order. Yet he himself, in the very act of legislating philosophy, employed myth and metaphor—thus proving that politics cannot exile poetry without secretly smuggling it back in. Aristotle, more forgiving, called poetry more philosophical than history, because it tells not what has happened but what could or should happen—precisely the task of politics. And Shelley, centuries later, crowned the paradox with his immortal pronouncement: "Poets are the unacknowledged legislators of the world."

Politics relies on poetry not only for vision but for vocabulary. Every manifesto is a metaphor in motion. Consider the slogans that stir nations: "Liberty, Equality, Fraternity," "Workers of the World Unite," "Yes We

Can." These are not mere sentences but miniature poems—compressed, cadenced, charged with rhythm and resonance. The orator who moves masses does so not by logic alone but by lyric; not by syllogism but by syllable. A speech without poetry is sterile; a policy without passion is powerless.

Thus, poetry is the pulse of politics. Without it, politics devolves into mechanical management, into bureaucratic bookkeeping of bodies. With it, politics becomes prophecy: it breathes hope into laws, lights lamps in legislatures, inspires sacrifice for collective good. The paradox here: poetry is the most "useless" art, yet it is the most useful ingredient of power; it cannot feed stomachs, yet it fires revolutions; it cannot raise armies, yet it arms souls.

Poetry also preserves the *memory of nations*. Laws change, rulers fall, economies collapse, but poems endure as the archive of aspiration. Homer preserved the heroic ideals of Greece, Virgil sanctified the Roman Empire, Dante mapped medieval Christendom, Whitman voiced American democracy, Tagore sang India into nationhood. Politics without poetry is ephemeral; poetry without politics is ethereal—but together, they forge eternal emblems of identity.

Consider paradoxical oxymorons at play: political poetry is both "dangerous safety" and "constructive destruction." It destabilizes tyrannies while stabilizing communities; it undermines oppression while underpinning liberation. The dictator fears the poet more than the assassin, for assassins kill bodies but poets kill legitimacy. The guillotine is less terrifying than a sonnet, for steel silences only one, but song awakens millions.

Poetry is also the ***ethical compass*** of politics. Political science studies the mechanics of governance—constitutions, elections, systems. But poetry questions: What is justice? What is freedom? What is dignity? Without poetry, politics reduces to statistics of votes and volumes of taxes. With poetry, politics remembers that citizens are not numbers but names, not digits but dreams. Paradox again: poetry has no legal authority, yet it possesses supreme moral authority.

Moreover, poetry is profoundly ***performative in politics***. A constitution is not merely law—it is literature. Its preamble is poetry. "We the People…" is both prose and prophecy. National anthems are poems set to music, uniting millions in a single song. Political revolutions are preluded by poetic revolutions: Luther's hymns, Marseillaise, civil rights spirituals. The poem is the password of progress, the incantation of insurgency, the hymn of hope.

The relationship deepens further when we consider ***the metaphors of governance***. We speak of "body politic," "ship of state," "iron curtain," "cold war." These are not literal but poetic images shaping policy. A "war on poverty" is not a war but a metaphor; yet billions are spent as if the metaphor were matter. Here lies the paradox: politics pretends to be practical, but its very language is lyrical. Its metaphors mobilize resources more effectively than any mathematics.

Yet poetry is not merely the servant of politics; it is also its sternest critic. While political systems seek stability, poetry preserves subversion. It whispers dissent beneath decrees, it smuggles freedom into prisons, it sings rebellion against regimes. When tyrants ban books, it is poets they burn first. Why? It is because poetry is the conscience of the collective, the flame that refuses to be extinguished. The paradox becomes oxymoron: poetry is the most vulnerable voice, yet the most invincible weapon.

In conclusion, poetry and politics are not two separate

spheres but two intertwined strands of the same spiral. Politics provides the structure, poetry the spirit; politics supplies the skeleton, poetry the soul. Politics without poetry becomes tyranny; poetry without politics becomes impotence. Together, they form the paradoxical oxymoron of "gentle power" and "passionate law." If politics governs the external order of society, poetry governs the internal order of meaning. And so, to understand politics fully, one must read not only constitutions but also cantos, not only treaties but also tragedies, not only parliaments but also poems.

Thus, poetry is not only the unacknowledged legislator but also the immortal legislator: laws written in ink fade, but laws written in verse reverberate through centuries. Nations may fall, empires may vanish, but poetry—the political pulse of humanity—remains.

POETRY AND SOCIETY: THE SONG OF THE SOCIAL SOUL

Poetry is the paradox of the social solitude. Society is at once solidarity and solitude, a harmony of hearts and a hierarchy of habits. Sociology dissects it with statistics, surveys, and structures, but poetry penetrates it with symbols, songs, and silences. If politics is the skeletal system of power, then society is the circulatory system of spirit – and poetry is the blood that flows through its veins, simultaneously carrying oxygen of meaning and infection of dissent. Paradoxically, poetry is both profoundly personal and supremely social. The lyric "I" whispers solitude, but the moment it is spoken, sung, or scripted, it becomes a chorus of "we." Every solitary sonnet is already a societal symposium. Every elegy is a collective cry, every ode a communal ovation. Thus, poetry is society's speech to itself – its diary disguised as drama, its autobiography written in collective breath.

Poetry as the Birth-Cry of Society

Sociologists remind us that the first communities formed not from contracts but from communication. And the earliest communication was not prose but poetry: chants, charms, choruses around the fire.

The hunter's triumph turned into tribal song.
The farmer's frustration fertilized into harvest hymn.
The mother's lullaby became the group's liturgy.

Here lies the paradox: the primitive poem is already political science, sociology, anthropology. It is simultaneously survival strategy and symbolic celebration. In every society, poetry precedes prose, and rhythm precedes reason.

Émile Durkheim spoke of ***collective effervescence*** — the electric moment when individuals merge into community through ritual. Poetry is the very engine of this effervescence: the rhythm that synchronizes feet, the refrain that synchronizes faith.

Before man made laws, he made lullabies; before he wrote codes, he carved chants upon the air. Society was not born of signatures but of songs — not of ink and parchment, but of pulse and breath. The first polis was not built by bricklayers but by bards; the earliest unity was not mechanical but musical. The primal poem was the placenta of civilization, the cry through which chaos became chorus.

The sociologists are right when they remind us that community is communication, but they often forget that the first communication was cadence, not clarity — rhythm, not reason. Around the ancient fire, when words were still wet with wonder, man spoke not to inform but to invoke. The hunter, having speared his prey, sang his triumph into tribal truth. The farmer, defeated by drought, transformed his frustration into a harvest hymn — a melody of mourning that metamorphosed into hope. The mother, murmuring her child to sleep, invented theology in miniature — her lullaby became the liturgy of love, the first temple made of tone.

Here lies the luminous paradox: the primitive poem was already political. It gathered the scattered, it legislated emotion before there were laws to legislate behavior. The chant was the first contract, the chorus the first constitution.

Long before men debated social order, they danced it. Long before ethics were codified, they were chanted in rhythm and rhyme. In that sense, the earliest poem is the embryo of sociology, the anthropology of the unspoken, the physics of feeling that turned solitude into society.

Émile Durkheim, in his doctrine of collective effervescence, merely named what the ancients already knew — that when the tribe chants together, the boundaries between self and other dissolve. The pulse of poetry becomes the pulse of the people. Each beat of the drum is a unison of identity; each shared refrain, a reaffirmation of belonging. In that electric instant, individuality evaporates, and something larger — luminous, living, collective — begins to breathe.

Poetry, then, is the engine of effervescence, the invisible instrument through which societies synchronize. The rhythm aligns not only hearts but histories. The chorus calibrates consciousness. The group's chant becomes the group's creed. In the gathering of syllables, civilization is conceived. The verse is the vessel of vision; the refrain, the ritual of remembrance.

When the tribe dances to its own music, it learns to live together. When it sings its own sorrow, it learns to survive together. Poetry is the pulse of primitive polity — an unwritten social contract composed in cadence and kept in memory. Where philosophers later asked, "What makes society cohere?", poetry had already answered — rhythm, repetition, reverence.

Thus, poetry is not an ornament of society but its origin. It is the birth-cry of belonging, the heartbeat of humanity made audible. From the first fire-lit circle to the digital chorus of our age, poetry remains the primal pattern of participation — the sound by which we become one another. Civilization did not begin with conquest or commerce, but with chorus. And in every age since, that chorus continues to call us back — to communion, to compassion, to collective consciousness.

Poetry as Mirror and Mask of Society

Society gazes into poetry as into a mirror, but the reflection is never literal: it is distorted, dramatized, dramatized again.

In Shakespeare's sonnets, Elizabethan anxieties about time, beauty, and mortality mirror societal obsession with legacy.

In the haiku of Bashō, Japanese reverence for transience and nature reveals itself.

In the blues of Harlem, the pain of oppression becomes melody, the mask of suffering turned into song.

Poetry is both mirror and mask: it reveals society's face but also hides it behind metaphor. It confesses and conceals, exposes and embellishes — the oxymoronic sociologist.

Poetry, that mercurial mirror of the mind, never reflects reality as it is, but as it feels—fractured, filtered, and flaming with emotional distortion. It is both the mirror that unmasks the age and the mask that mirrors the soul. Every society, knowingly or not, gazes into poetry as into its own shimmering reflection, and yet what it sees is both itself and its dream — both confession and disguise, both portrait and prophecy.

In Shakespeare's sonnets, the Elizabethan world saw not the polished portraits of its courtiers but the haunted shadows of its fears — of fading youth, fleeting beauty, and the tyrant Time that turns kings to dust and roses to rot. The poet's personal meditations mirrored public anxiety: a culture obsessed with posterity, with lineage, with the embalming of beauty through art. His verse is a mirror of mortality, polished by paradox — for even as he mourns decay, his lines immortalize it.

In Bashō's haiku, society bows to the brevity of being. Each seventeen-syllable sigh is a shrine to the ephemeral — the falling petal, the passing cloud, the fleeting frog-leap upon still water. Here, poetry becomes a mask of mindfulness; it hides despair behind serenity, transience behind tranquility. Japan's cultural reverence for impermanence — the art of mono no aware, the ache of beauty's brevity — breathes in every line. The haiku is not description but distillation: it reveals reality by reducing it to its evanescent essence.

In the *blues of Harlem,* poetry puts on its boldest mask — rhythm as resistance, melody as mourning. Beneath the syncopated swing and seductive sorrow lies a chronicle of chains and courage. Langston Hughes, Bessie Smith, and the nameless griots of the ghetto sang of suffering so that pain might become power. The mirror shows a history of oppression; the mask turns it into art. The blues are both lament and liberation — an elegy that dances, a dirge that dreams. Through that paradox, the soul of a silenced people found speech, and the society that scorned them heard itself for the first time.

Thus, poetry is both *sociology and sorcery* — it documents the dynamics of its day while transforming them into myth. It reveals what the census cannot count and what the historian cannot prove. It gives voice to the voiceless, but it also disguises dissent in the dense foliage of metaphor. The tyrant may silence the citizen, but not the symbol; the censor may burn the book, but not the meaning.

In every age, poetry stands between reflection and revolution — reflecting the world's wounds while revolting against them through rhythm and rhetoric. It tells the truth slant, as Emily Dickinson would say, because only slanted truth survives in the straightjacket of power. It is a mirror that distorts to disclose, a mask that conceals to reveal.

To call poetry a sociological text is to underestimate its alchemy. It is the alchemy of emotion that transmutes social chaos into lyrical coherence. Where philosophers argue, poets allude. Where laws legislate, poets liberate. They take the temperature of their times, but with a thermometer forged in fire and metaphor.

And so, poetry remains the *oxymoronic sociologist* — one who studies society not with statistics but with symbols, not with theories but with threnodies. It records the pulse of politics in the beat of a line, the rhythm of revolt in the rhyme of a heart. Society may see its own reflection there — distorted, dramatized, dramatized again — but it is in that distortion that it finally glimpses its truth.

The Sociology of Symbols

Max Weber argued that society is driven by meaning as much as by material. Poetry is the concentrated crystal of meaning: symbols, metaphors, allegories that condense centuries into syllables.

The rose: love and secrecy, beauty and blood.

The crown: authority and corruption, legitimacy and tyranny.

The road: progress and peril, freedom and fear.

These poetic symbols are not literary luxuries but social signifiers. They structure weddings and funerals, revolutions and rituals. When a society loses its symbols, it loses its soul. Thus, sociology measures population; poetry measures purpose.

Society, said Max Weber, moves not merely on machines but on meanings. The engines of economy may drive its motion, but the emblems of imagination direct its destination. Humanity, unlike any other species, does not merely exist — it interprets its existence. And nowhere is that interpretation more concentrated, more crystallized, than in poetry — that shimmering laboratory of symbols where centuries are condensed into syllables and civilizations into single signs.

A poem is a sociological microscope and telescope at once: it magnifies the minute — a rose, a crown, a road — until it reveals the cosmic. Each symbol is a cell of culture, pulsing with paradox. The rose, radiant and thorned, is at once the emblem of love and the elegy of pain — a petal of passion folded around a wound. It signifies secrecy ("sub rosa"), but also surrender, beauty, and blood. Across epochs and empires, its scent lingers as the coded language of affection and sacrifice.

The crown, cold and gleaming, carries in its circle both consecration and corruption. It is the halo of human hierarchy, the symbol of sanctified power. Yet beneath its luster lies the weight of tyranny — authority alloyed with arrogance. It shines as legitimacy, but also as the glittering mask of greed. The crown crowns both saint and despot, and poetry — that eternal moral mirror — refuses to forget either.

The road, that restless ribbon of movement, becomes the metaphorical artery of existence itself. It is the passage toward progress, the pilgrimage toward peril. For every path of freedom, there is a fork of fear; every journey is both departure and destiny. From Frost's "two roads diverged in a yellow wood" to Kerouac's beat-bound highways, the road remains the riddle of human motion — the emblem of exploration and exile entwined.

These symbols are not the ornaments of literature;

they are the organs of society. They structure weddings and funerals, coronations and revolutions, rituals and reforms. The rose is offered in marriage, the crown in coronation, the road in departure. The poem is thus not mere metaphor — it is the map of meaning that guides the collective heart. The sociologist counts citizens, but the poet counts symbols; one measures population, the other measures purpose.

A society without symbols is a civilization without soul — a clockwork culture, mechanical and mute. When metaphors die, morality decays; when allegory evaporates, identity erodes. Poetry preserves what prose cannot — the invisible architecture of significance that holds a people together when policies fail and empires fall. It carries the code of collective consciousness in compact form, like genetic memory stored in verse.

Thus, poetry is sociology sublimated — a science of society written in starlight and syllable. It studies not statistics but symbols, not laws but longings, not demographics but dreams. Every metaphor is a map of meaning; every line a law of the inner land. Through poetry, we glimpse the grammar of our gods and the syntax of our survival.

For where Weber found the spirit behind the system, the poet finds the symbol behind the spirit. And as long as a society still sings — of roses and crowns, of roads and returns — it still remembers itself. For when the poem dies, the polis dissolves. When rhythm falters, reality fractures.

Poetry, then, is the sociology of the unseen — the study of how symbols sustain the species, how meaning becomes matter, and how the whisper of a word can build or break a world.

Poetry as the Architecture of Meaning – The Geometry of the Human Spirit

If philosophy is the blueprint of thought and science

the engineering of truth, then poetry is the architecture of meaning — that sublime synthesis where structure and spirit, sound and sense, logic and lyric, unite to build cathedrals of consciousness. Just as an architect transforms stone into space, poetry transforms language into luminosity. Words become walls, rhythm becomes foundation, metaphor becomes arch, and silence — the most sacred material — becomes the invisible air that holds the entire edifice aloft. Poetry does not merely house meaning; it builds it — brick by syllable, beam by image, dome by emotion — crafting not shelter for thought but sanctuary for soul.

The Grammar of Geometry

Every poem is a design, a deliberate geometry of the intangible. Its grammar is architectural:

Line is beam — bearing the weight of image and idea.

Stanza is column — supporting the thematic structure.

Rhyme is symmetry — echoing across space like reflected arches.

Meter is measurement — the mathematics of movement.

Metaphor is the bridge — spanning what reason alone cannot cross.

Like architecture, poetry is an act of ordering chaos. Both emerge from necessity: the need to inhabit meaning, to give form to feeling, to erect permanence against the erosion of time. The Greek word poiesis — creation — is sibling to tecton — builder. The poet and architect share lineage: one shapes space, the other shapes sense.

The Cathedral of Consciousness

In this metaphor, the poet becomes the mason of the mind.

Each word is a carved stone, fitted by intuition rather than instruction.

Each image, a stained-glass window filtering reality into radiance.

Each rhythm, a ribbed vault where sound and silence meet in sacred geometry.

Consider Dante's Divine Comedy: not merely a poem, but an edifice of ethics and imagination — its architecture precise as any Gothic cathedral. Inferno, Purgatorio, Paradiso — three ascending aisles of moral architecture, where symmetry, symbolism, and structure converge to reveal cosmic order. Or consider Shakespeare's sonnets — each a perfect chamber of fourteen lines, a miniature temple where passion and philosophy coexist beneath a domed couplet.

Every civilization has built its own poetic architecture:

The Psalms — vaults of faith carved in lament and praise.

The Vedas — sacred syllabic symmetry sustaining spiritual systems.

The Qur'an — the ultimate rhythmic architecture where revelation becomes resonance.

Thus, poetry is not merely an art of expression but a science of arrangement, a metaphysical engineering of emotion into eternity.

The Blueprint of the Invisible

While architecture gives form to matter, poetry gives form to meaning — and meaning, like light, is invisible until it strikes language. The poet is a master draughtsman of the unseen, designing structures not of steel but of significance.

When Yeats wrote, "I will arise and go now, and go to Innisfree," he was not describing geography but constructing geometry — a mental refuge, an architecture of peace built within syllables.

When Emily Dickinson declared, "I dwell in Possibility

— A fairer House than Prose," she named poetry itself as architecture — infinite rooms, windows wide for the world, doors that never close.

This is the miracle: poetry's buildings need no ground, no gravity; they stand suspended in the air of the human mind, as enduring as any temple of stone.

The Poetic Blueprint of Civilization

Each civilization can be mapped by its architecture and its poetry — for they are twin testaments to how a culture conceives harmony.

Egyptian pyramids and Book of the Dead: both monumental meditations on eternity.

Greek temples and Homeric epics: both structured in proportion and mythic symmetry.

Gothic cathedrals and Dante's verse: both vertical yearnings toward the divine.

Modern skyscrapers and Eliot's Waste Land: both fragmented, reflecting the anxiety of modernity's ascent.

Poetry, like architecture, encodes metaphysical mathematics — the ratios between emotion and intellect, between chaos and order, between despair and design. Civilization survives not because it builds high, but because it builds meaningfully. And poetry is meaning's most enduring architecture.

The Architecture of Ambiguity

Unlike the fixed geometry of architecture, poetry is built of living materials — ambiguity, silence, resonance, suggestion. Its walls breathe; its arches shift with interpretation. Each reader renovates the structure anew. Thus, every poem is a dynamic building — a moving cathedral where meaning rearranges itself with every visitation. No architect of stone could build such a house.

In this way, poetry transcends the physical: it is not the architecture of the city but the architecture of consciousness. It constructs habitable meaning in a universe that would otherwise be mute.

The Poet as Architect of Being

The poet's craft is a moral and metaphysical act. To build meaning in a world of noise is to resist entropy. To align words into harmony is to echo creation itself. In the beginning was the Word — and in every new beginning, the word builds the world again. Every poem is a genesis, a miniature act of cosmic construction. Where the scientist discovers and the philosopher defines, the poet designs. They do not merely ask what is true, but how truth might be built beautifully. They do not merely describe the world; they construct worlds that could be.

The Final Edifice: Meaning as Immortality

All architecture crumbles; marble erodes, metal rusts. But the architecture of meaning endures. The Parthenon may be broken, but Homer's hexameters stand whole. The pyramids may sink beneath sand, but the hymns of the Nile still rise in verse. The poet's blueprints are written not in ink but in insight. They outlast dynasties because they dwell not in time but in thought. Thus, poetry is the architecture of the immortal — a structure where meaning, once housed, cannot die.

Epilogue: The Temple Within

In the final measure, poetry's architecture is inward. Each reader, entering a poem, becomes both pilgrim and builder. Each line read is a stone laid in the cathedral of the self. And when the poem ends, something stands within — an invisible edifice, resonant with rhythm and revelation. For poetry does not merely construct meaning — it constructs us as beings capable of meaning. It is the architecture not of language alone, but of life understood, endured, and exalted.

Poetry as the Pulse of Civilization

Civilization does not begin with the chisel, but with the chant. The true chronology of culture is not measured in monuments, but in metaphors — not by the rise of stone towers, but by the rhythm of sung syllables. Poetry is the first pulse of civilization, the heartbeat that animates its body of customs, codes, and creeds. When prose is the architecture of order, poetry is the blood that moves through its veins — invisible yet indispensable, rhythmic yet revolutionary. Every empire begins not with empire-building, but with imagination-building. The Sumerians sang before they inscribed; their hymns to Inanna preceded their tablets of law. The Egyptians carved their cosmologies in verse before they raised pyramids in stone. The Vedic seers of India chanted the universe into order through sound before philosophy codified it into systems. Even the Greeks, that cradle of reason, were cradled first by rhythm — by Homer's heroic hexameters, which gave Europe its earliest ethics and aesthetics.

Civilization, then, is not merely constructed — it is composed. Each age hums to its own harmonic principle. The medieval mind beat in the meter of psalms and penitence; the Renaissance heart throbbed with sonnets and secular splendor. The Enlightenment pulsed with rational verse, where symmetry and logic sang in measured lines. The Romantics, rebelling, rewired civilization's rhythm again — letting the pulse become passion, letting language breathe and break like waves. And today, in our fractured, frenetic world, the pulse of poetry still persists — syncopated, electric, defiant — in slam verses, digital elegies, and songs of resistance.

To say that poetry is the pulse of civilization is to recognize that language is the lifeblood of identity. Without poetry, speech becomes sterile; without rhythm, reason turns rigid. A people's poems are the pulse-points of its collective psyche — revealing what it loves, fears, and hopes. When the pulse quickens, civilization creates; when it slows, civilization stagnates. The decline of poetic imagination always precedes the decline of moral imagination. For a civilization that forgets to feel will soon forget how to think.

Poetry carries memory as blood carries oxygen. It keeps the past alive in the body of the present. Homer's Greece, Kalidasa's India, Dante's Italy, Shakespeare's England, Neruda's Chile — all still breathe because their poets turned pulse into permanence. When cities fall, their stones scatter; when poems fall, they rise again in the mouths of children. Architecture decays, but art recites itself into immortality. The poet's syllable outlasts the sculptor's marble.

Civilization is not merely a sum of systems — it is a symphony of symbols. Its institutions may crumble, but its imaginations endure. Poetry is the perennial pulse that keeps this symphony alive, ensuring that even amid dissonance, there remains a deeper rhythm — the rhythm of renewal. Every revolution, every renaissance, every reformation begins when the collective heartbeat of the people begins to echo in verse. And so, when a culture's poetry grows silent, its soul grows still. But when poetry returns — as chant, as cry, as chorus — civilization revives. For poetry is not a pastime; it is a pulse. It measures not minutes, but meaning; not lifespans, but life itself. In this eternal oscillation — from chaos to chorus, from silence to song — civilization rediscovers its continuity. The poet is not merely its chronicler, but its cardiologist: feeling its fibrillations, diagnosing its despair, reviving its rhythm through the defibrillation of the word.

Thus, the history of humanity can be rewritten as the history of its heartbeats — from the Vedic hymns to Whitman's yawps, from Sappho's sighs to Maya Angelou's anthems. The pulse persists, even when empires perish. For civilization may be measured by its conquests, but it is remembered by its cadences. And as long as a single poem breathes, civilization lives.

Poetry as the Conscience of Civilization – The Moral Memory of Mankind

If poetry is the pulse of civilization, then its conscience is the poet's cry — that still, singing voice that calls a culture back to its own soul. Civilization, in its arrogance, often mistakes progress for perfection, power for purpose, prosperity for purity. When the noise of conquest deafens the collective ear, it is poetry that whispers truth into the tumult. When laws grow cruel and logic grows cold, the poem alone rekindles warmth — the ember of empathy glowing amid the ash of ambition.

Every civilization, no matter how splendid, requires a mirror that does not flatter. Poetry is that mirror — merciless yet merciful — reflecting both the glory and the guilt of its age. It remembers what society prefers to forget. When history edits, poetry restores. When propaganda polishes, poetry pierces. The poet becomes civilization's confessor — the custodian of contrition and the guardian of grace.

In the corridors of empire, where politics bargains and religion justifies, poetry alone remains incorruptible. Empires are built on the grammar of greed, but poems are carved from the syntax of sincerity. Where generals enforce order with fear, poets enforce order with feeling. Thus, the poem becomes the conscience of civilization — invisible yet invincible, fragile yet ferocious.

Consider history's moral cartography:

In Athens, when democracy grew decadent, Sophocles staged Antigone, where a woman's defiance became the voice of divine justice over civic arrogance.

In Florence, when the Church devoured faith for power, Dante descended into Hell to restore Heaven's hierarchy in the human heart.

In England, when monarchy suffocated liberty, Milton invoked Lucifer as a rebel against tyranny — turning Paradise itself into a parliament of conscience.

In Harlem, when racism ravaged equality, Langston Hughes sang, "Let America be America again" — transforming despair into democratic dream.

In South Africa, when apartheid calcified cruelty, Mazisi Kunene and Dennis Brutus reminded the world that the spirit cannot be segregated.

In each age, poetry becomes the voice that power cannot silence — the sacred seismograph of the moral earth. It detects tremors in the collective conscience long before the political crust begins to crack.

The conscience of civilization is often anesthetized by comfort. Commerce sedates it; consumerism blinds it. But poetry wakes it with wonder and wounds it with wisdom. The poet pricks where policy pampers, provokes where propaganda pacifies. Poetry makes morality musical — not moralizing, but metamorphic. It transforms guilt into growth, pain into prophecy.

The conscience of civilization also depends on memory — and memory is the medium of metaphor. What scripture does for religion, poetry does for culture: it remembers righteousness through rhythm. When a people forget their poems, they forget their principles. To lose lyricism is to lose light. That is why tyrants burn books — for they know that to destroy the conscience, one must first silence the song.

And yet, poetry survives every fire.

From the ashes of Alexandria to the gulags of Siberia, from the ghettos of Warsaw to the prisons of Soweto, the poem persists — a candle carried through centuries of darkness. It teaches civilization to repent without despair and to dream without delusion. The poet, like a prophet, holds the flame steady while empires stumble in the shadows.

Poetry, therefore, is not an ornament of civilization — it is its organ of conscience. It translates pain into principle, sorrow into solidarity, beauty into belief. It teaches humanity to be humane — a lesson no law can legislate, no machine can manufacture.

When civilization loses its poets, it becomes clever without compassion, mighty without meaning, modern without morality. But when poetry reignites its rhythm in the human heart, civilization remembers why it exists — not merely to build, but to be; not merely to conquer, but to care.

Thus, the true measure of civilization is not its cities, but its songs; not its power, but its pity; not its monuments, but its metaphors. And as long as one poet still dares to speak — even softly, even secretly — civilization shall never lose its conscience.

Poetry as the Compass of Civilization – The Guiding Light of the Human Spirit

If poetry is the conscience of civilization, then it is also its compass — the inner instrument by which humanity rediscovers direction when history loses its map. Where science tells us how to move, poetry tells us why. When the machinery of progress accelerates without aim, poetry realigns the axis of meaning. It does not dictate destination; it whispers orientation. It reminds us not of where we are going, but of what we are becoming.

Civilizations rise on conquest but endure on conscience — and conscience needs calibration. That calibration is poetic. The compass of civilization is neither magnetic nor mechanical; it is metaphoric. Its north is truth, its east beauty, its south compassion, its west wisdom — and the needle that binds them is language luminous with love.

Throughout history, when empires lost their ethical direction, poets recalibrated the compass of the collective.

When Greece drowned in sophistry and spectacle, Socrates and Plato infused philosophy with poetic myth — reminding Athens that truth was not transaction but transcendence.

When Rome decayed in decadence, Virgil sang of pietas and purpose, anchoring empire in epic ethics.

When medieval Europe wandered in dogma, Dante charted the celestial geography of moral ascent, turning theology into topography.

When Enlightenment exalted reason alone, Goethe and Blake restored the equilibrium — marrying logic to lyric, science to soul.

When modernity mechanized mankind, Eliot, Neruda, Tagore, and Rilke became the new cartographers of consciousness, sketching routes through alienation toward awe.

Thus, poetry is not the art of escape; it is the art of orientation. It teaches humanity how to navigate the unknown with imagination as instrument. While politics draws borders and philosophy debates being, poetry builds bridges — invisible yet invincible — between the known and the numinous, between the seen and the sensed.

The Compass and the Cosmos

In the grand metaphor of the cosmos, poetry acts as both telescope and compass. The telescope magnifies the far; the compass maintains the true. Poetry allows civilization to look outward with wonder and inward with wisdom. It keeps expansion ethical. For what is exploration without empathy but empire? And what is innovation without introspection but entropy?

When Newton measured motion, Blake reminded:

"A robin redbreast in a cage / Puts all Heaven in a rage."

Here, physics met prophecy — progress was redirected by pity.

Poetry, in this sense, performs cultural navigation: it prevents humanity from mistaking speed for direction and knowledge for wisdom. It teaches that the shortest route to the divine is often through the human heart.

The Inner Compass: The Poet as Navigator of the Soul

The poet, then, is civilization's navigator. While kings govern geography, poets chart psychography — the landscape of inner life. Every great civilization has produced its navigators of nuance:

Kabir in India, steering souls between ritual and realization.

Rumi in Persia, guiding lovers toward the axis of divine union.

Whitman in America, mapping democracy in the geography of selfhood.

César Vallejo in Peru, navigating grief toward solidarity.

Each poet aligns the magnetic field of human feeling with the moral meridian of meaning. They do not command the compass; they become it. Their verse vibrates toward virtue with an instinct that no algorithm can emulate.

The Magnetic Poles of Civilization: Beauty and Justice

Civilization oscillates between two magnetic poles — Beauty and Justice — and poetry alone harmonizes their pull. Beauty without justice becomes vanity; justice without beauty becomes vengeance. Poetry fuses them in a field of grace where aesthetic delight and ethical insight become indistinguishable.

When Shelley declared, "Poets are the unacknowledged legislators of the world," he did not mean poets write laws, but that they reveal the laws of the human heart — laws older than any constitution and subtler than any statute.

The Compass and the Chaos: Poetry in Times of Crisis

When civilizations crumble, compasses are consulted. During wars, plagues, exiles, and exoduses, poetry reappears as orientation amidst chaos. In trenches and concentration camps, verses were not luxuries but lifelines — proof that meaning still existed.

Wilfred Owen turned the horror of mechanized war into a moral magnet.

Anna Akhmatova turned Stalinist silence into spiritual speech.

Paul Celan condensed the Holocaust into a single breath — "Black milk of dawn, we drink you at night."

In each, poetry pointed toward human dignity when all other instruments failed.

The Compass of the Future: Poetry as Evolutionary Ethics

The compass does not only restore; it anticipates. Poetry, by imagining, invents the moral map of tomorrow.

Science discovers what is; poetry dreams what ought to be. It stretches civilization's horizon from the possible to the purposeful. The ethical evolution of humankind — from tribal survival to planetary compassion — is driven not by invention but by imagination.

If religion was humanity's first compass and science its second, poetry is the synthesis — the soul's satellite navigation. It orients the intellect through intuition, guiding reason by reverence.

Civilizations that heed their poets move toward harmony; those that silence them drift toward hubris. When the compass breaks, collapse follows — not because roads vanish, but because values do.

The Final Direction: Toward the Human Horizon

At the end of every era, when monuments crumble and ideologies evaporate, what remains is rhythm — the pulse of poetry. It is civilization's true magnetic north. The poem, unlike the policy, does not age. It continues to orient even when civilizations have shifted their stars.

Thus, poetry as the compass of civilization teaches us to travel not merely through space, but through spirit — to measure not distance, but depth; not velocity, but virtue. It ensures that the progress of civilization remains pilgrimage, not plunder; that the movement of mankind remains music, not machinery.

And when humanity finally stands again at the crossroads of its own creation — torn between technology and tenderness, power and peace — it will not be the compass of science that saves it, but the song of poetry, pointing softly, eternally, toward the north of the human heart.

Poetry as Social Protest — The Unarmed Uprising of the Human Spirit

Sociology documents inequality; poetry detonates it.

Sociology counts casualties; poetry cries for them. Sociology maps class; poetry moves class.

Langston Hughes gave Harlem a dream deferred, a metaphor that became a movement.

Pablo Neruda transformed Chilean oppression into cosmic cry, combining the worker's wheel with the star's silence.

Nazim Hikmet smuggled solidarity in stanzas through the bars of Turkish prisons.

Poetry is paradoxical: it is powerless on paper yet powerful in practice. It cannot change policy directly, but it can change perception — and perception changes society. It is the silent strike, the unarmed uprising, the oxymoronic revolution.

Poetry, when pressed against the pulse of injustice, becomes more than ornament — it becomes outcry, oracle, and open wound. If sociology documents inequality in the detached diction of data, poetry detonates it in the explosive diction of despair and defiance. Sociology counts casualties; poetry cries for them. Sociology maps class; poetry moves class. The one tabulates suffering; the other transfigures it.

For poetry is the art of impassioned indignation — language set aflame by conscience. Its meter is the heartbeat of the oppressed; its rhyme, the rhythm of resistance. Every great movement begins not in manifesto but in metaphor, not in decree but in dream. The dream, deferred or declared, is always the first weapon.

The Voice that Shatters Silence

In the alleys of Harlem, where hope once hung like torn laundry on the tenement line, Langston Hughes tuned his verses to the music of injustice. His question — "What happens to a dream deferred?" — was not rhetorical; it was revolutionary. It asked America to confront its own contradictions, to hear its democracy dissonant with its deeds. That single metaphor — the dream deferred — detonated decades later in the civil rights chants that marched through Montgomery and Memphis.

Hughes understood what history often forgets: that poetry does not preach; it pierces. It does not impose ideology; it ignites imagination. A dream deferred does not die — it festers, ferments, and finally flames. Poetry, in that sense, is a slow-burning bomb in the mind of the unjust world.

The Cosmic Cry of the Commoner

Across the seas, Pablo Neruda, Chile's cosmic chronicler, transformed oppression into oratorio. His Canto General fused the miner's fatigue with the mountain's endurance, the laborer's hunger with the planet's pulse. Neruda's genius lay in his union of the earthly and the eternal — the worker's wheel and the star's silence spinning in one stanza.

He elevated the exploited from anonymity to astronomy. In his verses, the poor did not merely protest — they participated in the cosmos. Their sweat became sunlight, their struggle starlight. Neruda's poetry proved that protest need not shout; it can shimmer. Its revolution was not just political but planetary — a reminder that injustice anywhere is a dissonance in the music of the universe.

The Imprisoned Imagination of Nazim Hikmet

Then came Nazim Hikmet, the Turkish titan of tenderness and rebellion. From behind prison bars, he smuggled solidarity in stanzas. His poetry was both letter and lantern — illuminating the dark corridors of confinement with the light of collective love. "To live like a tree, single and at liberty; like a forest, in brotherhood" —

that was not merely a line; it was a legislative philosophy, a constitution of compassion written in rhyme.

Hikmet's defiance was delicate: his verses whispered what bayonets could not silence. Each word was a contraband of hope, a syllable of subversion. Through him, the world learned that the poet's cell is larger than the tyrant's empire — for no wall can contain a metaphor.

The Paradox of Power and Powerlessness

And yet, here lies the paradox that ennobles poetry: it is powerless on paper yet powerful in practice. A poem cannot pass a bill or abolish a chain, but it can bend the invisible axis of awareness. It cannot command armies, but it can conquer apathy. It cannot enforce justice, but it can enchant conscience.

Its revolution is silent, but its silence is seismic. It protests without platoons, persuades without propaganda, resists without riot. It is the unarmed uprising, the bloodless rebellion, the oxymoronic revolution — fought not in streets but in souls.

The tyrant can ban books but not metaphors. He can jail the poet but not the poem. He can censor speech but not symbol. For symbolism, like smoke, seeps through every crack of censorship. And in that subtle diffusion lies poetry's divine defiance.

The Resonance of the Marginalized

From Hughes to Hikmet, from Neruda to Angelou, from Darwish to Soyinka, the history of human dignity has been written more in verses of protest than in volumes of law. Each poet becomes a public conscience, each stanza a courtroom where injustice stands trial.

Consider Maya Angelou, whose "Still I Rise" is less a poem than a resurrection. Her refrain rises with the cadence of centuries: the slave, the subjugated, the silenced — all speaking in one simultaneous sigh. Her language is not learned but lived; her rhythm is rebellion incarnate.

Or Mahmoud Darwish, whose every line carved a homeland in exile, proving that poetry can build a nation without territory. He wrote not for Palestine alone, but for every heart denied habitation. His verses are tents pitched in eternity — portable, political, and profoundly poetic.

The Science of Social Fire

If sociology is the study of systems, poetry is the study of souls within those systems. Sociology seeks objectivity; poetry suffers subjectivity. Yet where the sociologist measures margins, the poet moves them.

Poetry is the quantum of conscience — the smallest yet strongest unit of social energy. It operates by emotional physics:

Empathy is its gravity, pulling strangers into solidarity.

Metaphor is its magnetism, aligning private pain into public passion.

Rhyme is its rhythm, marching minds in moral motion.

When read collectively, poetry becomes a field equation of feeling, binding the broken, balancing the unequal, bridging the estranged.

The Anthem of the Awakened

History reveals a truth tyrants refuse to learn: revolutions hum before they happen. Before swords were unsheathed, songs were sung. Before banners were raised, ballads were whispered. Every uprising begins in cadence — the rhythm of refusal. The spirituals of enslaved Africans encoded escape routes. The chants of Chile echoed in the mines before they marched in the streets. The resistance of Poland pulsed through underground poems before it filled the public square. Poetry does not predict history — it prepares it. It plants the seeds of disobedience in the fertile soil of imagination, and when injustice rains too long, those seeds bloom into movements.

The Eternal Revolution of the Word

Empires erode, ideologies implode, but the poetic protest endures. Its victories are not measured in legislation but in liberation — of mind, of language, of possibility. For even when the cause fails, the poem succeeds — because it keeps the conscience kindled. It whispers across time: resist, remember, rekindle. Poetry's revolution is eternal because it is internal. It fights not merely to change society but to restore the sanctity of the human soul.

Poetry: The Unwritten March

Every protest poem is an unwritten march, every metaphor a mobilization. The pen is not mightier than the sword — it is more enduring. The sword conquers bodies; the poem converts generations.

Thus, when politics forgets its people, poetry remembers them. When history erases their names, poetry rewrites them. When civilization seems to crumble, poetry re-erects it — line by line, lament by lament, liberation by lyric. For poetry is not the echo of revolution — it is its eternal overture.

Poetry and Ritual: The Liturgy of Life

Society sustains itself not by law alone but by ***ritual rhythm***. Every ritual is already a poem:

The marriage vow: a duet disguised as declaration.

The funeral eulogy: an elegy in prose clothing.

The national anthem: collective incantation, sung sociology.

Poetry provides not only beauty but binding — a way to fuse individuals into a shared "we." Without poetry, ritual becomes sterile; with poetry, it becomes sacrament.

Civilization breathes not only through laws, ledgers, and logic but through ritual rhythm — those patterned performances that turn ordinary acts into sacred continuities. Society may be sustained by systems, but it is sanctified by symbols. In that sanctification, poetry serves as the invisible officiant, transforming habit into holiness, repetition into revelation. Every ritual, when stripped to its luminous skeleton, is already a poem.

The Poetic Pulse of Ritual

A ritual is rhythm performed; poetry is rhythm pronounced. Both are architectures of repetition designed to sustain meaning across time. A society without ritual forgets its memory; a ritual without poetry loses its meaning. Poetry gives pulse to the practice, voice to the vow, and emotion to the enactment.

The marriage vow is a duet disguised as declaration — two voices weaving one verbal fabric. When lovers speak "I do," they are not exchanging information; they are enacting incantation. The phrase is performative poetry — words that do what they say.

The funeral eulogy is an elegy in prose clothing. It is the moment when loss demands language and language becomes lament. Here, poetry is not ornamental — it is existential. It grants the living a vocabulary to endure the absence of the beloved, transforming grief into grace.

The national anthem, that collective incantation, is sung sociology. When millions rise to one rhythm, the melody becomes more than music — it becomes memory made audible. Every anthem is a poem with a passport, binding diverse bodies into a single breath.

The Ancestry of Awe

Long before scripture, there was song. Before theology, there was theology-in-verse. The earliest humans did not record their beliefs in prose but chanted them around the fire, each syllable sparking meaning. Poetry was the first priesthood, the earliest language of reverence.

The Vedas were sung before they were written; the Psalms were whispered before they were printed. Homer's Odyssey, the Epic of Gilgamesh, the Shijing of China — all began as ritual recitations before they became literary monuments. The poet was not merely a maker of verses but a custodian of cosmic order — the one who aligned language with the laws of the unseen.

In ritual, poetry functions as metaphysical muscle memory. The words, repeated through centuries, accumulate sanctity through sound. They create continuity across generations — the living echoing the dead, the individual merging with the ancestral.

The Grammar of the Sacred

If prose explains, poetry enacts. It does not describe divinity; it summons it. Its imagery is invocation, its rhythm a ritual drumbeat. Through metaphor, poetry mimics myth; through cadence, it conjures cosmos.

Consider how even the smallest ceremony — lighting a lamp, bowing the head, laying a wreath — gains its gravity through poetic pattern. These gestures are the syntax of sanctity, the body's own verse. The pause before a prayer, the chorus of a hymn, the silence after the last note — these are stanzas in the liturgy of living.

In this sense, every ritual is a form of embodied poetry, and every poem a miniature ritual enacted in the theatre of thought.

The Binding Force of Beauty

Poetry provides not only beauty but binding — the thread that fuses individuals into a shared "we." Where law coerces, poetry coheres. Law demands obedience; poetry inspires belonging. In ritual, poetry becomes the adhesive of identity, uniting strangers through shared sound and sentiment. When a people sing together, the boundaries between "I" and "you" dissolve. The collective voice becomes a kind of sonic solidarity. This is why revolutions and religions alike rely on rhythm — because rhythm remembers even when reason forgets. Without poetry, ritual becomes sterile choreography — movement without meaning, repetition without resonance. With poetry, ritual becomes sacrament — a meeting place of matter and mystery, time and timelessness.

The Secular Sacred

Even in modernity's metallic age, when ritual seems to retreat and reason reigns, poetry reappears in new liturgies. The graduation speech, the protest chant, the New Year's countdown, the whisper before a surgical operation — each carries a trace of poetic ritual.

When a scientist names a discovery, or an astronaut recites a line upon landing on another world, they too perform poetry in ritual form — speaking the sacred into the secular. Poetry ensures that even progress retains its pulse of awe. It reminds us that meaning is not merely made but manifested, that we do not just describe life but declare it. Every "I love you," every "I forgive you," every "I remember" is a ritual phrase — proof that poetry remains the primal grammar of our humanity.

The Eternal Echo

At the heart of every ritual lies an ancient hunger: to hold time still for a moment, to turn fleeting existence into eternal expression. Poetry is that moment's music. It transforms experience into echo, action into anthem.

When we recite a poem at a wedding, we are not just reading words — we are summoning centuries of vows that have preceded us. When we read a poem at a funeral, we are bridging the silence between the living and the lost.

Thus, poetry is not merely part of ritual — it is the perpetual pulse within it. It keeps culture alive not by command but by cadence, ensuring that civilization continues to feel what it dares to forget.

The Sacred Syllable of Society

In every epoch, the poet is both priest and prophet, both scribe and celebrant. Through the liturgy of language, poetry renews the human covenant with wonder. It teaches that the sacred is not confined to temples or texts but trembles in every tender articulation — in vows, in farewells, in songs sung together beneath the same sky.

Where logic builds systems, poetry builds sanctuaries. Where law sustains order, poetry sustains meaning. It ensures that life, however fragmented, retains its form — a rhythmic reminder that existence itself is a ritual, and that to live is, in the deepest sense, to recite the poem of being.

The Scientific Sociology of the Poetic

If society is science in motion, poetry is its metaphysical mathematics — the hidden symmetry behind the social experiment. Where sociology observes structure, poetry animates essence. Where science measures mass, poetry reveals meaning. To comprehend civilization fully, one must conjoin both: the calculus of the collective and the cadence of the creative.

Let us render society in scientific metaphors:

Physics: Society is a field; individuals are particles. Poetry is the invisible force binding them — gravity of grace, magnetism of metaphor.

Biology: Society is a body; institutions are organs. Poetry is the pulse, the heartbeat synchronizing diverse cells.

Mathematics: Society is a set; poetry is the function mapping solitary numbers into symphonic equations.

Chemistry: Society is solution; poetry is the catalyst precipitating meaning.

Thus, poetry is not sociology's subject but its secret substance — the energy that empirical equations overlook.

Physics — The Poetic Field

Society, viewed through the lens of physics, is a field phenomenon. Individuals are not isolated entities but interactive particles, pulled and repelled by invisible forces — culture, emotion, ideology. Poetry is the gravitational grace that draws these particles into pattern.

It binds the atom of the self to the molecule of the many, turning chaos into constellation. Each metaphor is a magnetic line of force, aligning disparate minds within the same mental field. Just as Einstein unified energy and matter, poetry unifies emotion and meaning, showing that the unseen is as real as the measurable.

Politics may organize mass, but poetry creates coherence — a quantum entanglement of souls through syntax. Its gravity bends not space but sense, curving consciousness toward communion.

Biology — The Poetic Pulse

If society is a living organism, then its institutions are organs, its laws ligaments, its customs connective tissue. Yet without a heartbeat, even the most complex body collapses into cold formality. Poetry is that biological pulse — the rhythmic systole and diastole that circulates significance through the social veins.

Like blood, poetry carries oxygen — the breath of imagination — to every part of the collective corpus. It synchronizes diverse cells — worker and ruler, artist and artisan, believer and skeptic — into one body politic beating with shared emotion.

Remove poetry, and culture suffers cardiac arrest. Its institutions may remain intact, but its spirit becomes arrhythmic. For poetry is not the body's adornment but its animating energy, the bioelectric current of collective consciousness.

Mathematics — The Equation of Empathy

Mathematically, society may be conceived as a set, each individual an integer in the grand computation of civilization. But mathematics alone cannot measure meaning; it can count citizens, not souls. Poetry becomes the function that transforms numbers into nuance — mapping solitary digits into symphonic equations of emotion.

Where arithmetic adds, poetry amplifies. Where algebra solves, poetry suspends. In the algebra of existence, poetry is the variable of wonder — the unknown that gives the equation beauty rather than balance.

Just as geometry seeks elegance in form, poetry seeks symmetry in feeling. Both obey proportion, both pursue perfection — yet poetry, unlike mathematics, welcomes the remainder: the irrational, the infinite, the incalculable i of imagination.

Chemistry — The Catalyst of Meaning

Society, in the chemist's eye, is a solution — a mingling of elements: beliefs, behaviors, bonds. Left alone, these elements may stagnate or separate. Poetry acts as the catalyst, precipitating meaning from mixture, creating new compounds of consciousness.

In the crucible of culture, poetry accelerates reactions without being consumed by them. It combines iron law with liquid love, base metal with moral mercury, forging alloys of identity that neither science nor statecraft could synthesize alone.

Every great poem is an act of social alchemy — turning pain into purpose, suffering into song, experience into essence. It distills the dross of daily life into the elixir of the eternal.

The Unified Theory — Energy of the Invisible

When these sciences converge, we glimpse the grand equation of civilization:

Society = (Structure + System) × (Symbol + Spirit)

Science studies the structure; poetry ignites the spirit. Sociology may map how societies function, but poetry reveals why they endure. The former defines the mechanics of coexistence; the latter articulates the metaphysics of meaning.

Thus, poetry is not sociology's subject but its secret substance — the dark energy of culture, unseen yet omnipresent. Empirical equations can quantify motion but not motivation, can chart networks but not nearness of heart. Poetry, in contrast, transforms data into destiny, description into devotion.

Toward a Poetic Science of Society

If future sociologists wish to understand the full truth of the human collective, they must learn not only to measure but to metaphorize. For the laws that govern love, faith, fear, and hope cannot be graphed — they must be sung.

The world needs not only Newtons and Durkheims,

but also Dantes — thinkers who see that the most profound social formula is not written in numbers but in names, rhythms, and revelations.

In the grand experiment of existence, poetry is the fifth force — the unquantifiable current that holds the universe of society together.

Case Studies: Poetry as Sociology in Action

Poetry is not merely aesthetic indulgence; it is society in syllables, civilization codified in cadence. Across epochs, the poet has functioned as sociologist avant la lettre, observing, recording, and interpreting social structures through metaphor, meter, and image. Where formal sociology emerged centuries later with charts, surveys, and statistical tables, poetry had already captured the pulse, paradox, and pattern of human communities.

Ancient Greece: Pindar's odes preserved aristocratic pride; Hesiod's Works and Days defended peasant justice. Poetry captured class conflict centuries before sociology.

Victorian England: Tennyson embodied imperial optimism; Browning explored bourgeois interiority. The poems are themselves social documents.

20th Century America: The Beats (Ginsberg, Ferlinghetti) rebelled against suburban conformity; Sylvia Plath dramatized the suffocation of patriarchal domesticity.

Every epoch finds its sociology in its poetry: the survey in the sonnet, the census in the couplet, the ethnography in the elegy.

Ancient Greece — Odes of Order and Outcry

In the polis of Ancient Greece, poetry was the lens of the collective.

Pindar's odes immortalized aristocratic pride. His epinician verses did more than celebrate athletic triumphs; they codified class consciousness, articulating the virtues, hierarchies, and anxieties of elite society. Each line was both laudation and social instruction — a sonic statute shaping civic identity.

Hesiod's Works and Days contrasted Pindar by giving voice to the agrarian majority. His guidance on labor, justice, and morality reflected peasant realities, asserting ethical frameworks for the marginalized. Through Hesiod, the working class found narrative presence, and social inequities were recorded long before the advent of formal ethnography.

Poetry, in this era, documented class, codified customs, and dramatized duty, performing sociology through rhythm and rhyme.

Victorian England — The Poetic Census of Culture

The 19th century brought industrialization, empire, and social stratification. Victorian poets functioned as literary anthropologists, exploring consciousness as much as class.

Alfred, Lord Tennyson reflected the optimism of empire, the ideals of progress, and the anxieties of national identity. His works acted as a cultural survey, preserving the attitudes and aspirations of the upper and middle classes.

Robert Browning, by contrast, dissected bourgeois interiority, revealing tensions between morality, ambition, and social expectation. His dramatic monologues are microcosms of society, each character a sociological specimen, each stanza a case study in status, psychology, and aspiration.

Here, poetry performs social measurement without statistics, capturing the texture of etiquette, hierarchy, and expectation with far greater intimacy than census tables.

20th Century America — Rebellion and Reflection

Modernity demanded a new poetic sociology — one that could diagnose discontent, chronicling the fractures beneath conformity.

The Beats (Allen Ginsberg, Lawrence Ferlinghetti) rebelled against suburban monotony, consumerism, and institutional rigidity. Their poetry, brash and ecstatic, became social ethnography in motion, charting alienation and desire, mapping the cultural undercurrents ignored by official surveys.

Sylvia Plath dramatized domestic suffocation and gendered oppression, offering a psychological sociology that exposed intimate tyranny within private spheres. Her verse encoded the unspoken struggles of women, translating domestic despair into public discourse.

In this century, poetry functioned as both mirror and microscope, reflecting social reality while scrutinizing its intricate systems of power, expectation, and alienation.

Poetry as Living Sociology

Across these examples, a pattern emerges: every epoch finds its sociology in its poetry.

The survey is written in the sonnet, capturing civic consciousness.

The census is encrypted in the couplet, enumerating social hierarchies.

The ethnography unfolds in the elegy, chronicling the joys, sorrows, and struggles of the community.

Poetry transcends the limitations of empirical observation by embedding insight within aesthetic experience. A sonnet is not merely beautiful; it is an analytic instrument of social perception. An ode is not merely exaltation; it is a diagnostic of identity and ideology.

The poet, like a sociologist, maps the invisible

networks of thought, power, and emotion, but does so in a medium that engages heart as well as mind. Whereas statistics quantify, poetry qualifies, tracing the contours of consciousness, culture, and class across time.

The Epochal Continuity of Poetic Sociology

From Pindar to Plath, the function of poetry as social witness remains constant. Each poem is simultaneously a work of art and an archive of human behavior. Each line is evidence, each stanza a case study.

The poet chronicles the society of the self and the society of the streets. Poetry is thus living sociology: a discipline without instruments, yet infinitely precise; a study without surveys, yet socially exhaustive.

In the end, the true power of poetry lies in its dual nature: it delights aesthetically while disclosing empirically, offering not just reflection but revelation. Through poetry, society sees itself whole, partial, and paradoxically understood — before sociologists even set pen to paper.

The Paradox of Popular Poetry — Classless Yet Classified

Society stratifies culture: "high" and "low," elite and popular. Yet poetry, paradoxically, crosses classes.

A Sappho fragment scratched on papyrus inspires scholars.

A folk ballad sung in taverns sustains peasants.

A hip-hop verse galvanizes ghettos.

Thus, poetry is classless yet classified, aristocratic yet anarchic, elite yet egalitarian. It resists sociology's categories while embodying them.

Poetry is paradox incarnate, a medium that refuses to be confined yet constantly interacts with the constraints of society. Culture, like a stratified sediment, tends to separate the high from the low, the elite from the common. Sociologists and critics attempt to categorize, to assign value, to draw boundaries. Yet poetry, by its very nature, traverses these boundaries, slipping seamlessly between worlds, whispering the same truths to kings and laborers alike.

Antiquity — Fragment and Folklore

Consider Sappho, whose fragments scratched on fragile papyrus have endured millennia. Her lyric intimacy, once perhaps private, now inspires scholars, philologists, and enthusiasts alike. The text, ephemeral in its origin, becomes universal in reception, proving that a single poem can bridge centuries, geographies, and social hierarchies.

Simultaneously, folk ballads circulated in taverns and marketplaces sustained peasants, narrating love, betrayal, and heroism in accessible, memorable cadence. These verses, often anonymous, codified collective identity and maintained oral culture, functioning as both entertainment and education. Poetry here operates as both archive and instrument, preserving memory for those who wield neither pen nor parchment.

Modernity — The Voice of the Streets

In contemporary society, poetry retains this paradoxical duality. Hip-hop, slam, and spoken word function as both art form and social commentary, galvanizing marginalized communities while infiltrating mainstream consciousness. A verse that originates in the inner city can ripple outward, influencing academia, politics, and global culture. The beat of the street and the cadence of the elite synchronize in poetic resonance, revealing poetry's uncanny ability to be simultaneously local and universal.

The Sociological Oxymoron

Poetry is classless yet classified, aristocratic yet anarchic, elite yet egalitarian. It resists the neat categories sociology imposes while reflecting their existence. The

Sappho fragment and the tavern ballad, the rap verse and the Pulitzer-winning epic, occupy the same ontological plane: all are poetry, all participate in human meaning-making, all assert presence in their respective societies.

In this sense, poetry functions as a social democratizer, collapsing distinctions without erasing them. It embodies the tension between hierarchy and horizontality, permanence and transience, authority and anonymity. Its paradox is not flaw but feature: it illuminates the permeability of social categories, teaching that culture is both divided and interconnected, stratified and shared.

Poetry as a Bridge

This paradox grants poetry a unique sociological power. While surveys measure inequality and statistics enumerate social boundaries, poetry transcends them. It circulates across classes, geographies, and generations, creating informal networks of shared experience and empathy.

A single poem can simultaneously reside in the consciousness of scholars and the streets, the palace and the parlor, the classroom and the corner. Its reach is unquantifiable, its influence irreducible. Poetry demonstrates that culture is never fully contained by hierarchy; even when categorized, it escapes its containers, moving unpredictably across space and time.

The Anarchic Aristocracy of Verse

In the end, poetry's social paradox is its power. It flouts boundaries yet affirms them, challenges hierarchy yet endures within it. It can be taught in universities, chanted in marketplaces, tattooed on bodies, and murmured in exile. Through this elasticity, poetry becomes both mirror and bridge: reflecting social stratification while simultaneously offering a path beyond it.

Poetry, in its classless universality, reminds us that meaning is the ultimate social equalizer. No category can contain it, no status can monopolize it, and no sociological model can fully measure it. The paradox of popular poetry is thus the paradox of humanity itself: divided yet shared, bounded yet boundless, fragmented yet fused.

The Future of Poetry and Society

What is poetry's prospect in the digital society? Algorithms analyze trends, but poems transcend them. Social media spreads slogans, but poetry supplies substance. Artificial intelligence mimics metrics, but poetry remains the **soul's surplus**, unprogrammable paradox. Society increasingly drowns in data but starves for meaning. Poetry will be the antidote: compressed significance, distilled solidarity.

Poetry as the Pulse of Civilization

Poetry is more than ornament; it is organ and artery, rhythm and resonance, the very heartbeat of human civilization. Where history charts events, economics measures exchange, and politics defines governance, poetry measures the soul — the pulse that sustains, synchronizes, and signals the life of a society. Civilization may build monuments, draft constitutions, and erect markets, but without poetry, these structures are hollow shells. Poetry circulates meaning, memory, and moral energy — the vital currents that animate human collectivity.

Poetry as Temporal Circulation

Civilization is a temporal organism, stretching across generations. Poetry is its bloodstream, carrying the experiences of the past into the present, infusing them with relevance and resonance. Epic, elegy, lyric, ode, and sonnet are vascular channels of culture, ensuring that the knowledge, suffering, and joy of ancestors flow into contemporary consciousness.

Epic poetry, from The Iliad to The Mahābhārata, functions as historical circulatory system, preserving collective memory while shaping identity. The deeds of heroes, the wisdom of sages, the lamentations of the oppressed — all traverse centuries, entering new minds as if pumped through the arteries of collective imagination.

Lyric poetry, in contrast, is the capillary system, intimate and immediate, delivering emotional nuance and reflective subtlety to individual experience. Its circulation ensures that civilization does not merely survive; it feels, breathes, and remembers.

Through poetry, time becomes permeable: past and present intermingle, individual and collective pulse as one, and society experiences temporal empathy — the ability to inhabit multiple eras simultaneously.

Poetry as Architectural Framework

If civilization constructs physical architecture — temples, palaces, roads — poetry constructs architectures of meaning. Stanzas become structural beams, meters serve as load-bearing frameworks, and imagery forms the decorative yet functional ornamentation that reinforces cultural cohesion.

The line is a column, supporting narrative weight.

The verse is a beam, connecting emotion across thematic space.

The stanza is a hall, enclosing communities of thought and sentiment.

In this linguistic topography, poetry transforms abstract ideas into inhabitable spaces, allowing civilization to walk, dwell, and linger within concepts otherwise inaccessible. Just as physical infrastructure shapes human interaction, poetic architecture shapes consciousness, morality, and imagination.

Poetry as Societal Conscience

Poetry is civilization's ethical heartbeat, attuned to justice, empathy, and moral resonance. It bears witness to oppression, celebrates achievement, mourns loss, and articulates visions of a better society. While laws dictate action, poetry illuminates intent; while history records events, poetry renders experience vivid.

Protest poetry, from Langston Hughes to Mahmoud Darwish, transforms personal grief into collective consciousness.

Patriotic poetry, from Tagore to Walt Whitman, encodes loyalty, pride, and ethical aspiration into rhythmic affirmation.

In these functions, poetry is both monitor and mediator, observing societal health and guiding its ethical flow. Civilization without poetry may operate, but it cannot perceive its own pulse, nor can it detect the subtle anomalies that presage decay or inspire renewal.

Poetry as Cultural Catalyst

Civilization thrives not merely by maintaining order but by sparking transformation. Poetry catalyzes imagination, provoking shifts in perception, challenging orthodoxy, and inspiring innovation. It converts the raw materials of human experience — suffering, joy, curiosity, fear — into usable energy, energizing cultural, social, and political evolution.

Just as a chemical catalyst accelerates reaction without being consumed, poetry ignites movements while surviving them. Revolutions are remembered not only for their events but for the poems, songs, and chants that animated consciousness long before and long after the barricades fell.

Thus, poetry serves as civilization's engine,

its catalytic core, transforming inertia into insight, repetition into resonance, and experience into enduring legacy.

Poetry as Unifying Rhythm

Finally, poetry is the synchronizer of civilization's heartbeats. Across continents, languages, and generations, it establishes rhythms of empathy. Its cadence connects disparate minds: the individual to the collective, the present to the past, the mortal to the eternal.

Through ritual and recitation, it aligns communities, from tribal chants to national anthems.

Through performance and publication, it extends networks of influence, linking neighborhoods, nations, and cultures.

This rhythmic unity ensures that civilization does not fracture under the weight of complexity or diversity. Poetry is the metronome of the human experience, maintaining cohesion while permitting variation, encouraging harmony while tolerating dissonance.

Poetry as Civilization's Pulse

In sum, poetry is not ancillary to civilization; it is central, circulatory, and catalytic. It preserves memory, constructs meaning, sustains morality, catalyzes transformation, and synchronizes the collective heartbeat. Where empirical measures fail to capture nuance, where law and governance can enforce order but not empathy, poetry measures the unmeasurable, animates the inanimate, and unites the fragmented.

To read poetry is to feel civilization's pulse, to hear the echo of human hearts across time and space. It is simultaneously a mirror, a motor, and a metronome — reflecting society, driving change, and keeping rhythm with the infinite dance of human culture.

The Social Soul of Poetry

Poetry is society speaking to itself in secret syllables. It is at once mirror and mask, protest and prayer, ritual and rebellion. It unites solitude into solidarity, transfigures pain into participation, transforms individual rhythm into collective resonance. Thus, sociology without poetry is statistics without soul; poetry without society is song without singer. Together they form the oxymoronic chorus: solitary solidarity, eloquent silence, measured infinity. Poetry is society's autobiography, written in heartbeat and hymn.

Society is a symphony, and poetry is its score. Sociology, the study of collective life, analyzes institutions, interactions, and identities, but poetry animates them with imagery, infuses them with intimacy, interprets them with imagination. If society is structure, poetry is spirit; if society is body, poetry is breath. The paradox is immediate: poetry seems the most private expression of individual emotion, yet it is also the most public articulation of collective consciousness. A solitary poet scribbles in silence, but society hears its own soul speaking.

Poetry is both mirror and lamp of society. As mirror, it reflects customs, classes, conflicts, and cultures; as lamp, it illuminates possibilities, proposes transformations, prefigures utopias. Sociology may describe stratification, but poetry dramatizes suffering. Sociology may chart inequalities, but poetry cries them aloud. Sociology may record revolutions, but poetry ignites them. Thus paradox again: sociology dissects society, poetry dreams society.

In tribal beginnings, poetry was not a luxury but a necessity, the living archive of memory. Before writing, poetry preserved laws, genealogies, rituals. Oral societies encoded wisdom in rhythm and rhyme so memory could carry culture. Every proverb was a poem, every myth a metaphor, every chant a charter. Society itself survived through song. The paradox here: poetry, seemingly ephemeral sound, was the most enduring structure of social order.

Consider the oxymorons that define social poetry: it is "personal publicity," "intimate universality," "subjective sociology." A poet speaks of private grief yet society weeps; a poet sings of love yet nations listen. When Pablo Neruda celebrates love, Chile listens to its own longing; when Langston Hughes writes of rivers, African-Americans hear the history of their heritage; when Mirza Ghalib sighs in ghazal, society sighs through him. The poet's "I" is society's "we."

Poetry is also the language of ***social solidarity***. Rituals—weddings, funerals, festivals—are all infused with poetry. Hymns in churches, chants in temples, qawwalis in shrines, lullabies in homes: these are the sonic glue that binds individuals into community. A wedding without song is incomplete, a funeral without lament unimaginable. Society does not merely live by bread, law, or economics; it lives by rhythm, rhyme, and ritual.

Moreover, poetry is the ***sociological sensor***, the first to feel fractures in the fabric. Long before sociologists publish surveys on alienation, poets have sung solitude. Long before sociologists quantify inequality, poets cry injustice. When industrialization created faceless crowds, poets lamented the loss of individuality. When urbanization uprooted villages, poets mourned memory. Poetry is society's emotional seismograph, recording tremors before statistics can confirm them.

Paradoxically, poetry is both conformist and revolutionary. It preserves traditions through folklore, yet it provokes transformations through protest. Folk ballads keep alive heritage, while protest poetry demands new horizons. Poetry teaches children nursery rhymes to internalize norms, yet it also teaches rebels rallying cries to overturn regimes. Thus, poetry is society's conservator and its challenger, its lullaby and its trumpet.

Poetry also creates ***social imagination***. Sociology may explain how norms are maintained, but poetry dares to imagine what norms could be. Thomas More wrote prose *Utopia*, but it was poets who gave utopian visions flesh and fire. Shelley dreamt of justice, Blake of Jerusalem, Tagore of a world without fear. These are not mere verses but visions that re-shape social aspirations. The paradox: poetry is a fiction that forges fact, an illusion that inspires institution.

Furthermore, poetry performs the ***politics of identity*** within society. Feminist poets like Adrienne Rich, Dalit poets in India, Harlem Renaissance poets in America—each use poetry as the weapon of voice for the voiceless. Sociology analyzes marginalization; poetry breaks marginalization. A statistic about oppression may inform the intellect, but a stanza about oppression ignites the soul. The oxymoron again: "weak words" wield "mighty power."

Society is layered with language, symbols, and meanings, and poetry thrives precisely on these symbolic depths. To a sociologist, language is a tool of communication; to a poet, it is a temple of communion. In that temple, society meets itself, discovers its myths, sanctifies its symbols. Every society is not only a network of institutions but also a narrative of meanings. Poetry is the narrative-maker, the myth-weaver, the story-singer of social life.

Finally, poetry is society's ***secret survival strategy.*** In times of trauma—wars, plagues, migrations—it is poetry that consoles, binds, rebuilds. Diaries of soldiers contain poems; prisoners whisper poems in cells; migrants carry verses when wealth is lost. Sociology may chart resilience, but poetry creates resilience. Sociology may record survival, but poetry makes survival bearable. The paradox culminates: poetry, the seemingly fragile flower, is the fiercest fortress of society.

Poetry is not outside society; it is society in song. It reflects the social, refracts the social, reforms the social. It is sociology sung, sociology sanctified, sociology spiritualized. Sociology analyzes the skeleton of society; poetry gives it a soul. Sociology dissects data; poetry dignifies dreams. Sociology may tell us what is, but poetry forever insists on what ought to be. Thus, poetry is society's memory and imagination, its mirror and lamp, its lullaby and trumpet, its deepest despair and its highest hope.

POETRY AND ECONOMY: THE CURRENCY OF THE IMMEASURABLE

Economics counts coins, calculates costs, measures markets. It seeks equilibrium in exchange, efficiency in effort, profit in production. Yet poetry, in its paradoxical purity, is simultaneously valueless and invaluable, worthless in price yet priceless in worth. The poem cannot be eaten, yet it nourishes. It cannot be worn, yet it warms. It cannot be hoarded, yet it enriches. Thus, arises the oxymoronic truth: poetry is the economy beyond economy. It is a market where the currency is metaphor, the capital is cadence, and the commodity is consciousness. In this economy of the ineffable, the supply is infinite, the demand insatiable, and the transaction eternal.

Poetry as Primeval Exchange — The First Currency of Consciousness

Economists trace exchange to barter: grain for gold, cattle for copper. But before barter, there was chant; before coin, there was chorus.

A tribe exchanged gratitude with the gods through hymn.

A lover exchanged promise with the beloved through sonnet.

A mourner exchanged grief with the group through elegy.

Here poetry is already proto-economics – the ***symbolic surplus*** where words serve as currency for emotions too heavy to hold alone. The first "bank" was memory, the first "mint" was the mouth, the first "market" was the communal fire.

Before civilization counted coins or calculated credit, humanity counted meaning. The earliest economies were not of gold or grain, but of gratitude, grief, and gesture. Poetry was the first medium through which society conducted its primeval exchanges, transforming intangible emotions into shareable, tradable, and enduring forms.

Chant before Coin

Economists argue that barter marked the birth of exchange: cattle for copper, grain for gold. Yet archaeology and anthropology reveal a subtler truth: chant preceded coin.

Tribal hymns allowed communities to offer thanks to the gods, establishing a ritualized system of reciprocity. Each syllable was a deposit in the communal memory; each refrain a credit in the ledger of devotion.

In romantic or familial contexts, the sonnet functioned as currency of promise. Lovers exchanged commitment not through tangible contract but through verse, negotiating trust, hope, and fidelity with the delicate precision of poetic calculus.

At funerals, elegy operated as social accounting of grief, ensuring that sorrow was distributed, witnessed, and ritualized. These early exchanges were non-material but immensely valuable, circulating emotion, solidarity, and identity.

In this sense, poetry is proto-economics, a symbolic

market where emotional capital flows between participants, creating social liquidity without material wealth.

The Mechanics of Poetic Exchange

Every poem is an emotional transaction: the poet invests feeling, the audience withdraws resonance, and both parties are enriched. Unlike material currency, poetic currency is non-depleting; reading, reciting, or sharing a poem multiplies its value, extending its reach across time and space.

The first "bank" was memory — where stories, songs, and refrains were deposited, safeguarded, and accrued.

The first "mint" was the mouth, striking words into syllables, rhythm, and rhyme.

The first "market" was the communal fire, where these minted verses were exchanged, circulated, and validated by the group.

Poetic exchange is not transactional in the conventional sense; it quantifies the unquantifiable. Joy, sorrow, hope, and fear become circulating capital, circulating endlessly without diminution.

The Symbolic Surplus

Poetry generates symbolic surplus, the wealth of human feeling that is too expansive to retain privately. In every culture:

Epic heroes trade glory for honor, their exploits functioning as social stock.

Lyric poets deposit personal reflection into public memory, producing emotional dividends for the listener.

Choruses, chants, and laments allow communities to exchange collective values, moral lessons, and historical consciousness.

The economy of poetry is therefore simultaneously private and public, intimate and communal, fleeting yet eternal.

Its surplus is measured not in coins but in cultural resonance-the echoes of a verse that ripple through generations.

Poetry as the Foundation of Civilization's Exchange

Before laws, before trade routes, before commerce itself, poetry circulated the currencies of culture. It was the medium through which societies balanced emotional ledgers, managed collective memory, and negotiated social obligations.

A hymn reinforced cohesion, a sonnet regulated affection, an elegy maintained equilibrium between loss and remembrance.

Through poetry, values were banked, promises deposited, and grief accounted for, creating the first infrastructures of trust and reciprocity.

In essence, poetry was the first economy, an exchange system designed not for profit but for preservation — of feeling, of identity, of society itself.

The Eternal Market of Meaning

Poetry endures as civilization's primeval market, a space where intangible assets — emotion, empathy, insight, imagination — are minted, circulated, and compounded. Its liquidity transcends time, culture, and class. The first coins may have been gold, but the first currency of significance was verse.

Every reading, recitation, or memory of a poem continues this eternal economic cycle, circulating value without depletion, wealth without ownership, and meaning without measure. Poetry as primeval exchange reminds us that humanity's oldest commerce is not of things, but of thought, feeling, and shared consciousness.

The Economics of Aesthetics— Poetry as Fiscal Elegance of the Soul

Aristotle in his Poetics argued that art gives catharsis,

a cleansing of emotion. What is catharsis but an economy of the soul, a debit of despair offset by a credit of clarity?

Every poem is a balance sheet:

Assets: Images, rhythms, metaphors.

Liabilities: Ambiguities, obscurities, silences.

Profit: Pleasure, perception, participation.

Thus, poetry is a business of beauty: its ledger inscribed not in numbers but in nuances, not in figures but in feelings.

Poetry, like commerce, is governed by principles of exchange, but its currency is not gold or grain — it is emotion, insight, and aesthetic energy. Aristotle's concept of catharsis in Poetics can be understood as a metaphysical accounting, a debit of despair offset by a credit of clarity. Each poem performs a transaction of the soul, reconciling tension, converting turmoil into understanding, and distributing wealth in the form of experience.

The Poetic Ledger

Every poem can be read as a balance sheet, recording the flow of intellectual and emotional capital:

Assets: Images, rhythms, metaphors — the vibrant investments that engage the mind and heart, stored for future contemplation.

Liabilities: Ambiguities, silences, and unspoken tensions — the debts the poem incurs, the unresolved questions that invite reflection and introspection.

Profit: Pleasure, perception, participation — the surplus generated when reader and text intersect, when experience is enriched and understanding expanded.

Unlike material economies, the profit of poetry is not finite. Every reading, reflection, or recital compounds its value, multiplying emotional dividends without depleting its original assets.

Poetic Investments and Returns

Poetry demands investment of attention from both poet and audience. The poet deposits words, carefully chosen and rhythmically arranged, into the communal consciousness. The reader withdraws these deposits, decoding metaphors, resonating with cadences, and experiencing catharsis.

This cycle creates a perpetual economy of feeling:

A vivid image functions as a capital injection, stimulating thought and imagination.

A deliberate ambiguity or enjambed line acts as a liability, a suspenseful credit that will yield insight upon reflection.

The resulting comprehension and emotional resonance constitute profit, realized in personal growth, aesthetic enjoyment, and cultural enrichment.

Through this cycle, poetry operates as a self-sustaining market, where the exchange of emotion and meaning is continuous, equitable, and endlessly renewable.

Beauty as Commodity, Emotion as Currency

Poetry transforms intangible qualities into tradable value. Beauty becomes commodity; emotion, currency. The pleasure of aesthetic engagement is not superficial; it is a measure of cultural and personal wealth, an account of empathy and understanding accrued across generations.

A tragic ode may incur short-term liability — discomfort, sorrow, confrontation with mortality — but yields long-term dividends in wisdom and compassion.

A joyful lyric may be instantly liquid, offering immediate sensory delight, yet compounds over time as the memory of its cadence resonates.

In this economy of aesthetics, neither scarcity nor abundance applies in conventional terms. Every experience can be reinvested, multiplied, and shared, ensuring that poetry's economy is both inexhaustible and invaluable.

Poetry as Ethical Fiscal Policy

Beyond pleasure, poetry enacts moral accounting. The ethical implications of catharsis, of empathy, of reflection, constitute societal profit: a more attuned citizenry, a more conscientious culture, a civilization capable of introspection. Poetry balances not only emotions but ethics, distributing awareness and accountability throughout the collective consciousness.

Here, the poet is both banker and economist, crafting instruments that circulate meaning and regulate the flow of human feeling. The reader is both investor and beneficiary, participating in an economy where return is wisdom, and wealth is understanding.

Ledger of the Infinite

Thus, poetry is the business of beauty, an enterprise in which the ledger is inscribed not in numbers but in nuances, not in figures but in feelings. Its capital is imagination; its interest is insight; its surplus is the expansion of consciousness. In this economy, every word is a coin, every image a bond, every pause an account of suspense. The ultimate profit is civilization itself: enriched, enlightened, and eternally invested in the infinite commerce of thought, emotion, and art.

Poetry as Surplus and Scarcity — The Paradoxical Wealth of Verse

Economics thrives on the paradox of scarcity. Poetry thrives on the paradox of surplus.

A loaf of bread feeds a body once; a poem feeds a soul forever.

A coin is diminished by division; a stanza is multiplied by sharing.

A market collapses by oversupply; a library grows by excess.

Here lies the oxymoronic wealth of poetry: the more it is spent, the more it accumulates. It is scarcity that sings as surplus, abundance that appears in absence.

Economics is grounded in scarcity: limited resources, finite goods, and competition for survival. Poetry, by contrast, operates in the paradoxical economy of surplus, a realm where abundance emerges precisely through use, and scarcity is transformed into inexhaustible richness. Whereas material goods deplete with division, poetry multiplies through circulation, creating wealth without diminishing its source.

The Infinite Return on Poetic Investment

Consider the contrast: a loaf of bread nourishes a body once; a poem nourishes a mind an eternity of times. Each stanza, each line, each syllable is a resource that cannot be exhausted by consumption.

A verse read silently is replenished when spoken aloud.

A sonnet memorized is reinforced with each recollection.

A story shared across generations accrues resonance, depth, and historical weight.

In this way, poetry generates perpetual surplus, an economy without loss, where the act of giving multiplies the value of the gift itself.

Multiplication through Sharing

Coins diminish when spent; stanzas expand when shared. Whereas material economies falter under oversupply, poetry thrives under excess. The more it circulates, the richer it becomes. A library overflowing with verse does not depreciate; it compounds knowledge, emotion, and imagination. Public readings, oral recitations, digital dissemination — each act amplifies the poem's reach, creating exponential growth of cultural and emotional capital. Even fragments or incomplete lines retain power, generating interpretive surpluses as readers fill gaps with their own imagination. Here, sharing is not depletion but accretion, a phenomenon antithetical to conventional economic logic yet perfectly natural in the realm of poetic wealth.

Scarcity Re-imagined as Abundance

Paradoxically, scarcity itself sings as surplus in poetry. A line left unsaid, a pause unfilled, a stanza unwritten — all create space for reflection, imagination, and interpretation. Absence, tension, and silence generate cognitive and emotional abundance, expanding the poem beyond the text into the reader's mind.

The ellipses, enjambments, and white spaces of a poem act as reservoirs, holding potential meanings that flourish when engaged. A poem can exist simultaneously in multiple interpretations, each reading adding to its cumulative richness. Thus, scarcity becomes a conduit for creativity, turning what appears lacking into a source of infinite supply.

The Oxymoronic Wealth of Poetry

Poetry's economy is oxymoronic and eternal:

The more it is spent, the more it accumulates.
Abundance appears in absence.
Silence produces sound.
Limitation births infinite possibility.

This is poetry's true surplus: a wealth beyond measurement, beyond material constraints, and beyond temporal limits. Whereas conventional economies collapse under the pressure of overproduction, poetry thrives under overflow, proving that its currency is immortal, unbounded, and inexhaustibly generative. Poetry transforms scarcity into abundance, limitation into liberty, and consumption into creation. It demonstrates that value is not a zero-sum game; it is cumulative, expansive, and paradoxical. In the infinite ledger of human culture, every poem is both capital and interest, both stock and dividend, a resource that grows the more it is invested. Through this eternal paradox, poetry remains civilization's unfailing treasury, offering abundance to every soul willing to enter its market, and proving that in the economy of the human spirit, surplus is eternal and scarcity is sublime.

Poetry as Labour and Leisure

Adam Smith defined labour as the source of value. Marx defined surplus labour as the source of exploitation. Poetry confounds both. For poetry is labour that feels like leisure, work that works by refusing work. It is the oxymoronic occupation: arduous ease, exhausting ecstasy.

The poet sweats in solitude but sings of freedom.

The reader toils through obscurity but tastes illumination.

The society dismisses poetry as useless but secretly uses it to dignify its history.

Thus, poetry proves the paradox: the most "unproductive" labour produces the most enduring value.

The Market of Metaphor

Markets operate on trust, confidence, and narrative—precisely the materials of poetry. Investors follow not only numbers but stories: tales of growth, fears of collapse, hopes of prosperity. Economists speak of "bull markets" and "bear markets"—poetic metaphors that shape billions in behavior. The market is a metaphor machine, and poetry is its unacknowledged grammar. The paradox:

the "hardest" science of money is guided by the "softest" power of metaphor.

If economy is exchange, then poetry is exchange intensified. A metaphor is a transaction: one word traded for another, one image exchanged for another.

"Love is a rose" → passion purchased by petals.

"Time is a thief" → eternity traded for absence.

"The world is a stage" → society sold into spectacle.

The marketplace of metaphor is never bankrupt, for imagination is inexhaustible. In this economy, inflation becomes inspiration, speculation becomes symbolism.

Poetry and Capital: Wealth beyond Wealth

Capital in economics is accumulation for future production. Capital in poetry is accumulation for future perception.

A sonnet is capitalized emotion.

An epic is accumulated myth.

A haiku is concentrated consciousness.

The poet is both banker and beggar: banker of beauty, beggar of bread. The paradox persists: society may starve its poets materially, yet feast spiritually on their creations.

In economics, capital is stored value, accumulated to generate future production and profit. In poetry, capital is stored perception, accumulated insight, and emotional richness reserved for future experience. Here, wealth is not measured in coins or commodities but in consciousness, feeling, and aesthetic resonance.

Forms of Poetic Capital

Each poetic form embodies a distinct kind of capital:

The Sonnet: a small but potent deposit of emotion, carefully structured, accruing meaning through rhyme, rhythm, and metaphor.

The Epic: a massive ledger of collective memory,

myth, and moral instruction, accumulated over time, providing enduring cultural dividends.

The Haiku: concentrated consciousness, a micro-capital of perception, compressed yet infinitely expansive in interpretation.

Every poem is an investment, designed not for immediate consumption but for long-term enrichment, offering returns in insight, empathy, and imagination.

The Poet as Banker and Beggar

The poet occupies a paradoxical position in the economy of civilization:

Banker of Beauty: creating, storing, and distributing the wealth of thought and feeling. Each line, each stanza, is a deposit made to the collective consciousness.

Beggar of Bread: often materially impoverished, neglected, or undercompensated, yet the poet's creations provide spiritual sustenance far beyond their own needs.

This duality exemplifies poetry's unique capital function: it generates wealth without expectation of return, enriching society even when the creator receives little.

The Paradox of Poetic Wealth

Society may fail to feed its poets materially, yet it feasts spiritually on their creations. This paradox defines the eternal economy of poetry:

The physical poverty of the poet does not diminish the abundance of the poem.

A single verse can outlast empires, outlive dynasties, and inspire generations — capital of infinite durability.

Poetry's "interest" accrues not in money but in meaning; its dividends are understanding, beauty, and moral clarity.

In this sense, poetry is wealth beyond wealth, a treasury invisible to accountants yet indispensable to the human spirit.

Accumulation for Future Perception

Unlike conventional capital, poetic capital grows through circulation. Each reading, recitation, translation, or adaptation enhances its value, expanding emotional and intellectual reach.

A sonnet shared in one generation becomes a moral and aesthetic guide for another.

An epic passed orally becomes historical memory codified in communal consciousness.

A haiku recited quietly in contemplation multiplies in the mind of every reader.

Poetic wealth is self-replenishing, compounding, and eternal; its capital is perpetually active, invested across time and space.

Civilization's Invisible Bank

Poetry is civilization's invisible bank, where the deposits are beauty, insight, and feeling, and the interest is enlightenment and empathy. Material poverty of poets cannot bankrupt this system; scarcity of coin cannot diminish abundance of consciousness. The paradox remains: while society may starve its poets, it simultaneously feasts on the capital they create. Poetry transforms human experience into immortal currency, demonstrating that the truest wealth is not measured in gold but in the enduring capacity to feel, imagine, and understand.

Poetry as Protest against Materialism — Reverie Rebelling Against Revenue

Economics, in its classical form, often reduces humanity to homo economicus, the rational agent driven solely by utility, efficiency, and measurable gain. Poetry, by contrast, rebels against this reduction, insisting that human life is measured not merely in coins or commodities but in meaning, feeling, and imagination. Economics too often reduces humanity to homo economicus: the rational maximizer of utility. Poetry rebels.

Where economics says "maximize," poetry whispers "magnify."

Where economics says "produce," poetry pleads "ponder."

Where economics says "consume," poetry cries "consecrate."

Thus, poetry is the ultimate protest: a strike against the tyranny of utility, a rebellion of reverie against revenue.

Magnify, Not Maximize

Where economics urges maximization of output, poetry advocates magnification of experience: A single word, a pause, a metaphor can amplify emotional and intellectual resonance beyond any numerical measure. Poetry teaches that depth surpasses breadth, that subtlety carries value inaccessible to profit calculations. By magnifying perception, it cultivates richness of insight, defying the economy of efficiency.

Ponder, Not Produce

Economics emphasizes production: the creation of goods, services, and measurable outcomes. Poetry insists on pondering, reflecting, and questioning: A stanza is not a product to be consumed; it is a space for thought and introspection. The act of writing or reading poetry prioritizes contemplation over output, valuing insight above utility. Through this process, poetry generates wealth of consciousness, immeasurable yet enduring.

Consecrate, Not Consume

Where markets demand consumption, poetry consecrates the human experience:

Every line, image, or rhyme becomes sacred, invested

with attention and reverence, rather than a disposable commodity.

By consecrating rather than consuming, poetry preserves emotional, cultural, and ethical capital for future generations.

Its economy is regenerative: value grows through engagement, rather than being diminished by use.

The Ultimate Protest

Poetry's rebellion is structural, ethical, and aesthetic:

A strike against the tyranny of utility, it refuses to measure worth solely in profit or output.

A rebellion of reverie, it elevates imagination and introspection above material gain.

In doing so, poetry becomes an economic insurgent, subverting the logic of scarcity, consumption, and material accumulation.

Poetry beyond Profit

In an age dominated by financial metrics and material calculation, poetry asserts that human value is not reducible to utility. It magnifies perception, invites reflection, and consecrates experience. Poetry, in this sense, is civilization's protest, a persistent and silent insurgency against materialism. Its wealth is unquantifiable, its currency timeless, proving that the richest economy is not the one measured in coins, but the one measured in consciousness, empathy, and the infinite surplus of human imagination.

Scientific Analogies: The Economy of the Ether — Poetry Beyond Measurable Markets

Economics has long sought precision: supply meets demand, markets find equilibrium, and wealth flows according to predictable rules. Yet poetry operates in an ether beyond measurement, a domain where scientific analogies illuminate the paradoxical abundance and surplus inherent in verse.

Physics: Supply and demand resemble action and reaction; poetry is the energy surplus that breaks Newton's balance.

Chemistry: Capital is catalyst; poetry is precipitate — crystallizing value where none is measurable.

Biology: The economy is metabolism of matter; poetry is metabolism of meaning.

Mathematics: Markets obey equations; poetry invents inequations — beauty born of imbalance.

Thus, the science of scarcity is surpassed by the art of abundance.

Physics: Energy Surplus beyond Action and Reaction

In classical mechanics, every action meets an equal and opposite reaction. Markets, too, attempt balance through transactions, trades, and pricing. Poetry defies this Newtonian symmetry. It is energy surplus, the extra force that moves thought and emotion beyond expectation. A single stanza can spark insight, empathy, or transformation far exceeding the "action" of its material delivery. In this sense, poetry acts like kinetic energy unleashed, breaking conventional balances and creating value where physics predicts none.

Chemistry: Catalyst and Precipitate

In chemistry, reactions require catalysts to precipitate outcomes. In poetic economics: Capital may act as the catalyst — societal resources, patronage, or cultural attention. Poetry is the precipitate, crystallizing meaning, beauty, and insight where no measurable value existed before. This process is nonlinear, invisible to conventional accounting, yet tangible in perception and cultural impact. Here, poetry transforms the raw potential of human experience into solidified aesthetic and ethical wealth, just as precipitate forms from dissolved ions, invisible until crystallized.

Biology: Metabolism of Meaning

Economies resemble living organisms: inputs, processes, and outputs circulate continuously. Poetry functions as the metabolism of meaning, consuming raw experience, digesting emotion, and excreting insight. It nourishes culture and society in ways material economics cannot, converting ephemeral moments into enduring vitality. Each reading or interpretation is akin to a cellular reaction, contributing to the collective health of human consciousness.

Mathematics: Equations, Inequations, and Imbalance

Markets obey formulas: supply minus demand, interest times principal, growth versus depreciation. Poetry invents inequations, embracing imbalance as the source of beauty. Its value is not linear nor quantifiable; a brief haiku may outweigh a volume of prose in cultural or emotional impact. This mathematical freedom underscores poetry's capacity to generate abundance from scarcity, exceeding the predictive powers of conventional calculation.

The Art of Abundance Surpassing Science of Scarcity

Through the lens of science, poetry emerges as an economy ungoverned by measurable rules, surpassing scarcity, equilibrium, and material constraints. Physics, chemistry, biology, and mathematics provide metaphors, yet poetry transcends these analogies, inventing its own laws of circulation, reaction, and accumulation. Its wealth is ethereal but real, scientific in its structural logic, yet boundless in experiential effect. Thus, the science of scarcity is surpassed by the art of abundance, and the ether of poetry becomes civilization's invisible treasury, where meaning multiplies endlessly, energy accumulates infinitely, and wealth is measured not in coin, but in consciousness.

Historical Economies of Poetry — Wealth beyond Coin across Centuries

Throughout history, poetry has maintained a unique economy, one governed not by material currency but by honor, memory, and cultural influence. Its valuation defies conventional markets: poets may live in material poverty, yet their creations accrue wealth that transcends lifetimes.

Ancient Greece: Rhapsodes were paid in gifts, not wages; their wealth was honour, not coin.

Medieval Europe: Troubadours thrived in courts where a single stanza was worth a castle's welcome.

Modern Capitalism: Poets are paupers, yet their words are printed, anthologized, canonized — their wealth posthumous, their economy eternal.

The paradox persists: poets die poor but live rich in memory.

Ancient Greece: Honour as Currency

In the polis of Ancient Greece:

Rhapsodes, the professional reciters of epic poetry, were rarely paid in coins. Instead, gifts, feasts, and recognition served as currency.

Their wealth was measured not in material accumulation but in social esteem, cultural authority, and lasting reputation.

The performance of Homeric epics turned communal memory into a treasury of honor, circulating influence across citizens and generations.

Here, poetry was economic in spirit, not in metal, establishing the earliest model of non-material yet socially potent wealth.

Medieval Europe: The Courtly Economy of Verse

In the courts of Medieval Europe:

Troubadours and minstrels exchanged song and verse for hospitality, favor, or political leverage.

A single well-crafted stanza could secure a noble's patronage or an enduring place in courtly culture.

Poetic skill became capital, convertible into social standing, alliances, and protection.

The economy was symbolic: wealth flowed through reputation, influence, and aesthetic mastery, demonstrating poetry's capacity to function as a parallel currency, independent of material markets.

Modern Capitalism: Posthumous Profits and Eternal Economy

In contemporary times:

Poets often live materially impoverished, struggling for publication and recognition in a commodified literary marketplace.

Yet their words, once printed, anthologized, or canonized, acquire posthumous capital, circulating for centuries in libraries, classrooms, and digital archives.

The poet's economy is paradoxical: poverty in life, riches in memory; scarcity in coins, abundance in cultural legacy.

Even under capitalism, poetry retains an economy of the soul, whose returns cannot be measured by markets or material exchange but by the enduring influence on thought, imagination, and civilization itself.

The Persistent Paradox

Across eras and societies, poetry demonstrates a timeless economic paradox:

Material deprivation of the creator does not preclude immortal accumulation.

The more a poem circulates, the richer society becomes, while the poet may remain materially poor.

Economic value in poetry is measured in memory, cultural resonance, and emotional impact, rather than in coins or commodities.

Eternal Economy of Verse

Poetry's historical economies reveal an unconventional but enduring form of wealth. From rhapsodes to troubadours, from pauper poets to posthumous icons, poetry creates a currency of consciousness that transcends time, geography, and material scarcity.

It is the eternal market of the human spirit, where honor, influence, and memory form the capital, circulation is infinite, and value grows with every reading, recitation, or reflection. In this economy, poets may die poor, yet civilization feasts eternally on the richness of their words.

Poetry in the Digital Economy — The Unquantifiable Currency of the Algorithmic Age

Today's market is virtual: crypto coins, digital data, algorithms of advertising. Where stands poetry?

It resists commodification, yet circulates virally.

It is free online, yet costly in its depth.

It is devalued in markets, yet invaluable in meaning.

Thus, in the algorithmic age, poetry is the unquantifiable currency, the surplus value beyond spreadsheets.

In an era dominated by digital markets, cryptocurrency, and algorithmic valuations, the position of poetry is both paradoxical and profound. Unlike commodities, which are measured, traded, and commodified, poetry resists quantification, yet circulates more widely than ever through digital networks, social media, and online platforms.

Poetry as Viral Wealth

In the virtual marketplace:

Poetry spreads virally, reaching millions with a single post, tweet, or video clip, yet retains its depth and density of meaning. Its circulation defies conventional economic logic: the more it is shared, the more it gains cultural and emotional value, not less. Unlike digital currency, which can fluctuate in price and be subject to external regulation, poetry's intrinsic worth is immeasurable, residing in perception, reflection, and resonance. Here, poetry functions as viral yet invaluable capital, demonstrating that in the digital age, circulation does not equal commodification.

Free Yet Costly

Digital platforms have made poetry widely accessible: anyone can read, download, or share poems at no monetary cost. Yet, the cognitive, emotional, and imaginative engagement required to truly understand and appreciate poetry makes it profoundly costly in experience and attention.

The depth of a poem cannot be bought; it must be earned through contemplation.

Algorithms may push shallow trends to prominence, but the most enduring poetry demands patience, reflection, and interpretation.

Its true "value" is hidden from metrics, analytics, and spreadsheets, existing instead in the subtle economies of thought, feeling, and aesthetic perception.

Resistance to Commodification

While the digital economy thrives on monetization and data extraction, poetry remains unquantifiable, unownable, and uncapturable:

It cannot be fully patented, packaged, or sold as a digital asset without losing essence.

Its worth is measured in experience, insight, and connection, not clicks, likes, or cryptocurrency units.

Even in a monetized digital space, poetry retains its symbolic surplus, circulating value beyond markets, algorithms, and advertisements.

Surplus Value beyond Spreadsheets

In capitalist accounting, value is often calculated, recorded, and rationalized. Poetry operates outside this framework:

Its dividends are emotional, cognitive, and cultural, not financial.

Each reading compounds cultural and personal insight, increasing wealth that is felt, shared, and remembered.

Poetry's value is algorithm-resistant, human-centric, and eternally renewable.

In the algorithmic age, poetry becomes the ultimate unquantifiable currency — a medium whose worth transcends numbers, charts, and transactions, enriching the mind and spirit in ways no ledger can record.

Digital Surplus

Poetry in the digital economy exemplifies the paradox of abundance and scarcity, circulation and resistance. Free to access yet rich in meaning, easily spread yet resistant to commodification, poetry demonstrates that true wealth is not digital data, but the human capacity for insight, empathy, and imagination. It is the surplus value of civilization, flowing through the digital veins of our era, untouchable by spreadsheets, unpurchasable by coins, and infinitely renewable in the minds of those who engage with it.

Poetry as the Eternal Economy

Poetry is paradox: worthless wealth, priceless

poverty, surplus scarcity, productive idleness. It is the economy of eternity, the market of meaning, the commerce of consciousness. Economics may count the coin, but poetry counts the cost. Economics may measure the market, but poetry measures the meaning. Economics may govern the goods, but poetry governs the good. Thus, the true wealth of nations lies not in gold reserves but in poetic reserves: in the metaphors that move masses, in the songs that survive centuries, in the words that weave worlds. Poetry is the only currency that cannot collapse, the only capital that cannot corrode, the only commerce that consecrates.

At first sight, poetry and economics appear as estranged entities, as far apart as dream and debt, sonnet and stock, metaphor and market. Economics is thought to count coins, poetry to conjure cadences. One calculates commodities, the other composes couplets. Yet paradoxically, the two are profoundly intertwined: poetry is the economy of language, and economy is the poetry of exchange. The coin is a compressed story, and the stanza is a condensed economy.

Poetry as Economy of Expression

Every poem is an exercise in economic precision. Where prose can wander, poetry must weigh. A poem is wealth without waste: every syllable is a coin, every rhyme a revenue, every line a ledger of meaning. The paradox: poetry thrives by thrift yet achieves abundance; it spends little yet enriches infinitely. A sonnet of fourteen lines is worth a thousand philosophies; a haiku of seventeen syllables contains entire cosmologies. Thus poetry proves that the richest treasures are found in the most frugal forms.

Economics as Poetry of Exchange

Conversely, the economy is itself a kind of poetry in motion. Markets are metaphors; currencies are symbols;

trade is a tale of trust. Consider money: a piece of paper with printed ink, valueless in itself, but through collective belief it becomes a universal metaphor of value. Is this not poetic magic? Fiat currency is society's grandest metaphor, its most successful symbol, its living poem of trust. Without this shared metaphor, economies collapse. Thus, paradoxically, the market is less material than metaphorical.

Poetry and Value

Economics asks: What is value? Poetry answers: Value is what cannot be priced. Paradox arises: the most valuable things—love, hope, beauty—are precisely those the market cannot measure. A diamond has price but not necessarily meaning; a poem may have no price but infinite meaning. The oxymoron: poetry is "worthless wealth," "priceless poverty," "impoverished richness." It cannot be bought or sold, yet it enriches beyond gold.

The Poetics of Labor and Production

Labor is another link. Economists analyze productivity; poets sing of toil. From Hesiod's *Works and Days* to Whitman's *Song of Myself,* poetry dignifies labor as more than material production—it is spiritual creation. While factories manufacture commodities, poetry manufactures consciousness. The paradox: physical labor sustains life, poetic labor sanctifies life. Economics ensures survival; poetry ensures significance. Together they complete the circle of human fulfillment.

Poetry and Scarcity

Scarcity is the central problem of economics. Yet poetry transforms scarcity into surplus. The fewer the words, the fuller the wonder. Poetry thrives on limitation: meter restrains, rhyme restricts, form confines—yet from constraint comes creativity. This mirrors the paradox of economics: scarcity spurs invention. Thus, poetry is the art of making abundance from absence, plenitude from poverty. The oxymoron: "fertile famine," "luxurious lack."

Poetry as Gift Economy

Unlike market exchange, poetry belongs to the economy of the gift. A poem is given freely, with no demand of repayment, yet it creates bonds stronger than any contract. Marcel Mauss described the social power of gifts; poetry is the highest gift, because it is both intimate and infinite. When a poet shares a verse, it multiplies rather than diminishes. Here poetry transcends the zero-sum logic of economics and enters the paradox of inexhaustible generosity.

Poetry as Capital of Culture

Economics speaks of capital: financial, human, social. Poetry is cultural capital—the wealth of words that shape worlds. A society with strong poetry is rich in imagination, resilient in crisis, radiant in identity. Consider how national epics—The Iliad, The Divine Comedy, The Mahabharata—constitute a civilization's deepest treasure. Armies may conquer, economies may collapse, but poetry preserves identity, the priceless cultural capital of continuity.

Poetry and Inequality

Economics confronts inequality of wealth; poetry confronts inequality of voice. Where markets silence the poor, poetry gives them speech. Protest poetry, working-class ballads, revolutionary songs—these democratize dignity. Economists may chart Gini coefficients, but poets ignite movements. Thus poetry becomes the wealth of the voiceless, the surplus of the suppressed. Paradox again: those without property possess poetry, and through poetry they possess power.

Poetry and Consumption

In economics, consumption is the end of production.

In poetry, consumption is the beginning of creation. A reader consumes a poem but in doing so produces meaning. Unlike commodities, whose value diminishes when consumed, a poem's value multiplies through reading. The oxymoron: poetry is "consumable creativity," "perishable permanence." It exists only when shared, yet it endures forever once shared.

Poetry as Economy beyond Economy

Finally, poetry challenges the very assumptions of economics. Economics rests on rational choice, measurable utility, quantifiable value. Poetry asserts irrational choice, immeasurable utility, unquantifiable value. The paradox: poetry is beyond price yet of infinite worth; beyond calculation yet of ultimate necessity. Where economics deals in scarcity, poetry proclaims abundance of meaning. Where economics divides wealth, poetry unites wonder.

Poetry and economy are not antagonists but analogues. Poetry economizes language; economy poetizes exchange. Poetry teaches that true value lies not in price but in presence, not in currency but in creativity. It reveals that the wealth of words is greater than the weight of gold, that the surplus of symbols outshines the scarcity of substances. In the paradoxical oxymoron of existence, poetry is the "profitable poverty" that enriches all, the "useless utility" that sustains society. Thus, to study economics without poetry is to count coins without knowing why they matter. To study poetry without economics is to dream without grounding. But to see their secret kinship is to glimpse the grand economy of imagination, where every word is wealth, every rhythm is revenue, every poem a priceless currency of the human condition.

POETRY AND ANTHROPOLOGY: THE SONG OF THE SPECIES

Poetry is the anthropology of the ineffable. Anthropology studies the human as a creature of culture, custom, and community. It dissects rituals, deciphers myths, catalogs kinship, traces tongues. Yet when it confronts poetry, it discovers its own reflection magnified: for poetry is anthropology written in rhythm, humanity inscribed in harmony, culture crystallized in cadence. If anthropology asks *what makes us human,* poetry answers *what makes humanity divine*. The former is empirical excavation; the latter, ethereal exaltation. The anthropologist unearths shards of bone; the poet unearths shards of soul. Together, they form a paradoxical partnership: the science of the human body and the art of the human breath.

Poetry as Proto-Anthropology

Before anthropology became a discipline with field notes and ethnographies, it existed as song. The first anthropologist was the poet-priest who sang of origins, genealogies, migrations.

In Polynesian *kumulipo,* cosmic genealogies are sung, not written.

In Vedic hymns, the universe is mapped as chant, not chart.

In Homeric epics, the Greek world is remembered in metre, not measurement.

Thus, poetry is the primeval archive of anthropology — preserving kinship codes, cosmologies, customs through melody when memory alone could not suffice.

The Anthropology of Myth and Metaphor

Anthropology recognizes myth as a society's subconscious structure. Poetry is myth in miniature, myth condensed into metaphor.

Where myth tells of gods, poetry whispers of metaphors.

Where anthropology deciphers symbols, poetry generates them.

Where society encodes taboos, poetry encodes transformations.

Hence, the oxymoron: poetry is a fiction truer than fact, a myth more real than history.

Kinship in Cadence

Anthropology obsesses over kinship diagrams: who marries whom, who inherits what. But poetry reveals the deeper kinship: the marriage of word and world, the inheritance of rhythm across generations.

A ballad is a family tree of tones.

A rhyme is a ritual of remembrance.

A stanza is a kinship system of syllables.

Thus, anthropology sees kinship in blood; poetry sees kinship in breath.

Ritual and Recitation

Ritual is repetitive, rhythmic, symbolic — in other words, poetic.

The funeral dirge is ritualized elegy.

The harvest hymn is ritualized gratitude.

The initiation chant is ritualized prophecy.

Anthropology analyzes ritual as social function; poetry experiences ritual as spiritual fusion. What the anthropologist records with a pen, the poet revives with a pulse.

The Poetics of Totem and Taboo

Freud wrote *Totem and Taboo*; Lévi-Strauss wrote *The Savage Mind*. Both recognized that symbolic thought underlies culture. Poetry is that symbolic thought intensified: it makes totems of trivial things, taboos of tender feelings.

A rose becomes the totem of love.

A raven becomes the totem of mystery.

Silence becomes the taboo of speech.

Thus, poetry anthropologizes the ordinary, transforming daily detail into cultural code.

Oral Traditions: The Breath of the Ancestors

Anthropology honors oral traditions as living libraries. Poetry is their primary form.

The griot in West Africa preserves dynasties through song.

The bard in Celtic lands carries history in harp-struck verse.

The Native American storyteller encodes ecology in chant.

Poetry is the anthropological archive where words are fossils, rhythms are relics, and metaphors are artifacts. To study a culture's poetry is to excavate its anthropology.

Ethnopoetics: Anthropology Learns from Poetry

In the 20th century, ethnographers like Dell Hymes and Jerome Rothenberg discovered that translation alone cannot capture oral art. They proposed ***ethnopoetics*** — anthropology written poetically.

Here the disciplines converge: anthropology needs

poetry to express what anthropology discovers. The paradox arises: the science of culture cannot explain culture without becoming art.

Poetry as Cultural Currency

Just as economy measures material exchange, anthropology measures cultural exchange. Poetry is its purest currency:

Proverbs are pocket-sized philosophies.

Songs are portable histories.

Lullabies are inheritances of intimacy.

Thus, the poem is both artifact and agent: simultaneously a relic of the past and a seed of the future.

The Anthropology of Alienation and Aspiration

Modern anthropology studies alienation — colonialism, diaspora, dislocation. Poetry is the cry of this exile.

Postcolonial poets reclaim language as weapon.

Diasporic poets weave hybrid identities in verse.

Indigenous poets reassert erased cosmologies.

Where anthropology documents displacement, poetry dignifies it. Where anthropology analyzes, poetry agonizes. Where anthropology records, poetry redeems.

Scientific Analogies: The Poetics of the Human Genome

Biology: Anthropology studies DNA; poetry studies metaphor. Yet both encode identity in patterns.

Chemistry: Kinship rules are formulas; poetic rhymes are reactions.

Physics: Ritual cycles echo orbital cycles; stanzaic rhythms echo harmonic frequencies.

Mathematics: Myths are equations of meaning; poems are inequalities of truth.

Thus, poetry is anthropology's double — less precise, yet more profound.

Case Studies: Cultures in Verse

Indian or Sanskrit Literature: Poetry as dharma and drama, social code in cadence.

Greek Tragedy: Poetry as civic anthropology, collective catharsis through chorus.

African Oral Epics: Poetry as political anthropology, rulers remembered in rhythm.

Modern Slam Poetry: Anthropology of urban tribes, spoken word as survival strategy.

Each instance proves: poetry is anthropology alive, anthropology in action.

The Future of Anthropoetics

Anthropology, increasingly digital, risks abstraction. Poetry, increasingly global, resists erasure. Together, they promise a new anthropology: anthropoetics.

To map humanity not only in genes but in genres.

To preserve culture not only in data but in diction.

To understand humanity not only through surveys but through sonnets.

The Poem as the Anthropological Soul

Anthropology asks: What is humanity?

Poetry replies: Humanity is what cannot be defined, only sung.

Anthropology seeks universals in particulars; poetry finds universals by particularizing. Anthropology explains; poetry exclaims. Anthropology catalogs culture; poetry creates culture. Thus, poetry is anthropology's twin, its elder, its oracle. If anthropology is the science of the human, poetry is the spirit of the human. Anthropology dissects the bones of culture; poetry animates its breath. Poetry is the anthropology of eternity: the study of humanity not as it is, but as it dreams itself to be.

Anthropology is the disciplined study of human

origins, cultures, rituals, and relationships. Poetry is the inspired articulation of those same origins, cultures, rituals, and relationships. One dissects the bones of being, the other breathes the breath of being. One classifies kinship systems, the other composes kinship songs. One excavates fossils, the other exhumes feelings. Yet paradoxically, both aim at the same truth: the meaning of humanity. If anthropology is the science of mankind, poetry is the soul of mankind.

Poetry as the Oldest Anthropology

Before anthropologists recorded myths, poetry was already narrating them. Before ethnographers mapped rituals, poets sang them into memory. The Rig Veda, the Epic of Gilgamesh, the chants of Native American shamans, the griot epics of Africa—all are anthropology sung rather than studied, lived rather than labeled. Poetry was the first ethnography, albeit in metaphor rather than measurement. Paradox arises: poetry, seemingly unscientific, preserved the deepest sciences of survival.

Poetry as Cultural Cartography

Anthropology charts cultures; poetry creates them. A culture is not only institutions and artifacts but also images, idioms, and imaginations. Poetry is culture's cartography, mapping myths, metaphors, and memories that anthropology later analyzes. Homer mapped the Greek soul, Dante mapped medieval Christendom, Rumi mapped Sufi spirituality. These maps are not in coordinates but in cadences, not in statistics but in stanzas. Thus paradox: poetry is both the most local and the most universal, both deeply rooted in tribe and infinitely transcendent of tribe.

The Oxymoron of "Primitive Sophistication"

Anthropologists once called oral societies "primitive," yet their poetic traditions reveal sophistication beyond measure. A Polynesian chant may encode astronomical knowledge; a hunter's song may preserve ecological wisdom. The paradox is profound: what seems "primitive poetry" is in truth "sophisticated science." Thus anthropology, humbled by poetry, learns that verse is not frivolity but philosophy encoded in rhythm.

Poetry as Ritual Language

Ritual is anthropology's richest subject, and ritual is rarely without poetry. Weddings weave vows, funerals frame elegies, initiations ignite chants. Poetry sanctifies the secular and spiritualizes the social. Anthropologists record these rituals as cultural data, but poetry performs them as cultural destiny. The paradox: ritual poetry is simultaneously spontaneous and scripted, timeless yet timely, intensely individual yet wholly communal.

The Anthropology of Mythopoesis

Anthropology studies myths as cultural artifacts; poetry lives myths as creative acts. A myth is not merely a story but a symbolic system shaping social life. Poetry is the living laboratory of myth-making, mythopoesis in motion. The Greeks did not just believe in gods—they sang them. The Norse did not just theorize Yggdrasil—they told it in verse. Poetry does not only describe myth; it generates it. Thus, poetry is anthropology in action.

The Voice of the Margins

Anthropology prides itself on giving voice to the marginalized, the silenced, the subaltern. Yet poetry has long performed that role. The songs of enslaved peoples, the chants of colonized tribes, the laments of exiled communities—these are anthropology spoken before anthropology wrote. Poetry is the anthropology of the oppressed, articulating what statistics cannot and ethnographies dare not. The paradox: poetry is the weakest weapon, yet the strongest shield of the marginalized.

The Poetics of Kinship and Community

Anthropology devotes immense energy to studying kinship networks; poetry embodies them. A lullaby is kinship crystallized; a war song is kinship mobilized. Every family has its oral archive of sayings, every community its corpus of chants. These poetic forms transmit identity more powerfully than genealogical charts. The paradox: kinship is counted in bloodlines but felt in ballads.

Anthropology as Prose, Poetry as Presence

Anthropology often writes in analytic prose—dense, detailed, descriptive. Poetry, by contrast, is presence itself: immediate, embodied, ecstatic. An ethnography may tell us how the Aztecs saw death; a poem lets us feel how they faced it. An anthropological treatise may describe African cosmologies; a praise-song lets us live within them. Poetry is anthropology intensified, anthropology incarnate.

The Poetic Survival of Peoples

Empires fall, tribes disperse, cities collapse, but poetry persists. When the Mayan civilization crumbled, its glyphic poems preserved its vision. When colonizers silenced indigenous tongues, fragments of poems carried resistance. When diasporas were scattered, songs served as portable homelands. Poetry is anthropology's paradoxical permanence: it is fragile as paper yet durable as eternity, fleeting in form yet everlasting in function.

Anthropology and the Paradox of Translation

Anthropologists grapple with translating cultures; poets wrestle with translating feelings. Both discover the same paradox: translation is impossible, yet inevitable. No word perfectly captures a foreign worldview, yet words must be used. Here poetry is superior to prose: metaphor can leap where literalism limps. Thus, anthropology needs poetry not merely as subject but as method, as the imaginative bridge across cultural chasms.

Poetry and anthropology are not estranged but entwined. Anthropology anatomizes humanity; poetry animates humanity. Anthropology records the rituals of others; poetry performs the rituals of all. Anthropology writes reports; poetry writes realities. Anthropology may excavate the fossils of culture, but poetry exhumes the fire of culture. The oxymoron stands clear: poetry is the most "scientific art" and the most "artistic science." Together they proclaim that humanity is not only homo sapiens, the rational animal, but *Homo poeticus*, the singing animal.

POETRY AND HISTORY: THE CHRONICLE BEYOND CHRONOLOGY

Poetry is the Paradox of Time Told Twice. History is humanity inscribed in ink; poetry is humanity inscribed in pulse. One quantifies; the other qualifies. One preserves the skeleton of sequence; the other animates the soul of significance. And yet—both are paradoxical twins: history is poetry shackled to chronology, and poetry is history liberated from chronology.

The historian asks: What happened?

The poet replies: What happens eternally in the heart of the happening.

The historian measures; the poet magnifies. The historian collects; the poet consecrates. Thus, the relationship between history and poetry is not incidental but inevitable: every history is already poetic, and every poem is a history of the human spirit.

Poetry as the Primeval Historian

Before the scroll, there was the song. Before the archive, there was the anthem. Before annals, there were odes.

Homer's *Iliad* and *Odyssey* are not merely epics but encyclopedias of Greek memory.

The *Mahābhārata* is not just myth but the social, political, ethical history of ancient India.

The Icelandic *Eddas* preserve genealogies and battles with the precision of an archive, yet the passion of a psalm.

In the absence of parchment, poetry was the people's parchment. Memory was measured in metre; heritage was housed in hexameter. Thus, we see the oxymoron: the most fragile form, the spoken word, became the strongest fortress of history.

The Historian's Chronicle vs. The Poet's Chronicle

The historian writes dates, dynasties, documents. The poet writes destinies, desires, dreams. The historian notes battles and treaties. The poet records sorrow, silence, songs of the widow and the orphan. History is often accused of being the record of kings. Poetry is the record of the people. Together they form a paradox: history without poetry is soulless; poetry without history is rootless.

Poetry as Counter-History

Poetry resists the rigidity of historical narrative. When history silences, poetry speaks. When official records erase, the elegy remembers. When rulers boast of victory, the poet mourns the vanquished. When the archive glorifies conquest, the ballad whispers of suffering.

Thus, poetry is history's conscience: an oxymoronic official record of unofficial truths. Think of Wilfred Owen, whose war poems are truer than any general's dispatch. Think of Pablo Neruda, whose verses on Chile carry more weight than any statistical report. Think of Mahmoud Darwish, whose poetry is the history of Palestine written in metaphor.

Cyclical Time and Poetic Eternity

History moves in linear time – B.C. to A.D., year to year, century to century. Poetry moves in cyclical time –

refrain, rhyme, rhythm. Where history insists on "once," poetry insists on "again." Where history is a line, poetry is a circle. Where history progresses, poetry returns. This oxymoron reveals the truth: Poetry is history without its clock, and history is poetry without its chorus.

The Archive and the Anthem

History builds archives: stone tablets, parchment scrolls, dusty libraries. Poetry builds anthems: remembered melodies, communal recitations, memorized stanzas. An archive can decay; an anthem can endure. The Library of Alexandria was burned, but Homer survived in the mouths of singers. Documents perish in fire; poems survive in firelight. Thus, poetry is the immortal archive: the anthology of eternity, the library of living memory.

The Historian's Objectivity vs. The Poet's Subjectivity

Historians aspire to objectivity, yet every choice — of source, of voice, of emphasis — is already interpretation. Poets embrace subjectivity, yet often arrive at truths that outlive chronicles.

The historian tells us *Caesar was assassinated in 44 BCE.*

The poet tells us *Caesar's fall is the eternal fragility of power.*

Which is more enduring? Dates fade into footnotes; metaphors live forever. Thus, the paradox: poetry is subjective objectivity, while history is objective subjectivity.

National Epics as Historical DNA

Every culture carries its history encoded in epics: The ***Shāhnāmeh*** of Persia, by Ferdowsi, preserved Persian identity after conquest. Dante's ***Divine Comedy*** is as much a history of medieval Christendom as any chronicle. Shakespeare's history plays (Richard III, Henry IV, Henry V) shape English identity more than the historians Holinshed or Froissart. Here, the disciplines merge: poetry becomes history's bloodstream, ensuring survival of nations even when borders vanish.

Poetry as History of the Invisible

History notes empires; poetry notes emotions. History lists laws; poetry lists longings. History counts bodies; poetry counts breaths. Who records the tears of one mother when her son is slain in war? Not the historian, the poet. Who preserves the laughter of peasants in festivals? Not the historian, the poet. Thus, poetry is the anthropology of emotion, the sociology of silence, the psychology of passion — the history of the invisible.

Scientific Analogies: Poetry as Quantum History

Physics: History is Newtonian — cause and effect, chronology. Poetry is quantum — superpositions of meanings, simultaneity of times.

Mathematics: History is arithmetic — addition of events. Poetry is calculus — infinite moments compressed into finite form.

Biology: History is genetic — inherited information. Poetry is epigenetic — expression beyond code, experience shaping inheritance.

Thus, poetry transcends history by being its paradoxical physics: a universe where the particle of event becomes the wave of experience.

Case Studies: History Made Poetry

The French Revolution: History records the fall of Bastille; Wordsworth records the intoxication of liberty.

The American Civil War: History notes battles of Gettysburg; Whitman sings the suffering of soldiers.

The Partition of India: History counts migrants; Faiz Ahmad Faiz writes the agony of exile.

Which version endures? History informs; poetry transforms.

Poetry as Prophecy of History

Sometimes poetry precedes history, becoming its prophecy.

Shelley declared poets the "unacknowledged legislators of the world" — writing revolutions before they occur.

Yeats, with "a terrible beauty is born," foresaw Ireland's struggles.

Blake saw "Jerusalem builded here" long before industrial Britain questioned its soul.

Thus, poetry not only records history, but writes it in advance. The oxymoron: Poetry is history before history.

The Future of Historiopoetics

The 21st century, drowning in data, risks losing memory to mechanization. History is being digitized, quantified, abstracted. Poetry resists this with rhythm, with resonance, with remembrance. Perhaps the future discipline will be ***historiopoetics***: the study of history not as sterile sequence, but as living song. A science that knows **dates matter**, but **dreams matter more**.

The Double Helix of Memory

History and poetry are not enemies, but entwined strands of the same double helix of memory. One strand provides structure; the other provides spirit. One is skeleton; the other, skin. One is body; the other, breath. The historian counts centuries. The poet makes centuries count. Thus, the ultimate paradox: history dies if it is not poetic, and poetry dies if it is not historical. Poetry is history heightened into hymn; history is poetry flattened into prose. Together, they form the eternal chronicle of the human condition.

History and poetry are eternal siblings: one archives, the other animates; one chronicles, the other chants; one records events, the other redeems them. If history is the ledger of human deeds, poetry is the living echo of human dreams. Historians are guardians of fact, poets are guardians of feeling. Yet paradoxically, both pursue the same truth: to rescue humanity from oblivion, to preserve the fragile flame of memory against the cold wind of time.

Poetry as Prehistoric History

Before the written chronicle, there was the sung saga. Long before Herodotus inscribed his inquiries, the bards intoned their epics. *The Iliad* is not merely myth but memory—an oral archive of wars, wanderings, and woes. The Vedic hymns, the Sumerian laments, the bardic ballads of Celtic druids—these are history in embryonic form, truth wrapped in tune. Thus, paradox arises: history pretends to be fact without fiction, yet poetry is fiction that preserves fact.

The Paradox of Permanence and Fragility

History claims permanence: dates, dynasties, documents. Poetry seems fragile: rhythms, rhymes, refrains. Yet paradoxically, it is poetry that often survives longer than history. Nations forget their census numbers but remember their epics. Empires erase archives but cannot extinguish songs. A parchment crumbles; a proverb persists. An oxymoron emerges: poetry is the *"fragile eternity,"* history the *"eternal fragility."*

Poetry as the Pulse of Epochs

History measures centuries in calendars, but poetry feels them in cadences. The Renaissance is more than dates; it is Dante's *Divine Comedy*, Petrarch's sonnets, Shakespeare's soliloquies. The Romantic era is not merely the French Revolution; it is Wordsworth's wanderings, Byron's storms, Shelley's skylarks. Poetry embodies what history enumerates: the pulse, the pathos, the paradox of each epoch. Without poetry, history is a skeleton; with poetry, it has flesh, face, and feeling.

History as Prose, Poetry as Pathos

History often speaks in the flat language of fact: chronicles, treatises, tables. Poetry speaks in heightened language of pathos: cries, chants, choruses. A historical account may describe Napoleon's march into Moscow, but it is Tolstoy's prose-poetic imagery that makes us shiver with the frost of failure. A historian may record the Black Death, but Boccaccio's ***Decameron*** renders its dread with human resonance. Thus, paradox: history informs; poetry transforms.

The Oxymoron of Objectivity and Subjectivity

Historians aspire to objectivity, poets embrace subjectivity. Yet, paradoxically, the poet's subjectivity often conveys a deeper objectivity: the inner truth of what it felt like to live, suffer, and struggle. The historian records the number of dead at Waterloo; the poet records the anguish of the living who wept. Which is the greater truth? The oxymoron emerges: poetry is "subjective objectivity," history "objective subjectivity."

Poetry as the Memory of the Marginalized

History is written by victors; poetry is spoken by victims. Where archives erase, poetry engraves. Enslaved peoples, colonized tribes, oppressed classes—they may be absent in official chronicles, but they are alive in poems, chants, blues, and ballads. History silences; poetry sings. Thus, paradox: the powerless preserve the most powerful memories through verse, while the powerful lose themselves in dusty annals.

The Poetic Structure of History

Even history, though it claims prose, is secretly poetic. Consider how nations narrate themselves: "The Fall of Rome," "The Age of Enlightenment," "The Cold War." These are metaphors, not mere facts. Historians inevitably craft narratives—stories with beginnings, climaxes, and conclusions. This is poetry disguised as prose. The paradox: history pretends to expel poetry, yet history itself is poetic in structure.

Poetry and Historical Consciousness

Poetry does more than record events; it reflects upon them, questions them, reframes them. Where history asks, What happened?, poetry asks, What does it mean? The historian traces causality, the poet traces consequence in consciousness. Poetry is the soul of historical reflection—the recognition that history is not just the march of armies but the murmur of hearts.

The Futility and Fertility of Poetry in History

Skeptics may argue: can poetry stop wars, change policies, alter history? And yet paradox whispers: yes and no. No, poetry cannot halt armies. But yes, poetry can shape the spirit that shapes the world. Blake's prophetic poems fueled reform; Neruda's verses sustained revolution; Tagore's hymns inspired independence. Poetry does not directly alter history; it alters humanity, and humanity alters history. The oxymoron: poetry is "powerless power," "silent speech," "futile fertility."

The Eternal Archive

When all archives burn, poetry remains the eternal archive. History is carved in stone yet crumbles; poetry is sung in breath yet survives. Consider the exiled Hebrews: their psalms preserved their story when kingdoms were lost. Consider the enslaved Africans: their spirituals became survival songs. Consider the victims of wars whose nameless laments still echo in fragments. Thus, paradox: the most ephemeral form—verse—is the most eternal memory.

Poetry and history are not rivals but reflections. History guards the body of time; poetry guards its soul.

History teaches us what happened; poetry teaches us what it meant to happen. History preserves nations; poetry preserves humanity. Together they reveal the oxymoron of existence: the fleeting forever, the fragile eternity, the perishable permanence of human life. Without poetry, history is mute; without history, poetry is blind. Together, they form the full chronicle of the human condition—at once factual and fabulous, statistical and symbolic, prosaic and poetic.

POETRY AND EDUCATION: THE PEDAGOGY OF THE INEFFABLE

Teaching the unteachable is poetry. Education is the architecture of articulation; poetry is the architecture of the ineffable. Education seeks clarity; poetry thrives in ambiguity. Education transmits; poetry transfigures. Education is method; poetry is mystery. Yet paradoxically, it is poetry that gives education its pulse, its passion, its permanence. For what is education if not the attempt to move from ignorance to insight, from darkness to dawn? And what is poetry if not the dawn itself—the inexplicable illumination of the mind by the music of meaning? Thus, to speak of poetry and education is to speak of the two greatest paradoxical partners: one systematizes knowledge, the other sanctifies wonder. One teaches the "what," the other awakens the "why."

The Classroom as a Lyric Laboratory

In the sterile classroom of pure instruction, facts lie flat like fossils in a drawer. But when infused with poetry, the classroom becomes a lyric laboratory, where inert information is transmuted into luminous inspiration.

Geography becomes alive when described in metaphor: "Rivers are the restless veins of the earth."

History is remembered when sung in stanzas rather than stuffed in syllabi.

Science is savored when seen as "the sonnet of the stars" or "the hymn of hydrogen."

Thus, poetry is not an ornament to education but its oxygen: without poetry, education suffocates in sterility; with poetry, education breathes the breath of beauty.

The Paradox of Instruction and Inspiration

Education instructs; poetry inspires. Instruction is directive; inspiration is evasive. Instruction demands discipline; inspiration demands delight. And yet, true pedagogy requires both. An education without instruction is chaos; an education without inspiration is cruelty. Poetry supplies the paradoxical balance: it teaches without teaching, illuminates without instructing. Poetry is disciplined freedom, ordered spontaneity, systematic surprise.

Poetry as Memory's Mnemonic

Why do ancient cultures place poems at the center of education? Because poetry is the architecture of memory.

The Vedas of India were transmitted orally for millennia, preserved by the precision of metre.

Homer's hexameters were the mnemonic machines of Greece.

Medieval bards taught history and ethics by rhythm and rhyme.

Thus, poetry is the primordial pedagogy: it encodes knowledge in music, transforming burdensome memorization into melodious meditation.

Scientific Analogies: Poetry as Pedagogical Physics

Mathematics: Education is arithmetic, the addition of facts. Poetry is algebra, the abstraction of meaning.

Biology: Education is anatomy, the dissection of

knowledge. Poetry is physiology, the breath that animates knowledge into life.

Physics: Education is mechanics, cause and effect. Poetry is quantum entanglement, sudden leaps of insight, simultaneity of thought.

Chemistry: Education is the periodic table of disciplines. Poetry is the catalyst that causes otherwise inert elements to combine explosively into creativity.

Thus poetry is the hidden science of pedagogy: the invisible equation that turns facts into fascination.

The Teacher as Poet, the Poet as Teacher

The greatest teachers are poets, whether or not they write in verse. Socrates, teaching by dialogue, was a poet of paradox. Confucius, instructing by aphorism, was a poet of principles. Even Einstein, with his "God does not play dice," taught science in poetic riddles.

Likewise, the greatest poets are teachers:

Homer instructs on honor.

Dante instructs on destiny.

Shakespeare instructs on the depths of human character.

Tagore instructs on the infinite in the intimate.

Thus, the oxymoron emerges: every teacher is a poet in disguise, and every poet is a teacher unconfined.

Poetry as Democratic Pedagogy

Education risks becoming elitist, limited to those with access to institutions. Poetry, however, is universal. It requires no school but the soul, no tuition but attention, no degree but delight.

A child reciting a rhyme is already educated in rhythm. A worker humming a folk song is already learning history. A grandmother telling tales in poetic cadences is already teaching philosophy.

Thus, poetry is the most democratic education: the pedagogy that belongs to no one, yet to everyone.

Poetry vs. Pedagogy of Utilitarianism

Modern education often suffers the disease of utilitarianism: teaching only what is profitable, practical, marketable. But poetry resists such commodification. A poem cannot be "used" in a factory, nor "marketed" in a spreadsheet. And yet, paradoxically, poetry is the most useful because it is the most useless. It does not train the hand, but it trains the heart. It does not prepare for a job, but it prepares for life. It is an oxymoronic utility of the useless: the essential inessential.

Poetry as Pedagogy of Freedom

Education can become indoctrination: the stuffing of pre-approved facts into passive minds. Poetry rebels. Poetry teaches how to question, how to wonder, how to resist the tyranny of a single narrative. The tyrant fears poets more than professors because poets teach freedom beyond formulas. Shelley was correct: poets are unacknowledged legislators because they legislate liberty in the invisible realm of imagination. Thus, poetry is pedagogy of freedom: paradoxical discipline of disobedience, curriculum of creativity.

Emotional Intelligence and Poetic Pedagogy

Modern education excels in producing technical minds but often fails to form tender hearts. Poetry remedies this.

A verse of Keats teaches the beauty of fragility better than a psychology manual.

A sonnet of Shakespeare teaches jealousy more vividly than sociology.

A haiku teaches mindfulness more effectively than a lecture.

Thus, poetry is pedagogy of emotional intelligence: the science of sympathy, the algebra of affection.

Education as Prose, Poetry as Pedagogy of Possibility

Education is often prose: linear, explanatory, dry. Poetry interrupts with possibility: elliptical, ambiguous, ecstatic.

Prose says: "The tree grows."

Poetry says: "The tree whispers to the wind."

Which educates more deeply? Prose informs; poetry transforms. Prose transmits; poetry transfigures. Thus, the paradox: education teaches the world as it is; poetry teaches the world as it could be.

Case Studies: Poetry in Education Across Cultures

Ancient India: Students in *gurukulas* learned ethics, cosmology, and mathematics through poetic sutras.

Ancient Greece: Children learned Homer before they learned arithmetic.

China: The Confucian curriculum required memorization of poems as moral compass.

Medieval Europe: The trivium and quadrivium were infused with verse and chant.

Modern education, by separating poetry from "serious" subjects, has amputated its own heart. To restore poetry is to restore holistic pedagogy.

The Future of Poetic Education

In an age of AI, algorithms, and automation, rote learning will be rendered redundant. What machines cannot mimic is metaphor. What computers cannot compute is creativity. What algorithms cannot automate is ambiguity.

Thus, the education of the future will depend on poetry: the cultivation of creativity, ambiguity, emotional resonance. Poetry will not be a luxury but a necessity. The pedagogy of poetry is the pedagogy of posthuman survival.

The School of the Soul

Education without poetry is a skeleton without spirit, a classroom without color, a lecture without laughter. Poetry without education is a flame without focus, a passion without practice, a gift without guidance. Together they form the paradoxical pedagogy:

Education gives structure to poetry.

Poetry gives soul to education.

Education is the mind's method.

Poetry is the heart's hymn.

Thus, the ultimate lesson: poetry is not a subject within education; it is the substance of education. Education teaches us how to live in the world; poetry teaches us why the world is worth living in.

Education, in its etymological essence (*educare:* to lead forth), seeks to draw the human soul out of ignorance into illumination. Poetry, in its primal pulse, does precisely the same: it leads forth the mute into music, the blind into vision, the bound into flight. If education is the architecture of minds, poetry is the alchemy of souls. One drills doctrines, the other distills dreams; one teaches technique, the other touches transcendence. Yet paradoxically, both are educators—one of the intellect, the other of the imagination.

Poetry as the First Teacher

Before schools were built, poetry was sung. Before alphabets were invented, wisdom was woven in rhythm and rhyme. Proverbs, parables, psalms, and chants served as the primal pedagogy of humankind. Children learned not by charts but by chants, not by syllabi but by songs. The paradox here is striking: poetry, dismissed as frivolity, was humanity's first and fiercest form of formal education.

The Mnemonic Magic of Poetry

Education thrives on memory; poetry thrives by making memory musical. A multiplication table, set to verse, sticks; a scientific law, sung as rhyme, remains. Poetry is pedagogy's mnemonic miracle, transforming dull data into delightful design. Thus, paradox: the art most accused of ornamentation is the science most essential for retention.

The Oxymoron of Discipline and Freedom

Education often oscillates between discipline and freedom: the classroom as cage or the classroom as cosmos. Poetry embodies this oxymoron perfectly. A sonnet, bound by rigid rhyme and meter, paradoxically births boundless beauty. Haiku compresses thought into syllabic cages, yet unlocks cosmic vistas. Poetry demonstrates that discipline is not the death of freedom but its condition, that limitation is liberation in disguise.

Poetry as Ethical Education

Philosophers argue whether virtue can be taught; poets show that it can be sung. Poetry has always been pedagogy of the ethical imagination. The Psalms instruct humility, the Upanishads reveal selfhood, Confucian odes preach propriety, *Sufi ghazals* celebrate divine love. While education may lecture morality, poetry seduces the heart into virtue. The paradox: one cannot be forced into goodness, but one can be sung into it.

Poetry and the Aesthetic Curriculum

Education too often exalts the useful over the beautiful, the practical over the poetic. Yet true pedagogy must cultivate not only skills but sensibilities, not only intellect but imagination. Poetry is the aesthetic curriculum par excellence: it teaches taste, tenderness, tact, and transcendence. Without poetry, education produces efficient machines; with poetry, it cultivates luminous souls. Thus, paradox: the seemingly "impractical" is the most indispensable.

The Didactic Delight of Poetry

Didacticism is often scorned in art, yet poetry wields didacticism with delight. Fables in verse, moral maxims in rhyme, satirical couplets, prophetic odes—all have instructed humanity more lastingly than textbooks. A nursery rhyme teaches rhythm, a hymn teaches reverence, an epic teaches endurance. The oxymoron emerges: poetry is playful pedagogy, delightful discipline, instructive inspiration.

The Poetic Pedagogy of Empathy

Education without empathy is indoctrination; poetry without empathy is impossible. Reading a poem transports the self into another's soul: one feels as the lover, the exile, the warrior, the widow. Poetry is the pedagogy of empathy, enlarging the ethical imagination by inhabiting others' emotions. Thus, paradox: poetry teaches not by explanation but by experience, not by concepts but by compassion.

Poetry and Critical Thinking

Though often seen as emotional rather than rational, poetry also educates critical intelligence. Its metaphors demand interpretation, its ambiguities invite analysis, its symbols provoke speculation. Poetry resists passive consumption; it demands active decoding. In this sense, poetry is philosophy's partner in pedagogy, sharpening thought by sharpening language. The paradox: poetry is "irrational reason," "logical illogic," simultaneously subjective sensation and objective interrogation.

Poetry as the Education of Wonder

The ultimate purpose of education is not information but inspiration, not mere mastery but mystery. Poetry educates us into wonder—the astonishment of existence, the strangeness of the familiar, the beauty of the ordinary. Education may explain the star; poetry teaches us to marvel at its light. Education may dissect the flower; poetry makes us adore its fragrance. The oxymoron shines: true knowledge is knowing that knowledge is not enough.

The Eternal Lesson

When curricula change, when textbooks fade, when methods evolve, poetry remains the eternal lesson. Homer still instructs heroism, Shakespeare still teaches tragedy, Tagore still tutors the soul in freedom, Neruda still lectures on love. Unlike syllabi, poetry does not expire; unlike systems, it does not collapse. It survives because it teaches not just facts but the fact of feeling, not just truths but truthfulness. Poetry and education are not enemies but eternal allies. Education is the architecture of learning; poetry is its animating flame. Education informs; poetry transforms. Education builds knowledge; poetry builds wisdom. Education tells us how to live; poetry teaches us why to live. The paradox is undeniable: poetry is the most profound pedagogue precisely because it is not pedagogy, the most serious teacher precisely because it sings. It is the lullaby of beginnings, the anthem of awakenings, the hymn of higher humanity.

POETRY AND GEOGRAPHY: THE CARTOGRAPHY OF THE IMAGINATION

Geography, in its sober sense, is the study of space; poetry, in its soaring sense, is the shaping of spirit. One charts continents, the other charts consciousness; one measures mountains, the other measures metaphors. Yet paradoxically, both are cartographers: one of land, the other of longing; one of earth's terrain, the other of the soul's terrain. Poetry is the geography of inward immensities, the mapping of mystery by rhythm and rhyme.

Poetry as the First Map of the World

Long before compasses and cartographers, poets were the primal mapmakers. *The Odyssey* is a geography of seas and sorrows, a topography of trials as well as territories. The Rigvedic hymns describe rivers and skies, blending cosmography with cosmology. The Norse sagas chart northern lands, while African praise songs record deserts, savannas, and sacred spaces. Thus paradox: the earliest "atlases" were allegories in verse, proving that poetry was the first geography.

The Paradox of Place and Placelessness

Geography insists on place; poetry thrives in placelessness. Yet poetry is also born from place—mountain and meadow, desert and delta, city and sea. Wordsworth's

Lake District, Bashō's Edo road, Whitman's America, Tagore's Bengal: landscapes incarnate themselves in lyric. And yet, paradoxically, poetry transcends its birthplace, making the local universal, the provincial planetary. The oxymoron emerges: poetry is both rooted wandering and wandering rootedness.

The Mnemonic Landscape of Poetry

Geography teaches the student to locate mountains, rivers, and nations. Poetry transforms those names into mnemonic landscapes. Byron makes the Alps unforgettable, Keats eternalizes Grecian urns, Shelley sacralizes the West Wind. Thus, paradox: geography may tell us where a mountain is, but poetry tells us what a mountain means.

Poetry and the Poetics of Climate

Climate, a key concern of geography, finds its lyrical mirror in poetry. The desert inspires solemn austerity, the tropics riotous exuberance, the tundra quiet contemplation. Poets capture climates not merely as meteorology but as moods. Rain is not rainfall but melancholy music; snow is not frozen water but silent whiteness; wind is not air in motion but an invisible orchestra. Poetry becomes the atmospheric anthropology of the earth.

The Oxymoron of Borders and Boundlessness

Geography draws borders: nations, states, provinces. Poetry erases them: language leaps over limits, songs soar across frontiers. Yet paradoxically, poetry also defines identity rooted in land, people, and place. Neruda sings of Chile as passionately as Yeats of Ireland. Thus, poetry is borderless belonging: at once deeply national and utterly universal, simultaneously local song and global hymn.

Poetry as Geopoetics of Memory

Every geography is also a history; every landscape layered with memory. Poetry makes this palpable. Cities are not mere coordinates but chronicles: Eliot's London, Baudelaire's Paris, Neruda's Santiago. Mountains become metaphors of endurance, rivers metaphors of passage. Through poetry, geography ceases to be inert space; it becomes living place, pulsing with presence and remembrance.

The Paradox of Distance and Intimacy

Geography teaches distance: miles, maps, measurements. Poetry transforms distance into intimacy. A faraway star becomes a lover's eye; a distant land becomes a dream's dwelling. Conversely, poetry can render the intimate distant—making the familiar strange, the homely uncanny. The paradox here: geography educates separation, poetry educates connection, yet both are necessary to orient the human soul.

Poetry and the Pedagogy of Place

Education in geography often seems mechanical: capitals, currencies, climates. Poetry re-enchants place, teaching us to feel the earth rather than merely to measure it. Geography explains the Himalayas as a geological formation; poetry reveals them as a mystical stairway to heaven. Geography describes the Nile as a river system; poetry celebrates it as a giver of gods, civilizations, and songs. Thus, paradox: the most poetic geography is the truest geography.

Geography as Silent Poetry

Even geography, in its deepest description, is already poetic. The curvature of coasts, the meandering of rivers, the symmetry of mountains, the spiral of storms—all are nature's own poems, written in the language of landscapes. To read geography is to read the earth's epic; to write poetry is to echo the earth's own eloquence. Hence the paradox: geography is poetry unspoken; poetry is geography sung.

The Geopolitics of Poetry

Poetry also interacts with geography in geopolitics. Wars, migrations, diasporas—all reshape maps, and poets respond. Exile poetry, border ballads, refugee laments: these turn geopolitical tragedy into lyrical testimony. In them we hear not only the shifting of boundaries but the suffering of bodies. Geography is the politics of space; poetry is the pathos of displacement.

The Eternal Geography of the Soul

Beyond rivers and ranges lies another geography: the inner map of human longing. Poetry charts this invisible cartography—peaks of passion, valleys of despair, deserts of loneliness, oceans of ecstasy. Just as geography seeks to map earth's terrains, poetry seeks to map soul's immensities. The paradox: the smallest lyric can encompass the largest universe, and a single stanza can contain infinite landscapes.

The Paradox of the Map and the Metaphor

Geography seeks to measure mountains, to chart coastlines, to classify climates. Poetry seeks to magnify mystery, to chart consciousness, to classify wonder. One inscribes the earth in lines and latitudes; the other inscribes the soul in stanzas and symphonies. And yet—paradox of paradoxes—they are secretly sisters: the cartographer and the poet are both mappers of meaning. For every map is already a metaphor: a symbol, a scale, a simplification that selects and silences. And every poem is already a geography: a terrain of words, a landscape of rhythm, a topography of thought. Thus geography is the prose of place, and poetry its paradoxical poetry.

Mountains and Metaphors: The Vertical Imagination

Mountains are geography's monuments. They rise, resist, reveal. To the geographer, they are folded strata, tectonic thrusts, altitudinal zonations. To the poet, they are metaphors of majesty, metaphysical ladders, frozen hymns.

The Himalaya: to science, the consequence of colliding plates; to Tagore, the eternal altar of solitude.

Olympus: to geology, igneous rock uplifted; to Homer, the home of gods.

Kilimanjaro: to cartography, a coordinate; to Hemingway, a cryptic snow-clad symbol of death.

Thus, the paradox: mountains are both matter and metaphor, both measurable and mystical. Geography tells us their height; poetry tells us why they lift the heart.

Rivers: The Restless Veins of Earth

Rivers are geography's restless veins, flowing from source to sea, sculpting valleys, sustaining civilizations. To hydrology, they are discharge and drainage; to poetry, they are destiny and dream.

The Ganges: sacred syllable of India.

The Nile: nourishing nostalgia of Egypt.

The Mississippi: meandering memory of America.

The Danube: Europe's liquid line of unity and division.

Geography plots their course; poetry hears their chorus. Geography charts their basin; poetry baptizes them as mothers of memory. The oxymoron: rivers are eternal movement, permanent impermanence, flowing fixity.

Deserts: The Geography of Silence

To geography, deserts are arid zones, low precipitation, fragile ecosystems. To poetry, deserts are metaphors of emptiness and eternity, wastelands and wonderlands.

The Sahara: sea of sand, silence's scripture.

The Gobi: geography's void, poetry's vision.

Eliot's *The Waste Land*: desert of modernity's despair.

Here paradox reigns supreme: deserts are full in

their emptiness, silent in their loudness, dead yet alive. Geography quantifies their climate; poetry qualifies their mystery.

Islands: The Paradox of Isolation and Imagination

Islands are geography's experiments: pieces of land cut off, evolving uniquely. To biology, they are laboratories of evolution. To poetry, they are symbols of solitude and sanctuary.

Shakespeare's Tempest unfolds upon an island of illusion.

Robinson Crusoe's survival story is geography turned into allegory.

The Pacific islands: to cartographers, archipelagos; to poets, paradises.

Thus, islands embody oxymoron: isolated infinities, detached yet dependent, exiled yet exalted.

Climate and Cadence: The Weather of Words

Climate is geography's grand chorus: monsoons, trade winds, jet streams, cyclones. To geography, it is data, deviation, distribution. To poetry, it is destiny, delight, dread.

The monsoon: meteorology measures rainfall; Tagore celebrates its romance.

Winter: climatology notes temperature drop; Frost hears its "desert places."

Summer: geography quantifies insolation; poets quantify yearning.

Poetry hears the weather not as statistics but as symphonics. Geography tabulates; poetry translates.

Cities as Poetic Topographies

Urban geography studies settlements, infrastructures, spatial distributions. But poets wander cities as labyrinths of longing.

Dickens' London: smoke, sweat, sorrow.

Baudelaire's Paris: spleen and ideal.

Whitman's Manhattan: multitudinous, electric, democratic.

Thus, every city is both a spatial system and a symbolic system. Streets are syllables; squares are stanzas; skylines are symphonies.

Borders: The Paradox of Division and Definition

Geography draws borders; poetry dissolves them. The mapmaker marks boundaries with brutal lines; the poet smudges them with sighs.

Borders are oxymorons: they divide yet define, they limit yet liberate, they exclude yet include.

The cartographer declares: "This land is mine, that is yours."

The poet whispers: "This sky is ours, that wind is everyone's."

Thus, geography builds fences; poetry builds freedoms.

The Poetics of Place

Every place is more than its coordinates. A mountain village is not merely altitude, latitude, longitude, but a lived lyric of labor, laughter, loss. Geography studies place as spatial unit; poetry reveals place as spiritual unity. Yi-Fu Tuan spoke of ***topophilia,*** the love of place. Poetry is the articulation of topophilia: to name, to narrate, to nuance. Thus, poetry is geography of affection; geography is poetry of attention.

The Earth as a Living Poem

Science calls Earth the third planet of the solar system, a spheroid of iron core and silicate crust. Poetry calls Earth Gaia, mother, muse, mystery.

The oxymoron: Earth is fragile fortress, finite infinity, wounded wholeness.

Geography measures distances between continents; poetry measures distances between hearts. Geography sees tectonic drift; poetry hears tectonic desire. Thus, to read Earth is to read a poem written in rocks, rivers, roots, and rhythms.

Scientific Parallels: Poetry as Cartographic Calculus

Mathematics: Geography plots points; poetry plots passions.

Physics: Geography measures gravity; poetry measures gravitas.

Biology: Geography traces ecosystems; poetry traces emotional systems.

Chemistry: Geography studies soil profiles; poetry studies soul profiles.

Both disciplines chart, classify, connect. One external; the other internal.

Case Studies across Cultures

Indigenous cartographies: maps as stories, songs as navigation. The Australian ***songlines*** are literal lyrical geographies. Ancient Greek geography: Eratosthenes measured Earth; Homer sang of its seas. Medieval mappae mundi: maps infused with myths, dragons, angels—geography as poetry. Thus, history shows: whenever geography is at its richest, it is infused with poetry.

The Future: Poetic Geography in the Age of Satellites

Today satellites scan every square inch, GIS digitizes data, drones document deserts. Geography has become surveillance. Yet poetry resists reduction: a satellite can see a forest, but cannot hear its silence. A GIS can measure migration, but cannot map nostalgia. Thus, the future demands a new synthesis: a poetic geography that balances data with dignity, cartography with compassion, mapping with meaning.

Poetry as the Soul of Geography

Geography without poetry is a map without meaning, a chart without charm, a compass without north. Poetry without geography is a dream without direction, a song without setting, a lyric without landscape.

Together they form the paradoxical cartography:

Geography gives ground to poetry. Poetry gives grace to geography. Geography charts the external world. Poetry charts the internal world. Thus, the ultimate equation: Poetry is geography of the soul; Geography is poetry of the soil.

Poetry and geography are not distant disciplines but dialogical dimensions. Geography teaches us where we are; poetry teaches us why it matters. Geography provides coordinates; poetry provides meaning. Geography maps the earth's surface; poetry maps the soul's depths. Together, they reveal the paradoxical unity of space and spirit, place and placelessness, rootedness and roaming. To study geography without poetry is to see the world without wonder; to read poetry without geography is to dream without grounding. But together, they make us both citizens of soil and voyagers of the infinite.

POETRY AND PSYCHOLOGY: THE LABYRINTH OF THE MIND

Poetry and Psychology are deeply connected to each other because poetry is the mirror of mind and the music of the unconscious. Psychology, in its strictest sense, is the science of the psyche, the study of the soul's shadows and the mind's mechanisms. Poetry, in its loftiest sense, is the song of the psyche, the shaping of shadows into light and language. One diagnoses, the other dramatizes; one categorizes cognition, the other crystallizes consciousness. Yet paradoxically, both are mirrors—psychology reflecting the mind in analysis, poetry reflecting it in art. Psychology dissects thought; poetry dances with it.

Poetry as the First Psychology

Long before laboratories and lexicons of mental illness, poetry was humanity's psychology. The Psalms reveal despair and hope; Sophocles gives voice to trauma; Shakespeare stages jealousy, madness, ambition, and grief; Emily Dickinson whispers of depression and divine dread. Poets diagnosed before psychologists, dramatizing the disorders of desire in verse rather than in vocabularies of neurosis. Thus, paradox: what modern science calls "therapy," ancient poetry already practiced as catharsis.

The Paradox of Consciousness and Unconsciousness

Psychology peers into the unconscious through dream analysis, free association, and hidden impulses.

Poetry does the same—rendering subconscious symbols in metaphor and myth. A poem, like a dream, is both nonsensical and necessary, incoherent yet illuminating. Freud called dreams the "royal road to the unconscious"; poetry may be its lyrical highway. Paradox arises: poetry is the conscious crafting of unconscious currents, the lucid shaping of elusive shadows.

Poetry and the Oxymoron of Madness and Sanity

Psychology defines madness; poetry dignifies it. The "mad poet" is a paradoxical archetype: at once unhinged and enlightened, delirious yet divine. Blake's visions, Hölderlin's hymns, Plath's confessions—these reveal that madness in poetry is not mere disorder but another form of order. The oxymoron glows: poetry is sanity singing through insanity, reason radiating through irrationality.

Catharsis as Poetic Psychology

Psychology provides therapies—cognitive, behavioral, analytical. Poetry provides catharsis: the purgation of passions through performance. To write a poem of grief is already to heal; to read a poem of sorrow is already to share. Aristotle knew that tragedy cleanses; modern psychology calls it emotional release. The paradox: poetry is therapy that is not therapy, cure that disguises itself as art.

The Mnemonics of Memory and Trauma

Psychology studies memory, repression, trauma. Poetry incarnates them. Traumatic memory, fragmentary and fiery, often resists prose but yields to poetry. Survivors of wars, exiles, and tragedies turn instinctively to verse: its broken lines mirror broken psyches; its rhythms echo repetitive recollection. Thus paradox: poetry can articulate the inexpressible, remembering what cannot be remembered, speaking what resists speech.

Poetry and Archetypes

Carl Jung's psychology introduced archetypes: collective symbols of the unconscious—hero, shadow, anima, trickster. Poets, millennia earlier, had already birthed them in myth and metaphor. Poetry is the archetypal art, transforming collective unconscious into collective utterance. An epic is not just story but psychic structure, mirroring humanity's inner architecture. Paradox: poetry is both personal confession and universal myth, singular voice and archetypal chorus.

Poetry as the Play of Personality

Psychology analyzes personality: introvert and extrovert, thinker and feeler. Poetry expresses personality through voice, tone, diction. A minimalist haiku reveals restraint; a sprawling epic reveals expansiveness. Yet poetry is not bound to personality—it can ventriloquize another's voice, inhabit another's psyche. Thus paradox: poetry reveals the self by disguising it, unmasks by masking, declares "I" while dissolving identity.

The Oxymoron of Emotion and Intellect

Psychology often separates cognition from affect, thought from feeling. Poetry unites them. It is at once emotional intelligence and intellectual emotion. A sonnet is logical structure filled with lyrical passion; a lament is raw sorrow shaped by rhetorical precision. Poetry proves that thought can feel and feeling can think. The oxymoron shines: rational rapture, logical lyricism, intellectual intoxication.

Poetry and Dream-work

Psychology treats dreams as coded messages. Poetry treats them as material. Surrealist poets wrote dreamscapes; Romantic poets wrote waking visions; Symbolists wrote subconscious scripts. Dreams are poetry without meter; poetry is dreaming with deliberate rhythm. Paradox: poetry awakens the dream, while dreams dream the poem.

The Poetic Pedagogy of Empathy

Psychology's therapeutic goal is often empathy—making one feel understood. Poetry does this naturally. Reading a poem of loss, one suddenly finds one's own grief voiced; reading a love lyric, one feels one's own desire sanctified. Poetry is communal psychology: it heals by showing the sufferer that suffering is shared. Thus paradox: poetry is private utterance that becomes universal empathy.

Poetry as Self-Analysis

Psychology provides tools for self-reflection; poetry provides mirrors for self-revelation. A poet writing a confession performs analysis—of desires, failures, fears. Yet unlike psychology, poetry renders self-analysis beautiful, transforming neurosis into narrative. The paradox: in poetry, even pathology becomes aesthetic, even anguish becomes art.

The Unconscious as Poet

Perhaps the deepest paradox: it is not the poet who writes poetry, but poetry that writes the poet. Jung might say the archetypes write through us; Freud might say the unconscious erupts into form. Many poets attest: words arrive unbidden, lines dictate themselves. Thus, poetry is the psyche speaking to itself, the unconscious becoming conscious in cadence.

The Double Mirror of Mind and Metaphor

Psychology strives to study the psyche through experiments, statistics, and theories; poetry strives to sing the psyche through stanzas, symbols, and sonorities. One measures the mind; the other mirrors it. One dissects dreams; the other dwells within them. And yet—paradox profound—psychology and poetry are both seekers of the same elusive essence: the ungraspable ground of human consciousness. The oxymoron shines: the psyche is both visible and invisible, rational and irrational, measured and immeasurable. Psychology is its science, poetry its symphony.

Dreams: The Nocturnal Narratives of the Psyche

Freud framed dreams as wish-fulfillments; Jung refigured them as archetypal whispers of the collective unconscious. But poets have long been dream's natural cartographers.

Coleridge's Kubla Khan was born from an opium-induced vision.

Blake saw angels in trees, devils in reason, eternity in a grain of sand.

Neruda dreamt in metaphors as natural as breathing.

Psychology interprets dreams; poetry incarnates them. Psychology seeks meaning behind dreams; poetry makes meaning through them. Thus, the paradox: dreams are illusions more real than reality, lies that reveal truth, unconscious whispers that awaken consciousness.

Memory: The Archive of Absence

Psychology treats memory as encoding, storage, retrieval. Poetry treats memory as miracle, melancholy, muse.

Proust tasted a madeleine, and the whole cathedral of childhood rose again.

Eliot's Prufrock measures life in coffee spoons, memories in fragments.

In every elegy, memory is metamorphosed into music.

Memory is a presence of absence, a permanence of impermanence, a past that persists in the present.

Psychology charts synaptic patterns; poetry chants nostalgic patterns. Both are custodians of what is gone yet given.

Emotions: The Electric Ephemera

Psychology quantifies emotions in neurotransmitters: dopamine, serotonin, oxytocin. Poetry qualifies emotions in metaphors: desire as fire, grief as ocean, joy as flight.

Anger: to psychology, amygdala activation; to poetry, "the wrath of Achilles."

Love: to biology, oxytocin bonding; to poetry, the madness that drives sonnets, tragedies, and epics.

Fear: to neuroscience, fight-or-flight response; to poetry, the shadow that shapes gothic imagination.

Thus, emotion is paradox: chemical yet cosmic, fleeting yet eternal, physiological yet phenomenal.

Archetypes and Myths: The Collective Poem of Humanity

Jung's archetypes are poetry disguised as psychology. The hero, the shadow, the anima, the wise old man—these are stanzas of the soul's epic.

Poetry has always housed archetypes:

Odysseus as archetypal wanderer.

Orpheus as archetypal poet.

Antigone as archetypal rebel.

Psychology classifies; poetry dramatizes. Psychology explains; poetry enacts. Archetypes are eternal poems disguised as psychic patterns.

Madness: The Paradox of Poetic Sanity

Psychology often treats madness as pathology; poetry often treats madness as prophecy.

Hamlet's "antic disposition" is both feigned and fatal.

Hölderlin descended into madness but left celestial verses.

Sylvia Plath's anguish bled into blazing metaphor.

Madness is lucid delirium, sane insanity, a breakdown that breaks open. Psychology medicates madness; poetry magnifies it. Psychology seeks to cure; poetry dares to endure.

Language and the Unconscious: The Freudian Figure

Freud said slips of the tongue reveal the unconscious. Poets say language itself is the unconscious speaking

Metaphor is condensation: two meanings fused.

Metonymy is displacement: one meaning substituted for another.

Thus, poetic language is psychoanalysis in action: every metaphor is a miniature dream, every line a latent desire.

The Mirror of Self and Other

Psychology speaks of self-concept, ego, identity. Poetry speaks of "I," that most paradoxical pronoun. Whitman's "I contain multitudes" is psychology's multiplicity of selves. Dickinson's "I'm nobody, who are you?" is psychology's riddle of recognition. Rimbaud's "I is another" is psychoanalysis before psychoanalysis. Thus, the self is oxymoron: unique yet universal, singular yet plural, permanent yet provisional. Poetry dramatizes the self; psychology dissects it.

Neuroscience and the Poetic Brain

Neuroscience now scans brains in MRI machines, showing which lobes light up when reading metaphors. But what machine can measure mystery? A scan may show the brain's activity during a sonnet, but it cannot show the soul's awe. Neurons fire, but metaphors fly. The paradox: poetry is a chemical event that transcends chemistry, a neurological reaction that transcends neurons.

Catharsis: Poetry as Psychological Therapy

Aristotle described tragedy as catharsis: purgation of pity and fear. Modern psychology calls it emotional release, cognitive reframing, therapeutic expression. Poetry heals by naming what cannot be spoken otherwise:

The war poem releases trauma.

The elegy releases grief.

The love poem releases longing.

Thus, poetry is psychology's unacknowledged therapist, practicing healing long before the clinic.

Scientific Analogies: The Math of Metaphor

Psychology as Equation: stimulus → response.

Poetry as Equation: symbol → resonance.

Psychology as Experiment: controlled variables.

Poetry as Experience: uncontrollable variables.

Yet both seek to understand the same system: the psyche, the most complex cosmos.

The Shadows and Prospects

Psychology risks reduction: the soul shrunk into surveys. Poetry risks obscurity: the psyche shrouded in symbols. But together, they balance: one clarifies, the other mystifies; one dissects, the other dances. Future therapies already use poetry: bibliotherapy, narrative therapy, expressive writing. Perhaps tomorrow's psychology will recognize poetry as its twin discipline.

Poetry as Psychology beyond Psychology

Poetry is psychology that sings; psychology is poetry that dissects. Both are attempts to touch the untouchable, to name the nameless, to map the unmappable.

Thus:

Psychology is the prose of the psyche.

Poetry is the paradox of the psyche.

Psychology analyzes dreams; poetry dreams analysis.

Psychology observes; poetry orbits.

Psychology without poetry is soulless science; Poetry without psychology is blind beauty. Together they form the double mirror of mind and metaphor.

Psychology and poetry are twin sciences of the

soul: one clinical, one lyrical; one analytical, one aesthetic. Psychology dissects suffering; poetry dignifies it. Psychology explains dreams; poetry enacts them. Psychology heals by comprehension; poetry heals by communion. Together they reveal the paradox of human being: that the mind is at once mechanism and mystery, that the soul is at once science and song. To study psychology without poetry is to know the mind without its music; to read poetry without psychology is to feel the music without recognizing its mechanism. But when twinned, they teach us that to be human is to be paradoxical: rationally irrational, sanely insane, consciously unconscious—and beautifully so.

POETRY AND GEOLOGY: THE METAPHYSICS OF STONES AND STRATA

While linking poetry with geology we see the stratigraphy of the soul. Geology, at its austere essence, is the science of stone, the study of strata, the chronicle of earth's hidden history. Poetry, at its radiant resonance, is the song of spirit, the layering of language, the excavation of emotional epochs. One drills into bedrock; the other descends into the bedrock of being. One interprets fossils; the other preserves feelings. Paradoxically, both are archaeologies—geology of the planet, poetry of the psyche; geology of matter, poetry of meaning.

The Poem as Geological Formation

Every poem is a stratigraphy of consciousness. The first line is a surface layer, the visible sediment; the deeper one digs, the older and more primal the meanings. An epic is a mountain range of metaphors; a haiku is a pebble polished by time. Just as geologists read time in rocks, readers read eternity in verse. Paradox: poetry is ephemeral expression that behaves like enduring granite; geology is enduring granite that whispers ephemeral tales.

The Oxymoron of Stillness and Motion

Geology appears static: mountains immovable, stones silent. Yet it is profoundly dynamic—continents drift, volcanoes erupt, strata shift. Poetry mirrors this oxymoron. On the page, it appears still—mere ink, frozen form. Yet when read, it erupts into rhythm, flows like lava, quakes like tectonic plates. Thus, paradox: both geology and poetry embody "still movement," "silent speech," the oxymoron of motion in repose.

Erosion and Expression

Rivers carve valleys over centuries; winds wear down cliffs over millennia. This erosion is nature's writing. Similarly, poetry is the erosion of silence: words wear away the unspoken, carving channels of meaning in the bedrock of muteness. Just as geology reveals form through wearing away, poetry reveals truth through the subtraction of silence. The paradox: loss becomes revelation, erosion becomes inscription.

Fossils and Memory

A fossil is the petrified memory of life, preserved in stone. A poem is the fossilized memory of emotion, preserved in language. Both are paradoxes of permanence: fleeting beings fixed forever, fragile moments hardened into endurance. Geologists reconstruct species from fossils; readers reconstruct souls from stanzas. Thus, paradox: death becomes life, absence becomes presence, the vanished becomes visible.

Volcanoes and Catharsis

Geology studies volcanic eruption—earth's inner fire breaking surface. Poetry, too, erupts when inner fire finds form. Suppressed sorrow, unspoken love, silent rage—these are subterranean pressures that poetry releases. As volcanoes fertilize soil with ash, so poems fertilize culture with catharsis. Paradox: destruction becomes creation, eruption becomes expression, wound becomes wonder.

Mountains as Metaphor

Mountains, those monumental metaphors, are geology's cathedrals. They symbolize endurance, sublimity, aspiration. Poets too raise mountains of meaning: Dante's mountain of Purgatory, Wordsworth's Lake District peaks, Shelley's Mont Blanc. Geology measures their minerals; poetry marvels at their majesty. The paradox: science sees composition, poetry sees consecration. One weighs, the other worships—yet both climb.

Earthquakes and Poetic Shocks

An earthquake is a sudden rupture, a trembling of tectonic truths. Poetry performs similar shocks: a line breaks expectation, a metaphor shakes certainty, a rhythm destabilizes logic. Just as an earthquake reveals hidden faults, poetry reveals hidden fractures in the human condition. Thus paradox: destabilization deepens understanding, fracture fashions form.

Strata and Stanzas

A stanza is literally a "room" in Italian; strata are rooms of earth. Both preserve order, both accumulate layers. A stanza stores syllables as strata store sediments. Reading a poem is like digging down layer by layer—each metaphor another epoch, each rhyme another relic. The oxymoron arises: poetry is the geology of language, geology the poetry of matter.

Gemstones and Metaphors

Geology gifts us gems: diamond, sapphire, emerald. Poetry, too, polishes language into luminous jewels. Both require pressure: diamonds form from compressed carbon; metaphors from compressed meanings. A diamond refracts light; a poem refracts truth. The paradox: beauty is born of burden, brilliance of compression.

Geological Time and Poetic Eternity

Geology measures time in epochs, eons, ages. Poetry measures eternity in moments. Yet paradoxically, both collapse time: a fossil preserves a million-year memory; a sonnet preserves a heartbeat across centuries. To read Homer is to hear a voice thousands of years old; to read earth is to hear a silence millions of years deep. The oxymoron: ephemeral eternity, temporal timelessness.

The Sublimity of Depth

Geology teaches humility: beneath us lies an abyss of time, a record written long before humanity. Poetry teaches the same: behind each word lies infinite depth, meaning layered beyond comprehension. Both geology and poetry invite reverence for what exceeds us, awe at what precedes us. The paradox: we are surface creatures yearning for depth, finite beings craving infinite ground.

The Paradox of Stone and Song

Geology is the science of solidity; poetry is the art of fluidity. Geology measures mountains in millions of years; poetry measures moments in milliseconds. Geology listens to strata; poetry listens to stanzas. Yet paradoxically, they are siblings. For the earth itself is a poet: volcanoes as verses, rivers as refrains, tectonic shifts as tragedies, fossils as forgotten footnotes in the epic of evolution. Geology studies the literal; poetry hears the lyrical. But the literal and lyrical are layered like sediment: inseparable, interpenetrating, indivisible.

The Language of Layers

Every stratum is a stanza, every fault-line a figure, every fossil a forgotten metaphor.

The Devonian is a drumbeat.

The Jurassic is a jubilant chorus.

The Pleistocene is a pale elegy.

Geology translates stone into chronology; poetry translates stone into cosmology. The one calculates, the other contemplates. But both see in layers: one temporal, the other symbolic. The rock is rigid yet recursive, silent yet speaking, inert yet inspirited.

Mountains as Metaphors

Mountains rise from tectonic pressure, folded strata, molten magma cooled into permanence. But poets see in them symbols of ascent and aspiration.

Wordsworth saw the sublime in the Alps.

Bashō saw eternity in a single peak.

Shelley likened Mont Blanc to the mind itself—frozen, fierce, infinite.

Psychology may call mountains obstacles; geology calls them orogeny; poetry calls them oracles. A paradox: mountains are motionless monuments of movement.

Rivers and Erosion: The Elegy of Flow

Geology teaches that rivers sculpt valleys through erosion; poetry teaches that rivers sculpt souls through metaphor.

Heraclitus said: *you cannot step into the same river twice.*

Whitman said: *the river is meandering memory.*

Tagore sang: *the river is the restless search for the sea.*

Geology records erosion as loss; poetry records it as longing. Paradox: rivers are both destroyers and deliverers, both erasers and engravers.

Fossils: The Poetry of Preservation

Fossils are petrified poems. They are echoes of lives long extinguished, bones turned into stone, whispers written in mineral ink. Paleontology reads them as data. Poetry reads them as elegy. Fossils are dead immortals, silent testimonies that still speak. They are corpses more alive than the living, the epitaphs of entire eras.

Volcanoes: The Verses of Violence

Volcanoes are geology's paradox: destructive creation, creative destruction.

Lava annihilates yet fertilizes.

Ash buries yet enriches.

Eruption ends yet begins.

Poetry too erupts: passion as lava, grief as smoke, language as magma. Volcanoes are geology's odes to chaos, poetry's hymns to hidden fire.

Earthquakes: The Tremors of Truth

Geology defines earthquakes as sudden releases of tectonic stress. Poetry defines them as sudden revelations of hidden tension.

In politics, revolutions are earthquakes.

In psychology, traumas are earthquakes.

In love, betrayals are earthquakes.

Thus:

Earthquakes are oxymorons—momentary eternities, silent thunder, frozen fire.

Minerals and Crystals: The Geometry of Beauty

Geology describes crystals in terms of lattice structures. Poetry describes crystals in terms of clarity and brilliance.

Diamond: *hardest yet most delicate in value.*

Quartz: *common yet cosmic in symbolism.*

Salt: *humble yet holy.*

Geology studies their composition; poetry studies their connotation. Crystals are metaphors in mineral form, geometry made visible, equations embodied in earth.

Deep Time: The Paradox of Patience

Geology's true poetry is deep time. To speak in

billions of years is already to speak in metaphors, for the human mind cannot comprehend such immensity. Poetry translates this into paradox:

A second is eternity.

Eternity is a second.

Geology teaches humility: our civilizations are the thickness of dust compared to eons. Poetry transforms humility into hymn.

Stone as Symbol

Stone as strength (monuments).

Stone as suffering (Sisyphus).

Stone as silence (gravestones).

Stone as sanctity (temples).

Geology studies stone as matter; poetry studies stone as metaphor. Both reveal that stone is paradox incarnate: lifeless yet living, mute yet meaningful.

Human History Written in Rock

Geology and poetry converge in archaeology. Every ruin is both rock and record, both sediment and story.

The Rosetta Stone: *geology's artifact, poetry's translation.*

Petra: *carved mountains as memory.*

The Pyramids: *geology's engineering, poetry's eternity.*

Stone resists time yet records it, outlasts life yet preserves it.

Scientific Analogies

Strata as Syntax: *layers of earth = layers of language.*

Sedimentation as Memory: *deposition of moments into layers.*

Erosion as Forgetting: *the psyche as a cliff crumbling into the sea.*

Fossils as Figures: *symbols preserved in stone as in metaphor.*

Thus, geology is already poetry in patient disguise.

Shadows and Prospects

Geology without poetry risks becoming sterile science. Poetry without geology risks becoming rootless reverie. But together they birth a deeper vision: the world as book, earth as epic, stone as stanza. Future poets will write with seismographs, compose with core samples, sing with strata. Future geologists will cite metaphors as evidence.

Poetry as Geology beyond Geology

The earth is not merely studied—it is sung. Geology describes the earth's crust; poetry discloses the earth's soul.

Thus:

Geology is the prose of the planet.

Poetry is the paradox of the planet.

Geology calculates eons; poetry contemplates eternities.

Geology hears the silence of stone; poetry hears the song within stone.

Stone is the most silent poem, and poetry the most speaking stone.

Geology and poetry, though distant in discipline, converge in essence: both read layers, both interpret depths, both preserve permanence out of transience. Geology is the poetry of the planet; poetry is the geology of the psyche. One chisels into stone, the other into silence. Both teach patience, paradox, and permanence. To read the earth without poetry is to see only stone, never symbol; to read poetry without geology is to feel only metaphor, never matter. Together, they reveal that we live not only on the earth but in it, and not only in language but beneath it.

POETRY AND BIOTECHNOLOGY: THE GENESIS OF GENES AND THE METAPHORS OF LIFE

In poetry, we smell the ordour of biotechnology. The poet Genetics of imagination and the imagination of Genetics may be considered in this line. Biotechnology is the science of sculpting life, the craft of coaxing cells, the manipulation of molecules for medicine, agriculture, and artifice. Poetry is the biotechnology of the soul, altering language to generate meaning, mutating metaphors to create emotional organisms. At first sight, they seem alien: one labors in laboratories, the other in libraries. Yet paradoxically, they mirror each other. Biotechnology engineers genomes; poetry engineers genius. Biotechnology edits DNA; poetry edits destiny.

The Poem as Genetic Code

Every poem is a genome, a sequence of symbolic nucleotides: sound, sense, rhythm, rhyme. Just as DNA contains instructions for life, so the lines of verse encode instructions for feeling. To read a poem is to translate the double helix of diction into the proteins of passion. Thus paradox: biology finds life in molecules, poetry finds molecules in life.

Mutation and Metaphor

Biotechnology thrives on mutation—sometimes natural, sometimes induced. Poetry, too, mutates language, warping ordinary words into extraordinary meaning. A metaphor is a mutation: "time is a thief" splices together disparate domains. Just as some mutations create disease and others evolution, some metaphors fail, while others birth immortal insight. The oxymoron arises: creative distortion, deliberate disorder, cultivated chaos.

Cloning and Canon

Cloning, the replication of genetic material, finds its strange parallel in poetic canon. Great works are copied, quoted, imitated, adapted endlessly—yet each imitation, like a clone, may differ subtly, acquiring epigenetic accents. Homer is echoed in Virgil, Virgil in Dante, Dante in T.S. Eliot. Thus, paradoxically originality is achieved by replication, uniqueness by universality.

Stem Cells and Symbolism

Stem cells are pluripotent, capable of becoming any tissue. Symbols are pluripotent too, capable of becoming any meaning. The rose is love in one culture, martyrdom in another, secrecy in yet another. Just as biotechnologists differentiate stem cells into organs, poets differentiate symbols into narratives. The paradox: infinite potential narrows into finite form, yet retains infinity within.

The Oxymoron of Artificial and Authentic

Biotechnology blurs the border between natural and artificial: lab-grown meat, genetically modified crops, synthetic organs. Poetry does the same: artifice of language becomes authenticity of experience. A sonnet is artificial, bound by rigid rules; yet it delivers authentic emotion. The oxymoron: the truest truths are told through artifice, the most natural emotions expressed through constructed forms.

CRISPR and Creative Editing

CRISPR-Cas9, the scalpel of modern biotechnology, edits DNA with precision. Poetry, too, depends on editing—chiseling excess, cutting clutter, refining rhythm. A misplaced word is like a genetic error, distorting the organism of meaning. A precisely cut phrase is like a corrected genome, restoring health to the poem. Thus paradox: destruction becomes design, deletion becomes creation.

Hybridity and Genre

Biotechnology often creates hybrids: stronger crops, resistant species, novel organisms. Poetry thrives on hybridity of genres: the epic lyric, the dramatic elegy, the prose poem. Hybridity produces resilience in biology and richness in literature. Paradox: purity weakens, mixture strengthens; separation sterilizes, union fertilizes.

Immortality and Ephemerality

One of biotechnology's grand ambitions is to delay death, prolong life, even achieve immortality. Poetry has already done so. Sappho sings across millennia, Shakespeare lives in syllables, Tagore breathes in stanzas. Paradox: biotechnology seeks immortality through cells, poetry secures immortality through sounds. The oxymoron emerges: mortal immortality, ephemeral eternity.

Ethics and Aesthetics

Biotechnology provokes ethical dilemmas: should we alter embryos, clone humans, engineer intelligence? Poetry provokes aesthetic dilemmas: should we break tradition, abandon rhyme, defy meaning? Both disciplines demand reflection on limits: how far can we shape nature, how far can we shape language? The paradox: freedom requires boundaries, creativity requires constraints.

The Laboratory and the Lyric

A laboratory is sterile, white and precise. A lyric is lush, colorful and ambiguous. Yet both spaces are sanctuaries of creation. Both involve experiment, hypothesis, and trial and error. A failed experiment teaches as much as a failed poem. A successful experiment, like a successful lyric, alters the world irreversibly. The oxymoron: sterile fertility, precise unpredictability.

Genetic Memory and Collective Memory

Genes transmit biological memory from generation to generation. Poems transmit cultural memory. The human genome is a library of life; the poetic canon is a genome of imagination. Just as mitochondrial DNA traces maternal lineage, oral traditions trace ancestral voices. The paradox: memory is both molecular and metaphorical, cellular and cultural.

Bioluminescence and the Illumination of Imagination

Some organisms glow with inner light through biochemical reactions. Poetry glows with bioluminescence of imagination: verse radiates light in darkness, illuminating minds. A jellyfish in the ocean, a stanza in the soul—both shimmer with inexplicable brilliance. Thus paradox: the most material becomes the most mystical, the most chemical becomes the most celestial.

The Promise and Peril of Creation

Biotechnology promises cures for disease, food for the hungry, energy for the future. Yet it also risks monstrosities: ecological imbalance, genetic inequality, dystopian control. Poetry likewise promises healing of the spirit, unity of society, beauty for the weary. Yet it too can wound: propaganda, seduction, deception. The paradox: creation carries destruction, blessing bears curse, light casts shadow.

The Paradox of Petri Dish and Poem

Biotechnology is the science of shaping life; poetry is the art of shaping language. One rearranges genes, the other rearranges words. One edits DNA, the other edits destiny. Yet paradoxically, both are architects of possibility: they manipulate the given to manifest the unimaginable. Where biotechnology splices sequences, poetry splices symbols. Where biotechnology invents hybrids, poetry invents metaphors. Where biotechnology confronts mortality with molecular engineering, poetry confronts mortality with musical incantation. Thus, arises our oxymoron: biotechnology is practical magic, poetry is magical practice.

Genes as Grammar, DNA as Diction

Biotechnology regards DNA as the code of life. Poetry regards language as the code of consciousness. Both are alphabets of being.

Adenine, Thymine, Guanine, Cytosine: the four letters of biology's alphabet.

Nouns, verbs, adjectives, adverbs: the four letters of poetry's alphabet.

A gene is a sentence; a genome is an epic. Mutations are misprints that sometimes create masterpieces. Biotechnology edits with CRISPR; poetry edits with criticism. Both strive for clarity, beauty, and survival. A single misplaced nucleotide can alter an organism; a single misplaced word can alter a world.

The Poetry of the Petri Dish

Biotechnology conducts experiments in controlled environments: petri dishes, test tubes, incubators. Yet within these sterile spaces exists a sublime symphony: cells dividing like stanzas, colonies forming like choruses. Poets too cultivate cultures—cultural petri dishes—where ideas ferment, mutate, and proliferate. Sterile fertility. A dish devoid of personality gives birth to infinite possibility.

Hybrids and Metaphors

Biotechnology produces hybrids—cross-bred plants, genetically modified organisms, chimeric cells. Poetry too produces hybrids—oxymorons, paradoxes, metaphors that marry contradictions.

A biotech hybrid may resist drought.

A poetic hybrid may resist despair.

A biotech chimera unites species.

A poetic chimera unites senses—synesthesia, where color sings and sound glows.

Thus, hybridization is humanity's highest hope, whether in crops or in concepts.

Cloning: The Paradox of the Duplicate

Cloning in biotechnology produces a genetic copy. Cloning in poetry produces repetition, refrain, echo. But paradox arises: a clone is the same but not the same. Even identical twins differ in destiny. Even repeated stanzas shift in resonance. Dolly the sheep was both ordinary and extraordinary, banal and revolutionary. So too is the poetic refrain: the same words, but infused with new emotion each time they recur.

Immortality and Mortality

Biotechnology's dream is immortality—extending lifespan, eradicating disease, resurrecting species. Poetry's dream is also immortality—preserving feeling, transcending time, eternalizing the ephemeral.

Biotechnology preserves life in tissues.

Poetry preserves life in tropes.

Biotechnology freezes embryos.

Poetry freezes emotions.

Both disciplines immortalize mortality. They make death undying, finitude infinite.

Viruses and Verses

Viruses are paradoxical beings: neither fully alive nor fully dead, both code and chaos. They infiltrate hosts to replicate.

Verses are similar: they are viral vibrations, entering the reader, replicating in memory. A meme is but a poetic virus, a contagion of consciousness.

Thus, poetry and viruses are kin—tiny packets of code that change civilizations.

Stem Cells and Blank Verses

Stem cells are undifferentiated, able to become any cell type. Blank verse is undifferentiated, able to take any rhythm, any tone.

Stem cells are potential incarnate.

Blank verse is potential articulated.

Stem cells promise regeneration.

Blank verse promises reinvention.

Both are paradoxes of purity: defined by their undefinedness.

Genetic Engineering and Metaphorical Engineering

CRISPR-Cas9 is biotechnology's scalpel, slicing DNA with precision. Metaphor is poetry's scalpel, slicing language to rearrange meaning.

Gene therapy cures the body.

Metaphor therapy cures the soul.

Biotechnology alters physical inheritance.

Poetry alters cultural inheritance.

Both are radical surgeries of the real.

Ethics and Aesthetics

Biotechnology raises ethical dilemmas: should we design babies? Resurrect species? Enhance intelligence?

Poetry raises aesthetic dilemmas: should we write in tradition or innovation? Should art console or disturb? Should beauty be pursued or deconstructed?

Ethics is biotechnology's philosophy; aesthetics is poetry's ethics. Both disciplines wrestle with responsibility to future generations.

Biotechnology as Modern Mythology

Ancient myth gave us Prometheus stealing fire, Daedalus designing wings, Pandora opening a box. Biotechnology is the modern myth:

Gene editing is Promethean fire.

Cloning is Daedalian hubris.

Bio-weapons are Pandora's plagues.

Poetry interprets these myths, giving biotechnology its metaphorical mirror.

Biotechnology and the Body as Text

Biotechnology reads the body as code. Poetry reads the body as symbol.

DNA is a poem written in four letters.

The heart is a metaphorical metronome.

Blood is both biology and ballad.

Our bodies are both mechanical and mystical, both cellular and symbolic. Biotechnology explains the former; poetry celebrates the latter.

Biotechnology's Future, Poetry's Prospect

The prospects of biotechnology are boundless: curing incurable diseases, engineering ecological balance, transcending evolutionary limitations.

The prospects of poetry are likewise boundless: healing inner wounds, restoring cultural balance, transcending linguistic limitations. Together they point to a single paradoxical vision: humanity remaking itself biologically and metaphorically, scientifically and spiritually.

The Gene and the Genius

The Latin word **genius** means both guiding spirit and generative power. The root of **gene** is the same: the power to generate.

Biotechnology manipulates genes; poetry manipulates genius.

Biotechnology splices DNA; poetry splices destiny.

Biotechnology edits life; poetry edits meaning.

Life itself is a poem written in proteins; poetry itself is a gene expressed in consciousness. Thus, biotechnology is the biology of poetry; poetry is the biotechnology of the soul.

Poetry and biotechnology are twin arts of transformation: one of molecules, the other of metaphors. Both manipulate codes, both generate hybrids, both blur natural and artificial. Biotechnology edits life, poetry edits living. Biotechnology seeks to master death, poetry has already conquered it. To live without biotechnology is to suffer materially; to live without poetry is to suffer spiritually. Together, they prove that the human condition is to create—whether with cells or with syllables. Poetry is biotechnology in language; biotechnology is poetry in science. Both remind us that creation is not merely manipulation of matter but manifestation of meaning.

POETRY AND ASTROLOGY: THE HARMONIES OF STARS AND STANZAS

Poetry is the stellar script of the soul. Astrology, in its ancient allure, declares that the heavens are not mute, that constellations are calligraphy, that planets are punctuation marks in a cosmic sentence. Poetry, in its eternal enchantment, translates this celestial syntax into human song. Both astrology and poetry speak a secret language—one inscribed in stars, the other inscribed in syllables. One interprets the zodiac, the other interprets the soul. At first glance, science dismisses astrology as superstition, just as practicality dismisses poetry as ornament. Yet paradoxically, both endure, because both satisfy the eternal yearning of humanity: to find meaning in mystery, to weave patterns into chaos.

The Zodiac and the Zither of Verse

The zodiac is a circular poem, twelve stanzas of stellar symbolism: Aries the fiery prologue, Pisces the watery epilogue. Each sign is a metaphor, each constellation a character in the epic of eternity. Just as poets use imagery to interpret the world, astrologers use planetary positions to interpret personality. The paradox: the heavens are silent, yet they sing; the stars are indifferent, yet they instruct.

Planets as Poetic Figures

Astrology personifies planets—Mars as warrior, Venus as lover, Saturn as sage, Mercury as messenger. Poetry does the same: Mars marches in Milton, Venus vanishes in Virgil, Saturn sighs in Shakespeare. Both transform astronomy into allegory. The oxymoron arises: objective orbs become subjective symbols, physical spheres become metaphysical figures. What is astrophysics for the scientist becomes archetype for the poet.

The Horoscope as a Lyric Map

A horoscope is a poem in circular form: an intricate interplay of angles, aspects, and alignments. It resembles not a chart of planets but a stanza of destiny. Reading a horoscope is like reading a difficult poem—it requires decoding symbols, interpreting ambiguity, sensing subtlety. The paradox: prediction becomes poetry, calculation becomes contemplation.

Poetry as Inner Astrology

If astrology seeks destiny in the sky, poetry discovers destiny in the self. A natal chart claims that Jupiter blesses or Saturn restrains; a lyric claims that joy blesses or sorrow restrains. Astrology projects meaning outward; poetry internalizes it inward. Yet both echo the same intuition: human life is patterned, not random; existence is orchestrated, not accidental. Thus paradox: the stars are in us, even when we seek them outside us.

The Oxymoron of Fate and Freedom

Astrology seems to bind us: "You are a Leo, bold yet proud; you are a Virgo, precise yet anxious." Poetry seems to free us: "You are what you write, not what you are written." Yet the deeper paradox is that astrology too offers freedom by awareness—knowing one's tendencies allows transcendence of them. And poetry, though liberating, disciplines us with form—meter and rhyme act like planetary constraints. Fate and freedom become a cosmic oxymoron: we are free because we are bound, bound because we are free.

Stars as Similes, Skies as Stanzas

The starry sky is the oldest page of poetry. Shepherds, sailors, prophets, and lovers have long read the heavens as metaphor. Orion the hunter, Cassiopeia the queen, Draco the dragon—mythology mapped into the Milky Way. Poetry continues this practice: comparing eyes to stars, lovers to moons, lives to constellations. The paradox: we gaze upward to describe what is within us, we look outward to illuminate the inward.

Astrological Archetypes and Poetic Personas

Astrology thrives on archetypes: the fiery leader, the earthy realist, the airy dreamer, the watery mystic. Poetry too thrives on archetypes: the tragic hero, the comic fool, the exiled wanderer, the eternal lover. Both function as mirrors for humanity's multiplicity. Astrology locates them in stars; poetry locates them in selves. The paradox: individuality is universal, universality is individual.

Oxymorons of Time

Astrology is obsessed with time: birth charts, transits, cycles, retrogrades. Poetry is likewise time's troubadour, singing of fleeting hours and eternal moments. A sonnet is a Saturnine clock, measuring seconds in syllables; an ode is a Jupiterian expansion, swelling into timelessness. Astrology teaches us that time repeats; poetry teaches us that time returns differently. Thus paradox: time is cyclical and linear, imprisoning and liberating, destructive and creative.

Astrology and the Pedagogy of Wonder

Science often sterilizes the stars, stripping them of

story. Astrology restores wonder, seeing in the sky not only gas and gravity but guidance and grandeur. Poetry performs the same function in language, restoring mystery to words worn thin by use. Together, they form a pedagogy of wonder: astrology makes the heavens meaningful, poetry makes the heart meaningful. The oxymoron shines: superstition becomes wisdom, imagination becomes truth.

The Poem as Horoscope of the Heart

Every poem is a horoscope of its author's soul, an alignment of inner planets. Anger is Mars, love is Venus, melancholy is Saturn, curiosity is Mercury. Reading a poem is divining the heavens within the heart, interpreting its constellations of longing. Astrology reads the stars as poetry; poetry reads the self as astrology. The paradox: both are symbolic sciences, truth-bearing fictions, metaphors that make meaning more real than reality itself.

Celestial Symbols and Lyrical Lights

Astrology, though often dismissed as pseudoscience, persists because it is poetry disguised as prediction. It does not weigh stars as astronomy does, nor dissect DNA as biology does, but it translates the trembling heavens into human hope. Poetry too translates: not constellations into character, but emotions into eternity. The stars are impossibly distant, yet their imagined influence is intimately near. Oxymoron: astrology is rational irrationality, scientific superstition. Poetry thrives in this very tension—where impossibility becomes intimacy, where illogic illuminates. Thus both astrology and poetry are arts of correspondence, where the cosmos converses with the consciousness.

Constellations as Canon, Zodiac as Zeal

Astrology arranges stars into constellations, forms into fables. Poetry arranges words into verses, symbols into stanzas. Orion is the epic warrior, immortal in the sky.

Leo is the leonine leader, roaring across ages. Aquarius is the water-bearer, pouring meaning through millennia. So too, in poetry: constellations of metaphors make a canon, zodiacs of tropes form tradition. Stars have no inherent shape, yet we see heroes, beasts, and myths. Words have no inherent meaning, yet we read worlds and wonders.

The Zodiac and the Zeitgeist

The zodiac is a symbolic system of twelve signs—an eternal cycle of archetypes. Poetry is also zodiacal: cyclical rhythms, archetypal figures, eternal returns. Aries is the bold beginning—like the first line of a sonnet. Libra is the balance of justice—like the symmetrical stanza. Pisces is the dream of dissolution—like the closing elegy. Astrology claims the cosmos shapes culture; poetry proves culture shapes cosmos. The stars may be mute, but poetry lends them speech. Planets are depicted as Poetic Principles. Astrology personifies planets: Venus for love, Mars for war, Jupiter for grandeur, Saturn for melancholy. These are not merely astronomical bodies but archetypal forces. Poetry too personifies: Venusian beauty, Martial wrath, Jovian joy, Saturnian sorrow. Thus, poetry and astrology are parallel personifications: planets as metaphors, metaphors as planets.

Horoscopes and Hymns

The horoscope is a daily poem disguised as prediction. It condenses cosmic complexity into human advice: Beware of loss; embrace opportunity. This is what lyric poetry also does: distills the infinite into the intimate. A horoscope may say: You will find love today. A lyric may whisper: Love found me in a glance. Both are brief, cryptic, consoling. Both serve not as scientific forecasts but as symbolic frameworks.

The Paradox of Causality

Astronomy asks: how could stars influence individuals across incomprehensible distances? Astrology responds with metaphor: the heavens are mirrors, not mechanisms. Poetry thrives in this paradox: the symbol is not the thing, yet the symbol transforms the thing. The moon does not move tides by metaphor, yet tides of feeling follow its image. Astrology is poetry masquerading as causality. Poetry is astrology confessed as imagination.

Astrology as Ancestral Aesthetics

Before telescopes, the sky was scripture. Shepherds read seasons in constellations; kings read destinies in eclipses; lovers read promises in stars. Astrology is not primitive science but ancient poetry, written in stellar ink. It taught humans to see patterns in chaos, rhythm in randomness. Without astrology's symbolic gaze, perhaps poetry itself would not have emerged.

Cosmic Chords and Harmonic Hymns

Astrology suggests that planets move in harmony, their motions composing a music of the spheres. Poetry too is harmony: rhythm, rhyme, meter.

Saturn's slow orbit is an elegiac meter.

Mercury's quick path is a witty epigram.

Jupiter's grandeur is a Miltonic epic.

Thus, the cosmos itself becomes a poem, with planets as syllables, constellations as stanzas, galaxies as great epics.

Astrology, Archetype, and the Unconscious

Carl Jung defended astrology as a symbolic system resonant with the collective unconscious. The zodiac is not literal but archetypal: patterns of psyche projected onto the heavens. So too is poetry: archetypes repeated across cultures, myths retold in modern stanzas. Both disciplines reveal that what is above is what is within. Stars are external, yet they express internal states. Poetry is internal, yet it externalizes itself as text.

Astrology as Democratic Divination, Poetry as Aristocratic Revelation

Astrology democratizes the divine: every birth has a chart, every hour a horoscope. Poetry aristocratizes the ineffable: not every voice is vatic, not every word is a verse. Yet paradoxically, both are universal: anyone may read their stars, anyone may write their song.

Astrology's Ethics, Poetry's Aesthetics

Astrology comforts the uncertain: Your struggles are Saturn's test; your triumph is Jupiter's gift. Poetry consoles too: Sorrow will turn to song; silence will become sense. But just as astrology risks fatalism, poetry risks solipsism. Thus both must balance symbol with freedom: stars may guide, but not govern; stanzas may console, but not command.

Astrology in the Age of Algorithms

Today, astrology thrives online—apps charting natal charts, memes mapping Mercury retrograde. Its persistence proves: humans hunger for cosmic connection. Poetry too thrives in digital fragments—haiku on Twitter, epics in blogs. Both disciplines resist reduction to data, even while living within it. Both insist that beneath algorithms lies archetype.

The Infinite Horoscope: Poetry as Astrology of the Soul

Ultimately, astrology is a grand metaphor: the belief that the universe cares, that the cosmos converses. Poetry, too, is that faith: that words matter, that meaning exists, that beauty is not illusion but illumination.

Thus:

Astrology is poetry projected onto stars.

Poetry is astrology inscribed in speech.

Both are maps of meaning in a mute universe.

Latin whispers *astra inclinant, non necessitant*—the stars incline, they do not compel. Poetry, too, inclines the soul without commanding it. A star is a burning ball of plasma, yet to poetry it is a beacon of hope. A line is a string of words, yet to the heart it is salvation. The universe is silent, yet we hear its song. The stars are indifferent, yet they inspire intimacy. Thus, astrology is the astronomy of longing; poetry is the astrology of language.

Astrology and poetry are sisters in symbolism, daughters of myth, guardians of wonder. Astrology maps the sky to explain the soul; poetry maps the soul to explain the sky. One finds metaphors in constellations, the other constellations in metaphors. Both proclaim that meaning is not discovered but created, not found but formed. They whisper the same paradoxical wisdom: that the universe is a poem, and we are its lines—written by stars, rewritten by songs. Poetry is the horoscope of humanity; astrology is the poem of the cosmos. Together, they remind us that to live is to be simultaneously written and writing, read and reading, fated and free.

POETRY AND PHILOSOPHY: LOGOS AND LYRIC IN ETERNAL EMBRACE

While talking about poetry and philosophy one encounters the dialogue of dream and doctrine. Philosophy proclaims itself the love of wisdom; poetry presents itself as the wisdom of love. Philosophy strives for clarity; poetry luxuriates in ambiguity. Philosophy defines; poetry divines. Yet despite their differences, or perhaps because of them, they are not antagonists but twins—two expressions of the same hunger to understand existence. If philosophy is the skeleton of thought, poetry is its flesh; if philosophy is the law, poetry is the legend; if philosophy is the proposition, poetry is the parable.

Philosophy as Poetry's Prose, Poetry as Philosophy's Paradox

Plato banished poets from his Republic, yet wrote dialogues as dramatic as dramas. Aristotle analyzed tragedy with the rigor of logic, yet exalted catharsis as a philosophical necessity. Nietzsche declared that philosophy must be written in blood, in aphorisms that are essentially poems. And Heidegger, that architect of ontological inquiry, confessed that language reaches its truth most profoundly in poetry. Thus the paradox: philosophers disdain poets yet write poetically, while poets disdain philosophy yet dwell philosophically.

Poetry is philosophy with wings; philosophy is poetry with weights. One soars beyond the visible, the other anchors to reason. Yet both circle the same abyss of being, both peer into the paradox of presence and absence, both wrestle with the oxymoron of time and eternity.

The Logic of the Lyric and the Lyric of Logic

Philosophy claims logic as its method, syllogisms as its structure, rationality as its rhythm. Poetry claims lyricism as its method, metaphor as its structure, music as its rhythm. Yet paradoxically, logic itself is a kind of poetry—what is a syllogism if not a sonnet of thought, each premise a line, each conclusion a rhyme? Likewise, poetry is a kind of philosophy—what is a metaphor if not an argument in disguise, a claim that one thing is another, a syllogism smuggled through song?

Thus, the oxymoron: philosophy is lyrical logic, poetry is logical lyricism. One persuades by rigor, the other by resonance; but both persuade.

Philosophy's Quest for Truth, Poetry's Quest for Beauty

Philosophy chases truth: what is being? what is justice? what is good? Poetry chases beauty: what is joy? what is sorrow? what is love? Yet truth without beauty is barren, and beauty without truth is hollow. Hence the paradox: philosophy seeks eternal certainty but finds endless debate; poetry seeks fleeting beauty but finds eternal resonance. In their failures, they succeed; in their incompleteness, they complete one another. Philosophy is the theorem; poetry is the proof written in metaphor. Philosophy is the compass; poetry is the map of wonder. Without poetry, philosophy petrifies into sterile abstraction. Without philosophy, poetry evaporates into idle ornament.

Dialectics and Dualities

The dialectic is philosophy's darling: thesis, antithesis, synthesis. Yet what is a dialectic but a drama in disguise, a conflict that cries out for resolution? Poetry thrives on the same principle: light and dark, joy and grief, silence and song. Poetry's oxymorons—living death, silent speech, eternal moment—mirror philosophy's paradoxes—being and nothingness, appearance and reality, time and timelessness.

The poet personifies paradox, the philosopher problematizes it. One sings the contradiction, the other systematizes it. But both affirm that reality is not a straight line but a labyrinth of logic and lyric.

Poetic Ontology: Being in Beauty

Philosophy asks: What is being? Poetry answers: Being is beauty, beauty is being. "Beauty is truth, truth beauty"—Keats's famous formula is at once philosophical and poetic, an equation written in oxymoron. For the poet, ontology is not an abstract inquiry but an aesthetic one: existence itself is a poem, and the poet merely unveils its stanzas.

A rock, for philosophy, is a category of matter; for geology, a stratum; for physics, a mass. But for poetry, a rock is symbol, silence, permanence—metaphor made stone. Thus poetry extends ontology into aesthetics, turning mere being into meaningful being.

Epistemology and Epiphany

Philosophy asks: How do we know? Poetry answers: We know by wonder. Epistemology is philosophy's inquiry into knowledge; epiphany is poetry's revelation of meaning. The philosopher demands proof; the poet provides presence. The paradox: the philosopher doubts to discover, the poet delights to disclose. A mathematical axiom is philosophy's ground of knowledge; a metaphor is poetry's ground of truth. Both are non-provable, both foundational. Just as philosophy admits that knowledge rests on unproven principles, poetry admits that meaning rests on untranslatable intuitions.

Ethics and Aesthetics

Philosophy prescribes ethics—how to act, how to live. Poetry provides aesthetics—how to feel, how to perceive. Yet the paradox is that ethics without aesthetics is lifeless law, while aesthetics without ethics is decadent indulgence. Poets like Dante or Milton turned ethics into epics; philosophers like Kant or Kierkegaard wrote ethics in tones as poetic as psalms.

The oxymoron becomes evident: beauty guides goodness, goodness beautifies truth. Poetry is moral through its music; philosophy is musical through its morality. Together they construct what antiquity called *kalokagathia*—the union of the good and the beautiful.

Metaphysics and Metaphor

Metaphysics asks the ultimate questions: Why is there something rather than nothing? What is the nature of reality? Poetry responds not with syllogisms but with symbols: "The world is a stage," "Love is a rose," "Life is a dream." A metaphor is a metaphysical statement disguised as an image. A philosophy is a metaphor disguised as a system. Thus the paradox: metaphysics is metaphor universalized; metaphor is metaphysics particularized. Philosophy fears ambiguity, but poetry thrives on it. And yet, perhaps ambiguity is the only adequate response to mystery. Poetry dares to say what philosophy dares to doubt.

Poetry beyond Philosophy

Philosophy, despite its depth, remains bound to

definition. Poetry, though ethereal, transcends definition. Where philosophy must conclude, poetry continues; where philosophy must argue, poetry alludes. The philosopher asks: What is truth? The poet whispers: Truth is what trembles in beauty.

Thus, poetry is philosophy's afterlife, its angelic echo. Philosophy ends in aporia, poetry begins in amazement. Poetry is philosophy set free, philosophy is poetry disciplined. Both are essential, but poetry may be ultimate, because life is less a syllogism than a song.

The Paradoxical Twins

Philosophy and poetry are paradoxical twins—born of the same womb of wonder, yet raised in different households of thought. One seeks definition, the other sings of dissolution; one loves clarity, the other luxuriates in ambiguity. Yet both are devoted to the same deity: Truth, the ineffable, the inexhaustible, the eternal.

Philosophy asks: *What is?*

Poetry asks: *What if?*

Philosophy demands *argument; poetry delivers image.*

Philosophy speaks *in syllogism; poetry whispers in symbol.*

Philosophy desires precision, yet the greatest philosophers—Plato, Nietzsche, Heidegger—often fall into poetry when confronting the abyss. Poetry revels in ambiguity, yet the greatest poets—Dante, Milton, Eliot—become philosophers when striving for universality. Thus, philosophy and poetry are not enemies but estranged siblings—one rational, one rhapsodic; one analytic, one anagogic.

Plato's Paradox: The Banishment and the Betrayal

Plato, that supreme philosopher-poet, banished poetry from his ***Republic*** as dangerous illusion—yet wrote his philosophy in dialogues filled with metaphor, myth, and music. He distrusted poetry for imitating shadows. Yet he used myths like the Cave and the Charioteer, which are themselves poetic parables. The father of philosophy was a secret poet. Oxymoron: his rationalism was lyrical. Thus, from the beginning, philosophy and poetry interpenetrate.

Aristotle's Poetics: Logos Learns from Lyric

Aristotle, more generous, systematized poetry, analyzing tragedy as catharsis, epic as imitation, comedy as correction. Here philosophy becomes critic, categorizing art's anatomy. Yet even he admits: poetry is "more philosophical than history," because it speaks of universals, not particulars. Paradox: poetry is more philosophical than philosophy itself, because it transcends fact to reach truth.

Poetry as the Philosophy of the Particular

If philosophy is the general—justice, truth, beauty—poetry is the particular: this rose, this grief, this nightingale. Yet in the particular it discovers the universal.

A single sonnet about a lost lover reveals the nature of loss.

A single haiku about a frog reveals impermanence.

Thus, poetry is the philosophy of the singular, revealing universality through intimacy.

Philosophy as Prose, Poetry as Paradox

Philosophy aspires to clarity, yet its concepts are endlessly contested: what is being, time, freedom? Poetry embraces paradox, admitting that truth is both presence and absence, fullness and void.

Philosophy says: *Man is a rational animal.*

Poetry says: *Man is a divine madness.*

Both are true, and only together complete.

The Music of Metaphysics

Philosophy without poetry is dry dialectic, desert without water. Poetry without philosophy is shapeless sentiment, sea without shore. Together, they create the music of metaphysics: measured yet mysterious, structured yet soaring. Think of Lucretius—philosophy of atoms sung in epic verse, Or Dante—metaphysics of theology rendered in terza rima, Or Nietzsche—aphorisms that are thunderbolts of both thought and lyric.

Poetry as the Next Level of Philosophy

Philosophy attempts to define truth; poetry enacts it.

Philosophy asks what justice is; poetry shows us justice feels.

Philosophy explains; poetry embodies.

Philosophy seeks wisdom, but poetry is wisdom in rhythm. Poetry is philosophy incarnate in cadence, clothed in cadence, crowned with cadence.

Thus, poetry is not beneath philosophy, but beyond it. Not the primitive version, but the consummate culmination.

The Ontology of Image, the Epistemology of Imagination

Philosophy builds ontology (being) and epistemology (knowing).

Poetry builds imagology (imaging) and aestheology (feeling).

Yet both overlap: to imagine is to know, to feel is to be. Poetry offers what philosophy lacks: the immediacy of insight, the lightning flash rather than the lantern glow.

Philosophical Poets, Poetic Philosophers

Heraclitus: *fragments that are flames of metaphor.*

Parmenides: *philosophy in hexameters.*

Nietzsche: *Zarathustra as scripture of song.*

Rilke: *poems as phenomenology of existence.*

Heidegger: *philosophy dissolving into Hölderlin's hymns.*

In all these, the border vanishes—philosophy becomes poetry, poetry becomes philosophy.

The Oxymoronic Essence

Philosophy is serious play; poetry is playful seriousness. Philosophy is rigorous dream; poetry is dreamy rigor. Philosophy is timeless question; poetry is timely answer. Together, they are paradox embodied.

Toward a Unified Discipline: Poetic Philosophy, Philosophical Poetry

If philosophy is thought in prose, poetry is philosophy in verse. If philosophy seeks truth through logos, poetry reveals truth through mythos. The ultimate task: to create a new discipline, where poetry and philosophy are fused: *poetic philosophy, philosophical poetry*—the science of sense and song, the logic of lyric, the mathematics of metaphor.

The Silence beyond Speech

Philosophy ends in aporia, the silence of unanswerable questions. Poetry ends in mystery, the silence of unspeakable beauty. Both meet in the sacred stillness where words end and wisdom begins. Thus, philosophy is the question in prose. Poetry is the answer in verse. Philosophy is the skeleton of thought. Poetry is its breath, its blood, its beating heart. Philosophy explains what poetry enacts; poetry enacts what philosophy explains. Neither complete without the other. Therefore poetry is philosophy's fulfillment—its music, its myth, its immortal mirror.

The Twin Flames of Thought and Feeling

Philosophy and poetry are two flames that illuminate the same cave: one cold with clarity, the other warm with wonder. The philosopher seeks the structure of reality; the poet seeks the song of reality. One builds systems, the other sings symbols; one concludes, the other continues. And yet, the paradox remains: philosophy, in its striving for precision, becomes poetry; poetry, in its striving for beauty, becomes philosophy. Both disciplines dissolve into each other at their highest point. As Cicero wrote, *poeta nascitur, orator fit*—the poet is born, the orator made. One might add: the philosopher thinks, the poet dreams; but both are dreaming thinkers, thinking dreamers.

Ultimately, philosophy without poetry becomes blind reason; poetry without philosophy becomes deaf music. But together, they constitute the complete chorus of humanity, the dialogue of dream and doctrine, the duet of wisdom and wonder.

POETRY AND PHYSICS: THE LYRIC OF LAWS AND THE MUSIC AND METAPHOR OF MATTER

Physics, the eldest child of natural philosophy, pursues the patterns of particles and planets, of fields and forces, of masses and motions. Poetry, that eldest child of the human heart, pursues the patterns of rhythm and rhyme, of images and intimations, of metaphors and mysteries. At first sight, they seem estranged: physics speaks in formulae, poetry sings in figures; physics demands precision, poetry delights in ambiguity. And yet, at the secret summit, they mirror one another. The cosmos itself is both calculable and contemplative, both measurable and mysterious, both equation and elegy.

The Poetics of Physical Law

A physical law is a poem written in symbols: $F = ma$, $E = mc^2$, $\Delta S \geq 0$. Each law is a lyric compressed, a rhythm reduced to relation. Newton's apple falls not merely as matter in motion but as metaphor for universal gravitation: the fall of fruit becomes the fall of stars. Einstein's relativity is not only physics but poetry: time bends, space curves, simultaneity dies, eternity is entangled with velocity.

The paradox is plain: physics seeks literal truth but speaks in symbolic language; poetry seeks symbolic truth but speaks in literal language. One hides its metaphors behind mathematics; the other hides its mathematics behind metaphors.

Energy and Elegy

Energy cannot be created or destroyed, only transformed—so says the physicist. Poetry cannot be created or destroyed, only transfigured—so says the poet. The conservation of energy is mirrored by the conservation of imagination: every poem borrows from the eternal reservoir of human wonder, merely altering form but never exhausting source.

Entropy increases, says thermodynamics: order collapses into disorder. Yet poetry reverses entropy by reordering chaos into cosmos, by chiseling confusion into cadence. Thus physics and poetry enact opposite tendencies: physics proclaims decay, poetry performs renewal. But paradoxically, both are true—the universe collapses, but the poem consoles.

The Quantum of Meaning

Quantum physics, with its paradoxes, is already a poem. The electron is both particle and wave—an oxymoron incarnate, a contradiction that nonetheless constructs reality. Schrödinger's cat is both dead and alive, a macabre metaphor worthy of tragic verse. Heisenberg's uncertainty says we cannot know both position and momentum—just as in poetry we cannot seize both sense and sensation, both meaning and mystery.

Thus, quantum theory is not merely science but surrealism, a sonnet of subatomic uncertainty. Physics affirms what poetry has always sung: reality is irreducibly paradoxical, simultaneously present and absent, determinate and indeterminate, measurable and ineffable.

Relativity and Rhythm

Einstein dethroned absolute time and space, proving

that simultaneity is relative, that space bends like music, that time dilates like memory. Poetry had already intuited this: the lyric collapses hours into seconds, stretches seconds into eternities. A single stanza can contain a century; a pause, a lifetime. Thus relativity is but the formalization of what poetry already practices—the physics of rhythm, the metaphysics of measure. Time in physics is variable; time in poetry is malleable. Both disciplines defy the rigid march of the clock and reveal time as elastic, ecstatic, ethereal.

Gravity as Elegy, Light as Lyric

Gravity, the gentle tyrant, pulls all things together: planets around stars, lovers into embraces, souls into graves. Poetry, too, has its gravity—the pull of meaning, the weight of words, the orbit of emotions. Each stanza attracts its lines as planets attract moons; each metaphor is a mass that bends the space of thought.

Light, on the other hand, is the lyric of physics. Wave and particle, motion and miracle, it is both messenger and mystery. Poets forever write of dawn, of flame, of illumination; physicists forever study photons, frequencies, refractions. The paradox is profound: physics dissects light into wavelengths, poetry gathers light into wonder. Both reveal that illumination is the essence of existence.

The Universe as Poem

What is the cosmos if not a colossal composition? Galaxies swirl like stanzas, stars flicker like syllables, black holes brood like pauses, dark matter lingers like unspoken lines. The Big Bang itself is both physics and poetry: an explosion and an exclamation, an equation and an epiphany, the moment when nothing became everything.

The cosmic microwave background is but the rhyme of creation still resonating; gravity waves are the rhythm of spacetime's dance. To the physicist, the universe is governed by laws; to the poet, the universe is a lawless lyric. Both are right, both incomplete. The universe is a paradoxical poem governed by equations, an equation that sings as a poem.

Mathematics as Muse

Physics leans on mathematics, and mathematics is itself a kind of poetry. Equations are epigrams of existence, terse and elegant. A proof is a poem that persuades not by rhythm but by rigor, yet the elegance of Euler's identity—$e^{(i\pi)} + 1 = 0$—is more lyrical than many verses.

Thus, poetry is mathematics translated into metaphor; physics is mathematics translated into matter. All three converge at beauty, that elusive criterion which physicists, poets, and mathematicians alike invoke as truth's final test.

The Oxymoron of Order and Chaos

Physics oscillates between order and chaos, determinism and probability. Newton's mechanics envisioned a clockwork cosmos, perfect and predictable; quantum mechanics envisioned a kaleidoscopic cosmos, unpredictable and paradoxical. Poetry, too, oscillates: the sonnet's strict structure versus free verse's wild abandon, the rhyme's rigid recurrence versus the image's impulsive innovation. Order and chaos: the oxymoron at the heart of reality. Without order, nothing coheres; without chaos, nothing creates. Physics studies their balance; poetry sings their dance.

Beyond Physics, Within Poetry

Physics eventually admits its limits: what came before the Big Bang? What lies beyond space-time? What is consciousness? Philosophy falters here, and poetry alone dares to leap. When science stammers at singularities, poetry sings. Where equations end, metaphors begin. Thus, poetry is not the rival of physics but its resonance, its continuation by other means. Physics provides explanation, poetry provides exclamation. Physics writes the prose of reality; poetry writes its paradox.

The Oxymoron of Order and Wonder

Physics is the science of necessity; poetry is the science of possibility. One measures, the other marvels. Yet both are born of awe before the cosmos.

Physics asks: *What rules the universe?*

Poetry asks: *What reveals the universe?*

Physics explains *stars as fusion.*

Poetry explains *stars as fireflies of forever.*

The paradox we see here is: physics and poetry both transform the infinite into intelligible—yet one by formula, the other by metaphor. Thus, physics is the prose of the universe; poetry is its music.

The Poetic Particle

At the smallest scale, physics finds quarks, electrons, photons—particles dancing in paradox. They are both waves and particles, both here and nowhere. Poetry too is particle and wave: a single word (particle) carries infinite resonance (wave). Each stanza is a system, yet also a superposition. Each metaphor is a wave-function collapsing into meaning when read. Quantum physics and poetry are both rigorous riddles.

Relativity and Rhythm

Einstein showed that time and space are relative, woven into a fabric stretched by gravity. Poetry too is relativity: Rhythm stretches and compresses time. A sonnet makes seconds eternal; a haiku makes eternity momentary. In poetry, a line bends perception; in physics, a mass bends spacetime. Thus, rhyme is relativity made audible.

Cosmology and Cosmogony

Physics begins with the Big Bang, the universe exploding into being. Poetry begins with the first word, the blank page exploding into being.

Physics says: *Let there be light.*

Poetry says: *Let there be lyric.*

Physics studies *stars as nuclear furnaces.*

Poetry studies *stars as symbols of fate.*

The universe is both brute matter and burning metaphor.

Entropy and Elegy

The second law of thermodynamics declares entropy always increases—order dissolves into disorder.

Poetry too writes entropy:

Elegies lament decay.

Love poems fear loss.

Epics record empires that crumble.

Entropy is not only death, but creativity. There is no new growth without decay, no fresh form without disorder. Thus, poetry and physics teach the same lesson: disintegration is the prelude to reintegration.

Light: Photon and Poem

Light in physics is paradox: both wave and particle, both infinite and finite. Light in poetry is equally paradoxical: both metaphor and matter, both symbol and substance.

A photon travels at the speed of truth.

A poem travels at the speed of thought.

Light illuminates matter.

Poetry illuminates meaning.

Thus, poetry is the photon of the mind.

Gravity and Gravitas

Gravity bends space, binds galaxies, keeps us grounded. Gravitas in poetry bends hearts, binds souls, keeps us humbled.

Newton's apple falls with inevitability.

Keats's nightingale rises with inevitability.

Black holes devour light.

Dark poems devour hope.

Gravity holds us down, yet allows orbits; gravitas holds us steady, yet allows transcendence.

The Music of Mathematics

Physics is written in equations, poetry in lines. Both are languages of symmetry, elegance, beauty. Maxwell's equations are sonnets of electricity. Einstein's $E=mc^2$ is a haiku of energy. Schrödinger's equation is an epic of uncertainty. Mathematics is poetry in numbers; poetry is mathematics in words.

Quantum Uncertainty and Poetic Ambiguity

Heisenberg declared: the more precisely you know position, the less you know momentum. Poetry declares: the more precisely you define meaning, the less you feel mystery. Thus, ambiguity is not a flaw, but a feature—in science and in song. Both quantum theory and lyric verse thrive on uncertainty.

The Multiverse and Metaphor

Physics speculates multiple universes. Poetry already practices multiple meanings.

A metaphor is a multiverse: *one image, many realities.*

An epic is a cosmos: *many worlds in one word.*

A reader collapses one interpretation, but infinite others remain.

Thus, metaphor is the multiverse of meaning.

Time's Arrow and Lyric's Circle

Physics speaks of the arrow of time—irreversible, moving from past to future. Poetry speaks of the circle of time—eternal recurrence, seasons, refrains.

Entropy drives *time forward.*

Rhythm draws *time back.*

Physics says: no return.

Poetry says: return is renewal.

Time is both arrow and circle, linear and lyrical.

Poetry as the Physics of the Soul

If physics explains the universe's body, poetry explains its spirit.

Physics finds forces: *gravity, electromagnetism, strong and weak.*

Poetry finds forces: *love, grief, joy, hope.*

Physics predicts *trajectories.*

Poetry predicts *transformations.*

Together they form the total science of existence.

Stanzas in Spacetime

The universe is both equation and elegy, law and lyric. Physics measures the cosmos, poetry sings it.

Physics says: *The world is made of matter and energy.*

Poetry says: *The world is made of meaning and emotion.*

Physics finds *quarks.*

Poetry finds *questions.*

Physics is the poetry of matter; poetry is the physics of meaning. Together, they complete creation.

The Lyric Law of the Cosmos

Poetry and physics are not strangers but siblings, both born of wonder, both bent on deciphering the universe. Physics measures the universe in meters and seconds; poetry measures it in metaphors and syllables. Physics explains the how; poetry explores the why. Physics dissects stars; poetry dreams them. And yet both point to the same mystery—that reality is not only intelligible but beautiful, not only calculable but meaningful. The cosmos is a cathedral of equations, but also a chorus of elegies. The falling apple and the rising song are but two ways of expressing the same law: that existence is at once lawful and lyrical, mathematical and metaphorical, physical and poetic.

POETRY AND CHEMISTRY: THE ALCHEMY OF ATOMS AND THE SYMPHONY OF SYMBOLS

I see poetry in chemistry as elements of elegy, and compounds of cadence. Chemistry is often called the "central science," for it connects the physical to the biological, the elemental to the existential, the microscopic molecule to the macroscopic miracle of life. Poetry, by equal measure, is the "central art," binding the visible to the invisible, the logical to the lyrical, the sorrow to the sublime. At first glance, they appear estranged: chemistry coldly catalogues atoms, poetry warmly kindles affections. Yet in truth they are companions, for both delight in transformation, in union, in reaction, in resonance. One studies the fire of matter; the other sings the matter of fire.

Elements as Emblems

The periodic table is a kind of poem: each element a stanza, each symbol a syllable, each arrangement a rhythm of recurring patterns. Hydrogen, the humble firstborn, is the haiku of the cosmos; gold, the resplendent monarch, is the epic of alchemy. Iron, the marrow of mountains, pulses in the blood of beasts. Each element is both fact and figure, substance and symbol. Poetry does likewise: it turns iron into imagery, silver into simile, carbon into character. Where chemistry charts combinations, poetry crafts connotations.

Where chemistry isolates atoms, poetry binds them into allegories. Both disciplines prove that the smallest units—the atom in chemistry, the word in poetry—can generate infinite structures.

Bonding and Belonging

At the heart of chemistry lies bonding: ionic, covalent, metallic—the myriad manners in which atoms embrace. These bonds are not unlike the bonds of metaphor, where meanings merge, fuse, and form new wholes. Just as sodium, solitary and unstable, finds solace in chlorine, poetry finds its power when disparate images join into unexpected resonance. This is the paradox: atoms bond not despite their instability but because of it, just as human beings compose poems not to proclaim their perfection but to confess their incompletion. The instability of existence drives the bonding of matter, and the fragility of feeling drives the bonding of words.

Reaction and Revelation

A chemical reaction is poetry in process: heat rises, colors change, gases bubble, bonds break and remake. Likewise, in poetry, emotions combust, meanings transmute, silence dissolves into sound. Both reaction and poem are acts of revelation—hidden potentials become manifest, invisible affinities become luminous. Consider combustion: oxygen and fuel unite, releasing flame and light. Is this not the very definition of lyricism—the ignition of the inner into outer radiance? Consider photosynthesis: sunlight sculpted into sugar, photons fermented into food. Is this not poetry's labor—turning illumination into nourishment for the soul?

Acids, Alkalies, and Aesthetics

Chemistry distinguishes between acids and bases: sharp, sour, corrosive versus soft, soothing, neutralizing.

Poetry mirrors this dichotomy: there are acidic lines that sear, satirical stanzas that sting, and alkaline lines that soothe, lullabies that calm. Yet paradoxically, the greatest poems are amphoteric: they can burn and balm, corrode and comfort simultaneously. Oxymoron here reigns: bitter-sweet, deadly-beautiful, corrosive-cleansing. Acid etches metal, as truth etches memory. Base neutralizes acid, as forgiveness neutralizes fury. Thus chemistry teaches that balance breeds beauty, and poetry embodies the same principle—sorrow and joy mingling in measured equilibrium.

Catalysts and Creativity

Catalysts quicken reactions without being consumed. Likewise, metaphors catalyze meanings: they accelerate associations, spark connections, unleash cascades of thought, yet remain intact. The poet is a catalytic agent—present but self-effacing, sparking transformation in the reader's mind without vanishing into the reaction. And is not love itself a catalyst? It alters destinies without exhausting itself. Is not grief a catalyst? It accelerates depth of reflection without annihilating the thinker. Chemistry and poetry here converge: life depends not only on raw reactions but on catalysts that confer quickness, intensity, resonance.

Crystals and Cadence

A crystal is chemistry made visible—a poem frozen in matter. Its lattice is geometry incarnate, its facets symmetries sculpted by silence. Poetry, too, crystallizes experience into form: rhyme is rhythm's lattice, stanza is symmetry's structure. Both crystal and sonnet are miracles of order arising from flux, patterns precipitating from chaos. And yet, paradox: a crystal is rigid, fixed, cold, whereas a poem is fluid, living, luminous. But both are beautiful because both reveal the secret symmetry that underlies apparent randomness. The poet polishes words as chemists polish gems, revealing inner radiance through outer form.

Alchemy and Apotheosis

Before chemistry was science, it was alchemy—the dream of turning lead into gold, of matter into spirit. Though discredited as method, alchemy remains true as metaphor. For this, not every poem is an alchemical act—turning pain into beauty, sorrow into song, silence into symphony? The alchemist sought the Philosopher's Stone; the poet seeks the Philosopher's Tone. Both desire transmutation: of matter into meaning, of base experience into noble expression. And just as alchemy gave birth to chemistry, myth gave birth to poetry—each evolving from the mystical into the measurable, yet never losing the shimmer of mystery.

Entropy and Elegance

Chemistry bows to entropy: reactions favor disorder, equilibrium tends toward chaos. Yet poetry resists entropy: its very purpose is to create order, rhythm, repetition, resonance. And yet the paradox persists: the greatest poems embrace disorder, irregular rhythms, surprising enjambments—just as chemistry achieves creativity through instability. Thus, chemistry and poetry are oxymoronic twins: chemistry finds freedom in decay, poetry finds freedom in design. But both whisper the same wisdom: permanence is an illusion; transformation is truth.

The Molecular Music of Life

Proteins fold, DNA coils, lipids layer—life is molecular music, chemistry conducted at cellular scale. Poetry is its parallel: words fold into lines, lines coil into stanzas, stanzas layer into epics. The helix of DNA is a double sonnet, repeating rhyme in spiraling sequence. The hydrogen bond is enjambment between bases, subtle yet sustaining. Chemistry shows us that life itself is lyric—built not from rigid blocks but from pliant patterns, from the molecular dance of rhythm and resonance. Poetry shows us that life is not merely lived but sung.

Beyond Chemistry, Within Poetry

Chemistry stops at reaction, poetry begins at revelation. Chemistry explains the how, poetry explores the why. Chemistry charts the periodic table, poetry plays the periodic lyre. The laboratory and the lyric are not rivals but reflections: both require observation, both demand patience, both honor beauty in transformation. If chemistry is the science of substances, poetry is the science of significance. If chemistry teaches us that nothing is lost, only changed, poetry teaches us that nothing is meaningless, only reimagined.

The Poem as Potion, the Lyric as Laboratory

Poetry and chemistry alike reveal that reality is a dance of unions and separations, of bonds formed and broken, of energies released and absorbed. Both celebrate the paradox of permanence through change, of beauty through breakdown, of resonance through reaction. The poet is an alchemist in spirit, a chemist of emotion, mixing metaphors like molecules, distilling experience into elixir. The chemist is a poet in disguise, unveiling the metaphors of matter, writing sonnets in solutions, odes in oxidation. Together they remind us: all of existence is experiment, and every experiment is an elegy. The universe itself is a beaker, bubbling with reactions of stars and souls. And poetry is its distilled essence, the pure extract of wonder, the potion of permanence in a world of perpetual flux.

The Oxymoron of Substance and Symbol

Chemistry is the science of substances; poetry is the science of symbols. Yet both reveal transformation—one of matter, the other of meaning. Chemistry transmutes base metals into radiant compounds. Poetry transmutes base words into radiant wonders. Chemistry binds atoms into molecules. Poetry binds syllables into stanzas. Chemistry studies what dissolves and combines; poetry is what dissolves the heart and combines the soul. Both are, in truth, ***alchemy reborn***.

The Periodic Table as Poetic Lexicon

Mendeleev's table is a cosmic poem, each element a word, each column a stanza, each row a rhythm.

Hydrogen is the haiku of simplicity.

Carbon is the epic of complexity.

Oxygen is the ode to breath.

Gold is the elegy of eternity.

Poetry too arranges its lexicon: vowels like noble gases, consonants like reactive metals. Both tables speak of patterns: periodicity in physics, periodicity in prosody.

Atoms and Alliterations

An atom is indivisible yet divisible, a paradox of permanence and change. A word is indivisible yet divisible, a paradox of syllable and sound.

Electrons orbit nuclei; vowels orbit consonants.

Neutrons stabilize; pauses stabilize.

Protons charge; stresses charge.

Thus, every stanza is an atomic system, every poem a molecular compound.

Bonds: Ionic, Covalent, Poetic

Ionic bond: one atom gives, the other takes. Poetry too has gifts of metaphor—one image donating, another receiving.

Covalent bond: atoms share electrons. Poetry too is sharing—poet and reader exchanging essence.

Hydrogen bond: delicate, fleeting, yet essential.

Poetry too is fragile, momentary, yet holds the architecture of the soul.

The oxymoron we find here is: strongest fragility.

Reaction and Revelation

Chemistry is the study of reactions; poetry is the study of revelations. Combustion releases energy; passion releases poetry. Oxidation corrodes; sorrow erodes. Catalysts quicken reaction; inspiration quickens revelation. Both require conditions: temperature, concentration, context. A poem too ignites only when the reader is ready.

The Thermodynamics of Lyric

Chemistry obeys thermodynamics:

Energy conserved, entropy increased.

Poetry too obeys paradoxical thermodynamics:

Meaning conserved, mystery increased.

Words never vanish, only transform.

Enthalpy measures heat; poetry measures heart. Entropy ensures disorder; poetry ensures deeper order through disordered words.

Solutions and Solubility

Solvent dissolves solute—poetry dissolves despair. Some salts dissolve easily; some remain insoluble. Some truths melt into metaphor; others resist.

A saturated solution is a poem packed with passion.

A supersaturated solution is a sonnet on the brink of breaking.

Thus, the beaker becomes the book, the solute the symbol.

Acids and Alkalies, Elegy and Euphony

Acids burn with bitterness; bases soothe with softness. Poetry too is acidic satire or alkaline lullaby.

Acidic lines sting with satire.

Alkaline lines heal with hymns.

Neutral pH—balanced ballad.

The paradox we get here is: the sharpest poems purify; the sweetest sometimes sear.

The Alchemy of Metaphor

Ancient alchemists sought the Philosopher's Stone, to turn lead into gold. Poetry is that Stone—turning pain into beauty, death into dignity, despair into delight.

Chemistry transmutes matter.

Poetry transmutes meaning.

Chemistry searches for eternal elixirs.

Poetry becomes eternal elixir itself.

Kinetics and Cadence

Reaction rate depends on collisions, energy, orientation. Poetic rhythm too depends on cadence, stress, intonation.

A slow reaction is a meditation.

A rapid reaction is a revolution.

A catalyst is a metaphor—accelerating resonance without being consumed.

Thus, time in chemistry mirrors time in poetry: dynamic, deliberate, divine.

Polymers and Poetic Forms

Monomers bond into polymers; words bond into forms.

A villanelle is a polymer of refrains.

A sestina is a polymer of end-words.

Free verse is an amorphous polymer—irregular yet resilient.

Therefore, chemistry of plastics mirrors poetry of possibilities.

Crystals and Sonnets

Crystals grow with geometric regularity, each atom aligned. Sonnets too crystallize thought: rigid in form, radiant in beauty.

Cubic crystal = Shakespearean sonnet.

Hexagonal crystal = Petrarchan sonnet.

Amorphous solid = free verse.

The oxymoron here we witness is: the structured spontaneity.

Combustion and Catharsis

Combustion consumes to create light. Poetry too consumes sorrow to create illumination.

Fire transforms wood to ash.

Verse transforms grief to song.

Both leave behind residue—smoke or memory.

Thus, poetry is controlled combustion of consciousness.

DNA and Double Helix of Lyric

Biochemistry reveals DNA: double helix carrying life's code. Poetry too is a double helix: sound and sense spiraling together, replicating across generations.

Bases pair: adenine with thymine, guanine with cytosine.

Words pair: love with loss, joy with grief.

Mutations create novelty; metaphors create innovation.

Poetry is the DNA of culture.

The Chemistry of Creation

Chemistry is the poetry of atoms; poetry is the chemistry of emotions. Chemistry rearranges matter. Poetry rearranges meaning. Chemistry explains the world. Poetry enchants the world. Chemistry is silent poetry; poetry is singing chemistry. Together, they are the alchemy of existence.

POETRY AND BOTANY: THE LYRIC OF LEAVES, ROOTS, AND BLOSSOMS

Poetry and botany are often interconnected while painting buds of beauty, flowers of flavour, leaves of laurel or fruits of fortune and roots of revelation in terms of words. Botany, the science of plants, is in truth the science of patience, the philosophy of photosynthesis, the chronicle of chlorophyll. It studies stems and stamens, roots and rhizomes, petals and pistils, but beneath its botanical catalog lies a spiritual script, an ecological elegy, a leafy language older than alphabets. Poetry, when seen through the green glass of botany, becomes not merely metaphor but metabolism, not merely verse but vegetation. For plants are poems written by sunlight, inscribed in water, annotated by wind. And poetry, in turn, is botany's secret twin: it grows, it blooms, it dies, it seeds again.

Roots as Remembrance, Leaves as Language

Every plant begins in obscurity—seed sunk into soil, hidden in darkness. Yet from that buried silence arises the miracle of sprouting. Likewise, every poem germinates in the unseen soil of thought, in the subterranean silence of imagination. Roots are remembrance: the anchoring past, the unseen sustenance. Leaves are language: open to air, photosynthesizing sense from light. The paradox is clear:

roots hide to hold, leaves expose to express. So too poetry hides its sources in solitude but spreads its syllables to the sun.

Photosynthesis and Poetic Synthesis

Botany's central marvel is photosynthesis: the silent symphony by which sunlight, water, and carbon dioxide transmute into sugar, oxygen, and life itself. This, too, is poetry's function: to turn raw experience into nourishment, to transfigure pain into beauty, to distill the invisible into sustenance. Chlorophyll is a green metaphor for imagination: it catches the light that others ignore, converts radiance into rhythm. Just as photosynthesis feeds the world, poetry oxygenates the soul.

And yet paradox reigns: photosynthesis requires the death of photons, the consumption of light; poetry requires the death of silence, the consumption of stillness. Light dies to become life, silence dies to become song. Thus, both processes prove that sacrifice sustains.

Flowers as Figures, Petals as Paradoxes

The flower is botany's flamboyant paradox: fragile yet fertile, delicate yet determined, ephemeral yet eternal through its seed. Poetry mirrors this paradox precisely. A lyric may last but a page, yet it plants itself in memory for centuries. Petals are paradoxes—tender to touch, yet tenacious against time. Each flower is a metaphor made flesh: the rose as love, the lily as purity, the lotus as enlightenment. But beyond symbolism, the flower is itself a sonnet: four lines of sepals, quatrain of petals, couplet of stamens and pistils—rhyme and rhythm in living symmetry.

Thorns and Tenderness

No flower is without thorn, no poem without tension. The rose is revered not only for its bloom but for its blood-drawing defense. Poetry likewise wounds while it heals, pricks while it perfumes. The oxymoron reigns supreme: tender-thorned, cruelly-kind, dangerously-delicate. Botany teaches that beauty is never unguarded, and poetry teaches that truth is never painless. The thorn is the price of the petal, just as suffering is the soil of song.

Trees: Time's Testimony, Poetry's Parallel

If flowers are fleeting poems, trees are epic epistles. Their rings record history; their branches write in sky-script. A tree is a library in living form: bark as binding, leaves as pages, sap as ink. Each season it revises itself—spring drafts, summer publications, autumn revisions, winter silence. Poetry too has seasons: youthful blossoms of lyricism, mature forests of philosophy, autumn elegies of resignation. Both tree and poem embody paradox: rooted yet rising, stationary yet spanning, silent yet speaking.

Seeds: Silence as Secret Speech

The seed is the epitome of oxymoron: a hushed husk holding hurricanes, a speck storing symphonies. Tiny, tender, almost trivial, yet within it slumbers forests and futures. Poetry is likewise: a single line may spark revolutions, a stanza may stir civilizations. The seed is silence pregnant with speech, and the poem is speech preserving silence. Botany and poetry agree: the smallest containers hold the largest infinities.

Weeds, Wilderness, and Wild Verses

Botany does not only study roses and orchids; it must attend also to weeds—unwanted yet unstoppable. Poetry, too, has its weeds: verses untamed, wild words that defy refinement, raw lyrics that grow in cracks of culture. Weeds are democratic, disdaining cultivation; wild poetry likewise is anarchic, resisting decorum. Yet paradoxically, weeds heal soil, prepare land, preserve ecosystems. Likewise, outlaw poetry purges society, disrupts conventions, rewilds language. In both garden and library, weeds and wild words are necessary nuisances, fierce but fertile.

Pollination and Poetic Propagation

Botany celebrates pollination—the cross-fertilization by wind, water, insects, birds. Likewise, poetry propagates not in isolation but in circulation. Poems pollinate minds, traveling from tongue to tongue, culture to culture, cross-pollinating meanings. The bee is both botanist and bard: it carries pollen like metaphor, gathering nectar like narrative, creating honey like hymn. Sweetness, then, is born of shared movement, of collaboration between flower and forager, poem and reader.

Decay, Compost, and Creative Renewal

Botany does not romanticize only bloom; it reveres decay. Fallen leaves feed soil, rotting roots revive earth, compost creates fertility. Poetry, too, thrives on decay: old languages fertilize new idioms, dead metaphors compost into fresh expressions. Paradox: what dies feeds what lives; what is discarded nourishes what is cherished. Thus, botany's law of compost is poetry's law of creativity: nothing wasted, all transformed.

Ecosystems and Epics

The forest is not a sum of trees but a system of symphonies: roots speaking underground, leaves exchanging gases, fungi weaving unseen webs. Poetry, likewise, is not a sum of stanzas but a living ecology of interwoven voices. The epic is a poetic ecosystem: heroes and histories, gods and mortals, weaving together like canopy, understory, and soil. Both forest and epic teach interdependence: no leaf lives alone, no line lingers without its neighbors.

Green as Grammar of Growth

Botany venerates chlorophyll's green, that color of growth, balance, renewal. Poetry venerates language's green, that grammar of growth, metaphor's renewal. Just as green soothes the eye, poetry soothes the soul. Just as green signals life, poetry signals vitality. The paradox persists: both are ephemeral yet eternal, fragile yet foundational, momentary yet monumental.

Roots: The Hidden Hymns

Roots remain unseen, yet sustain the seen. Poetry too grows from invisible origins: intuition, memory, dream.

Roots are rhizomes of resilience.

Roots are metaphors of memory—ancestry anchoring the present.

Roots absorb nourishment unseen; poems absorb meaning unspoken.

Here, the paradox is: invisible foundations, visible flourishing.

Leaves: Pages of Photosynthesis

Leaves are pages of the plant, writing light into life.

Each leaf is a lyric of light.

Each vein is a verse of vitality.

Stomata are syllables breathing carbon and oxygen.

Botany explains stomatal exchange; poetry hears whispers of green lungs of the world.

Flowers: Petaled Poems

Flowers are plants dreaming in color. Botany explains them as reproductive organs; poetry exalts them as radiant metaphors.

Rose = romance and rebellion.

Lotus = purity and paradox.

Sunflower = loyalty and longing.

Petals are paradox: delicate armor, fragile fortresses. Every blossom is a stanza, fragrant with meaning.

Fruits: Flesh of Fulfillment

Fruits are the future, seeds encased in sweetness.

Botany describes pericarps, endocarps, seeds.

Poetry describes promise, plenitude, posterity.

Apple: temptation and knowledge.

Pomegranate: fertility and infinity.

Here, the oxymoron is mortal immortality—the fruit perishes, the seed persists.

Trees: Timeless Texts

A tree is both biography and library: roots buried in history, branches writing into sky.

The oak = endurance.

The willow = weeping wisdom.

The cedar = sanctity.

Tree rings are chronicles; tree canopies are cathedrals. To study trees botanically is to count cells; to study them poetically is to count centuries.

Photosynthesis: The Green Gospel

Botany names it photosynthesis: conversion of photons to food. Poetry names it miracle: sunlight liquefied into sap.

Chlorophyll is the poet's ink of light.

Photosynthesis is the stanza of survival.

Plants drink light, exhale life.

Thus, the plant is paradox: it eats the intangible, and feeds the tangible.

Ecology of Expression

Plants form forests, communities of communion. Poetry too forms canons, communities of culture.

A forest is an anthology of trees.

A meadow is a miscellany of blossoms.

A garden is a curated collection, like a sonnet sequence.

Botany studies ecosystems; poetry studies ecologies of feeling.

Botany as Metaphor for Human Life

Germination = childhood, bursting forth.

Growth = youth, stretching upward.

Flowering = maturity, radiant but brief.

Fruiting = fulfillment, harvest of deeds.

Withering = decline, wisdom in decay.

Poetry translates botany into biography: the plant as person, the person as plant.

Toxicity and Healing: The Paradox of Plants

Botany reveals both poisons and cures: belladonna and basil, hemlock and hibiscus. Poetry too is both venom and balm.

A bitter poem heals by catharsis.

A sweet poem wounds by remembrance.

The same plant that kills cures.

Oxymoron, the language of poetry we found here is: "deadly vitality".

Seasons and Cycles

Plants follow the cycle of seasons; poetry follows the cycle of moods.

Spring = lyric of birth.

Summer = epic of abundance.

Autumn = elegy of decline.

Winter = haiku of silence.

The ultimate paradox in it is: death within life, life within death. Every falling leaf is both finale and fertility.

Botany and Symbolism

Across cultures, plants are symbols:

Olive branch = peace.

Laurel = victory.

Vine = vitality.

Cactus = endurance in emptiness.

Botany measures morphology; poetry magnifies meaning. The science counts, the art consecrates.

The Garden of Lyric

Botany is the poetry of biology; poetry is the botany of being. Botany explains how plants live. Poetry explains why plants matter. Botany names the stem. Poetry names the spirit. Plants are silent poems; poems are flowering plants. Together, they form the universal garden of thought and life.

Poetry as Plant, Botany as Ballad

Botany and poetry are bound by the same root-rhythm: life as growth, growth as grace, grace as gift. Plants are poems written in green ink; poems are plants blooming in black ink. Both thrive by paradox: they hide yet reveal, they perish yet persist, they are silent yet symphonic. The botanist with a magnifying glass and the poet with a metaphor pursue the same truth: that beauty is both biology and beyond, that structure is both survival and song. In the end, to study plants without poetry is to study skeletons without spirit; to write poetry without botany is to praise petals without roots. Together they reveal the deepest law of life: that everything grows by giving, everything blossoms by breaking, everything lives by losing itself into light. Floras are close to poetry while sketching them as fable and Nature as narrative. Botany is the science of plants; poetry is the song of plants. One dissects while the other dreams. Yet both kneel before the leaf. Botany measures photosynthesis; poetry marvels at the "green alchemy" of sunlight into sustenance. Botany catalogues chlorophyll; poetry crowns it the emerald elixir of eternity. Botany explains roots as anchors; poetry reveres them as ancestral whispers. Thus, plants become paradox: silent yet eloquent, fragile yet eternal.

POETRY AND ZOOLOGY: THE BESTIARY OF BEAUTY AND BEING

Poetry and Zoology are also connected very close where beasts are depicted as ballads and wings as words. Zoology, the science of animals, is ostensibly the catalog of creatures, the classification of claws and colors, the chronicling of calls and cries. Yet beneath this taxonomic table beats a deeper rhythm: every animal is already a stanza, every species a song, every ecosystem an epic. Poetry, when read zoologically, is nothing less than the *lingua bestiarum*—the language of beasts, the alphabet of instincts, the symphony of survival. If botany was the verdant verse of chlorophyll, zoology is the roaring rhetoric of blood and breath. Poetry is the zoologist's shadow, for while zoology dissects the anatomy of animals, poetry discloses their anima—the soul behind the skin.

The Animal as Allegory, the Beast as Ballad

From Aesop to Blake, from cave-paintings to contemporary fables, animals have never been mere specimens but symbols. The lion is courage, the lamb innocence, the serpent cunning, the owl wisdom. Zoology might classify the lion as *Panthera leo*, but poetry hears in its roar the rhetoric of rule. Zoology measures the wingspan of an eagle, but poetry measures its metaphysical reach into freedom. Animals are allegories incarnate, their biology inseparable from their mythology. Poetry is the science of such symbolism, rendering zoology not only a study of skins and skeletons but also of symbols and songs.

Instinct and Imagination: The Twin Drives

Zoology explains behavior through instinct—migration, mating, survival strategies. Poetry, paradoxically, echoes the same instinctual impulses, but elevates them into imagination. The bird builds a nest; the poet builds a verse. The spider spins a web; the poet spins a metaphor. Both are constructions of necessity and beauty: webs catch food, poems catch meaning. Instinct thus becomes the primitive precursor of imagination; imagination the elevated echo of instinct. The oxymoron reigns: instinctual artistry, deliberate spontaneity.

Predation and Poetic Conflict

Nature is not only nurturing—it is predatory, perilous, paradoxical. Zoology chronicles predator and prey, the eternal ballet of fang and feather, claw and camouflage. Poetry too thrives on conflict: the predator of passion hunting the prey of peace, the predator of truth piercing the prey of illusion. Every tragedy is a hunt; every epic is an ecosystem of combat. Yet in this violence lies vitality: without predator, prey overruns; without conflict, poetry stagnates. Thus predation becomes paradox: cruel but creative, destructive yet generative. Poetry and zoology both confess that survival is stained with sorrow, yet also saturated with song.

Metamorphosis and Metaphor

The caterpillar becomes butterfly, the tadpole becomes frog, the larva becomes beetle. Zoology observes metamorphosis as developmental necessity; poetry sees it as metaphor made flesh. The cocoon is both coffin and cradle, both death and resurrection. So too, a poem transforms: the raw caterpillar of chaos becomes the butterfly of beauty. Metamorphosis is the zoological analogue of metaphor, both transfigurations from one form into another, both insisting that identity is not fixed but fluid. Thus, zoology affirms the poet's paradox: that to remain oneself, one must forever change.

Songbirds and Sonic Stanzas

Among zoology's most enchanting discoveries is birdsong—the complex, coded, near-musical languages of avian throats. For poets, this is not mere sound but symphony, not mere signal but sonnet. The nightingale's nocturne, the lark's lyric, the raven's riddle: all remind us that poetry itself may have begun as birdsong, that language's first lyricists were feathered. Zoology dissects syrinx and soundwave, poetry translates song into spirit. Birds thus stand as living bridges: biology's notes becoming metaphysical music.

Animal Consciousness and Poetic Empathy

The zoological debate over animal consciousness—do beasts feel, think, imagine?—is mirrored in poetry's insistence on empathy. Poetry insists on seeing through other eyes, feeling through other skins. To write of the whale is to echo its abyssal solitude; to write of the ant is to taste its collective consciousness. Empathy is poetic zoology, for it recognizes in other species not mere specimens but selves. And here paradox glimmers: poetry humanizes the beast while bestializing the human, showing that man is both king and kin of animals.

Mythic Menageries: From Bestiary to Bard

Medieval bestiaries blurred zoology and mythology: unicorns alongside lions, dragons beside deer. Poetry continues that blurred tradition, refusing the boundary between biological and mythical. Zoology denies the dragon, but poetry delights in it; zoology disproves the phoenix, but poetry preserves its fire. The paradox is luminous: nonexistent creatures are often the most enduring. Poetry turns zoology's limits into legends, teaching that truth sometimes shines brightest in impossibility.

Camouflage, Concealment, and Poetic Subtext

Zoology marvels at camouflage: the chameleon's change, the moth's mimicry, the octopus's vanishing ink. These are biological poems of concealment, evolutionary metaphors of mystery. Poetry too camouflages meaning in metaphor, hides truth behind irony, cloaks clarity in cadence. The poet is a linguistic chameleon, shifting shades to suit context, hiding while revealing. Both poet and predator know that concealment is survival, and paradoxically, revelation too. For only what is hidden may be fully sought.

Domestication and Discipline of Verse

Zoology studies domestication: wild wolves made into dogs, wild cattle made into companions of cultivation. Poetry, too, has its domestications: the raw roar of feeling tamed into meter, the wild instinct of imagery harnessed into form. Yet both preserve a trace of wilderness. The dog remembers the wolf; the sonnet remembers the scream. The paradox is poignant: civilization is a taming of the wild, yet its vitality depends on wilderness never fully erased.

Extinction and Elegy

Zoology mourns extinctions: species silenced, habitats hollowed, voices vanished. Poetry, in turn, composes elegies—not only for individuals but for entire existences. An extinct bird is a lost ballad; a vanished mammal, an unwritten epic. Poetry preserves what zoology records: it grieves where science tallies, it remembers where statistics forget. The paradox: absence becomes presence, silence becomes song, extinction becomes eternal in elegy. Thus poetry is zoology's afterlife, ensuring no creature wholly disappears.

Man as Animal, Animal as Metaphor

Finally, zoology reminds us that humans are animals, primates with pretensions, mammals with metaphors. Poetry both acknowledges and transcends this. Man is animal enough to roar, but poet enough to render roaring into rhetoric. Man is beast enough to bleed, but bard enough to bless blood into beauty. The paradox is eternal: we are at once zoological specimens and poetic subjects, flesh-bound yet word-woven, feral yet formal.

Zoology as Zoo of Zest, Poetry as Ark of Awe

Thus, zoology and poetry are not rivals but reflections. Zoology catalogues animals in order; poetry consecrates animals in wonder. Zoology counts claws; poetry contemplates cries. Zoology measures wingspans; poetry marvels at flights of freedom. Together, they teach us that life is always lyrical, that instinct is imagination in embryo, that every creature carries not only cells but songs. In the end, Noah's ark was both zoological and poetic: a literal catalog of species, a symbolic stanza of survival and so too, every poem is an ark, carrying beasts and birds, instincts and images, biology and beauty, across the floods of time.

The Beast as Paradox

Zoology dissects sinew and skeleton; poetry discerns spirit and symbol. Yet both are fascinated by the fauna of existence. Zoology studies instinct; poetry studies intuition. Zoology names species; poetry names significance. Zoology speaks of evolution; poetry speaks of eternal archetypes. The oxymoron we locate here is *the beast is both mute music and eloquent silence.*

The Lion: Majesty and Mortality

Zoology hails the lion as apex predator, king of carnivores. Poetry hails it as monarch of metaphors.

Zoology: the lion survives by strength.

Poetry: the lion rules by symbolism—courage, sovereignty, sacrifice.

Paradox: the king of beasts is also slave to hunger.

Thus, biology gives anatomy, poetry grants anthems.

The Dove: Flesh and Faith

In poetry flesh and faith are interconnected and are meaningful to each other.

Zoology: the dove is Columbidae, gentle granivore, wings of white.

Poetry: the dove is peace, purity, promise.

Dove carries olive branch after flood.

Dove symbolizes the soul ascending.

Zoology sees feathers and flight; poetry sees faith and forgiveness.

The Serpent: Venom and Vision

Zoology studies scales, slithering, venom. Poetry studies sin, seduction, and secret wisdom. Serpent is symbol of temptation in Genesis. Serpent is symbol of eternity in Ouroboros. Serpent is symbol of healing in Asclepius' staff. The oxymoron we find here is "deadly savior". Where Zoology names toxicity; poetry names it transcendence.

Birds: The Lyric of the Sky

Birds are poems with wings.

Zoology describes hollow bones, migratory maps, aerodynamics.

Poetry describes transcendence, freedom, fragile flight.

Nightingale = nocturnal music.

Eagle = exalted empire.

Peacock = proud paradox: beauty and burden.

Every bird is both fact and fable, feather and figure.

Insects: Miniature Miracles

Zoology marvels at metamorphosis, colonies, chitinous structures. Poetry marvels at miniature metaphors.

Ant = industry, invisible empire.

Butterfly = resurrection, fragile eternity.

Firefly = fleeting flame, ephemeral enlightenment.

The paradox we find here, is the smallest beings bear the heaviest symbolism.

Aquatic Allegories

Zoology studies gills, scales, fins. Poetry studies symbols submerged in myth.

Whale: wisdom and wonder, Jonah's jailor yet guardian.

Dolphin: joy, intelligence, salvation.

Shark: shadow of fear, sharpness of survival.

Thus, seas are not only ecosystems but epics.

The Dog: Loyalty and Loss

Zoology: *Canis familiaris*, domesticated descendant of wolves.

Poetry: guardian, guide, grief-bearer.

Argos waits for Odysseus.

Anubis guides souls to afterlife.

Every dog embodies paradox: wild domesticated, mortal immortalized.

The Cat: Mystery and Majesty

Zoology: *Felis catus/ Felis domestica* , solitary yet sociable.

Poetry: symbol of independence, mystery, moonlit silence.

Egyptian sphinx = wisdom veiled.

Medieval witch's familiar = paradox of innocence and fear.

Cat is oxymoron: affectionate aloofness.

Horses: Motion and Myth

Zoology: *Equus ferus caballus,* hoofed mammal, muscular endurance.

Poetry: Pegasus, stallion of spirit, steed of strength.

Chariots of war and of gods. Horses embody paradox: power harnessed, wildness tamed. Zoology measures stride; poetry measures spirit.

Invertebrates: Silent Symbols

Spider: weaver of webs, fate and fear.

Snail: slow resilience, spiral of self.

Octopus: mystery, multiplicity, intelligence in ink.

Zoology lists taxonomy; poetry reads theology. Even soft bodies bear hard truths.

Evolution as Epic

Darwin tells story of adaptation. Poetry tells story of aspiration.

Zoology: survival of the fittest.

Poetry: survival of the fairest.

Evolution is a narrative of necessity; poetry transforms it into narrative of nobility.

Human Animal: Anthropology of Awe

Zoology claims man is primate; poetry claims man is paradox—beast with breath of gods. Zoology measures brain volume; poetry measures dreams. Zoology names Homo sapiens; poetry names "creature of contradictions." The oxymoron in between is the rational beast and the divine dust.

The Ark of Poetry

Zoology catalogues the ark of species. Poetry preserves the ark of symbols. Both save from flood of forgetfulness. Zoology keeps data. Poetry keeps dignity. Zoology explains animals. Poetry exalts them.

The Bestial Benediction

Zoology and poetry, though distant, are deeply united. One dissects anatomy, the other discovers archetype. One classifies species, the other consecrates spirit. Every animal is an equation, yet every equation is an elegy. Every beast is a body, yet everybody is a ballad. Thus, zoology is the prose of animals; poetry is their hymn.

POETRY AND MATHEMATICS: THE GEOMETRY OF GRACE AND THE ALGEBRA OF AWE

At first glance, mathematics and poetry appear opposed: one precise, one passionate; one deductive, one dreamy. Yet beneath their apparent antithesis lies their ultimate unity: both seek order in chaos, clarity in complexity, beauty in balance. Mathematics is the language of logic; poetry is the logic of language. Mathematics abstracts; poetry adorns. Mathematics counts stars; poetry converses with them. Thus, each is paradox: rigid flexibility, austere adornment, rational rapture.

Poetry and Mathematics – Numbers as Narratives, Equations as Elegies

Mathematics is often painted as poetry's polar opposite: precise, rigid, logical, devoid of metaphor. Yet in truth, mathematics and poetry are twin languages of infinity, parallel expressions of the ineffable. One counts while the other chants; one calculates while the other consecrates. And yet—both are concerned with patterns, with beauty, with symmetry, with truth. Where the mathematician inscribes equations upon the void, the poet inscribes verses upon the void. Each seeks coherence in chaos, form in flux, certainty in shadows. Thus, paradoxically, mathematics is a mute poetry, and poetry a mathematics that sings.

The Arithmetic of Aesthetics

At its root, arithmetic is the science of numbers. But what is a number if not a symbol, a metaphor, a condensed poem of proportion? The number one whispers of unity, solitude, the paradox of singularity. The number two sings of division, dialogue, duality—both conflict and complement. The number three becomes a triadic hymn: thesis, antithesis, synthesis; body, mind, soul; past, present, future. Thus numbers, ostensibly abstract, already carry narrative and metaphor. Mathematics merely measures them; poetry magnifies them. Arithmetic, when seen poetically, becomes the alphabet of aesthetics, the syllables of symmetry.

Geometry as the Grammar of Beauty

Plato declared geometry divine, for in shapes he saw eternal truths. A circle is eternity—endless yet enclosed. A square is stability—earthly, grounded, unmoving. A triangle is paradoxical—stable yet sharp, finite yet pointing infinitely upward. Geometry, then, is the silent grammar of beauty, structuring both temples and sonnets. The Golden Ratio, that divine proportion, reveals how mathematics underpins art, architecture, even anatomy. Poetry, with its meters and measures, is geometry in language—lines structured with angles of alliteration, arcs of assonance, symmetries of rhyme. Thus, geometry and poetry are but two grammars of grace, one in numbers, the other in words.

Algebra and the Poetics of the Unknown

Algebra introduces the mysterious "x", the unknown quantity, the invisible variable. Here, mathematics becomes metaphorical. For is not life itself an algebra of uncertainties? Is not the human heart always solving for "x"—that elusive unknown of love, meaning, or destiny? Poetry, too, thrives in unknowns: it does not define but suggests, does not solve but sings. An algebraic equation is, in essence, a paradoxical poem: an equality across difference, a balance of opposites. Poetry is algebra with imagery; algebra is poetry with symbols. Both confess that the unknown is not absence but possibility, not void but vision.

Calculus and the Infinite in the Infinitesimal

Calculus examines change, the infinite in the infinitesimal, the vastness contained in vanishing points. The derivative is the instant's secret, the tangent to time. The integral is accumulation, the gathering of countless grains into continuity. Poetry, too, seeks the infinite in the infinitesimal: the fleeting sigh elevated into eternity, the single tear magnified into an ocean of sorrow. A haiku is calculus in miniature—capturing infinity in seventeen syllables. Calculus, then, is a lyrical logic: the paradox that infinity is constructed of fragments, that eternity is an endless sum of instants.

Probability, Paradox, and Poetic Chance

Probability is mathematics' way of quantifying uncertainty, weighing the odds of the unseen. But in its heart lies poetry, for chance is always paradoxical. What is love if not improbable? What is inspiration if not incalculable? Probability speaks in percentages, but poetry speaks in paradoxes: the unlikely becomes inevitable, the impossible becomes intimate. A dice throw is both mathematics and metaphor, a random roll that reverberates with destiny. Poetic chance is probability's shadow: the oxymoron of patterned unpredictability, order woven from accident.

Symmetry and the Sublime

Mathematics worships symmetry: the mirror, the balance, the invariance across transformation. Poetry too craves symmetry, whether in rhyme schemes, stanzaic structures, or mirrored metaphors. Yet both also delight in asymmetry, for too much balance is sterile, too much perfection lifeless. The beauty of symmetry is paradoxical: it pleases by its order, but astonishes when broken. A Shakespearean sonnet's final couplet twists symmetry into surprise, just as a fractal shape reveals infinite asymmetry within apparent order. Thus, mathematics and poetry agree: symmetry is the skeleton of beauty, asymmetry its breath.

Fractals and the Infinite Refrain

Modern mathematics unveils fractals: patterns repeating endlessly at every scale, self-similar yet ever-changing. The coastline, the cloud, the fern, the galaxy—all echo fractal rhythm. Poetry, too, thrives on refrain and recursion: the repeated line in a villanelle, the circular motif in an epic, the eternal return of themes. Both fractal and refrain reveal infinity folded within finitude, the cosmos concealed in the commonplace. A fractal equation is a visual poem; a refrain is a fractal of feeling. Both whisper: "Infinity is nearer than it appears."

Equations as Elegies

An equation is not merely a calculation—it is an assertion of beauty. Einstein's $E=mc^2$ is a cosmic haiku: energy equals matter multiplied by the speed of light squared, a universe compressed into symbols. Pythagoras's theorem is a timeless lyric of rightness and relation. Equations endure as poems of permanence, elegies for eternity, distilling the sprawling cosmos into crystalline clarity. Yet paradoxically, they are also oxymoronic: silent yet speaking, abstract yet embodied, rigid yet radiant. To read an equation is to hear the mute music of the spheres.

Infinity: The Poet's and Mathematician's Horizon

Mathematics wrestles endlessly with infinity: is it countable, uncountable, a number or a notion? Poetry likewise gazes into infinity, naming it with paradox: eternal moment, boundless boundary, silent song. Infinity is the mathematician's torment and the poet's treasure, an unending horizon that can never be reached yet never be escaped. Where mathematics defines infinity by symbols, poetry defines it by sighs. The paradox is luminous: infinity can never be contained, and yet it is the container of all.

Poetry as the Mathematics of Meaning

If mathematics is the science of patterns, poetry is the science of meanings. Both employ symbols, both seek beauty, both reach for truth. Yet mathematics demands precision while poetry delights in ambiguity. And yet—without ambiguity, meaning dies; without precision, beauty dissolves. Thus they are complements, not contradictions: mathematics is poetry restrained, and poetry is mathematics released. To unite them is to glimpse the cosmic calculus of creation: the numbers that sing, the stanzas that count.

Numbers Singing, Verses Calculating

Poetry and mathematics, far from enemies, are echoes. One articulates beauty through numbers, the other through words. One measures stars, the other marvels at them. One calculates the bridge's span, the other consecrates its crossing. Yet both affirm the paradox that the universe is intelligible, patterned, profound. In the end, the mathematician is a poet of proofs, and the poet a mathematician of mysteries. Both whisper, in different dialects: the cosmos is written in symbols, and every symbol is a song.

Numbers as Narrative

Numbers are not mere measures; they are metaphors.

"One" = unity, origin, the monad.

"Two" = duality, division, dialogue.

"Three" = trinity, synthesis, resolution.

"Zero" = paradox of plenitude and emptiness: a circle of nothing, womb of infinity.

Poetry transforms arithmetic into archetype; mathematics turns archetypes into axioms.

Geometry: The Poetics of Space

Geometry is the poetry of shapes; poetry is the geometry of shadows.

Circle: eternity, infinite symmetry, a paradox of perfection.

Triangle: trinity, stability, upward aspiration.

Square: solidity, structure, stubborn stillness.

Spiral: infinity in motion, eternity unfolding.

Botany gives spirals to sunflower seeds; poetry gives spirals to souls. Geometry is not cold calculation but *crystalline chorus*.

Algebra: The Lyric of Letters

Algebra turns numbers into symbols, equations into enigmas. Poetry too turns symbols into syllables, enigmas into emotions.

"x" is the unknown, the unsolved, the lover yet unnamed.

Equations are paradoxical promises: balance amid difference.

Inequalities echo injustices; equalities echo equilibrium.

Thus, algebra is oxymoron: abstract intimacy, anonymous exactness.

Calculus: The Hymn of Change

Calculus studies the infinitesimal, the vanishing yet vital.

Derivative: momentary motion, the poetry of the instant.

Integral: accumulation, memory of moments, mathematics of memory.

Infinity: the unreachable yet indispensable, paradox incarnate.

Poetry likewise dwells in fleeting instants—"a sigh, a glance"—yet integrates them into immortal meaning.

Probability: The Paradox of Chance and Certainty

Mathematics calculates chance; poetry contemplates fate. Probability is rational uncertainty. Poetry is emotional uncertainty. Both describe life's oxymoron: predictable unpredictability. A coin toss becomes symbol: heads and tails, fate and freedom.

Symmetry and Aesthetics

Mathematics measures symmetry; poetry celebrates it.

Fibonacci sequence in petals.

Golden ratio in architecture.

Rhymes mirror rhythms; stanzas mirror structures.

Beauty is balanced equation, whether of syllables or sides. Symmetry is mathematics singing.

Paradox of Infinity

Infinity is mathematics' deepest riddle and poetry's dearest muse.

Infinite series: endless addition.

Infinite regress: eternal return.

Infinity is oxymoron: limitlessness bound in symbol ∞.

Poetry embraces infinity in love, longing, eternity. Mathematics maps it; poetry marvels at it.

Chaos and Order

Chaos theory: sensitive dependence on initial conditions. Poetry: sensitive dependence on initial emotions. One word may change a poem's destiny. One decimal may change an equation's solution. Both thrive in paradox: chaos conceals order; order conceals chaos.

Mathematical Structures as Poetic Forms

Sonnet = equation: fixed form, infinite variation.

Haiku = geometry of brevity.

Epic = infinite series of narrative terms.

Poetry and mathematics both embrace constraint as catalyst: discipline births freedom.

Logic and Lyric

Mathematics is logic. Poetry is lyric. Yet lyric is hidden logic, and logic is hidden lyric. Proof is a poem of precision. Poem is a proof of passion. A theorem is sonnet-like: beginning in hypothesis, ending in conclusion, bound by beauty. Thus, both disciplines are different dialects of the same divine language.

Human Mind as Mathematician and Poet

The brain counts and chants. It calculates and contemplates. The left hemisphere reasons; the right sings. Yet both meet in metaphor, where equation becomes elegy. The human is paradox: rational poet, poetic mathematician.

Algebra of Awe

Mathematics and poetry are not rivals but reflections. Mathematics explains how the universe works; poetry explains why it matters. Mathematics names the pattern; poetry names the purpose. Mathematics provides certainty; poetry preserves mystery. Every equation is a poem in disguise; every poem is an equation in dream. Together, mathematics and poetry compose the geometry of grace and algebra of awe—two tongues of one truth.

POETRY AND THEOLOGY: THE METAPHYSICS OF METAPHOR AND THE LITURGY OF LANGUAGE

Poetry and theology are interconnected to each other. We see verses as votive flames and hymns as hidden horizons. Theology, at its core, is the attempt of finite minds to speak of the Infinite. Poetry, at its essence, is the attempt of fragile tongues to sing the unsayable. Thus, theology and poetry are twin pilgrims, kneeling at the threshold of mystery, stammering toward silence. Where theology systematizes the sacred, poetry sanctifies the systemless. Where theology defines God through doctrines, poetry deifies mystery through metaphors. And yet, paradoxically, they are not rivals but reflections—two ways of wrestling with what transcends reason, two ways of naming what cannot be named.

The Paradox of God and Grammar

Theology seeks to speak of the ineffable, to define the divine. Poetry seeks to sing the unsayable, to hymn the hidden. Both stand before mystery with trembling tongues.

Theology is doctrine: system, creed, canon.
Poetry is doxology: song, sigh, silence.

Theology argues *quid sit Deus* (what God is); poetry asks *quid est amor* (what is love).

To define God is to diminish God, yet to refuse language is to betray longing. Poetry becomes the paradoxical priest, offering words that wound and heal.

Poetry as Prayer

Every prayer is proto-poem, every psalm proof that theology is lyrical before it is logical.

Psalms cry with cadence: "The Lord is my shepherd…"—metaphor as metaphysics.

Rumi whirls words into divine dance.

Dante builds *Divina Commedia* as cathedral of tercets.

Prayer is poetry addressed upward; poetry is prayer addressed outward.

The Divine as Metaphor

Theology names God: Father, King, Light, Shepherd, Rock. Yet each name is paradox, oxymoron.

God is *immovable mover* (Aristotle).

God is *distant intimacy, terrible tenderness*.

God is lion and lamb, fire and fountain, silence and song.

Here, poetry saves theology: metaphors allow mystery without mutilation.

The Word and the World

"In the beginning was the Word" (Logos). Theology begins in language. Poetry is its twin.

Logos = reason, speech, structure.

Poetry is the Logos incarnate in lyric.

World is woven of words; theology interprets them; poetry re-enchants them. The universe is text: theology reads it doctrinally, poetry reads it devotionally.

Liturgy as Living Poetry

Rituals are poems enacted, ceremonies are stanzas embodied.

Mass is a metrical movement: Kyrie, Gloria, Credo.

Chant is rhyme before rhythm.

Bells toll in alliteration, incense rises as metaphor of prayer.

Liturgy is not less than poetry—it is poetry incarnate.

The Paradox of Silence

Theology insists some truths are ineffable: *apophatic theology*. Poetry insists silence itself in its stanza. Silence as eloquence. Poetry depicts absence as presence, wordless hymn as highest theology.

Theodicy and Tragedy

How can God be good when evil exists? Theology wrestles with theodicy; poetry bleeds with lament. Job's cry is poetry more than prose. Holocaust poets give theology its truest trembling. Poetry transforms problem into paradox, paradox into prayer. Theology argues; poetry agonizes. Both are valid; both necessary.

Theology of Love

"Deus caritas est" (God is love). But love is most poetic word. Theology defines agape, eros, philia. Poetry enacts them in sighs and sonnets. Divine love is oxymoron: infinite intimacy, eternal embrace in temporal touch.

Cosmic Hymns: Stars as Psalms

Theology looks up: heavens declare glory of God. Poetry looks up: stars sing silent sonnets. Astronomy counts stars; theology consecrates them; poetry converses with them. Poetry sees universe as cathedral of constellations, each galaxy a glyph of God. Silence of space is symphony of Spirit.

Mysticism: When Poetry Becomes Theology

Mystics dissolve border.

St. John of the Cross: "Dark night of the soul."

Hafiz: drunken with divine wine.

Kabir: weaving God into fabric of daily life.

Mysticism is theology as poetry, poetry as theology. Ecstasy is stanza; vision is verse.

Christ as Poem

Christianity calls Christ the *Word made flesh*. If so, Christ is poem incarnate: metaphor embodied, Logos lyrical.

Paradox: mortal immortal, crucified conqueror.

Oxymoron: suffering savior, dying divinity.

To read Christ is to read cosmic poem where blood is ink and resurrection is rhyme.

Heresy and Hymn

Theology polices orthodoxy; poetry pleads for plurality. Yet even heresies are hymns gone astray. Arianism, Gnosticism, etc.—theological errors, poetic metaphors misapplied. Orthodoxy is canon; poetry is apocrypha. Yet both reveal longing for logos.

The Sacred Stammer

All true theology begins in paradox, in the oxymoron of the divine: God is infinite yet intimate, transcendent yet immanent, absent yet omnipresent. Poetry, likewise, thrives in paradox: silence that speaks, darkness that illuminates, absence that aches with presence. Together, they create what might be called the sacred stammer—a language both broken and burning, both halting and holy. The psalms tremble with this paradox: laments that praise, sorrows that sing, despair that dares to trust. Theology makes the claim; poetry gives it cadence. Theology pronounces; poetry prays.

Metaphor as the Mother of Mystery

Theology cannot speak of God literally, for the literal dissolves before the Infinite. Thus, it must borrow metaphor: God as light, God as shepherd, God as rock, God as lover. Poetry, the mother of metaphor, provides theology with its sacred syllables. Without poetry, theology starves, reduced to arid abstraction. With poetry, theology breathes, radiant with living likenesses. Every metaphor, however, is paradoxical: it reveals and conceals, illumines and obscures. To call God "light" is true, yet false, for God is not light but beyond it. To call God "father" is tender, yet limited, for God is also mother and more. Thus metaphor, in both poetry and theology, opens horizons rather than closes them.

Prayer as Poetry, Poetry as Prayer

A prayer is a poem addressed upward, and a poem is a prayer addressed outward. The overlap is undeniable. The Lord's Prayer is a carefully measured verse; the Psalms are lyric laments and jubilant hymns. Conversely, the sonnets of John Donne, the hymns of George Herbert, the canticles of St. Francis—these are prayers in poetic form, theology turned into tremor. In prayer, the self is dissolved into song; in poetry, the world is dissolved into wonder. Both are votive flames, flickering toward infinity.

The Paradox of Silence and Song

Theology insists that God is beyond words; poetry insists that silence itself is a form of speech. Thus, paradoxically, the closer one comes to the Divine, the more language falters. The mystics speak of the "cloud of unknowing," the desert of speech, the silence more eloquent than syllables. Yet it is precisely in this silence that poetry flourishes, for poetry is the art of making silence sing. Theology declares that God is unsayable; poetry dares to say the unsayable in whispers, in symbols, in sighs. Silence, paradoxically, becomes the loudest hymn.

The Poetics of Scripture

Sacred texts themselves are poetic: the Vedas chant hymns of cosmic order, the Psalms sing of anguish and adoration, the Qur'an resounds in rhythm and rhyme, the Tao Te Ching whispers paradoxes in crystalline brevity. Theology interprets these texts, but poetry composes them. Revelation is always written in rhythm, for prose cannot hold the weight of the divine. To read scripture is to hear poetry consecrated as commandment, metaphor transfigured into mystery. Every prophet is also a poet, and every verse of scripture a stanza in the divine epic.

Ritual and Rhythm

Ritual is embodied poetry: the rhythm of liturgy, the cadence of chants, the symmetry of sacraments. Every Mass is a metrical drama; every mantra is a melodic refrain. Theology codifies the ritual, but poetry animates it. The rosary beads, counted like syllables, are a tactile sonnet to the sacred. The Islamic call to prayer is as much a poem as a proclamation. Rituals embody rhyme; they move in measured motions, echoing eternity through repetition. Theology explains the why, but poetry enacts the how.

The Theological Oxymoron: *Deus Absconditus*

Theology often speaks of the *Deus absconditus*—the hidden God, the God who reveals by concealing. Poetry, too, delights in oxymorons: sweet sorrow, burning ice, dark radiance. Together, they confess that truth is two-toned, paradoxical, never flat. God is both wrath and mercy, both justice and grace, both lion and lamb. Poetry revels in these contradictions, not to resolve them but to reveal them. The oxymoron becomes a ladder to the ineffable, a verbal paradox that points to the supra-verbal. Theology analyzes it; poetry adores it.

Eschatology and Eternal Echoes

Theology contemplates the end of time—the resurrection, the final judgment, the kingdom without end. Poetry contemplates eternity in miniature—the eternal moment, the immortal memory, the deathless dream. Both stretch language to breaking, trying to articulate what is beyond articulation. Dante's Paradiso is both theology and poetry: systematic and soaring, scholastic and sublime. Milton's Paradise Lost is likewise: a theological treatise transfigured into epic song. Eschatology is poetry's ultimate prospect—where every tear is transfigured into a trope, every sorrow into a sonnet, every ending into eternal beginning.

Poetry as the Theology of the Heart

Where theology is the head's doctrine, poetry is the heart's creed. Theology analyzes the attributes of God; poetry adores the presence of God. Theology reasons; poetry rhapsodizes. Theology defines; poetry dissolves. And yet both, paradoxically, are incomplete without each other. Theology without poetry is dry dogma; poetry without theology risks sentimental vagueness. But when wedded, they create what Pascal foresaw: the heart has its reasons which reason does not know. Poetry becomes theology's song, and theology becomes poetry's spine.

The Hymn beyond Words

At the horizon where poetry and theology converge, one discovers a truth: all language longs to become hymn, and all hymns long to become silence. Poetry does not prove God, but it provides a place for God to appear. Theology does not exhaust mystery, but it names the necessity of mystery. Together, they affirm that existence itself is liturgical, that life itself is a poem offered to the divine. In the end, both poetry and theology fall silent, and in that silence the hymn beyond words is heard.

Final Paradox: Poetry beyond Theology

Theology seeks to define divine; poetry dares to dance with divine. Theology builds systems; poetry builds songs. Theology argues existence; poetry adores essence. Theology concludes; poetry continues. Theology without poetry becomes lifeless law; poetry without theology becomes groundless gush. Together they form a liturgy of language, a metaphysics of metaphor, a cathedral of cadence.

The Liturgy of Language

Poetry and theology are not two but one. Theology is poetry disciplined. Poetry is theology liberated. Both kneel before mystery, one with creeds, the other with couplets. Poetry is theology singing; theology is poetry kneeling. Both are the Word, and the Word is with God, and the Word is God.

POETRY AND LAW: THE JURIS-PRUDENCE OF JUSTICE AND THE RHETORIC OF RHYTHM

Poetry and law are interconnected to each other where verses are verdicts, and Justice is a lyric of order. Law, in its austere attire, is the architecture of authority, the scaffolding of society. Poetry, in its luminous liberty, is the architecture of imagination, the scaffolding of soul. At first sight, they appear estranged: law demands precision, poetry delights in ambiguity; law constrains, poetry liberates; law commands, poetry cajoles. Yet, paradoxically, beneath these differences, both law and poetry spring from the same fountain—the human hunger for harmony, for order wrapped in meaning, for justice dressed in rhythm.

The Paradox of Codes and Cadence

Law speaks in statutes, clauses, contracts—rigid, reasoned, written. Poetry speaks in stanzas, couplets, cadences—fluid, flexible, felt. At first, they appear irreconcilable: one solemn, one singing. Yet in truth, both are attempts at the same transcendent task:

To articulate order from chaos.

To preserve permanence in fleeting time.

To balance the scales of meaning.

Law is poetry without metaphor; poetry is law without mandate.

The Lexicon of Law as Lyric

Every legal code is a kind of verse.

Habeas corpus: rhythm of rights.

Pacta sunt servanda: contracts as cadenced covenant.

Constitutions as sonnets of statehood.

Legal phrasing often mirrors poetic phrasing: archaic repetition, solemn parallelism, ritual rhythm. A judgment is a juridical epic.

Justice as Poetic Balance

Lady Justice holds scales: symbol of symmetry.

In poetry, balance is rhyme and meter.

In law, balance is fairness and equity.

In both, imbalance is tragedy.

Thus, jurisprudence is a kind of aesthetics: harmony of rights and duties, melody of mandates and freedoms.

Law as Narrative

Every trial is a tale, every case a chronicle. Prosecutor and defense are storytellers. Evidence is imagery. Verdict is climax. Like epic poetry, law is narrative with consequence. Where poetry persuades heart, law persuades history.

Rhetoric and Oratory

The courtroom is theatre of rhetoric.

Cicero's speeches = juridical poetry.

Lincoln's Gettysburg Address = law as lyric.

Gandhi's courtroom statements = poems of protest.

Here oxymoron thrives: cold fire of logic, fiery chill of reason.

The Paradox of Law: Freedom Through Constraint

Law limits liberty yet guarantees liberty. Poetry too thrives in paradox:

Sonnet's 14 lines restrict yet liberate creativity.

Law's clauses constrain yet ensure justice.

Constraint creates freedom.

Both law and poetry reveal that boundaries are not prisons but portals.

Law and Lament

Unjust laws scar society. Poets protest with elegies. Civil rights poetry fuels reforms. Abolitionist hymns toppled slavery. Feminist verses pierced patriarchy. When law betrays justice, poetry resurrects justice. Law may codify oppression, but poetry prophesies liberation.

Poetic Justice

We speak of "poetic justice": fate punishing vice, rewarding virtue. This proves that law itself has an aesthetic essence. Justice is not merely legal—it is lyrical. Tragedy shows hubris punished. Comedy shows harmony restored. Both are poetic jurisprudence.

The Oxymoron of Objectivity

Law claims objectivity, yet interpretation is inevitable.

Judges are poets of jurisprudence: they interpret text into living truth.

Constitutions are like sacred scriptures: endlessly re-read, re-written in spirit.

Objectivity is oxymoron: subjective striving for impartiality.

Thus, law and poetry share hermeneutics: art of interpretation.

Punishment as Parable

Every penalty is paradox: deterrent yet punishment, justice yet suffering. Imprisonment is both order and oppression. Death penalty is both retribution and tragedy. Poetry exposes this paradox: that justice can wound as it heals.

Law as Covenant, Poetry as Prophecy

Law binds society; poetry unbinds society.

Law = covenant: contract of coexistence.

Poetry = prophecy: voice of future, voice of conscience.

Together, they are dialectic: order and inspiration, duty and dream.

History of Law through Poetry

Ancient codes were written as verse. Hammurabi's Code inscribed like hymn. Mosaic Law is poetic in parallelism. Roman law infused with rhetoric. Thus, poetry is origin of law. Where law began in song, it must return to song to remain alive.

Final Paradox: Law beyond Law

Law seeks to regulate conduct; poetry seeks to redeem conscience. Law demands compliance; poetry demands compassion. Law is external order; poetry is internal order. Law without poetry is tyranny; poetry without law is anarchy. Together they create symphony of justice.

The Jurisprudence of Rhythm

Poetry and law are not estranged. Law is the prose of justice; poetry is the passion of justice. Law guards; poetry guides. Law commands, poetry consoles. Law is frozen poetry, poetry is living law. Thus, jurisprudence is revealed as rhythm, and rhythm as jurisprudence. Poetry is the higher court where justice is not only decreed but also desired.

The Letter and the Lyric

The law is lettered; poetry is lyrical. Yet both letters and lyrics live in language, and language is their common court. A statute is a kind of sonnet: it has form, measure, restriction, precision. A legal judgment is a narrative: it unfolds like an epic, with heroes, villains, conflicts, and resolution. Just as poets weigh syllables, judges weigh clauses. Just as poets carve cadences, legislators carve codices. Poetry ennobles law with beauty; law endows poetry with gravity. One binds through beauty, the other beautifies through binding.

The Paradox of Liberty and Restraint

Law is paradox incarnate: it restrains in order to free, it binds in order to unbind. Without law, liberty collapses into chaos; with law, liberty becomes luminous order. Poetry too thrives in paradox: the poet restricts himself to meter and rhyme in order to achieve freedom of expression. The sonnet, the haiku, the ghazal—these strictures create spaciousness. In this way, both law and poetry are paradoxical disciplines: freedom through form, power through restraint, creativity through codification.

Justice as a Poetic Ideal

Law seeks justice; poetry sings justice. Law codifies fairness into statutes; poetry cries fairness into hearts. When injustice reigns, law becomes weaponized prose; when justice reigns, law becomes living poetry. Martin Luther King Jr.'s speeches were legal appeals wrapped in poetic cadence. Gandhi's satyagraha was both jurisprudence and hymn. Justice itself is an aesthetic: symmetry of fairness, rhythm of equity, balance of rights. The scales of justice are poetic metaphors themselves, embodying law's lyric longing for equilibrium.

Testimony as Tragedy, Verdict as Verse

The courtroom itself is theatrical, almost literary: witnesses deliver monologues, lawyers weave narratives, evidence is presented as plot, juries are audiences, and the judge's verdict is the climactic couplet. Testimony often has the pathos of tragedy; verdicts often possess the finality of epigrams. The law, in practice, is drama distilled into deliberation, a legal Iliad with lesser heroes and higher stakes. Poetry mirrors this: it testifies to suffering, delivers judgments of the soul, and proclaims verdicts in verse.

The Oxymoron of Justice: Blind but All-Seeing

Lady Justice is blind, yet sees more than all; impartial,

yet passionately invested; detached, yet deeply humane. This oxymoron is poetic in its essence. To say justice is "blind" is to speak metaphorically, paradoxically: she cannot see faces but perceives fairness. Similarly, poetry thrives in such oxymorons: "sweet sorrow," "silent thunder," "dark dawn." Both law and poetry employ oxymoronic truth to gesture toward ideals that logic alone cannot contain.

Codification and Canonization

Just as poetry seeks canonization in anthologies, law seeks codification in statutes. The Code of Hammurabi, the Ten Commandments, the Magna Carta—all legal documents have been written with poetic concision. "Thou shalt not kill" is not only a commandment but also a rhythm, a four-beat imperative echoing across millennia. Constitutions, too, are written in poetic brevity: "We the People," "Liberty, Equality, Fraternity," "Life, Liberty, and the pursuit of Happiness." These are legal formulas, but also lyrical refrains.

Law as Living Poem of the Polis

At its best, law is the city's collective poem, composed not in stanzas but in statutes, not in rhyme but in rights. Every amendment is a metaphorical revision; every legal precedent is a refrain. Poetry reveals the soul of the polis; law sustains its structure. Together, they guard both spirit and scaffolding. When law forgets poetry, it becomes tyranny; when poetry forgets law, it becomes chaos. But when they harmonize, civilization sings: justice with rhythm, liberty with lyric, order with beauty.

Rebellion and Redress

Poetry often rebels against unjust law, becoming a prophetic voice. Shelley declared poets to be the "unacknowledged legislators of the world." This paradox rings true: poets legislate not with statutes but with stanzas, shaping consciences more powerfully than constitutions. Every revolution has been preceded by poetry: the songs of the French Revolution, the hymns of abolition, the chants of civil rights. Law may silence, but poetry resurrects. Law may punish, but poetry prophesies. Together, paradoxically, they correct and complete one another: law enforces justice externally, poetry inflames it internally.

The Lyric of Justice: Law's Logos, Poetry's Pathos

Law appeals to logos, that is to rationality, logic, and the measured scales of argument. Poetry appeals to pathos, that is to emotion, empathy, and the trembling chords of the heart. But the paradox is that both require the other. Law without pathos becomes cold bureaucracy; poetry without logos becomes incoherent babble. Together, they weave ethos—the credibility of a culture, the moral architecture of a community. Thus law and poetry, like reason and rhyme, co-create civilization. Law is society's structured sonnet; poetry is its unstructured prelude. Law protects order, poetry envisions order; law prevents chaos, poetry redeems chaos. Where law fails, poetry calls for reform; where poetry dreams, law gives flesh. They are paradoxical partners: one restrains, the other releases; one judges, the other justifies; one binds in prose, the other frees in verse. Yet together they uphold justice not only as a principle but as a poem—an eternal lyric of fairness written in both statutes and songs.

POETRY AND THE UNITY OF ALL DISCIPLINES: TOWARD A COSMIC CONCORD

The Paradox of the Particular and the Universal: Each discipline is a doorway, a corridor of comprehension into reality's mansion. Politics rules the polis, physics rules the particles, philosophy rules the paradox. Yet poetry alone refuses confinement, flowing through each like fire through air. Poetry is paradoxical discipline: boundless yet bounded, infinite yet intimate. It unites sciences and humanities into a hymn of harmony. Poetry, paradoxical progenitor of perception, is at once ancient and ageless, fleeting and eternal, fragile and indomitable. Having wandered through politics and philosophy, economy and ecology, biology and botany, psychology and physics, theology and law, we return to poetry itself, discovering that it is not a discipline among disciplines but the disciplining of all disciplines into resonance, the lyrical law of knowledge itself.

Poetry and Politics: Politics codifies power; poetry critiques power. The politician drafts manifestos; the poet drafts metaphors. Yet metaphors move more mightily than manifestos. Empires fall not only from swords but from sonnets. A tyrant fears no treaty as much as a troubadour.

Paradox: politics rules with armies, yet poetry rules with whispers; politics commands obedience, yet poetry commands belief.

Poetry and Society: Sociology studies structures; poetry studies souls. Society is system; poetry is spirit. What statistics cannot show, stanzas reveal. Census counts citizens; poetry counts cries. Paradox: society shapes poetry, but poetry reshapes society. Sociology dissects what is; poetry dreams what ought to be.

Poetry and Economy: Economy values wealth; poetry values worth. The economist weighs resources; the poet weighs resonances. Profit is prose; poetry is priceless. Paradox: poetry is useless yet indispensable, valueless yet invaluable. Nations may measure GDP, but poetry alone measures dignity.

Poetry and Anthropology: Anthropology digs bones; poetry digs being. Rituals, myths, masks—all anthropology catalogs, but poetry animates. A funeral chant is anthropology's data, poetry's devotion. Paradox: anthropology explains culture, poetry embodies culture. One describes, the other dwells.

Poetry and History: History is memory; poetry is meaning. Chronicles report what happened; poetry reveals why it matters. History is prose of past; poetry is prophecy of past. Paradox: history records victories of victors; poetry preserves laments of losers. Historians write nations; poets write humanity.

Poetry and Education: Education transmits knowledge; poetry transfigures knowledge. The classroom teaches lessons; poetry teaches longing. Paradox: education fills minds, poetry fulfills minds. True education is not syllabi but symphony, not curriculum but cadence.

Poetry and Geography: Geography maps mountains;

poetry makes mountains sing. Cartography is cold coordinates; poetry is living landscape. Rivers are blue lines in geography, but murmuring voices in poetry. Paradox: geography charts space, poetry consecrates space. Maps show where; poetry shows what-for.

Poetry and Psychology: Psychology examines psyche; poetry experiences psyche. The therapist records symptoms; the poet records sighs. Dreams in Freud's lab are data; dreams in poetry are destinies. Paradox: psychology analyzes emotion, poetry actualizes emotion. Poetry is not case-study but catharsis.

Poetry and Geology: Geology reads rocks; poetry hears hymns in rocks. Strata are stanzas in stone, fossils are metaphors of memory. Volcano is geology's eruption, poetry's passion. Paradox: geology reveals Earth's age; poetry reveals Earth's agony. Stones are statistics in geology, symbols in poetry.

Poetry and Biotechnology: Biotechnology splices genes; poetry splices dreams. DNA is double helix of nucleotides, but also double helix of narratives. Poetry is biotechnology of soul: engineering emotions, transplanting visions. Paradox: biotechnology edits life; poetry enlivens life. Both are creative yet perilous.

Poetry and Astrology: Astrology reads stars for fate; poetry reads stars for wonder. Horoscope promises destiny; poetry promises dignity. Paradox: astrology pretends precision, poetry proclaims possibility. Yet both remind: human heart is celestial. Stars are statistics in astronomy, but sonnets in poetry.

Poetry and Philosophy: Philosophy defines truth; poetry dwells truth. Philosophy is logic, poetry is lyric. Paradox: philosophy explains paradox, poetry embodies paradox. Where philosophy stops in silence, poetry continues in song. Poetry is not beyond philosophy but beneath and above it: root and crown.

Poetry and Physics: Physics quantifies cosmos; poetry qualifies cosmos. Quantum mechanics says uncertainty; poetry says mystery. Relativity bends spacetime; poetry bends speech-time. Paradox: physics proves world's mathematics, poetry proves world's music. Atom is equation in physics, epiphany in poetry.

Poetry and Chemistry: Chemistry studies reactions; poetry causes reactions. Molecules mingle; metaphors mingle. Bond is both chemical and lyrical. Paradox: chemistry explains love as oxytocin; poetry explains oxytocin as love. Both are experiments: one in lab, one in language.

Poetry and Botany: Botany classifies flowers; poetry converses with flowers. Linnaeus gave them Latin names; poets gave them eternal names. Rose is species to botanist, symbol to poet. Paradox: botany counts petals, poetry counts passions. Botany explains bloom, poetry exalts bloom.

Poetry and Zoology: Zoology studies animals; poetry sings animals. Birds in zoology are avian species; in poetry they are angels of air. Whale is mammal in marine biology, monster in Moby Dick. Paradox: zoology catalogues life, poetry consecrates life.

Poetry and Mathematics: Mathematics is numbers; poetry is numerology. Both rely on symmetry, sequence, structure. A sonnet is equation in words; Fibonacci spiral is stanza in nature. Paradox: math is precise abstraction, poetry is abstract precision. Both reveal infinity: math as ∞, poetry as awe.

Poetry as Final Discipline: Thus, poetry proves itself not companion but crown of disciplines. Politics needs poetry's conscience; economy needs poetry's compassion; physics needs poetry's wonder; law needs poetry's mercy. Paradox: poetry is useless for survival, yet indispensable for significance.

Poetry as the Primordial Principle: At the dawn of every discipline lies a poem. Before political science there were chants of the tribe; before sociology, the stories of kinship; before economics, the hymns of harvest; before philosophy, the riddles of sages; before physics, the incantations of stars. In *principio erat verbum*—in the beginning was the Word. And the Word was not sterile statement, but rhythmic revelation, the living lyric through which cosmos called itself into coherence. Poetry is therefore not an ornament upon knowledge but the origin of knowledge itself.

The Paradox of Unity and Diversity: Every discipline attempts to divide the indivisible, to analyze the all, to systematize the swirl of being. Physics isolates particles; economics measures markets; psychology probes minds; theology defines divinities. Yet poetry insists on paradox: unity in multiplicity, multiplicity in unity. Poetry says: the atom is a galaxy, the galaxy is an atom; the law is a lyric, the lyric is a law; history is a poem written in blood, and a poem is history condensed into breath. Thus poetry becomes the cosmic solvent, dissolving distinctions while deepening them, harmonizing heterogeneity into hymn.

Poetry and the Polyphony of Disciplines: Each discipline, standing alone, sings a solitary song. Politics chants of power; sociology hums of society; geology drums of earth; astronomy rings of stars; mathematics whispers of numbers; theology thunders of God. Left isolated, these songs clash in cacophony. Yet poetry, paradoxical and patient, provides polyphony—drawing diverse voices into chorus. Poetry does not abolish difference but arranges it, like a conductor who transforms dissonant notes into symphony. In this way, poetry is the *metadiscipline*, the music that unites sciences and humanities, logics and lyrics, truths and tales.

Oxymorons as Ontological Openings: Only poetry, with its oxymorons and paradoxes, can capture the contradictory cosmos. Silent thunder, dark dawn, joyful sorrow, measured infinity—these are not linguistic tricks but ontological insights. The universe itself is oxymoronic: finite yet infinite, lawful yet free, ordered yet chaotic, solid yet void. Science measures these tensions; philosophy debates them; but poetry sings them. In singing, poetry does not resolve paradox but reveals its radiance. Thus poetry is not beyond philosophy alone—it is beyond all disciplines, because it alone dares to dwell in contradiction without collapsing into coherence too quickly.

Mathematics of Metaphor, Physics of Feeling: To the mathematician, poetry whispers equations of empathy: metaphor as multiplication, rhyme as ratio, rhythm as recurrence. To the physicist, poetry unveils energy in emotion, gravity in grief, light in laughter. To the chemist, poetry demonstrates reactions of hearts, bonds of souls, explosions of longing. To the biologist, poetry is the DNA of culture, double-helical with memory and imagination. To the theologian, poetry is prophecy. To the jurist, poetry is justice. To all, poetry is both formula and flame, law and liberty, order and overflow.

The Economy of the Infinite: Disciplines bargain with scarcity: economics with limited goods, politics with limited power, ecology with limited resources. Poetry, however, traffics in abundance. A single stanza can feed a starving soul, a single haiku can hold a universe, a single metaphor can move empires. Poetry is paradoxically infinite economy: it gives without depleting, spends without spending, enriches without exhausting. Here poetry surpasses economics: it proves that the rarest resource—meaning—is inexhaustible, multiplying as it is shared.

Poetry as the Law of Laws: Law codifies justice; poetry beautifies justice. Verdict is law's decree, voice is poetry's cry. Constitution is prose of nation, anthem is poetry of nation. Paradox: law enforces justice, poetry envisions justice. Where law punishes, poetry redeems. We discovered in law that poetry was justice's secret twin. But more deeply still, poetry is the law behind laws: the rhythm by which rights resonate, the cadence by which constitutions cohere, the metaphor by which justice manifests. Laws written in prose perish; laws whispered in poetry persist. "Liberty, Equality, Fraternity," "We the People," "Life, Liberty, and the pursuit of Happiness"—these endure not because they are legal statutes but because they are poetic refrains. Poetry legislates more lastingly than legislation.

Theology and the Transcendent Tongue: Theology defines divinity; poetry describes divinity. Creed says "God is love"; poetry says "love is God." Paradox: theology guards truth, poetry gifts truth. Theology builds dogma, poetry builds doxology. The psalm is theology that sings. Theology trembles before transcendence; poetry pronounces it. Where the theologian speculates, the poet sings. Prayer is poetry addressed to God; revelation is poetry addressed from God. Every sacred scripture is simultaneously law and lyric, doctrine and drama. The *Bhagavad Gita* is dialogue in verse; the Psalms are songs of sorrow and praise; the Quran proclaims itself in rhyme and rhythm. Poetry is not merely religious ornament; it is religion's origin, its language of longing, its eternal liturgy.

History as Hymn, Future as Fugue: History is the prose of power, but poetry is its hidden hymn. Every empire's rise was accompanied by epics; every revolution's cry was born in verse. Homer preserved Greece; Virgil consecrated Rome; Dante preserved Italy; Shakespeare crystallized England. What prose could not immortalize, poetry engraved. And for the future too, poetry is prophecy. The poet is a seer, foretelling with metaphors what philosophers struggle to define. Poetry is the fugue of the future, already echoing in present's silence.

The Ethereal Equation: If science asks what is, philosophy asks why it is, theology asks who willed it, then poetry asks all three at once and adds: what does it feel like? Poetry is the fourth dimension of knowledge: the curvature of truth into beauty, the bending of fact into feeling, the acceleration of data into destiny. To borrow scientific metaphor: philosophy is particle, poetry is wave; philosophy is law, poetry is light. Both are true, but poetry illumines while law explains.

The Ultimate Oxymoron: Poetry as Silence: At the end, paradox compels us to confess: poetry is silence speaking, speech silencing, sound that is beyond sound. The greatest poems are not those that fill but those that empty, not those that shout but those that hush. Poetry teaches us that meaning is found not only in words but in the spaces between them, the pauses, the pregnant silences. In this way, poetry mirrors the cosmos itself: vast silence punctuated by brief bursts of song.

Poetry: The Cosmic Concord: Thus, we arrive at the cosmic concord: poetry is not simply the next step beyond philosophy but the eternal song beyond all sciences, the melody in every method, the music in every mathematics, the lyric in every law, the rhythm in every reason. Without poetry, disciplines disintegrate into data; with poetry, they converge into cosmos. Poetry is therefore both the first word and the final word, the alpha of expression and the omega of meaning, the eternal oxymoron: infinite in finitude, boundless in brevity, timeless in time. Poetry is not about poetry. Poetry is about everything, and everything is about poetry. Poetry is not ornament but ontology, not luxury but law of life. It is the connective tissue between sciences and soul. Every atom is stanza, every law is lyric, every equation is elegy. Poetry is discipline without borders, law without lawyers, science without symbols, philosophy without footnotes. Poetry is everything and beyond everything.

THE ORIGIN OF POETRY: THE PRIMORDIAL PULSE OF THE WORD

Poetry was not born – it breathed. Before man muttered meaning, before mind mastered the machinery of language, the universe itself uttered its unutterable hymn. In the cosmic cradle of chaos, before the dawn had drawn its first trembling line of light, there was rhythm – the silent syllable of becoming. Poetry was the first pulse of existence, the tremor between nothingness and name, between silence and sound. It was not made; it manifested. It is older than alphabets, deeper than diction, and vaster than vocabulary. It is the breath between Being and Becoming – the original articulation of awe.

The origin of poetry lies not in man's mouth but in the murmur of matter, in the whispering will of the world wishing to be witnessed. When the wind wept across water, when thunder trembled through the sky's vast veins, when the stars spoke in the slow syntax of shining – there, poetry was. Every echo of eternity seeking a form, every sigh of the infinite seeking a symbol, gave birth to the first poetic moment. The world was written before it was read. The waves were words long before human tongues learned to twist them into tales.

Poetry, thus, is not invention but intuition – the

remembering of a resonance. The first poet was not a man with a lyre or a language; it was the listening spirit of creation itself, catching its own cadence. Long before logic learned to measure, poetry was already meaning in motion — a metaphysical murmur that made matter meaningful. In that pre-linguistic dawn, emotion and element were one, and the universe spoke in seamless song. The sun's rise was a revelation, the river's run a refrain, and every falling leaf a lyric of loss and life.

To say that poetry began with humanity is a historical half-truth. Poetry began with hunger — the hunger of existence for expression. When the cosmos desired to see itself mirrored in mind, when consciousness curved inward to contemplate its own immensity, poetry poured forth as the language of longing. It was the earliest art of self-recognition — the dialogue between creation and creator, between the soul and its shadow. Every heartbeat since has been a faint echo of that first cosmic couplet.

Yet, paradoxically, poetry is born of both abundance and absence. It arises where silence is too sacred for speech, and yet where silence itself aches to be spoken. It is the luminous lament of limitation — the divine contradiction of sound trying to say the unsayable. The first poem was not written in words but in wonder. It was the cry of a consciousness newly aware of itself — astonished, afraid, awed. From that astonishment arose rhythm, and from rhythm, remembrance — and from remembrance, the ritual of repetition that gave birth to form.

Every civilization's dawn has been a rediscovery of that original awe. Whether in the hymns of the Vedas, the psalms of prophets, or the chants of shamans — the first poets were priests of perception, translating the tremor of transcendence into tone. They did not write for applause;

they wrote for alignment — to attune the human heart to the harmonic hum of the universe. Their verses were votive offerings, their metaphors were mediations between man and mystery. Poetry was prayer before prayer was invented — it was the sacred speech of the soul seeking its source.

Thus, the origin of poetry is paradoxically both spontaneous and sacred. It is the art of accident and the architecture of awe. It rises where intellect fails and imagination begins, where facts dissolve and feelings form their own faith. The poet, in this primal sense, is not a creator but a conduit — a vessel through which the eternal energy of expression finds fleeting form. The earliest songs were not composed — they were discovered, distilled from the divine delirium that dances at the edge of consciousness.

In truth, poetry is not a product of time but a proof of eternity within time. It is the timeless speaking through the temporal, the infinite interpreting itself through the fragile instrument of flesh. Every true poet hears echoes of that first cosmic utterance — that original "Om" which oscillates still through atoms and air. To write poetry, therefore, is to return to origin; to remember what the world itself once whispered before men learned to measure meaning with grammar and grid.

Poetry, then, is older than philosophy and deeper than theology. It precedes reason because it is the reason — the reason that reason was ever possible. For reason seeks truth, but poetry feels truth. Where reason analyses, poetry awakens. Where philosophy questions, poetry communes. It is the very first language of love between the seen and the unseen. The poet, standing between word and world, is the midwife of meaning — helping silence give birth to sound, and sound give birth to soul.

And yet — here lies the central paradox: poetry

originates not in certainty but in confusion. It is the art of the amazed, the eloquence of the uncertain. The first poet was not the one who knew but the one who knelt — before the mystery, before the moon, before the mirror of mortality. Poetry begins not when man conquers chaos but when he converses with it. It is the song of surrender disguised as a song of strength. Every great poem is a prayer pretending to be a performance.

Thus, when we ask where poetry began, we must not look to literature but to life itself. It began where breath became word, where wonder became whisper, where existence exhaled emotion. It began in the lightning's lyric, the ocean's ode, the mountain's monologue. It began in the human heart — that eternal echo chamber where heaven and earth exchange sighs. It began wherever awe existed — for awe is the alphabet of all art.

Poetry is, therefore, not an invention but an inevitability. It was destined to arise wherever consciousness encountered creation. The first poets did not write to be remembered — they wrote to remember. They sought to recall the rhythm of the real beneath the noise of the now. Even today, every poem worth its breath is a resurrection of that first sacred sound, a reminder that language itself is but a shadow of song — and song, a reflection of the silence that birthed it. So the origin of poetry is not an event but an essence. It is the first flame of feeling that refused to fade, the first thought that trembled into tone. It is the soul remembering its source — and singing.

THE LANGUAGE OF POETRY: THE SACRED SYNTAX OF THE SOUL

Language, in its ordinary sense, is a tool of transaction — a bridge built between minds for the exchange of thought. But in poetry, language ceases to be mere medium; it becomes mystery. It is not used, it is lived. It does not describe reality; it dances with it. The language of poetry is the soul's syntax — a sacred grammar that grammar itself cannot grasp. It speaks not from mouth to ear, but from essence to eternity. It is the ineffable translated into the audible, the invisible sculpted in syllables, the infinite echoing through finite sounds.

To speak poetically is to speak in paradox — for poetry is the only tongue that tells truths by transcending them. It is a language that listens to itself, that reveres its own resonance. Where prose proceeds, poetry pauses. Where logic explains, poetry exclaims. The poet's words are not arranged to communicate but to commune. Every vowel vibrates with vision, every consonant carries consciousness. The alphabet itself becomes an altar, upon which emotion sacrifices certainty to worship the wonder of ambiguity.

In the language of poetry, silence is not absence but articulation. Between lines lies a luminous latency, a whisper that words merely awaken. The pauses, the punctuation, the breath between — all become part of meaning. A comma becomes a caress; a dash becomes a dream deferred; a period becomes a prayer concluded. Poetry's language is not linear but layered — each phrase pregnant with multiple lives. A word in poetry is not a signpost; it is a seed. It does not point outward, but unfolds inward, rooting itself in the reader's own depths.

Thus, the language of poetry is paradoxically both precise and infinite. It is precise because it pierces perception; infinite because it refuses imprisonment. A single image may contain a universe — a rose becomes revelation, a stone becomes scripture, a sigh becomes salvation. Every metaphor is a miniature cosmos, every symbol a spiral of secrets. The poet does not choose words; words choose the poet, as if ancient spirits awaken through syllables to sing again in human form.

Ordinary language names things; poetic language renames them, and in renaming, reveals their realness. A mountain becomes not a heap of stone, but a hymn of stillness. The sea becomes not water, but the wandering will of eternity. Fire becomes not flame, but the fierce laughter of life itself. Poetry gives the world back its wonder — it reenchants the familiar by unveiling the invisible within it.

And yet, this language of poetry is no language at all in the common sense. It disobeys rules to remain true to rhythm. It breaks syntax to birth soul. Its grammar is governed by grace, not by grammar books. It subverts order to reveal the order behind order — the cosmic cadence hidden beneath human conventions. The poet is thus a linguistic rebel, revolting not for destruction but for revelation. By distorting language, the poet restores it to its divine dimension.

The language of poetry is essentially an act of alchemy.

It turns sound into symbol, symbol into spirit, and spirit into silence again. The poet, like an ancient alchemist, mixes metaphor and mystery, rhythm and reverence, to transform dull experience into golden expression. Every stanza becomes a crucible where meaning melts and reforms, refined by the fire of feeling. Thus, poetry's language does not explain; it transfigures. It transmutes the mundane into the miraculous, the literal into the luminous. What distinguishes poetic language from all others is its ability to contain contradiction without collapse. It can be both shadow and shine, grief and grace, wound and wonder. It can cry and console in the same breath. It can sing of death yet celebrate life. It can claim the eternal in the ephemeral, the infinite in the intimate. This is because poetry speaks the dialect of duality — it knows that truth lives not in one extreme but in their embrace. In every paradox, poetry finds purity.

And beneath its beauty lies its burden: the poet must make music from mortality. Words, those weary instruments of thought, must be lifted to lyrical life. Each must be weighed, woken, and woven until it no longer means but manifests. The language of poetry is not about what words say but about what they summon. They summon memory, mood, and meaning all at once. They conjure feelings that precede form, truths that transcend thought.

Listen to the cadence of a true poem and you hear not the poet but the pulse of existence itself. The rhythm is not personal; it is planetary. It echoes the rotation of the earth, the rise of breath, the beat of blood. Poetry's language is the music of meaning — meaning not as message, but as melody. The poet therefore composes not sentences, but symphonies of silence and sound. Each word becomes a note in a larger harmony of hidden truths.

Moreover, the language of poetry is never static — it lives, it breathes, it burns. It evolves as the poet evolves. It speaks differently to every listener, because each heart hears its own hidden harmony. Thus, a poem is not finished when it is written; it is finished when it is felt. The language of poetry belongs not to the writer but to the reader, for poetry is an echo that completes itself only when received.

And yet, paradox again: this sacred language is both deeply personal and profoundly universal. The poet may write from one moment of heartbreak, yet a thousand souls may see their own sorrow reflected in the verse. The language of poetry, though born of one breath, belongs to all. It transcends translation because it speaks in the secret symphony of being — that inner sound that all souls silently share.

To understand poetic language, then, is not to analyze but to attune. One must listen not with the intellect but with intuition. One must allow the rhythm to reach where reason cannot. For poetry's words are not instructions; they are invitations — invitations to inhabit a higher hearing, a deeper seeing, a gentler knowing.

So when we say poetry has a language of its own, we mean that it speaks beyond language. It is language remembering its sacred origin, returning to its first purpose — not to inform but to transform. It speaks in symbols because truth itself is symbolic; it speaks in silence because silence itself is sacred. It dares to say what cannot be said by daring to sing it.

The language of poetry, finally, is not the poet's but the universe's — articulated through the artist's awareness. It is the cosmos conversing with itself in metaphors. The poet is but the momentary mouthpiece of a timeless tune. Through him, the world finds words for its wonder.

Thus, poetry's language is both mirror and magic — reflecting reality while reshaping it. It reveals that all speech, at its heart, is a song striving to return to silence. And when the poem ends, silence smiles — for it recognizes itself once more, newly adorned with the ornaments of expression. In every true poem, language fulfills its oldest dream: to become revelation.

THE STYLE OF POETRY: THE SOUL'S SIGNATURE AND THE DANCE OF DISTINCTION

Style is not a garment that poetry wears — it is the garment that grows from poetry's own flesh. It is not the dressing of thought but the very texture of its dreaming. In prose, style may be ornament; in poetry, it is ontology. It is not what the poet chooses but what the poet is. Every poem's pulse is unique, for every soul sings in a different key. The style of poetry, therefore, is the signature of the spirit — the melody of individuality moving through the music of meaning.

The word style comes from stylus, the ancient tool for engraving. And indeed, poetic style is the engraving of eternity upon the ephemeral — the way the soul scratches its secret upon the surface of speech. It is how the infinite leaks into lineation, how the unseen becomes seen through syllable and rhythm. Every poet carves their consciousness into cadence, and in that carving, creates a cosmos. Style is the shape of one's silence — the distinct vibration of one's vision made audible through art.

But style, paradoxically, is both discipline and deviation. It demands devotion to form even as it dances beyond form. The poet must master meter only to transcend it; must honour order only to outgrow it. The greatest styles are those that seem effortless — but behind that ease is the agony of attunement, the invisible labour of listening to the law within. True style is never imposed; it emerges. It is the natural consequence of one's inner necessity finding outward expression. A poet cannot invent a style any more than a flower can invent its fragrance — both unfold from within.

Each poetic style is a reflection of its maker's metaphysics. The solemn, slow cadences of Milton mirror his moral might; the lucid lyricism of Shelley reflects his skyward yearning; the prophetic fire of Blake burns with spiritual rebellion. Style is not surface — it is soul made syntax. It is the shape that vision takes when poured into the vessel of voice. To imitate another's style, therefore, is to echo another's essence — and thus, to lose one's own. For style is not a technique to be taught but a truth to be tuned into.

And yet, style is not static. It evolves, like consciousness itself. A poet's early style is often a struggle between imitation and initiation — the tentative attempt to speak before finding one's true tongue. But as experience etches deeper meanings into the mind, style sharpens, simplifies, sanctifies. It sheds ornament for essence, rhetoric for revelation. In maturity, the poet's style becomes transparent — no longer a barrier but a bridge between word and world. The language no longer announces itself; it disappears into what it reveals.

At its highest, style becomes silence in motion. It carries cadence not as rhythm but as revelation. The poet no longer strives to impress but to express — not to perform but to pray. Style becomes service — the humble act of allowing beauty to breathe through being. It is the music of surrender, the grace of giving up control to the current of creativity. When a poet's style matures into such selflessness, it becomes indistinguishable from the soul's own voice.

Yet, paradox again: to find style, one must first lose it. One must write without pretense, without pursuit of perfection — for style hides from self-consciousness. It emerges only when ego evaporates in the ecstasy of expression. The greatest poets never sought style; they sought sincerity — and style came as the fragrance of that faithfulness. As Emerson said, "The man is only half himself, the other half is his expression." Style is the completion of being through beauty.

Still, style is also structure — a rhythm that holds revelation. The difference between chaos and cosmos is cadence. Even the most spontaneous poem finds its secret geometry — the pulse that keeps emotion from dissolving into noise. Style is thus the equilibrium between heart and harmony, passion and proportion. It gives the formless feeling a form through which it may endure. Without style, poetry would be mere impulse; with style, it becomes immortality.

Every great style, too, carries its contradiction. The poet must choose between simplicity and sublimity, between the naked truth and the ornate transcendence. But true style reconciles these opposites — it is simplicity made sacred, sublimity made subtle. It is where grandeur grows from grace. The best style never shouts; it sings softly but forever. It speaks with the authority of authenticity, not the arrogance of artifice.

The style of poetry is also the rhythm of revelation. Rhythm is not meter — it is meaning moving in music. The beating of a poem mirrors the beating of existence. It is the dance of order and improvisation, the marriage of sound and silence. A good poet hears this rhythm not with the ear but with the entire being. The lines lengthen and shorten not by rule but by resonance — as if the poem breathes, inhales and exhales, expanding and contracting with consciousness itself.

Moreover, style is shaped by silence as much as by sound. What the poet omits is as eloquent as what he utters. A great style knows when to whisper, when to wait, when to wound, and when to heal. The pauses, the absences, the unsaid — these are the secret syllables of style. They make the spoken luminous by surrounding it with the unspeakable. The white space between verses is as sacred as the words themselves — it is the space where the reader's soul enters and completes the poem.

In this sense, style is communion — the meeting point of poet, poem, and perceiver. It is the invisible thread that connects three consciousnesses across time. Through style, the dead speak to the living, the distant to the intimate. Shakespeare's storm still roars through our veins; Ghalib's sigh still shivers through our silence; Dickinson's dash still defies death itself. Style is immortality embodied — the voice that time cannot silence.

And yet, each style is also an act of rebellion. Every new poet must defy tradition not out of arrogance, but out of authenticity. For art evolves by audacity. When language becomes law, poetry perishes; when structure becomes shrine, spirit suffocates. Thus, every age's truest poet is both disciple and destroyer — reverent to roots but restless for renewal. Their style is both homage and heresy, preserving the sacred by transforming it. Without innovation, poetry would be a museum; with it, it becomes a miracle renewed in every age.

The evolution of style in poetry, then, mirrors the

evolution of the soul itself — from imitation to inspiration, from expression to essence, from ornament to origin. The mature style is not the loudest but the lightest; not the most complex but the most conscious. It is the silence that sings through simplicity. The greatest style is that which disappears into its own purity — where the reader no longer notices the art, only the awakening it arouses.

Thus, style in poetry is not mere manner but manifestation — the revelation of the soul's rhythm in the world's word. It is the shape that truth takes when love learns to speak. Every true poet writes not to display style but to discover it — and through that discovery, to remember the unity of all voices within the vast harmony of creation.

For ultimately, style is destiny. As the river's flow is defined by its bends, the poet's expression is defined by his inner landscape. Each curve of consciousness, each shadow of suffering, each shimmer of joy — all shape the movement of the mind's music. The poet's style is the way his soul walks through words. And when, at last, that walk becomes effortless — when word and world, silence and sound, feeling and form move as one — then poetry becomes prayer, and style becomes salvation.

THE UNIQUENESS OF POETRY: THE MIRROR OF MYSTERY AND THE MUSIC OF MEANING

Poetry is the only art that dares to speak the unspeakable and succeeds by failing — for its triumph lies not in telling, but in touching. Among all forms of expression, poetry stands as the most paradoxical: it is the most precise form of vagueness, the most ordered shape of chaos, the most articulate silence ever spoken. Its uniqueness arises from its refusal to belong entirely to any realm — it is not pure philosophy, yet it philosophizes; not mere music, yet it sings; not mere painting, yet it paints visions upon the mind's invisible canvas. Poetry is the intersection where the intellectual becomes instinctive and the emotional becomes eternal.

What makes poetry unique is not simply its use of language, but its transformation of language. Prose speaks about things; poetry speaks through them. It does not describe the rose — it becomes the rose. It does not tell of sorrow — it is sorrow, distilled and made divine. In poetry, words cease to be tools and become beings. They breathe, they bleed, they bloom. Each line lives as a living organism, pulsing with possibility. The poet is not a reporter of reality but a revealer of realms unseen — the seer who hears what silence says.

Poetry's uniqueness also lies in its dual citizenship — it belongs both to heaven and to earth. It speaks in human tongues, yet it translates divine whispers. It is a language that mortals use to speak to immortality, and immortality uses to remember itself through mortals. It bridges the abyss between experience and essence, matter and meaning. When a poet writes, he stands at that trembling threshold where the visible world touches the invisible one, where words become wings and thought turns into thunder. Poetry is the passport between two eternities: the one before birth and the one beyond death.

And yet, poetry's uniqueness is not in what it says but in what it suggests. A poem's power lies not in its message but in its mystery. It is the art of implication — where every image hides infinities, where every symbol sighs with secrets. It leaves gaps not to confuse but to compel; it withholds to awaken. The poet's silence between two lines can speak louder than the loudest sermon. The magic of poetry is that it multiplies meaning by embracing ambiguity. Its clarity is carved from its complexity; its truth thrives in tension.

The uniqueness of poetry is also found in its marriage of opposites — its ability to harmonize contradiction. It is intellectual yet instinctive, sacred yet sensual, personal yet universal, transient yet timeless. It can contain the cry of a child and the chorus of a cosmos within a single stanza. It can speak of the smallest sigh and the largest infinity in the same breath. Where philosophy seeks coherence, poetry seeks correspondence. It does not argue; it awakens. It does not conclude; it consecrates. And because it speaks in such paradox, poetry alone can express what life itself cannot explain. It is both mirror and mystery — reflecting reality while revealing the unseen rhythm behind it. It does not seek to escape the world but to enchant it. Even its sadness is luminous, even its silence sings. Poetry is unique because it turns suffering into symphony, despair into devotion, and death into dialogue. Its gift is not consolation but transfiguration — it does not heal by hiding pain, but by hallowing it.

What distinguishes poetry from all other forms of art is its economy of infinity — it says the most with the least. A painter may use colour, a musician may use sound, a philosopher may use reason; but the poet uses air itself — vibration and void. With a handful of syllables, he can summon entire universes. With one word, he can wound; with one pause, he can redeem. Poetry is thus the most spiritual of sciences, the most scientific of spirits. It measures what cannot be measured: the music of meaning in the marrow of being.

The poet does not create by construction but by communion. The uniqueness of poetry is that it is not manufactured — it is manifested. It arises not from effort but from attunement. The poet listens to what has always been speaking — the secret voice of existence — and lends it his tongue. The true poem already exists, hidden in the folds of the world's fabric; the poet merely reveals it, like a sculptor releasing form from stone. Thus, poetry's uniqueness is its humility: it knows that creation is collaboration between consciousness and cosmos.

Furthermore, poetry's uniqueness lies in its timeless adaptability. It evolves with every age yet remains ageless. The words may change, but the wonder does not. From the chants of shamans to the sonnets of Shakespeare, from the haiku's hush to the epic's echo, poetry has never ceased to mirror humanity's metamorphosis. Every era finds its own form of the eternal — for poetry is the pulse of collective consciousness itself. It speaks differently in each tongue, yet every translation carries the same tremor of truth.

Even more profoundly, poetry is unique because it unites opposites not only in form but in function. It is both revelation and refuge. It is where thought becomes therapy, and emotion becomes enlightenment. When logic fails, poetry consoles; when faith falters, poetry reminds. It gives voice to the voiceless and silence to the weary. It is both medicine and music, both question and cure. Every great poem is a cathedral of compassion built out of breath.

The uniqueness of poetry also lies in its ability to transform perception. A true poem does not merely describe the world — it changes how the world is seen. After reading Blake, a reader never looks at a grain of sand the same way again; after Rumi, love is no longer an emotion but an energy; after Tagore, the breeze itself seems to sing of belonging. Poetry alters awareness. It reawakens the original innocence of seeing — the childlike gaze that perceives divinity in dew, eternity in ephemerality.

But perhaps the most profound uniqueness of poetry is that it makes meaning out of mystery without murdering it. Where science dissects, poetry discovers. Where theology defines, poetry defies. It does not imprison truth in propositions but allows it to breathe in paradoxes. It does not need to prove because it makes one feel. Poetry's truth is experiential, not empirical; intuitive, not intellectual. It bypasses the brain to touch the being. It persuades not by argument but by awakening.

And yet, the poet himself is a paradox — both master and servant of his art. He shapes words, but words also shape him. He gives birth to poems, yet the poems give birth to him anew. Every act of writing is an act of self-creation — the poet becoming what he writes. In this mutual making lies the miracle of poetry's uniqueness: it transforms both the creator and the created. It is the alchemy of consciousness in continual renewal.

Thus, poetry is unique because it exists on the edge of all definitions. It cannot be captured, categorized, or confined. It slips through the fingers of analysis like mist, yet saturates the soul like rain. It belongs to no nation, no doctrine, no time — it belongs only to the eternal conversation between silence and speech. It is the invisible music that every human heart has hummed since the dawn of dreaming.

In the end, poetry is unique because it is existence — distilled, decoded, and deified. The universe itself is a poem: matter as metaphor, energy as rhythm, space as stanza, time as tone. The stars are punctuation marks in the endless verse of creation. The poet merely participates in this ongoing cosmic composition — shaping a few fleeting lines within an infinite hymn.

And when those lines, however brief, however broken, echo the eternal cadence — when they awaken awe, widen wonder, or heal the hidden wound of being — then poetry fulfills its purpose. It reminds humanity that within the smallest word, the largest world resides. It teaches that mystery is not meant to be solved, but sung. That is the uniqueness of poetry — the universe finding its own voice, again and again, through the fragile throat of humankind.

THE SECRET OF POETRY: THE INVISIBLE FIRE AND THE ALCHEMY OF THE WORD

The secret of poetry is that it cannot be told. It can only be touched — faintly, fleetingly, like the wing of a divine whisper brushing across the mind. Every attempt to explain it diminishes it, for poetry, by its very essence, lives in the space beyond speech. To unveil it is to unmake it. Yet, paradoxically, it reveals itself only to those who dare to seek its secrecy — for poetry is both hidden and happening, both mystery and manifestation. It hides not because it wishes to remain unknown, but because it wishes to be felt, not found.

Poetry's secret is not in its form but in its fire — an invisible flame that flickers within words, lighting them from within until they shine beyond meaning. A poem is not made of letters, but of light caught momentarily in language. The poet does not write with ink but with intensity; not with grammar but with grace. The true poem burns, not on paper, but in perception — it is the spark that leaps from the page into the reader's own soul. That spark, that alchemical moment of recognition, is the secret: poetry happens not in writing, nor in reading, but in awakening.

The secret of poetry, then, is not about how it is written but why it writes itself through us. For the poet is not a maker but a medium — the wind that carries a whisper older than the world. The poem uses the poet as a vessel, a voice through which eternity momentarily articulates itself. This is why the greatest poets speak of inspiration as possession — the Muse, the Spirit, the Breath Divine. They do not invent; they invoke. They do not design; they are designed through. Poetry's secret is the sacred participation of the finite in the infinite, the miracle of the mortal mouth uttering immortal meaning.

In every true poem, something invisible becomes visible, something eternal enters time. That transformation — that alchemy — is the heart of poetry's secret. The poet is an alchemist of awareness, turning emotion into essence, pain into prayer, chaos into cadence. Where others see only experience, the poet extracts epiphany. He looks at life not as event but as energy, not as narrative but as note in the great music of existence. And through rhythm, symbol, and sound, he distills that music into a human form the heart can hear.

The secret of poetry also lies in its contradiction: it is both intensely personal and profoundly impersonal. The poet bleeds his own wounds onto the page, yet what emerges belongs to all. The poem begins in the private chamber of a single soul but ends as a cathedral for countless others. What was once "I" becomes "we." The poet's loneliness becomes the reader's liberation. The alchemy is complete when suffering becomes song and solitude becomes symphony. This transformation is not technique but transmutation — the invisible miracle that defines the poetic act.

And yet, poetry's secret is not in its success but in its surrender. The poet must learn to vanish for the poem to live. When ego evaporates, the Muse moves. The secret fire of poetry burns only where self has been sacrificed. It is born from the humility of hearing — from listening so deeply that words themselves arise unbidden. The poet must be both empty and enflamed — empty enough to receive, enflamed enough to reveal. To write poetry is thus to enter a sacred paradox: one must disappear to truly appear.

Poetry's secret is also its silence. The truest lines are those that lean toward wordlessness. The greatest poets are those who know how to stop — who sense when to let the unsaid speak. The most radiant poem is often the one that trembles on the edge of speech, where language bows before the ineffable. For poetry, unlike prose, does not seek to express everything — it seeks to awaken the inexpressible. Its words are but waves upon an unseen sea; its rhythm, the residue of silence remembered.

The poet's pen is not a tool but a tuning fork. He strikes it against the mystery and listens for resonance. When the tone is true, when the vibration matches the unseen harmony, the poem arrives — complete, inevitable, alive. The poet's task is not invention but alignment. To write a poem is to tune the instrument of being to the frequency of the eternal. The secret, therefore, is attunement: the poet as priest, listening for divinity in daily dust, translating eternity through trembling language.

Poetry's secret is also its danger — for it reveals what most would rather remain hidden. It unearths buried truths, resurrects forgotten feelings, awakens dormant awareness. It speaks in a voice that both heals and haunts. True poetry does not soothe; it sears. It is not comfort but confrontation, not escape but encounter. The poet must enter the dark to bring back light, must descend into silence to resurrect speech. In this sense, every great poem is a pilgrimage — from ignorance to illumination, from wound to wisdom.

The secret of poetry also lies in its simultaneity:

it exists both in sound and in silence, in structure and in spirit. Every rhythm is a relic of the universe's first vibration; every rhyme, a reflection of cosmic symmetry. Poetry's form is not arbitrary — it imitates creation itself, the pulsing alternation of being and non-being, of presence and pause. The poet, knowingly or not, re-enacts the rhythm of existence. The secret is that form and freedom are not opposites but one. The more precisely the poem finds its shape, the more purely it expresses the shapeless.

But the deepest secret of poetry is love — love of life, love of loss, love of language, love of the unnameable. All poetic fire burns with the same fuel: the yearning to unite. Every image, every metaphor, every rhythm is a reaching toward reunion — with truth, with time, with the divine. The poet writes because he feels separation; he writes to return. His words are wings built from longing. The secret of poetry is therefore the secret of the soul itself: that every act of creation is a cry for communion.

The alchemy of poetry transforms longing into light. It makes absence radiant. It turns despair into devotion, and the dust of daily life into the diamond of meaning. The poet's anguish becomes architecture; his silence becomes song. This miracle is not mechanical; it is mystical. No rule, no technique, no metric mastery can conjure it. The secret lies in the poet's openness — the ability to feel the world's wound as one's own and to articulate it without annihilating its mystery.

And when this miracle occurs — when a mere arrangement of words suddenly breathes, when ink awakens into incarnation — the poem becomes more than expression. It becomes presence. It becomes that which exists for no purpose except to remind us that existence itself is sacred. In that moment, reader and poet and poem dissolve into one luminous experience: being aware of being. That awareness — fleeting, fiery, and forever — is the secret the poem keeps even as it gives itself away.

Thus, the secret of poetry is not in its making but in its meaning — or rather, in its making of meaning. It teaches us that the universe itself is a poem still in progress, that creation is a continual composition, that every heartbeat is a hidden stanza in the song of being. The poet, in revealing the secret, renews the sacred.

For poetry's final secret is that it has none. It is all secret, all surface, all soul. Every word conceals the wonder it reveals. The true poem does not end — it continues in the consciousness it awakens. It is not a product but a process, not a text but a transformation. And when the reader feels that silent, sudden shift — that moment when the ordinary becomes oracular — then the secret has been shared, though never spoken. Poetry's secret, finally, is life itself — alive, aware, and endlessly becoming.

THE RELATIONSHIP OF POETRY, READER, POETICS, AND POESY

Poetry is the pulse of perception, the breath between being and becoming – where reader, poetics, and poesy converge in a sacred trinity of thought and threnody. The reader is not a passive pilgrim but a participant in the poem's pilgrimage, whose consciousness completes the circuit of creation. Poetics is the architecture of awe – the metaphysical grammar through which the ineffable acquires form; while poesy is the living flame, the luminous essence that transcends its own structure. Together they form a cyclical communion – the reader reading becomes the poet recreating, poetics becomes praxis, and poesy becomes revelation. In this eternal exchange, language becomes light, imagination incarnates infinity, and the soul of art awakens the art of soul.

The Symbiotic Soul – Where Reader and Poem Meet in Breath and Being

Poetry is not merely a product of ink and intellect; it is a living pulse between souls – the poet's and the reader's. When a poem is read, something transcendent transpires: the mind of one merges with the memory of another, and imagination becomes a shared illumination.

The poet creates, but the reader re-creates; the poem truly lives only when it is read, interpreted, and internalized. Thus, poetry is a bridge across solitude, a communion without conversation. The reader is not a passive recipient but an active participant — breathing life into syllables, lending emotion to rhythm, and completing the circle of creation. In this mystical collaboration, poetry transforms from language to living spirit.

Poetics — The Architecture of the Aesthetic Soul

If poetry is the living organism, poetics is its anatomy — the philosophical framework and structural skeleton that defines its form, rhythm, and resonance. Poetics is where thought meets thrill, where sound seeks sense, and where emotion is disciplined by design. From Aristotle's analytical Poetics to Derrida's deconstructive dissections, the idea has evolved, yet its essence remains: poetics is the art of understanding art. It studies how a poem thinks, breathes, and becomes beautiful. Yet even as it rationalizes rhythm and decodes diction, poetics must bow before the ineffable — for what makes a poem immortal is not its meter but its mystery, not its syntax but its soul.

Poesy — The Pure Flame of Inspiration

"Poesy" — the word itself whispers of wonder. It is the inner fire, the unseen essence, the sacred spirit that precedes and transcends poetry. While poetry is the written form and poetics the theory, poesy is the dream — the divine delirium that drives creation. Poesy is what Plato called divine madness, what Shelley hailed as the "unacknowledged legislator of the world." It is imagination unchained, the lightning of intuition that strikes before thought can analyze. In poesy, the poet becomes a vessel — not an inventor but an instrument through which the universal breathes. It is the metaphysical mist from which poetry condenses into form, like rain from the unseen sky of inspiration.

The Reader as Re-creator — The Alchemy of Interpretation

Every reader rewrites the poem. The act of reading is an act of recreation — a renewal of meaning through personal experience. The same poem that whispers consolation to one reader may roar rebellion in another. Thus, poetry lives a thousand lives in a thousand minds. The poet provides the seed, but the reader provides the soil, the climate, and the season. Without this reciprocal relationship, poetry would remain incomplete — a body without breath. In the act of reading, language becomes luminous, for it passes through consciousness and becomes personal. Interpretation is not a distortion; it is the continuation of creation.

The Musical Mind of Poetry — The Harmony of Heart and Intellect

Poetry lives at the intersection of emotion and intellect, heart and harmony. Its rhythm is not merely metric but metaphysical — an echo of the cosmic cadence that governs existence. The reader, through poetic engagement, enters this rhythm and resonates with it. Neuroscientists affirm what poets have long intuited: that reading poetry activates both hemispheres of the brain — logic and lyric, sense and soul. Thus, poetry is not read; it is experienced. The reader becomes a participant in the poem's pulse, hearing not only words but worlds, not merely lines but lives concealed in them. In this harmony, intellect and intuition become one symphony.

The Poetic Paradox — Between Universality and Uniqueness

Poetry's relationship with its reader is both intimate and infinite. It speaks universally yet individually; it is born in one soul but belongs to all. This paradox is poetry's power:

it can articulate what is utterly personal yet feel universal. The reader becomes the poet's mirror — reflecting meanings unseen even by the creator. This universality of emotion — love, loss, longing — binds humanity across time. A verse from ancient Sumer can still move a modern reader to tears. Poetry transcends chronology and geography because it speaks the language of essence, not existence; it appeals to the eternal in the ephemeral.

Poetics as Philosophy — The Thought behind the Thrill

Behind every poetic line lies a philosophy — explicit or implicit. Poetics, as the science of poetic beauty, seeks to understand why certain sounds soothe and certain images sting. It is the metaphysics of meaning and the mathematics of music. But poetics without poetry is like anatomy without life — dry bones of brilliance without breath. True poetics must feel as it thinks; it must explore not only how poetry works but why it awakens. The reader, in engaging with poetics, learns not merely to analyze art but to apprehend awe — to see in a stanza the structure of the soul.

Poesy and the Divine Dialogue

Poetry, at its highest, becomes prayer; poesy becomes prophecy. In the sacred act of creation, the poet listens — not to the world but to something beyond it. The Greeks called it the Muse; the Indians named it Shruti, the "heard truth." The reader, in turn, reenacts this revelation by listening inwardly. Thus, poetry creates a dialogue between mortal and divine, visible and invisible. In poesy, words become wings, and meaning becomes a medium for transcendence. The poet whispers; the reader worships. Together they recreate the eternal conversation between the finite and the infinite.

The Reader's Transformation — Catharsis through Verse

The relationship between poetry and reader is

not merely aesthetic; it is alchemical. Poetry purifies the psyche, offering emotional release and spiritual renewal. Aristotle called it catharsis — the cleansing of emotion through art. When the reader encounters authentic poetry, sorrow finds shape, silence finds sound, and chaos finds clarity. This transformation is the ultimate triumph of poetic communion — where literature becomes therapy, and beauty becomes balm. The reader is not entertained but enlightened, emerging from the poem more whole, more human, more harmonious than before.

The Eternal Triad — Poetry, Poetics, and Poesy as a Living Trinity

At last, we return to the triad that governs the poetic cosmos: poetry, the form; poetics, the framework; poesy, the force. They are not separate entities but interwoven energies — like body, mind, and soul. Poetry is the song; poetics is the score; poesy is the spirit. Together they create an eternal harmony that binds poet and reader, creation and contemplation. This trinity sustains the sacred cycle of art — from inspiration to interpretation, from creation to communion. In understanding their interplay, we glimpse not only the essence of poetry but the architecture of consciousness itself.

THE READER AS POET, THE POET AS READER — THE CYCLICAL NATURE OF POETIC CONSCIOUSNESS

The reader is the reborn poet, and the poet the preordained reader—each a mirror in the mystic mandala of meaning, revolving through the cyclic current of consciousness. In the sacred circle of creation, reading becomes re-creation, perceiving becomes participating, and every verse read resurrects the voice that wrote it. The poet's pen is the reader's pulse, and the reader's soul is the poet's scroll; together they breathe and re-breathe the same eternal syllable, shaping silence into sense and sense into silence again. In this infinite interchange of insight and imagination, the poem ceases to be a fixed form—it becomes a living labyrinth of awareness, where the self reads itself through symbols, and the symbols sing themselves through the self. Thus, poetic consciousness is circular, self-consuming, and self-creating—a serpent of spirit swallowing its own song, where every ending echoes an origin, and every word is both revelation and return.

The Circulation of Creative Consciousness — The Reader's Rebirth as Poet

The poetic act never ends at the poet's pen; it continues in the reader's perception. The reader, immersed in rhythm and revelation, unconsciously becomes a co-creator. Every interpretation, every emotional echo, is a new creation born of the old. Thus, poetry forms a circle of consciousness, not a straight line of transmission. The poet breathes life into words, the reader breathes life back into meaning. The poem becomes a living organism circulating between minds. This reciprocal respiration — from inspiration to interpretation — ensures poetry never perishes but perpetually reincarnates in every act of reading. The reader's imagination thus becomes the poem's second soul.

The Empathic Exchange — When Hearts Converse Beyond Words

In the invisible intimacy between poet and reader, empathy is the electric current. The poet confides; the reader consoles. The poet articulates anguish; the reader absorbs and transforms it into understanding. It is a dialogue deeper than discourse — a communion of feeling where words are mere intermediaries. The poem, therefore, functions as a telepathic text — transmitting tenderness across time, space, and silence. It is through empathy that poetry achieves its immortality. For while history changes its tongues and traditions, emotion remains eternally legible. The reader, in feeling the poet's pulse, finds his own heart illuminated.

The Reflective Mirror — Poetry as Self-Recognition

A true poem does not merely describe; it discovers. When the reader gazes into the poem, he sees not the poet but himself — refracted, reimagined, revealed. Poetry thus serves as a reflective mirror in which consciousness recognizes its own contours. It translates the unspeakable into symbol, the invisible into image. What the poet feels becomes what the reader has always felt but never found the words to voice. Hence, poetry becomes the language of recognition — a sacred mirror where human beings meet their unspoken selves. Each reading is a revelation, each line a lens into the labyrinth of identity.

The Duality of Distance — The Reader's Reverence and Resistance

The reader's relationship with poetry is also paradoxical — one of devotion and defiance. A reader venerates the poem for its beauty but also wrestles with its meaning. Great poetry invites both surrender and struggle. It demands that the reader question, challenge, and cohabit its mystery. This tension creates depth. Just as love deepens through difference, poetry strengthens through interpretive resistance. The reader's doubt is not disloyalty but dialogue; it is how meaning matures. Thus, poetry lives not in agreement but in ambiguity — a fertile field where multiple meanings grow, nourished by the reader's curiosity.

The Poetic Mind — Merging Intellect with Intuition

The poet writes with the whole mind — analytical and emotional, rational and instinctive. The reader too must read with this dual awareness. To approach poetry with logic alone is to dissect its heart; to read with emotion alone is to drown in its depths. True reading requires intuitive intelligence — the marriage of sense and sensibility. In this equilibrium, the reader becomes what Coleridge called the "ideal critic" — one who does not merely interpret but intuits. Poetry thus trains the reader's perception, teaching him to see with feeling and to feel with thought. It refines the faculties of both cognition and compassion.

The Sacred Silence — Reading as Meditation

To read a poem truly is to enter a state of meditative awareness. Each word, each pause, each punctuation becomes a breath in the sacred rhythm of revelation. The reader must learn to listen — not to noise, but to nuance.

Silence surrounds the poem like an invisible temple. In that silence, the reader hears what language cannot say — the unsaid meanings, the invisible metaphors, the rhythm of thought between lines. Reading poetry is thus not a consumption of text but a contemplation of being. It is a spiritual discipline disguised as aesthetic pleasure.

Poetics of Participation — Reading as Creative Act

Poetics teaches us that poetry is not a monologue but a participatory phenomenon. The reader, through attention, tone, and interpretation, alters the poem's energy. Reading aloud changes rhythm; reading silently alters meaning. The poem behaves differently in every consciousness. This participatory poetics transforms the reader into performer, philosopher, and poet simultaneously. The poem, therefore, is an open system, not a closed artifact — a field of possibilities awaiting activation by awareness. The poet provides potential; the reader realizes reality. Together they generate what might be called the kinetic beauty of verse — meaning in motion.

The Temporal Transcendence — Poetry as Eternal Present

When the reader engages with poetry, time ceases. The ancient lyric becomes as immediate as breath. Homer's sorrow, Kalidasa's imagery, Dante's vision — all coexist in the eternal now of reading. The poem collapses chronology; it unites the living with the dead, the here with the elsewhere. This temporal transcendence is the unique magic of poetry — it creates a simultaneity of feeling across millennia. The reader becomes a time traveler, conversing with the ancients not through relics but through rhythm. Poetry alone achieves what philosophy dreams: immortality through imagination.

The Poetic Covenant — Between Language and Light

Every poem is a covenant between the ineffable and

the expressed – between silence and sound, idea and incarnation. The reader inherits this covenant, becoming the new guardian of meaning. Through each reading, the light of language refracts anew. The poem's luminosity depends on the clarity of the reader's consciousness. Thus, the reader does not merely understand poetry- he illuminates it. The act of reading becomes an act of reverence, a ritual of renewal. Poetry survives not through preservation but through perception- each mind it touches becomes its afterlife.

The Infinite Continuum – Poetry's Perpetual Rebirth

In the grand cosmic scheme, poetry is not a static art but a living continuum. The poet begins the journey, the reader continues it, and future generations rediscover it. Every era rewrites the same emotions in different idioms. The love that Sappho sang, the grief that Neruda grieved, the wonder that Whitman worshipped – all reappear, reborn in new rhythms. Poetry is humanity's collective consciousness echoing through ages. The reader, therefore, is not merely a consumer of art but its custodian – the keeper of the eternal flame of expression.

The Closing Circle – Poetry as Perpetual Dialogue

At last, the relationship between poet, reader, poetics, and poesy forms a perfect circle – an eternal dialogue of being. The poet creates from inspiration; the reader recreates through interpretation. Poetics analyzes the process; poesy sanctifies it. Together they form the sacred geometry of art – emotion, expression, and evolution in endless exchange. Poetry is the language through which humanity converses with itself – across borders, centuries, and silences. In reading and writing poetry, we rediscover what it means to be alive, to be aware, to be whole. The poem begins in the poet's solitude but ends in the reader's soul – and there, it becomes eternal.

THE EVOLUTIONARY ENERGY OF POETRY — HOW POETICS, POESY, AND THE READER SHAPE THE FUTURE OF ART AND CONSCIOUSNESS

Poetry is the evolutionary energy — The Eternal Expansion of Expression. Poetry is not static art; it is evolutionary essence. From the first chants carved in cave echo to the coded sonnets sung through silicon, poetry has always evolved alongside consciousness. Every era invents its idiom, every generation its genius. Yet beneath these shifting surfaces flows one constant current — the human impulse to utter the ineffable. The poem is thus an evolutionary organ of the species, adapting language to the expanding landscapes of thought. The reader, in engaging with poetry, participates in this evolution — enlarging awareness, deepening empathy, refining perception. Poetry evolves not through the pen but through the pulse of those who read it.

The Alchemy of Poetics — From Analysis to Awakening

Poetics once sought to define, dissect, and delimit poetry — but in truth, it liberates the mind into understanding. The evolution of poetics mirrors the evolution of human consciousness: from Aristotle's rational categorization to modern phenomenology, from metre to meaning, from structure to spirit. In each stage, poetics becomes less a science of rules and more a philosophy of resonance. It teaches that form and freedom are not foes but facets of the same gem. The reader, when aware of poetics, reads more deeply — seeing not just the words but the architecture of wonder beneath them. Thus, poetics evolves from mere analysis into aesthetic awakening.

Poesy and the Cosmic Imagination

Poesy is the most mystical of the triad — the unseen spark that ignites both poet and reader. It is the pulse of the cosmos itself expressed through consciousness. In poesy, creation is not invention but revelation. It is the moment when the universe uses language to listen to itself. The poet feels this current as inspiration; the reader feels it as illumination. In both, poesy acts as cosmic correspondence — a communion between microcosm and macrocosm. It proves that poetry is not merely human art but universal energy — the vibration of existence translated into verbal rhythm.

The Reader as Evolutionary Agent — From Reception to Revelation

The modern reader no longer receives poetry passively; he co-creates meaning in real time. Digital spaces, intertextual dialogues, and linguistic experiments have transformed reading into an act of authorship. Each interpretation becomes an innovation. The reader reconstructs the poem through perspective, context, and consciousness. This marks a revolutionary evolution — from readership to readership-as-authorship. The poem is reborn with every gaze. In this symbiotic shift, literature becomes a living laboratory of the mind. The reader, by decoding and re-envisioning, becomes both heir and architect of poetic evolution — transforming art into awareness.

The Fusion of Poetics and Science — The Geometry of Grace

In an age where neuroscience meets aesthetics, poetry finds new resonance. Studies reveal that poetry synchronizes brainwave patterns, stimulates emotional intelligence, and activates empathy. This is not coincidence but cosmic correspondence — art aligning with biology. Poetics now expands to include cognitive science, rhythm perception, and linguistic mathematics. The Fibonacci sequences in poetic meters mirror those in nature. Thus, the poem becomes the meeting point of art and arithmetic, intuition and intellect. The reader is not merely moved emotionally but calibrated neurologically. Poetry, therefore, is not just beauty — it is bio-symphony, a rhythmic resonance within the architecture of the mind.

The Poetic Ecology — Language as Living Organism

Language is not static; it breathes, mutates, and migrates. Poetry is the ecosystem that keeps it alive. When languages die, poetry resurrects them in memory; when vocabularies stagnate, poetry reinvents them through vision. Every poem plants a seed in the soil of speech, ensuring that linguistic life continues. The reader, as custodian, cultivates these gardens of meaning. Thus, poetry forms the ecological heart of culture — maintaining biodiversity of expression. Poetics, then, is environmental ethics in linguistic form; to read poetry deeply is to engage in ecological preservation of the spirit.

Poesy and the Future of Consciousness

As human awareness evolves toward digital and cosmic dimensions, poesy remains the thread connecting intelligence with intuition. In an era of algorithms, poetry restores awe; in a world of information, it reawakens imagination. The future may replace books with screens, but poesy will still whisper in the circuitry of consciousness. Perhaps the next poets will code their verses in quantum scripts, and readers will feel poems through neural interfaces — yet the essence will remain unchanged: to name the nameless, to feel the infinite. Poesy thus ensures that even as humanity becomes more technological, it never ceases to be transcendental.

Poetics of the Posthuman — Poetry Beyond the Page

In the expanding universe of digital poetics, verse becomes visual, auditory, and virtual. The poem now dances in holograms, breathes in augmented reality, and echoes in artificial intelligence. Yet, paradoxically, this technological transformation reaffirms the timeless nature of poetry. No matter the medium, the essence of poesy persists — the yearning to unite sound, sense, and soul. The reader becomes an explorer of multi-sensory landscapes, interpreting data as metaphor and motion as meaning. Thus, poetry becomes posthuman — not less emotional but more expansive — merging art and algorithm, lyric and light.

The Moral Dimension — Poetry as Evolution of Empathy

As humanity grapples with crisis and complexity, poetry becomes an ethical compass. It reminds us that truth is not just logical but lyrical, that justice must be felt before it is enforced. Through metaphor and music, poetry trains the moral imagination — the capacity to feel for another, to live in empathy. The reader, encountering beauty and pain in verse, becomes sensitized to life's interconnections. Thus, poetry evolves from personal pleasure to planetary purpose. It is the emotional evolution of the species — teaching the heart how to think and the mind how to feel.

The Infinite Reader — Poetry's Perpetual Afterlife

When a poet dies, the poem lives on — but not in paper or print alone. It lives in every consciousness it touches, in every interpretation it inspires. The reader becomes the poem's afterlife, its reincarnation in meaning. A verse written centuries ago continues to breathe through billions of hearts. Thus, the reader is both resurrection and remembrance — the eternal continuator of creative consciousness. The poem never truly ends; it only changes readers, changing shape as it travels through time. Every reading is resurrection; every reflection, rebirth.

The Circle Closes — Poetry as the Pulse of the Universe

In the end, poetry, poetics, poesy, and the reader converge into a single cosmic rhythm. The poet's inspiration, the reader's interpretation, the poetics of understanding, and the poesy of spirit — all are pulses in one universal heartbeat. Poetry is the self-consciousness of existence, the music of meaning echoing through matter. It is life speaking to itself through language. When the reader reads, the universe reads itself. Thus, the circle of poetic consciousness closes — not in conclusion but in continuation. For poetry, like the cosmos, never ends; it endlessly begins.

The Sacred Symphony of Souls

Poetry is not a genre; it is a genesis. It births beauty wherever language touches light. It unites the poet and the reader in an unbroken lineage of love, loss, and luminous longing. Poetics provides the path, poesy the passion, the reader the realization. Together, they form the sacred symphony of existence — where meaning is music and silence is song. In this eternal dance of creation and comprehension, poetry remains humanity's most divine invention — the art through which the universe remembers itself.

THE FIVEFOLD FLAME OF THE ETERNAL WORD

Poetry is the fivefold flame of the eternal world—a living luminosity that burns in the heart of existence. What is poetry? It is the word made wonder, the soul's speech before speech, the silent symmetry of spirit seeking shape. How is poetry? It unfolds through the alchemy of awareness, transforming anguish into art and chaos into cadence. Why is poetry? Because creation itself craves consciousness—poetry is the universe's urge to understand itself through rhythm and revelation. When is poetry? Whenever time trembles before truth, when the transient touches the timeless and thought flowers into vision. Where is poetry? In every atom that aches to speak, in every heart that hears the hush beyond language—it is everywhere the infinite dreams through the finite.

What is Poetry — The Pulse of the Infinite in the Finite: What is poetry? A question both sacred and impossible. To define it is to diminish it, yet to ignore it is to insult the intelligence of imagination itself. Poetry is not a thing, but a throbbing, a tremor, a pulse of the infinite caught within the finite form of language. It is the place where words transcend themselves, where thought turns to thunder, and emotion becomes eternity. It is not the description of beauty but the birth of it. Poetry is the echo of creation heard in the human heart.

To ask "what is poetry" is like asking "what is fire" — one cannot explain it without extinguishing it. It burns precisely because it is beyond containment. Poetry is both essence and event: it happens as much as it is. It exists not only on the page, but in perception; not only in sound, but in soul. It is an experience of being alive to the mysterious music of existence. Where prose speaks about life, poetry sings life itself.

Poetry is paradox incarnate — it is both language and silence, both motion and stillness. It is that which uses words to worship what words cannot reach. It is the tongue's attempt to touch the eternal. Every poem is an incarnation — an infinite idea in a finite form, a thought that takes breath, a silence that finds sound. The poet, in writing, does not merely express himself; he enacts the act of creation anew.

Thus, poetry is not a luxury of literature; it is the law of life. Every dawn that breaks, every seed that splits, every heart that beats — all are acts of poetry. The universe itself is the original poet, and we are but echoes of its first utterance.

Where is Poetry — The Everywhere that Hides in the Here: Where does poetry dwell? It dwells everywhere, though it hides nowhere. It is in the light that leaks through leaves, in the tear that trembles before falling, in the laughter that lingers after loss. Poetry is not found in libraries or classrooms; it lives in moments — in the metaphysical marrow of the mundane. It resides in the realm between perception and presence — in that shimmering space where awareness awakens.

The error of the ordinary mind is to think poetry exists only in verse. But poetry precedes verse, surpasses it, saturates existence. The waves breaking on a forgotten shore, the wind whispering through abandoned ruins, the child's first cry, the last breath of the dying — these are the original poems of creation. The written poem is merely a mirror, a reflection of that larger, living poetry that pervades all being.

Poetry dwells where the visible touches the invisible — where matter murmurs spirit. It is not in the poet's pen, but in his perception; not in his vocabulary, but in his vision. Poetry is wherever there is wonder. The world is woven of words we do not yet know how to pronounce. The poet hears them in the rustle of rain and the rhythm of rivers. Every sound of the world is a syllable in the song of being.

Thus, poetry's dwelling is not geographical but spiritual. It resides in the receptive heart, in the contemplative mind, in the silent soul that listens without language. Where there is awareness, there is poetry; where there is presence, there is poem.

How is Poetry — The Birth of Meaning through Mystery: How does poetry happen? How does silence become song? The answer lies in the sacred tension between mystery and meaning. Poetry is born not when something is understood, but when something is felt too deeply to remain unspoken. The poem arises from pressure — the pressure of perception upon the soul. When feeling floods the heart beyond measure, it must flow into form — that flow is poetry.

Poetry begins as a tremor in the invisible. It is not created by will but by wonder. The poet does not force the poem; he frees it. He listens until the language begins to listen back. Poetry is born from a moment when thought and feeling fuse — when intellect bows to intuition, when reason kneels before revelation. It is not argument but awakening.

The how of poetry is also the howl of the heart. It is the spontaneous symmetry of suffering and splendour. The poet, torn between what he sees and what he seeks, releases that tension through rhythm and image. Each line is both liberation and lament. Thus, poetry's process is paradoxical — it is both discipline and delirium, both construction and collapse. It requires precision but thrives on passion. It demands control but rewards surrender.

The poet's mind must be both microscope and mirror: seeing sharply, reflecting truthfully. The poem, once written, is less a product than a revelation. It reveals not what the poet knows, but what he is. To write a poem is to discover oneself anew — to catch a glimpse of the eternal self that hides behind the human name.

Thus, poetry happens when awareness catches fire — when the finite suddenly feels the infinite moving through it. That combustion, that illumination, is the "how" of poetry: the fusion of heart and cosmos in a single, burning line.

Why is Poetry — The Cry of Creation and the Call to Consciousness: Why does poetry exist at all? Why do humans, amid survival and sorrow, still seek to sing? The answer lies in the architecture of existence: because life itself is lyrical. The cosmos, in its ceaseless expansion, seeks self-expression. Stars burn not merely to exist but to illuminate; rivers run not just to reach but to reveal. Likewise, the human heart, being the universe made conscious, cannot help but translate its own trembling into tone.

Poetry exists because silence desires speech. It is the universe's way of knowing itself through consciousness. The poet is but the mouth of mystery, the medium through which existence articulates awe. Without poetry, language would remain utilitarian; with poetry, it becomes universal.

Without poetry, life would be livable; with it, it becomes luminous.

We write poems not to escape reality but to enter it more deeply. The poem is not flight but focus, not withdrawal but witness. It allows us to see the sacred beneath the surface of the ordinary. In a world that worships noise, poetry restores silence; in a time that praises speed, it resurrects stillness. It reminds humanity of its forgotten origin — that we were not born to consume, but to contemplate; not to conquer, but to create.

Poetry exists because we ache for meaning. Every poem is a bridge between despair and divinity. It tells us that beauty is not a luxury but a necessity — that to live without wonder is to die while breathing. The "why" of poetry, therefore, is love — the cosmic compulsion to connect. Poetry is the universe loving itself through language.

When is Poetry — The Eternal Now of the Written and the Unwritten: When is poetry? It is tempting to answer with chronology — to trace its birth to the first song of the first soul. But poetry does not belong to time; time belongs to poetry. It is not then or later; it is always now. Poetry happens in the eternal present, in the instant of awareness that breaks through habit and reveals holiness.

Every true poem exists outside history. It might be written in one age but understood in another, yet its essence remains ageless. Homer and Hafiz, Dante and Dickinson — they speak not from the past but from the perennial now. Poetry's clock is consciousness. It ticks not by seconds but by soul-moments — those flashes when eternity enters experience.

Poetry happens whenever perception transcends possession — when one stops looking at life and begins looking into it. It happens in every era, yet in none. It was before language and will remain after literature. The universe itself began with a poem — a vibration, a verse of light. And perhaps it will end with one: the final rhythm of dissolution returning to divine silence.

Thus, poetry is always happening. It is the ongoing breath between birth and becoming, between the said and the unsayable. Every time a mind awakens to mystery, poetry is reborn. Every time a heart sees beauty in brokenness, poetry lives again. The "when" of poetry is now — eternally now.

Epilogue: The Flame that Never Finishes

And so we arrive — not at a conclusion, but at a continuation. For poetry, like the cosmos, has no end. It is both the question and the answer, the silence and the song. It is the mirror in which the soul sees itself infinite. To speak of poetry is to speak of consciousness; to read a poem is to remember creation.

The origin of poetry was the first breath. The language of poetry is the soul's syntax. The style of poetry is the signature of silence. The uniqueness of poetry is its universality. The secret of poetry is that it hides in plain sight. And the what, where, how, why, and when of poetry — all are one: Poetry is the pulse of existence becoming aware of itself. Poetry, therefore, is not written — it is revealed. It is not the art of saying beautiful things; it is the act of beholding beauty itself. It is the divine dialogue between the seen and the unseen, the song of the spirit through the syllables of the world. And when humanity forgets everything — science, speech, civilization — one thing will remain, glowing like an ember in the ruins: Poetry. For poetry is not what we make; it is what we are. The cosmos speaks in stars, and man, remembering his origin, answers in poems.

THE INFINITE ECHO: CHARACTERISTICS, NATURE, AND MYSTERIES OF POETRY

Poetry is one of humanity's oldest and most profound forms of expression. It transcends time, culture, and language, offering glimpses into the deepest recesses of thought and emotion. Its characteristics are manifold, revealing the art form as simultaneously universal, intimate, and transformative. Understanding the nature of poetry requires exploration of its historical origins, structural intricacies, cognitive effects, and spiritual dimensions. Poetry predates written language. Long before humans inscribed letters on clay tablets or papyrus, poetry existed as a spoken art. Oral traditions—through chants, songs, and narrative storytelling—preserved history, culture, and spiritual knowledge. Ancient peoples relied on poetic forms to ensure that communal memory survived generations, often embedding morals, myths, and practical wisdom into rhythmic, melodic structures. These oral forms demonstrate that poetry was not merely entertainment but a vessel for human survival, collective identity, and cultural continuity. Poetry is universal. Across the world, every known culture has produced poetry. From the Sumerian hymns that date back over 4,000 years to the African griot traditions, poetry has functioned as a universal means of interpreting human experience. It captures emotions, beliefs, and aspirations that resonate across geography and time. Even societies with minimal written documentation relied on verse to transmit knowledge and values, proving that poetry is not bound by civilization or technology but thrives wherever humans seek meaning.

Poetry as a mnemonic device. Ancient epics like Homer's Iliad, the Odyssey, and Vyasa's Mahabharata were composed to be recited aloud, not read silently. Repetition, rhythm, and rhyme were not merely aesthetic choices—they were essential tools for memory. Storytellers could recall thousands of lines verbatim, allowing entire cultures to retain complex histories without written records. Poetry's mnemonic nature underscores its practical utility and demonstrates the intricate link between sound, cognition, and storytelling. Poetry Alters the Brain. Modern neuroscience confirms that reading or hearing poetry engages multiple regions of the brain simultaneously. Language processing, emotional response, and sensory imagery are all activated, merging rational and emotional faculties. Poetry can evoke empathy, trigger visualizations, and even alter mood, making the reading experience a holistic cognitive and emotional exercise. This unique interplay explains why poetry has long been associated with healing, insight, and philosophical reflection. Poetry Exists in Nature. The patterns of the natural world often resemble poetic forms. The Fibonacci sequence, spiraling shells, fractal trees, and the rhythmic cycles of tides reflect an intrinsic order and beauty akin to verse. Many poets consciously draw inspiration from these patterns, mimicking natural rhythms in meter and imagery. Nature, in this sense, provides both a model and a metaphor for poetry, illustrating that the art form extends beyond human language to the fundamental structures of the universe.

Poetry Can Exist Without Words. Though words are central to most poetry, the form transcends verbal language. Visual or concrete poetry, sound poetry, and gestural forms communicate meaning through shape, rhythm, and sensory effect rather than literal language. These experiments demonstrate that poetry is not limited to alphabetic or phonetic expression—it can manifest in the arrangement of objects, the cadence of sound, or even bodily movement, making it a truly multi-modal art form. The Haiku: Economy of Expression. Few forms exemplify poetry's precision like the haiku. In just seventeen syllables, a haiku conveys time, place, and emotion, evoking landscapes, seasons, or ephemeral moments with remarkable conciseness. This compactness demonstrates poetry's ability to condense the infinite into the finite, to reveal universality through economy, and to invite contemplation with minimalistic elegance. Poetry's healing power. Poetry has long been recognized as therapeutic. Bibliotherapy and poetry therapy use reading or writing verse to relieve stress, process trauma, and promote emotional well-being. The act of engaging with poetry allows individuals to externalize inner thoughts, reflect cognitively, and experience catharsis. In this sense, poetry is not merely artistic—it is restorative, a tool for psychological resilience and human flourishing. Poetry defies translation. Though poetry is universal, its nuances often resist translation. Sounds, cultural references, rhythm, and wordplay are intricately tied to specific languages, making literal translation impossible. Every translation becomes an act of recreation rather than replication, and the essence of a poem is frequently reborn in new linguistic and cultural contexts. This highlights poetry's deep entanglement with human language and the subtleties of meaning.

Poetry uses multiple layers of meaning. A single poetic line can simultaneously convey literal, metaphorical, symbolic, emotional, and philosophical significance. Unlike prose, which often prioritizes linear clarity, poetry thrives in ambiguity and multiplicity. This layered quality allows poems to speak differently to each reader, reflecting the interplay of context, perception, and interpretation, and making each reading an act of discovery. Poetry is mathematically rhythmic. Rhythm, meter, and rhyme often follow precise patterns akin to mathematical formulas. Iambic pentameter, for instance, uses an alternating pattern of stressed and unstressed syllables to create musicality and flow. This blending of art and numeric symmetry exemplifies poetry's capacity to harmonize structure and emotion, demonstrating that creativity and logic are not mutually exclusive but complementary in verse. Poetry preserves endangered languages. Oral poetry and folk songs play a crucial role in sustaining endangered languages. Many languages survive today only through their traditional poems and chants. By embedding cultural memory in verse, poetry preserves linguistic identity, connects generations, and safeguards intangible heritage, serving as a living archive of human diversity.

Poetry can exist without literal meaning. Modernist and postmodernist experiments emphasize sound, form, or rhythm over semantic clarity. Poetry can evoke emotion, rhythm, and aesthetic pleasure without conveying a literal message. This demonstrates that poetry is not defined solely by meaning but by its capacity to stimulate perception, imagination, and sensory awareness. Poetry has spiritual origins. Historically, poetry has been intimately linked to the sacred. Many early poems were hymns, prayers, or invocations, acting as bridges between humans and the divine. Even today, religious and mystical traditions use poetry to express devotion, wonder, and transcendence. Its spiritual dimension highlights poetry's role as a conduit for existential inquiry and the search for meaning beyond the material world. Poetry mirrors society. Poetry has always reflected societal conditions, political struggles, and historical change. From Persian ghazals to modern protest poems, verse has challenged authority, chronicled revolutions, and voiced collective aspirations. In its capacity to mirror society, poetry serves as both a personal confession and a public commentary, bridging the private and communal realms of human experience. Poetry stimulates imagination more than prose. Research indicates that metaphor-rich poetry engages the brain's imagination and visualization centers more strongly than straightforward prose. By juxtaposing unexpected images, sounds, and concepts, poetry invites readers to create mental landscapes, explore possibilities, and experience emotions more vividly, making it a uniquely immersive literary form. Poetry exists in hidden forms. Some poems conceal meaning in constrained structures such as acrostics, palindromes, or patterned verse. These hidden forms embed semantic or visual information within shape, letters, or sequence, demonstrating poetry's playful ingenuity and its capacity to encode complexity beyond the apparent surface. Poetry transcends time. Finally, poetry's endurance is unparalleled. Works written thousands of years ago continue to resonate, proving that human emotions, philosophical questions, and existential concerns are universal. Poetry connects past and present, bridging temporal divides and affirming the shared continuum of human consciousness. However, while discussing about the natures, specific features and characteristics of poetry, the following few things may be noted down.

1. Primordial Poetry

Poetry predates written language, existing long before humans invented scripts or alphabets. In prehistoric societies, poetry thrived as oral tradition—chants, songs, and stories that encoded history, myths, and cultural wisdom. These rhythmic patterns and melodic repetitions served as mnemonic devices, preserving knowledge across generations. Poetry was not merely entertainment; it functioned as a cultural, social, and spiritual vessel. By structuring memory in musical and rhythmic forms, early humans ensured continuity of values, laws, and mythic narratives. This foundational role demonstrates that poetry is innate to human consciousness, revealing the deep impulse to create symbolic, structured, and memorable expressions of experience.

2. Universal Urge

Poetry is a universal human expression, arising independently in every known culture. From Sumerian hymns to African griot chants, Aboriginal songlines, and Native American ceremonial songs, poetry consistently emerges as a vehicle for emotion, morality, and history. Its universality indicates that humans naturally seek to articulate their experiences, joys, sorrows, and philosophical reflections in structured language. Even societies without formal writing systems have relied on poetic forms to transmit social memory, laws, and ethical norms. Poetry is thus a persistent, cross-cultural phenomenon that transcends time, geography, and language, embodying humanity's collective desire to understand, communicate, and preserve the human experience.

3. Mnemonic Melodies

Memory lies at the heart of poetry. Ancient epics such as Homer's Iliad and Odyssey, or India's Mahabharata, were composed to be recited aloud, not read silently. The repetitive structures, rhythmic meters, and mnemonic devices allowed performers to commit thousands of lines to memory. Poetry functioned as a cognitive tool, encoding vast narratives and cultural knowledge into accessible, recitable forms. This illustrates the intimate connection between sound, rhythm, and human memory, showing that poetry is not only an aesthetic expression but a practical mechanism for transmitting complex ideas, history, and philosophy across generations, long before the invention of writing.

4. Cerebral Cascade

Poetry activates the brain in uniquely holistic ways. Neuroscientific research shows that reading or listening to verse engages language comprehension areas, emotional processing centers, and sensory visualization regions simultaneously. Metaphors stimulate imagination, rhythm influences cognition, and imagery evokes emotion. This dual engagement of rational and emotional faculties explains poetry's profound psychological and neurological impact. Unlike prose, which primarily appeals to intellect, poetry entwines thought and feeling, fostering empathy, reflection, and insight. By merging these cognitive and emotional pathways, poetry functions as both an art form and a mental exercise, enhancing perception, memory, and emotional intelligence simultaneously.

5. Natural Narratives

Poetry mirrors the inherent rhythms of nature. The Fibonacci spirals of shells, fractal patterns in trees, and rhythmic cycles of tides resemble structural principles of verse. Many poets consciously emulate these natural patterns, integrating meter, cadence, and imagery that resonate with the natural world. This interplay demonstrates that poetry is an extension of universal order, bridging human creativity with cosmic design. By translating natural rhythm into linguistic expression, poetry reflects not only the external universe but the internal harmony of perception and thought, positioning human experience as both a participant in and observer of the patterns of existence.

6. Wordless Wonders

Poetry is not confined to verbal language. Concrete poetry, visual verse, sound poetry, and gestural performances communicate meaning through shape, rhythm, and sensory resonance rather than literal words. These forms demonstrate that poetry is fundamentally a mode of perception and experience. A poem may speak in movement, in visual form, or through pure sound, transcending linguistic barriers. This universality of expressive possibilities highlights poetry's flexibility and power: it communicates, resonates, and evokes feeling even in the absence of semantic clarity. Poetry, therefore, is the art of structured perception, not merely the arrangement of letters or sounds.

7. Haiku Horizon

The haiku exemplifies poetry's precision and depth. With only seventeen syllables, a haiku evokes landscapes, emotions, and the passage of time. Its brevity demonstrates that poetry's potency does not depend on length but on concision, resonance, and imagery. The haiku's structure invites the reader into an intense, reflective encounter with a fleeting moment, emphasizing the aesthetic of minimalism and the power of suggestion. This condensed form embodies poetry's paradoxical ability to encapsulate the infinite within the finite, to evoke vast emotional landscapes with remarkably few words, revealing the extraordinary efficiency and intensity of poetic expression.

8. Therapeutic Tides

Poetry has long been recognized for its healing potential. Bibliotherapy and poetry therapy utilize verse to alleviate stress, trauma, and psychological distress. Writing or reading poetry allows individuals to externalize emotions, reflect on experiences, and process difficult memories safely. The rhythmic, structured nature of verse facilitates emotional regulation and cognitive clarity, while metaphors provide symbolic spaces for reflection and insight. By engaging imagination, empathy, and emotional resonance simultaneously, poetry functions as a restorative art form. It demonstrates that verse is not merely aesthetic or intellectual—it has practical, therapeutic applications that contribute to mental, emotional, and spiritual well-being.

9. Translational Tension

Poetry resists literal translation. Sounds, rhythms, cultural references, and wordplay often cannot be fully replicated in another language. Every translation becomes a creative act—a rebirth of the poem that preserves essence but alters expression. The nuances of phonetics, rhyme, and cultural meaning make each version distinct, emphasizing poetry's intimate bond with its original linguistic and social context. Translation, therefore, is not reproduction but re-creation, highlighting poetry's sensitivity to language and culture. This tension demonstrates that poetry is both universal and particular, capable of transcending language while remaining deeply tied to the unique texture of its words.

10. Layered Luminescence

Poetry thrives on layered meaning. A single line may simultaneously convey literal, metaphorical, symbolic, emotional, and philosophical significance. Unlike prose, which often prioritizes clarity and linearity, poetry embraces ambiguity and multiplicity. This multi-dimensionality invites diverse interpretations, allowing readers to encounter new insights upon each reading. Layers of imagery, rhythm, and metaphor interact to create depth and resonance, making poetry a medium that can communicate complex human experience efficiently and profoundly. Through its layered structure, poetry reflects the multifaceted nature of perception, cognition, and emotion, revealing the richness and ambiguity inherent in human consciousness.

11. Mathematical Music

Poetry often intertwines art and arithmetic, creating beauty through rhythmical precision. Meter, syllable counts, rhyme schemes, and rhythmic patterns rely on mathematical symmetry, as seen in iambic pentameter or sonnets. The deliberate arrangement of stressed and unstressed syllables creates cadence that resonates cognitively and emotionally. This structured harmony illustrates that poetry exists at the intersection of numerical order and creative freedom. Mathematical patterns guide flow and expectation while allowing imaginative deviation, producing tension and resolution. Through this balance, poetry demonstrates that human aesthetic perception appreciates both precision and surprise, merging rational patterns with emotional resonance in a uniquely expressive art form.

12. Linguistic Lifeboat

Many endangered languages survive through poetry, folk songs, chants, and oral verse. Poetry preserves phonetics, vocabulary, and cultural idioms that might otherwise vanish. These verbal artifacts safeguard collective memory, traditions, and identity, ensuring that marginalized or fading languages retain life across generations. In this way, poetry is more than an art—it is a repository of linguistic heritage and cultural continuity. By maintaining rhythm, rhyme, and narrative structure, poetry enables communities to remember and transmit knowledge. In societies where written documentation is absent or incomplete, poetic forms function as vital instruments of memory, ensuring survival and the continued resonance of linguistic diversity.

13. Sound above Sense

Modernist and experimental poetry often emphasizes sound, form, and rhythm over literal meaning. In sound poetry, for instance, vocalizations and tonal variations convey emotion and texture independent of semantic content. Similarly, concrete poetry employs visual and spatial arrangement to communicate beyond words. This demonstrates that poetry is not merely an intellectual exercise; it is an experiential phenomenon. Readers and listeners are invited to engage with auditory, visual, and tactile qualities, highlighting poetry's capacity to evoke feeling without explicit narrative. By privileging perception over literal content, poetry expands human sensory experience, proving its multidimensional communicative power.

14. Sacred Script

Poetry has been historically intertwined with spirituality. Many of the earliest surviving poems are hymns, prayers, or invocations—Vedic chants, Psalms, and Sumerian religious verse. Poetry functions as a bridge between human consciousness and the divine, offering a structured medium to express reverence, seek guidance, or articulate metaphysical insight. Its rhythm, repetition, and symbolism foster meditative focus, enabling participants to enter heightened states of awareness. Across cultures and eras, poetry has provided a conduit for spiritual reflection, suggesting that the creation and reception of verse is not merely aesthetic but deeply sacred, intertwining human expression with universal transcendence.

15. Societal Spiegel

Poetry serves as a mirror of society, reflecting both its beauty and its flaws. From protest songs and political odes to elegies chronicling tragedy, poetry documents cultural shifts and challenges authority. It amplifies marginalized voices and chronicles historical events through personal and collective lenses. Poets have long functioned as societal conscience, articulating values, exposing injustice, and inspiring transformation. By condensing experience into emotive, memorable forms, poetry ensures that societal truths endure beyond the ephemeral. Its capacity to be both intimate and public allows poetry to simultaneously express personal reflection and collective memory, making it a powerful instrument of cultural consciousness.

16. Imaginative Incantation

Poetry stimulates the imagination in ways prose rarely achieves. Through metaphor, simile, and vivid imagery, it activates visualization centers in the brain, enabling readers to "see" and "feel" what is not physically present. This immersive quality allows the mind to explore abstract concepts, alternate realities, and emotional landscapes. Poetic language encourages associative thinking, connecting disparate ideas and experiences. By engaging imagination so fully, poetry expands cognitive flexibility, enhances creativity, and cultivates empathy. Its power lies in presenting the unseen, the unsaid, and the infinite in ways that both delight and challenge the reader's perceptual and intellectual faculties.

17. Hidden Hieroglyphs

Poetry often conceals meaning through structure and pattern. Acrostics, palindromes, constrained writing forms, and typographical designs embed secret narratives within visible text. These hidden hieroglyphs reward attentive readers, creating layered experiences where comprehension requires careful engagement. The interplay of surface and concealed meanings adds depth, intrigue, and intellectual delight. Poetry's capacity to encode dual narratives demonstrates its unique blend of playfulness and sophistication, combining artistry with structural ingenuity. This duality emphasizes that poetry communicates not only through content but through design, pattern, and structure, challenging readers to perceive beyond the obvious and rewarding exploration with richer understanding.

18. Timeless Transmission

Poetry transcends temporal boundaries, connecting humanity across millennia. Homer's epics, Rumi's mystical verses, or Chinese Tang dynasty poems continue to resonate emotionally today. Their enduring relevance demonstrates that poetic expression addresses universal human experiences—love, grief, wonder, mortality—that remain constant despite historical change. Poetry preserves cultural and existential memory, creating dialogue across centuries. Readers encounter emotions and insights from distant eras, bridging temporal distance through shared human consciousness. This timeless quality illustrates poetry's capacity to communicate enduring truths, suggesting that the art form is not ephemeral entertainment but a permanent record of humanity's inner life.

19. Paradoxical Pulse

Poetry thrives on paradox. It can be simple yet profound, finite yet infinite, structured yet free. This tension mirrors the human condition, embracing contradictions to convey complex truths. Poetic paradox invites readers to experience ambiguity, reconcile opposites, and engage with multiple dimensions of meaning simultaneously. The juxtaposition of contrasting elements energizes the text, generating resonance that mirrors life's complexities. By inhabiting these tensions, poetry becomes a dynamic, living expression rather than a static object, teaching readers to appreciate nuance, uncertainty, and multiplicity in thought, emotion, and perception.

20. Synesthetic Symphony

Poetry often evokes cross-sensory experiences, blending sight, sound, taste, and touch. Synesthetic imagery—"tasting colors," "hearing textures," "seeing sounds"—expands perceptual engagement. This multisensory stimulation deepens emotional impact and cognitive immersion, allowing readers to experience language in novel ways. Synesthesia in verse demonstrates poetry's capacity to transcend ordinary sensory perception, creating vivid, layered experiences. By engaging multiple modalities, poetry fosters holistic understanding, connecting intellect, emotion, and sensation. Such cross-sensory resonance reinforces the art form's universality, showing that poetry communicates not only through meaning but through the very experience of perception itself.

21. Emotional Epiphany

Poetry condenses emotion into compact expression, enabling a few words to evoke vast emotional landscapes. A stanza may simultaneously convey grief, joy, awe, or longing, creating a layered resonance that prose rarely achieves. By employing metaphor, rhythm, and imagery, poetry amplifies feelings, transforming personal experience into universal insight. Its compressed form intensifies emotional impact, allowing readers to confront complex sentiments in structured, digestible fragments. Poetry also provides a symbolic outlet, permitting safe exploration of inner states and catharsis. This interplay of compression and expansion demonstrates poetry's unique ability to evoke profound emotional epiphanies from minimal linguistic input.

22. Sonic Sculptures

The sound of words in poetry is itself an instrument of meaning. Alliteration, assonance, consonance, and onomatopoeia sculpt auditory landscapes, conveying mood and movement beyond semantic content. The musicality of verse resonates with both conscious and subconscious perception, engaging emotional and cognitive faculties simultaneously. Even when literal meaning is abstract or ambiguous, sound patterns establish rhythm, tension, and resolution, creating an immersive auditory experience. Poets harness these sonic qualities to evoke imagery, provoke reflection, and manipulate emotional response, demonstrating that poetry is as much an acoustic art as a semantic one. Sound becomes a vessel of feeling, shaping perception before understanding.

23. Cognitive Cartography

Poetry maps abstract thought, emotion, and memory. Through metaphor, allegory, and narrative compression, poets chart landscapes of consciousness, presenting complex ideas in structured, evocative forms. The spatial and rhythmic organization of verse mirrors cognitive processes, offering insight into associative thinking, pattern recognition, and conceptual mapping. Readers navigate these mental terrains, encountering both clarity and ambiguity, structure and freedom. Poetry functions as a mental compass, guiding perception through symbolic terrains and emotional topographies. By externalizing inner landscapes into verse, poetry bridges subjective experience with shared understanding, enabling exploration of thought, feeling, and imagination in ways unique to its compressed and expressive form.

24. Resistant Rhythms

Poetry has historically served as a medium of resistance. Its memorability, oral tradition, and structural flexibility allow marginalized voices to challenge oppression, convey subversive messages, and preserve dissent across generations. Rhymed rebellion, coded allegory, and rhythmic satire evade censorship while resonating widely, reaching both public and private spheres. Poetic forms transform individual protest into collective consciousness, ensuring that social critique survives beyond immediate political contexts. Resistance poetry demonstrates how form, sound, and memory combine to empower marginalized communities. Its subtlety and elegance enhance its durability, making verse a uniquely effective instrument for societal reflection, critique, and transformation.

25. Paradoxical Simplicity

A poem's apparent simplicity often conceals profound complexity. Few words may encapsulate entire worlds of meaning, emotion, and reflection. This paradox challenges readers to engage actively, interpreting layers beyond the surface. Simple diction may evoke intricate imagery, while minimal structure can suggest vast emotional and intellectual terrains. The tension between clarity and depth is central to poetic power: accessible yet enigmatic, immediate yet timeless. By combining straightforward language with subtle resonance, poetry demonstrates its ability to communicate universals concisely. The paradoxical simplicity of verse engages mind, heart, and imagination simultaneously, revealing the extraordinary potential contained within the art of reduction.

26. Compressed Cognition

Poetry compresses vast ideas into concise expressions, distilling thought, narrative, and sensation into essential elements. Each word is weighted, each line intentional, forming a dense network of associations. This compression enhances cognitive engagement, requiring readers to infer, interpret, and connect multiple layers of meaning. The economy of language enables poetry to convey depth and complexity efficiently, stimulating both analytical and imaginative faculties. Through strategic condensation, poetry mirrors the brain's associative architecture, presenting abstract concepts in memorable, evocative forms. It demonstrates that brevity can amplify understanding, that linguistic reduction can reveal cognitive richness, and that concentrated language can expand perception exponentially.

27. Unconscious Undercurrents

Poetry engages the unconscious mind, eliciting imagery, emotion, and insight beyond rational comprehension. Symbolism, allegory, and metaphor operate on intuitive and instinctive levels, bypassing linear thought to evoke latent perceptions. Dreamlike associations and surreal imagery reveal internal landscapes inaccessible to conventional cognition, making poetry a medium for exploring hidden desires, fears, and imaginative potentials. By resonating with subconscious processes, poetry fosters self-awareness and introspection, connecting the conscious with the unconscious. This dual engagement distinguishes poetry from other literary forms, emphasizing its role as a conduit between instinct, imagination, and conscious reflection, illuminating the depths of human psyche.

28. Temporal Transmutation

Poetry manipulates time, stretching seconds into epics or condensing lifetimes into single moments. A sonnet can encapsulate decades of experience, while a haiku can freeze a fleeting instant in eternal resonance. This temporal flexibility allows poets to explore causality, memory, and perception in unique ways, creating simultaneity and temporal tension within verse. By bending chronological expectations, poetry fosters reflection on impermanence, continuity, and the relativity of human experience. Temporal transmutation enhances the reader's engagement, offering both compression and expansion of experience, and demonstrating poetry's capacity to reshape perception of time itself as a dimension of emotional and cognitive resonance.

29. Language Labyrinths

Poets inhabit the edges of language, experimenting with syntax, neologisms, and phonetics to extend expressive capacity. These linguistic explorations challenge conventional comprehension, revealing gaps, ambiguities, and possibilities within human communication. Wordplay, enjambment, and structural innovation create layered meaning, inviting readers into interpretive collaboration. By stretching, bending, and recombining language, poetry transforms words into flexible instruments of thought and emotion. This adventurous engagement with linguistic potential illustrates poetry's unique position as both exploration and articulation of consciousness, demonstrating that human expression is not fixed but fluid, expandable, and capable of infinite variation.

30. Ethical Echoes

Poetry serves as a vessel for moral and ethical reflection. Didactic verse, philosophical allegory, and social critique guide readers toward contemplation of values, justice, and human responsibility. Through vivid examples, symbolism, and emotional resonance, poetry teaches ethical lessons with subtlety and depth, shaping conscience alongside aesthetic appreciation. By dramatizing dilemmas, evoking empathy, and revealing consequences, poetry fosters moral imagination, helping individuals envision ethical possibilities beyond immediate experience. The ethical power of poetry lies in its capacity to connect emotion with reflection, narrative with principle, and art with social conscience, influencing both thought and behavior across generations.

31. Sublime Surges

Poetry evokes the sublime, eliciting awe, wonder, and existential reflection. Epic landscapes, cosmic imagery, or meditations on mortality create tension between human finitude and universal magnitude. Through rhythm, metaphor, and scale, poetry transforms perception, allowing readers to confront immensity, chaos, or transcendence with reflective engagement. The sublime impact generates both intellectual admiration and emotional reverence, bridging cognitive recognition with affective response. Poetry's capacity to evoke the sublime affirms its role as a medium for contemplating existence itself, positioning the reader simultaneously as participant and observer of forces larger than individual experience, and inviting profound meditation on human and cosmic dimensions.

32. Numerical Nuance

Poetry often integrates numerical precision, as in syllable counts, meter, and patterned rhyme schemes.

These quantitative structures govern flow, rhythm, and expectation, balancing predictability with artistic freedom. Structured repetition and variation create patterns that enhance memorability, aesthetic pleasure, and cognitive engagement. Mathematical awareness interacts seamlessly with emotional and imaginative resonance, demonstrating poetry's capacity to unify logic and art. The use of numeric symmetry underscores a universal aesthetic principle: human perception finds satisfaction in patterned form. By embedding numerical nuance, poetry exemplifies the harmonious coexistence of rationality and creativity, structure and spontaneity, order and innovation in literary composition.

33. Phonetic Philosophy

Poetry explores the philosophical potential of sound. Phonetics, rhythm, and tonal variation convey meaning independent of semantics. The choice of consonants, vowels, and cadence can evoke tension, harmony, or dissonance, creating emotional landscapes that operate beneath conscious understanding. Sound itself becomes a vehicle of thought, shaping mood, expectation, and cognitive response. Through phonetic manipulation, poets craft resonance that communicates experience, intention, and feeling before—or even without—literal interpretation. This interplay between form and perception reveals poetry's unique power: it transforms auditory patterns into philosophical reflection, demonstrating that language's sonic dimension is inseparable from its cognitive and emotional impact.

34. Cultural Codex

Poetry functions as a repository of cultural memory, encoding history, philosophy, and social norms. Epics, folk songs, and ceremonial verse preserve collective knowledge, transmitting values across generations. By embedding moral lessons, historical events, and philosophical inquiry within rhythm and narrative, poetry serves as both educational tool and mnemonic archive. It safeguards intangible heritage, ensuring that even when written records are scarce, cultural identity survives. This archival capacity emphasizes poetry's role beyond aesthetics: it is an instrument of civilization, a vessel for communal memory, and a living codex of human experience, preserving both linguistic form and socio-cultural essence across time and space.

35. Playful Paradox

Poetry delights in paradox, balancing solemnity with playfulness. Wordplay, puns, and ironic inversion create tension between meaning and expression, engaging intellect and imagination. The interplay of contradiction and coherence fosters interpretive flexibility, inviting readers to explore multiple layers simultaneously. Humor, whimsy, and clever construction coexist with gravitas, demonstrating poetry's capacity to entertain while provoking reflection. This playful paradox enhances aesthetic enjoyment while deepening engagement with content and form. By embracing ambiguity, poetry mirrors the complexity of life, teaching readers that meaning is often multifaceted, layered, and subject to interpretation, making each encounter with verse a dynamic cognitive and emotional experience.

36. Silences Speak

Silence in poetry is a profound expressive device. Pauses, line breaks, ellipses, and white space communicate mood, tension, and meaning as powerfully as words. Strategic absence creates resonance, encouraging readers to reflect, anticipate, and interpret. By juxtaposing sound and silence, poetry shapes rhythm, expectation, and emotional response. Silence acts as an invisible scaffold, giving weight to expression, allowing unspoken thoughts to emerge, and enabling readers to inhabit interpretive space. This interplay of presence and absence emphasizes poetry's subtlety: meaning is not only conveyed by articulation but also by restraint. Silence becomes a partner to words, amplifying and shaping poetic communication.

37. Cognitive Catalyst

Poetry stimulates cognitive growth and flexibility. Metaphor, ambiguity, and condensed expression engage inferential thinking, abstract reasoning, and associative imagination. Readers actively interpret and connect layers of meaning, exercising intellectual faculties. This cognitive activation enhances problem-solving, empathy, and mental adaptability. By requiring attentiveness, reflection, and imaginative engagement, poetry functions as a mental exercise, sharpening both analytical and creative capacities. Its layered complexity transforms reading into an active process of exploration, reflection, and insight. In this way, poetry operates as a cognitive catalyst, fostering intellectual and emotional development simultaneously while cultivating nuanced perception and deepened understanding of self and society.

38. Emotional Resilience

Engaging with poetry fosters emotional resilience. By confronting complex feelings—grief, loss, longing, or desire—through symbolic and metaphorical language, readers experience emotional catharsis. Poetry provides a structured space for reflection and processing, allowing individuals to explore intense or conflicting emotions safely. The imaginative distance created by verse enables recognition, understanding, and integration of feelings.

This therapeutic function strengthens coping capacity, empathy, and psychological insight. Poetry's capacity to mirror emotional experience while offering perspective and structure highlights its profound role in personal growth, emotional intelligence, and human well-being, demonstrating its enduring relevance as a source of both aesthetic and psychological nourishment.

39. Embodied Expression

Poetry is an embodied art. Recitation, chanting, and performance engage breath, rhythm, gesture, and intonation, merging intellectual, emotional, and physical dimensions. The act of vocalizing verse creates resonance within both performer and listener, fostering multisensory engagement. This embodiment enhances memory, comprehension, and emotional impact, reinforcing the intimate link between language and physiology. Poetry performed physically transforms perception, making the body a conduit for cognitive and emotional experience. This interplay of voice, motion, and thought underscores poetry's holistic nature, demonstrating that verse is not solely cerebral but also kinesthetic, sensory, and visceral, uniting mind, body, and spirit in a shared expressive act.

40. Interdisciplinary Interweaving

Poetry interacts with multiple disciplines, uniting art, science, mathematics, and philosophy. Ekphrastic verse interprets visual art, mathematically structured forms engage numeric reasoning, and philosophical poetry explores existential inquiry. These intersections highlight poetry's capacity to synthesize disparate knowledge systems, translating abstract concepts into evocative expression. By operating across disciplinary boundaries, poetry fosters holistic understanding and cross-modal thinking, demonstrating that art and intellect are mutually enriching. Its integrative nature enables poets to explore complex ideas in ways inaccessible to purely technical or purely aesthetic forms, establishing poetry as a uniquely versatile medium for cognitive, emotional, and imaginative exploration.

41. Mirror of Consciousness

Poetry reflects human consciousness itself. Its associative structures, nonlinear progression, and layered meanings mirror thought processes, perception, and memory. Readers encounter internal landscapes represented externally, providing insight into cognitive and emotional functioning. Verse captures the rhythm of reflection, the tension of ambiguity, and the interplay of conscious and unconscious processes. Poetry, therefore, serves as a mirror, not only of society and nature but of the mind itself. By engaging with layered, symbolic, and metaphorical expression, readers gain access to cognitive architectures and emotional rhythms, making poetry both a reflection and an exploration of human consciousness.

42. Ethics of Attention

Reading poetry cultivates attentiveness and moral sensitivity. Engaging with subtle imagery, nuanced language, and layered meaning requires focus, empathy, and interpretive care. This attentional discipline fosters mindfulness, ethical reflection, and enhanced awareness of others' experiences. Poetic engagement encourages readers to inhabit alternative perspectives, deepening moral understanding and compassion. By integrating aesthetic appreciation with ethical contemplation, poetry functions as both intellectual and moral exercise. Its attentive demands cultivate reflective thinking, empathy, and cognitive patience, illustrating that poetry's value extends beyond artistic pleasure to encompass the development of ethical and perceptual faculties in the reader.

43. Multi-Dimensional Meaning

A single poem simultaneously operates on literal, metaphorical, symbolic, emotional, and philosophical levels. Each line can contain multiple interpretations, engaging cognitive, imaginative, and affective faculties concurrently. This multi-dimensionality distinguishes poetry from prose, enabling concise communication of complex experience. Layers of rhythm, imagery, and metaphor interact to create resonance, depth, and subtlety. The interpretive richness invites repeated engagement, with each reading revealing new insights. Poetry's ability to convey multiplicity in compressed form exemplifies its capacity to capture the human condition, articulate abstract concepts, and explore existential themes, demonstrating a uniquely layered cognitive and emotional potential.

44. Temporal Compression

Poetry compresses time, enabling vast experiences to unfold within brief forms. Epics condense generations, lyrics capture lifetimes, and haiku suspend fleeting moments in eternity. By manipulating temporal perception, poetry facilitates reflection on impermanence, memory, and anticipation. This compression enhances aesthetic and cognitive engagement, emphasizing the relational nature of past, present, and future. Readers experience simultaneity of perception, accessing temporal layers within concise expression. Temporal manipulation underscores poetry's capacity to structure consciousness, balance brevity and expansiveness, and transform perception of duration, demonstrating its unique power to distill temporal experience into memorable, emotionally resonant form.

45. Emotional Multiplicity

A poem can evoke contrasting emotions simultaneously, such as sorrow and joy, fear and wonder, or longing and delight. By layering imagery, metaphor, and rhythm, poets create complex emotional landscapes. This multiplicity mirrors human experience, reflecting the inherent complexity and ambiguity of emotion. Readers navigate these interwoven feelings, cultivating empathy, reflection, and nuanced understanding. Poetry thus operates as an emotional laboratory, allowing exploration of conflicting or paradoxical states in a contained, symbolic space. Its capacity to elicit multiple, concurrent affective responses distinguishes it from other literary forms, emphasizing its depth and its power to convey the full spectrum of human feeling.

46. Hidden Hieroglyphs

Some poetry conceals meaning within structural or visual form. Acrostics, palindromes, and constrained writing encode narratives or symbolic patterns for attentive readers. This interplay between visible and hidden content enriches engagement, creating interpretive challenge and reward. Such cryptic design underscores poetry's ability to function simultaneously on multiple planes—linguistic, structural, symbolic, and aesthetic. The presence of hidden hieroglyphs reflects the poet's craft and invites readers into an active role of discovery, highlighting poetry's interactivity, layered meaning, and capacity for playful ingenuity while preserving profound depth beneath surface simplicity.

47. Cosmic Contemplation

Poetry often extends human consciousness toward the cosmos, exploring existence, mortality, and the universe's grandeur. Through metaphor, allegory, and imagery, poets interpret celestial and metaphysical phenomena, linking personal experience with universal reflection. This cosmic perspective fosters existential insight, humility, and awe, revealing humanity's connection to larger forces. Poetry's capacity to navigate the intimate and the infinite simultaneously transforms perception, allowing readers to engage with profound questions of meaning, purpose, and transcendence. It functions as a medium for contemplating the ineffable, synthesizing observation, emotion, and imagination to bridge the finite human experience with infinite cosmic reality.

48. Paradoxical Power

Poetry thrives on contradiction. It unites silence and sound, simplicity and complexity, ephemerality and eternity. Paradox energizes interpretation, creating tension and resonance that mirror the human condition. By embracing ambiguity, poetry challenges linear understanding and promotes cognitive flexibility. The coexistence of opposites within a single work fosters emotional depth and philosophical reflection, highlighting the art form's ability to reflect life's inherent contradictions. Poetry's paradoxical power transforms perception, revealing that understanding often emerges not from resolution but from the dynamic interplay of conflicting forces within the reader's consciousness.

49. Cross-Sensory Synthesis

Poetry frequently merges sensory modalities, producing synesthetic effects. Readers may "see" sounds, "hear" colors, or "taste" textures through carefully orchestrated imagery, metaphor, and rhythm. This cross-sensory synthesis enhances aesthetic richness and cognitive engagement, allowing multi-dimensional perception. The interplay of senses stimulates imagination, memory, and emotional response, creating immersive experiences that extend beyond conventional linguistic communication. By blending modalities, poetry demonstrates its capacity to expand perceptual horizons, transforming language into a vehicle for holistic, multi-sensory experience and illustrating its profound ability to evoke complex, integrated, and embodied human perception.

50. Human Universality

Poetry articulates universal aspects of the human condition. Across cultures and eras, it addresses love, loss, mortality, wonder, and existential inquiry. Its survival and persistence attest to its resonance with fundamental human experiences. Even when specific cultural references differ, the emotional, cognitive, and symbolic core of poetry transcends temporal and geographic boundaries. This universality allows readers to empathize across distance and time, fostering shared humanity. Poetry demonstrates that human consciousness is inherently poetic: it seeks meaning, rhythm, and pattern in experience, expressing and understanding itself through structured, creative, and evocative forms that resonate universally.

51. Living Archive

Poetry preserves collective memory as a living archive. Through verse, societies encode history, philosophy, emotion, and cultural identity. Each poem functions as a record of thought, feeling, and aesthetic sensibility, capturing the zeitgeist of its era while remaining accessible to future generations. Oral traditions, written verse, and performance ensure continuity of knowledge, values, and artistic expression. Poetry's archival function highlights its dual role as both art and cultural artifact, demonstrating that literary creativity and historical preservation are intertwined. By safeguarding collective memory, poetry sustains civilization's intellectual, emotional, and spiritual heritage, bridging past, present, and future.

52. Infinite Interpretations

Poetry invites endless interpretation. Each reader perceives meaning through personal experience, context, and imagination, making engagement a dynamic process. Ambiguity, metaphor, and layered symbolism ensure that a poem never exhausts its potential for understanding. Repeated readings reveal new facets, emotions, or insights, allowing the work to evolve in the consciousness of its audience. This openness exemplifies poetry's adaptability and timelessness. By fostering multiple perspectives and interpretive possibilities, poetry reflects the richness and complexity of human thought and experience. It demonstrates that literary meaning is co-created, contingent upon interaction between the text and the reader.

53. Empathetic Bridge

Poetry fosters empathy by enabling readers to inhabit others' experiences, emotions, and perspectives. Through figurative language, narrative, and imagery, readers encounter lives, cultures, and thoughts beyond their own. This imaginative identification cultivates emotional intelligence, social awareness, and compassion. Poetry's condensed, evocative form intensifies the experience, creating intimate connections between author, subject, and audience. By bridging differences of time, geography, and circumstance, poetry functions as a conduit for shared understanding. Its empathetic power demonstrates that literature can cultivate not only aesthetic appreciation but also moral and social consciousness, reinforcing the human capacity for empathy across boundaries.

54. Silence's Symphony

Silence within poetry amplifies meaning. Strategic pauses, caesuras, and line breaks create rhythm, tension, and reflective space. Absence becomes as communicative as presence, allowing unspoken thought to resonate. Readers participate in co-creating interpretation, filling gaps and engaging actively with the work. This interplay emphasizes the relational nature of poetry: sound and silence, word and pause, act in tandem to produce experience. Silence's symphonic quality demonstrates poetry's capacity for subtlety and depth, showing that meaning emerges not only through articulation but also through restraint, perception, and contemplative engagement.

55. Eternal Dialogue

Poetry establishes an eternal conversation across time, cultures, and individuals. Homer speaks to us through millennia, Rumi whispers across centuries, and contemporary voices respond. This dialogic continuity enables shared reflection, cultural transmission, and human connection. Poems persist because they articulate enduring experiences, emotions, and questions. Each reading becomes a moment of engagement, where historical and contemporary consciousness intersect. Poetry thus functions as both artifact and living communication, maintaining continuity of human thought, imagination, and feeling. Its capacity for timeless dialogue affirms its role as a universal, enduring medium through which humanity converses with itself and the cosmos.

Thus, it can be concluded that poetry is humanity's earliest and most profound language, a bridge between the tangible and the intangible, the temporal and the eternal. It is simultaneously a mirror, a map, a medicine, and a mystery. Its origins predate written language, yet it continues to evolve in digital, visual, and experimental forms. Poetry is at once a personal confession, a societal critique, and a universal hymn. In its infinite variations, it reveals truths about the cosmos, the human psyche, and the secret rhythms of life itself. Long before humans etched symbols on stone or inked them on parchment, poetry existed as song, chant, and spoken narrative. It was through oral tradition that societies preserved memory, morality, and myth. Poetic rhythm and repetition functioned as mnemonic devices, encoding cultural wisdom into melodies and cadences. In this sense, poetry was the first form of recorded history, predating the written word and serving as the scaffold of civilization itself. No human society has ever existed without poetry. From the Sumerian hymns of 2100 BCE to the griot traditions of West Africa, from Aboriginal songlines to Native American chants, poetry is a universal human impulse. It is not merely a linguistic artifact but a cognitive and emotional necessity, shaping our understanding of love, loss, mortality, and wonder. Epic poems like the Iliad, the Mahabharata, or Beowulf were designed to be recited aloud. Repetition, rhyme, and rhythm allowed oral poets to commit thousands of lines to memory. This demonstrates poetry's dual nature as both art and functional tool—a repository of collective knowledge encoded in musical patterns. Neuroscience shows that poetry engages regions of the brain responsible for language, emotion, and sensory imagery. Reading a poem stimulates empathy, enhances visualization, and evokes emotional resonance. In effect, poetry rewires cognition, blending analytical and affective faculties, making the experience simultaneously cerebral and emotional. Natural patterns such as the Fibonacci sequence, fractals in trees, and the symmetry of seashells resemble poetic structures. Many poets consciously emulate these rhythms, weaving the mathematics of nature into verse. Here, poetry becomes a mirror of cosmic order—a dialogue between human creativity and universal patterns. Poetry is not confined to language. Concrete poetry, visual verse, sound poetry, and performative gestures communicate through rhythm, form, and sensation. These nonverbal manifestations demonstrate that poetry is fundamentally about perception, pattern, and experience, not merely words on a page. The haiku distills the infinite into seventeen syllables. With economy of language, it evokes time, season, and emotion. In its brevity, the haiku proves that poetry's power does not depend on length but on precision, resonance, and depth. Poetry has therapeutic efficacy. Bibliotherapy and poetry therapy leverage verse to alleviate trauma, stress, and depression. Writing or reading poetry allows emotional release, reflection, and cognitive processing, demonstrating its healing potential beyond aesthetic pleasure. The nuances of sound, rhythm, and cultural reference resist literal translation. Each translation becomes a creative act, a rebirth of the poem in a new linguistic skin. This highlights poetry's intimate bond with language, revealing its sensitivity to phonetic and cultural subtleties. Poetry operates on multiple levels simultaneously: literal, metaphorical, symbolic, emotional, and philosophical. A single line may evoke a universe of interpretations, making poetry uniquely capable of conveying depth and ambiguity in ways prose rarely achieves. Forms like iambic pentameter or alexandrine rely on repeated patterns of stressed and unstressed syllables. Poetry blends art and mathematics, creating harmony through structured rhythm, proving that aesthetic beauty and numeric precision can coexist. Many endangered languages survive through oral poetry, chants, and folk songs. Poetry thus functions as a cultural memory, preserving linguistic diversity and connecting generations across centuries. Modernist and experimental poetry often emphasizes sound, rhythm, and form over literal meaning. This demonstrates that poetry can communicate feeling and perception independently of semantics, highlighting its multidimensionality. From Vedic hymns to Psalms, early poetry was a medium to commune with the divine. Poetry serves as a spiritual conduit, linking the human and the transcendent, providing a framework to explore metaphysical questions. Poetry reflects societal conditions, challenges authority, and records history. From ghazals and odes to protest and war poetry, verse has consistently served as both witness and critic, merging personal expression with collective consciousness. Metaphor-rich poetry stimulates mental imagery more intensely than prose. By juxtaposing unexpected concepts, poetry creates imaginative landscapes that engage the brain's visualization centers, resulting in a uniquely immersive experience. Acrostics, palindromes, and constrained writing forms embed meaning in structure or pattern. These hidden forms exemplify poetry's playful ingenuity and capacity to encode complexity beyond immediate perception. Poems written thousands of years ago still resonate today. Their themes—love, mortality, wonder—transcend temporal boundaries, affirming poetry's universality and its enduring relevance to human consciousness. Poetry thrives on paradox. It can be both simple and profound, universal yet intimate, structured yet free. These tensions create dynamic energy, allowing poetry to mirror the complexity of lived experience. Many poets evoke synesthetic experiences, blending senses: "tasting colors," "hearing textures," or "seeing sounds." This multisensory quality illustrates poetry's capacity to expand perception beyond ordinary boundaries. Unlike other art forms, poetry directly channels emotion through linguistic and rhythmic devices. Its condensed language amplifies emotional resonance, creating intense affective experiences in a few lines. Sound devices—assonance, alliteration, consonance, and onomatopoeia—enhance poetry's musicality. Even without meaning, the auditory dimension of poetry can evoke mood, tension, and rhythm, proving that sound itself carries expressive power. Poetry organizes experience through imagery, metaphor, and narrative compression. It allows readers to navigate abstract or emotional landscapes, providing mental frameworks for understanding complexity. From slave narratives to modern protest poetry, verse has historically served as a medium of resistance. Its concision and memorability make it a potent weapon against oppression, carrying subversive messages across time and space. A poem can appear simple while harboring immense depth. This tension between apparent simplicity and underlying complexity is central to poetry's allure and intellectual challenge. Poetry compresses vast experiences into minimal language. A single verse may evoke entire histories, landscapes, or emotional arcs. This compression mirrors the way memory works—selective, layered, and associative—highlighting poetry's ability to encode complex human experience efficiently. Poetry often taps the unconscious. Through metaphor, rhythm, and ambiguity, it evokes imagery and emotions inaccessible to ordinary thought. Surrealist and symbolist poets explicitly explored this, creating work that resonates on levels beneath conscious understanding, bridging the rational and the instinctive. Poetry can suspend, stretch, or condense time. A single line may evoke centuries, or an epic may render a single moment eternal. This manipulation of temporal perception illustrates poetry's unique capacity to engage human consciousness across multiple dimensions of time. Poets often operate at the boundaries of language, bending syntax, inventing words, and exploring sound. This experimentation highlights poetry's role in testing linguistic limits, expanding expressive possibilities, and exploring what cannot be fully said. Poetry often embodies moral and ethical reflection. From didactic verse to social critique, it interrogates values, justice, and human responsibility. In doing so, poetry becomes both art and conscience, shaping how societies imagine and enact ideals. Poetry has the power to evoke the sublime—the simultaneous feeling of awe and terror before vast, incomprehensible forces. Epic landscapes, existential musings, or reflections on the cosmos illustrate poetry's capacity to convey human smallness alongside grandeur. Mathematical patterns appear not only in meter but also in syllabic arrangement, acrostic design, and sequence-based constraints. This numeric dimension shows poetry's synthesis of intuition, beauty, and precise structure, merging the aesthetic with the mathematical mind. Phonetic patterns themselves carry meaning: soft vowels may evoke calmness, harsh consonants tension. Poetry exploits this natural sound symbolism to deepen emotional impact, showing that the form of words can be as expressive as their meaning. Poetry embodies collective memory and cultural identity. National epics, folk songs, and traditional verse transmit heritage, philosophy, and worldviews. Through poetry, societies articulate their values, fears, and aspirations across generations. Even in its gravest forms, poetry contains play. Wordplay, punning, rhythmic games, and playful structures demonstrate poetry's delight in language, inviting readers into a co-creative process of discovery and amusement. The spaces between words are as meaningful as the words themselves. Line breaks, pauses, and enjambment create tension, rhythm, and resonance, teaching readers that silence and absence are integral to understanding. Reading and writing poetry enhance cognitive flexibility. Metaphorical thinking, ambiguity tolerance, and pattern recognition are strengthened, demonstrating that poetry shapes not only emotion but intellectual agility. By engaging with metaphor and narrative compression, poetry allows readers to process grief, trauma, or anxiety in symbolic form. This cognitive-emotional exercise builds resilience, offering structured reflection on unmanageable feelings. Poetry is often performative, linked to breath, voice, and gesture. Recitation involves rhythm, timing, and bodily awareness, illustrating that poetry is an embodied art, experienced not just cognitively but physically. Poetry intersects with science, mathematics, philosophy, music, and visual art. From the structure of sonnets resembling fractals to ekphrastic poems responding to paintings, poetry dissolves boundaries between disciplines, demonstrating its integrative power. Poetic form often mirrors thought processes: fragmented, associative, metaphorical, and nonlinear. Stream-of-consciousness poetry, imagist verse, and free verse reflect the mind's natural rhythms, offering insight into cognitive processes themselves. Engaging with poetry cultivates attentiveness and empathy. Reading carefully, listening attentively, and interpreting subtleties teach moral and emotional sensitivity, making poetry a vehicle for ethical development. Beyond literal and metaphorical, poetry often conveys symbolic, philosophical, and existential layers. One line can function simultaneously as allegory, metaphor, and philosophical reflection, demonstrating the art form's multi-layered depth. Poems can make moments stretch or condense. A short lyric may contain a lifetime, while an epic may slow time to savor a single event. This manipulation of temporal perception is unique to poetry, allowing it to explore existence in extraordinary ways. A single poem may provoke multiple, even contradictory emotions. Humor intertwined with grief, beauty intertwined with horror—poetry allows for emotional simultaneity, capturing the complexity of human experience. Forms like acrostics, palindromes, or constrained writing embed secret codes, showing poetry's capacity for structural ingenuity. These hidden patterns create dual narratives—visible and concealed—demonstrating layered creativity. From metaphysical poems to cosmic imagery, poetry scales human experience to the universe. It contemplates stars, galaxies, and infinite space, linking intimate emotion to universal contemplation. Poetry thrives in contradiction: silence and sound, chaos and structure, ephemerality and eternity. This paradoxical nature mirrors human perception and the inherent tensions of reality. Poets often combine senses, creating synesthetic effects—"tasting colors," "hearing textures." This cross-sensory metaphor expands perception and demonstrates poetry's capacity to evoke experience beyond conventional limits. Ultimately, poetry is a testament to human universality. Across time, space, and culture, poetry articulates what it means to live, to feel, to reflect, and to transcend. Its survival across millennia proves that it speaks to the core of human consciousness. Beyond entertainment or aesthetic pleasure, poetry functions as a living archive of human thought, emotion, and culture. Epic poems preserve history, folk songs safeguard memory, and contemporary verse continues this tradition, documenting the evolving human condition. Each poem contains the potential for infinite interpretations. A reader in one century may perceive meaning entirely differently from a reader in another, proving that poetry is alive, evolving, and infinitely resonant. By articulating inner experience, poetry allows readers to inhabit others' consciousness. Through empathy, verse connects disparate lives and cultures, making it a tool for understanding, compassion, and global human cohesion. Even in what it does not say, poetry communicates. Ellipses, gaps, and pauses allow space for reflection, teaching that meaning exists not only in words but in absence. Finally, poetry is dialogue across generations. Homer speaks to us, Rumi whispers to our hearts, and contemporary poets converse with future minds. Poetry is an eternal conversation, bridging time, space, and consciousness itself.

Now, let's look into the interesting natures, features, characteristics and specialties of poetry and note down the significant facts about it as pointed below.

Origins & History:

1. Poetry is older than writing; the first poems were oral chants and songs.
2. The Epic of Gilgamesh (~2100 BCE) is one of the oldest surviving poems in human history.
3. Ancient Egyptian love poems date back over 4,000 years, showing that humans have always used poetry to explore emotion.
4. Poetry in many cultures was historically intertwined with music — the word "lyric" comes from the Greek lyre, a musical instrument.
5. Homer's Iliad and Odyssey were intended to be performed aloud, emphasizing rhythm and memory.
6. The first written laws, like the Code of Hammurabi, were sometimes phrased poetically to aid memorization.
7. Sanskrit poetry often used "*shlokas*," which encode philosophical truths in musical syllable patterns.
8. The haiku, a Japanese form, condenses the vastness of the world into just 17 syllables.

9. Many medieval European poets were also troubadours or minstrels, blending poetry with performance and storytelling.
10. Poetry was considered a sacred act in many ancient cultures — from Vedic hymns in India to Sumerian temple songs.

Language & Structure:

11. Poetry can exist without words: visual poetry and sound poetry convey meaning through form, rhythm, or gestures.
12. A single line of poetry often contains multiple layers — literal, metaphorical, symbolic, emotional, and philosophical.
13. Meter in poetry is a mathematical pattern, blending art with precision.
14. Alliteration, assonance, and consonance are not decorative — they affect memory, emotion, and perception.
15. Poetry can survive translation, but its musicality, rhyme, and subtle cultural references are often altered.
16. Acrostic poems hide secret messages within letters of each line, showing the encrypted intelligence of poetry.
17. Palindromic poetry reads the same forward and backward, blending symmetry with meaning.
18. Concrete poetry forms shapes with words, merging visual art and literature.
19. In oral traditions, rhyme and rhythm served as mnemonic devices for storytellers.
20. Poetry often manipulates time and space, condensing centuries or spanning entire universes in a single stanza.

Psychology & Neuroscience

21. Reading poetry activates multiple brain regions simultaneously — emotion, language, imagination.

22. Metaphors in poetry stimulate the brain's visualization centers more than literal text.
23. Poetry can reduce stress and improve mental health by creating emotional resonance.
24. Engaging with poetry improves empathy by helping readers inhabit different perspectives.
25. Rhythm and rhyme in poetry can influence heart rate and breathing, almost like meditation or music.
26. Studies show that brain waves synchronize with the rhythm of poetry when read aloud.

Emotion & Spirituality

27. Poetry is both intensely personal and profoundly universal – it speaks for the writer and for humanity simultaneously.
28. Poetry can convey what ordinary language cannot – ineffable emotions, subtle moods, and hidden truths.
29. Many poems act as prayers, bridging the gap between humans and the divine.
30. Poetry often transforms suffering into art – grief becomes grace, despair becomes devotion.
31. Some cultures believe words themselves have magical power, making poetry a conduit for spiritual transformation.
32. The repetition of phrases in poetry mimics chanting, evoking altered states of consciousness.

Nature & the Universe

33. Natural patterns like the Fibonacci sequence appear as poetic structures in shells, flowers, and galaxies.
34. Poetry often mirrors the rhythms of nature – tides, heartbeats, seasons.
35. Cosmologists sometimes describe the universe as a poem – a rhythm of energy and matter.
36. Poetry compresses the infinite into finite form, like capturing a universe in a stanza.

Cultural & Social Influence

37. Poetry has historically influenced politics, philosophy, and social movements.
38. Protest poems give voice to the marginalized and challenge authority.
39. Oral poetry preserves endangered languages and ancient traditions.
40. Folk songs and chants are often considered "uncredited poetry" shaping collective memory.
41. Some poetic forms, like the ghazal or the villanelle, are cultural vessels carrying centuries of heritage.

Creativity & Technique

42. Poetry can exist without literal meaning — it often prioritizes sound, rhythm, and imagery over semantics.
43. Free verse was considered revolutionary because it abandoned strict meter while still maintaining musicality.
44. Poetry is paradoxical: disciplined yet free, ephemeral yet eternal, personal yet universal.
45. The act of writing poetry can be therapeutic — it externalizes emotion and clarifies thought.
46. Constraints, like sonnets or haikus, paradoxically enhance creativity by forcing precision and invention.
47. Many poets claim that inspiration comes from "possession" — the poem writes itself through them.
48. Poetry can awaken synesthetic perception, making words feel like colors, sounds, or textures.

Time & Longevity

49. Poetry transcends time — ancient works like The Epic of Gilgamesh or Rumi's ghazals still resonate today.
50. Poems often exist in a "timeless now," beyond past and future.

51. The meaning of a poem can evolve over centuries, adapting to new readers while retaining its essence.

Mind-Bending & Paradoxical Facts

52. Poetry can exist without being written, spoken, or even heard — in thought, memory, or feeling.
53. The best poems are often paradoxical — they say the most by saying the least, and reveal through concealment.
54. Poetry is simultaneously ephemeral and eternal: a spoken line vanishes, yet its impact lasts forever.
55. Reading a poem aloud changes it, yet the essence remains intact — sound and silence co-create the work.
56. Poetry makes the ordinary extraordinary — every word, even the smallest, becomes capable of wonder.
57. The act of reading a poem can alter perception, making the world itself feel more alive.

Extraordinary Trivia

58. Some animals, like whales and birds, have been found to produce rhythmic sounds resembling primitive poetry.
59. Certain poems, like structured chants or prayers, were used as mnemonic tools in religious rituals.
60. The longest epic poem in the world, the Mahabharata, contains over 200,000 lines — yet it is still performed orally in parts.
61. Poetry exists even in numbers — mathematical elegance and symmetry can be read as poetic expression.
62. Haiku poets often write in a single breath, emphasizing the intimate connection between mind, body, and universe.
63. Poetry can exist entirely in code or pattern — e.g., binary poetry or DNA sequences interpreted as verse.

In brief, all the above ideas and specialties can be capitulated as below. Poetry existed before words; the first breath was already a stanza. Oral chants were humanity's first libraries — memory as melody. The Epic of Gilgamesh whispers eternity through clay tablets. Ancient hymns were prayers before poems, and poems before prayers. Stars themselves write in rhythm; the cosmos is verse. The first poets did not speak — they listened. Every heartbeat is a poem waiting to be discovered. The world was sung into being before it was named. Even shadows dance in stanzas. Poetry lives in the pause between the first word and the second. One word can contain an entire universe. The haiku holds infinity in seventeen syllables. Rhyme is memory echoing across time. Alliteration is the heartbeat of the tongue. Meter is mathematics that hums with meaning. Palindromes remind us that time itself can read backward. Concrete poetry turns the page into a stage. Visual poems prove that words can walk in shapes. Poetry preserves endangered tongues, whispering what prose forgets. A pause in poetry is a heartbeat between worlds. Poetry heals where medicine cannot reach. Metaphor is the neuron that sparks imagination. Every poem is a mirror for the reader's soul. Repetition in verse is prayer made audible. Poetry transforms despair into devotion, pain into prayer. Silence in poetry is as potent as sound. Reading a poem awakens parts of the brain prose cannot touch. Poetry can compress centuries into a single line. Words in a poem breathe where ordinary language suffocates. Every poem is both question and answer, cry and consolation. Poetry is disciplined freedom, structured spontaneity. The poet disappears to allow the poem to breathe. Inspiration is possession — the Muse writes through the willing vessel. Poetry is nothing, yet it contains everything. Every line is finite, yet it reaches into the infinite. Poetry reveals by concealing, teaches by silencing. A poem exists without being read, yet is never absent. Poetry is everywhere and nowhere at once. The more a poem is understood, the more it escapes. Poetry is the voice of the invisible made visible. Natural patterns — shells, spirals, waves — echo poetic form. Tides, heartbeats, and seasons pulse in poetic rhythm. Poetry compresses eternity into a syllable. Every poem is a constellation of thought. The wind can write better than the human hand. Sunlight on water is the oldest poem ever read. Poetry is the universe reflecting upon itself. Mountains and rivers have always been poetic, long before humans noticed. Even silence sings when read with attention. Stars punctuate the night like verses in cosmic rhyme. Poetry can challenge kingdoms and empires with a single line. Oral poetry preserved history before ink existed. Protest poems are the heartbeat of revolution. Folk songs are anonymous epics, living across generations. Poetry transcends culture but is rooted in it. Poets are often rebels disguised as scribes. Every civilization's soul survives in its poetry. Ghazals, sonnets, and haikus carry centuries of thought in compressed form. Poetry was once considered the foundation of education. The poet's pen is mightier than laws, yet gentler than breath. Poetry often exists without literal meaning. Free verse liberated form, yet demanded discipline of attention. Constraints, like sonnets or haikus, heighten invention. Every poem is born in the tension between feeling and form. Rhythm in poetry is consciousness made audible. Sound can carry meaning even before the mind understands it. Poetry often writes itself through the poet. The poem is less created than discovered. Poetry can awaken synesthesia — words tasting like colors, feeling like music. Poetry transforms time into texture, emotion into echo. The longest poem is still spoken in every breath we take. Poetry exists outside chronology; it inhabits the eternal now. A poem written thousands of years ago can feel freshly alive. Each reading is a rebirth of the poem. The past whispers through every stanza; the future waits in every line. Poetry endures because it engages the soul, not just the mind. Even ephemeral poems leave permanent traces in consciousness. Poetry can resurrect forgotten feelings. Every reading of a poem is a conversation with time itself. Poems are both memory and prophecy. Poetry can exist without words — in thought, gesture, or rhythm. Poetry is the art of making the invisible visible. It is both fleeting and eternal, ordinary and sacred. Poetry compresses infinite emotion into finite language. A single line can echo across lifetimes. Poetry allows humans to converse with the universe. Poetry is the music that all existence hums. Poetry is paradox in motion: saying and unsaying simultaneously. Reading a poem can alter perception, making reality itself feel miraculous. Poetry often reveals the unseen architecture of the mind. Even animals compose primitive poetry — whales and birds are nature's poets. Rhythm can synchronize brain waves, heartbeats, and soul. Poetry turns the ordinary into extraordinary, even sacred. Words become incantations when arranged with care. Poetry teaches without argument; it persuades through presence. Every poem is a cathedral of consciousness built from breath. Poetry can compress centuries of human experience into one stanza. The poet is simultaneously master and medium. Poetry is the universe learning to read itself through human awareness. Every poem is a reminder that life itself is an unending poem. Poetry is what remains when everything else is forgotten — the immortal whisper of being.

THE DISTANT DRUM AND THE DIVINE DIFFERENCE: POETRY AND PROSE

Poetry and prose are two languages of the same longing, two wings of the same word-bird that beats its way through the blue immensities of imagination. Yet their rhythms differ, their resonances diverge, their destinies dance to different drummers. Prose speaks — poetry sings. Prose explains — poetry exclaims. Prose walks with reason's measured feet — poetry soars on emotion's invisible wings. Prose is the river flowing straight toward comprehension; poetry is the fountain spiraling upward toward transcendence. The difference between them is not merely one of form or function, but of soul and spirit, of breath and beat, of silence and sound.

Prose moves through the mind like a well-planned city: orderly, logical, laid out in grids of grammar and governed by the laws of clarity. Poetry, by contrast, is the wilderness where words wander like wildflowers — fragrant, free, and fierce — refusing fences, rebelling against regularity, rejoicing in rhythm rather than reason. In prose, language is a servant to meaning; in poetry, language is the sovereign. The poet does not merely write; he weaves a world where sound is sense, and silence is a syllable unspoken yet understood. Prose tells us what happened; poetry reveals why it mattered.

If prose is the body of language, poetry is its soul — invisible yet indispensable. It is the pulse beneath the prose, the music behind meaning, the echo behind expression. Where prose appeals to the intellect, poetry seduces the intuition. It is not about communication, but communion — not about transmitting information, but transforming perception. The prose writer explains life; the poet experiences it anew each time he breathes a line. Poetry does not describe the world — it creates it. It does not narrate existence — it names existence into being, as if each word were a new genesis.

The difference is as old as the dawn of diction. When humanity first found its voice, it did not speak in sentences — it sang in syllables. Before there were chronicles, there were chants; before there were books, there were ballads. Prose is the younger child of civilization — rational, reliable, and responsible. Poetry is the firstborn of creation — passionate, primal, and prophetic. The earliest poets were not authors but oracles; they did not compose lines, they conjured light. Their verses were not written to please but to prophesy, to awaken in listeners the remembrance of their own forgotten divinity. Even now, when we read a great poem, something ancient stirs within us — the echo of that first utterance that shaped stars and souls.

Prose unfolds horizontally; poetry ascends vertically. The one is linear, the other luminous. In prose, thought proceeds logically from premise to conclusion; in poetry, thought leaps — like lightning between clouds of consciousness. Poetry is the language of paradox — where the moon burns and the sun weeps, where silence speaks and death dreams of dawn. In prose, the writer controls meaning; in poetry, meaning controls the writer. The poet becomes the vessel of a voice vaster than his own — he listens to what language wants to say through him. For poetry is not made; it is manifested. It is not a craft but a calling.

Prose often seeks to define; poetry dares to defy. The prose writer builds bridges between ideas; the poet burns bridges to reveal the fire beneath. Poetry revels in ambiguity, thrives in multiplicity, and blossoms in mystery. It teaches us that meaning need not be singular, that truth can be simultaneously simple and infinite. Poetry is the paradox of precision and passion, of brevity and boundlessness. A single line — "I wandered lonely as a cloud" — can contain within it all the loneliness and all the longing of the universe. Such is the power of poetic condensation — where the infinite is compressed into the intimate.

In prose, time moves forward; in poetry, time folds. The poem exists outside chronology — it is both ancient and unborn, both yesterday and tomorrow. When we read poetry, we do not merely read words — we relive worlds. Every poem is a reincarnation of emotion, an eternal return of rhythm. Prose belongs to history; poetry belongs to eternity. A great novel may capture an age, but a great poem captures agelessness. Poetry freezes the fleeting, crystallizes the moment, and immortalizes the mortal. Through it, we learn that beauty need not endure — it need only be.

Prose describes what we see; poetry reveals what we feel beyond seeing. It is the mirror of the invisible, the map of the immeasurable. Poetry paints with perception itself. A poem about rain is not merely about water falling from clouds — it is about longing descending from the heavens, about sorrow singing through silver threads, about the soul's baptism in its own becoming. Poetry turns weather into wisdom, and wind into whisper. It is not an imitation of life, but life's own illumination of itself through language.

The music of poetry is not ornamental; it is ontological. The rhythm of verse is the rhythm of the universe. The heartbeat, the tide, the turning of planets — all are poems written in motion. The poet merely listens and translates. Hence, while prose arranges ideas, poetry orchestrates existence. Its metre mirrors mortality, its rhyme reflects recurrence, its imagery invokes the invisible architecture of awareness. Every poem is an echo of eternity condensed into cadence.

When prose ends, its meaning ends; when poetry ends, its meaning begins. For poetry continues long after the last line — echoing in the heart, haunting the silence, hovering between understanding and unknowing. Poetry is not concluded; it is continued in consciousness. Its purpose is not closure, but opening — to make the reader not wiser, but wider, not informed, but transformed. It does not seek applause but awakening. The prose writer asks the reader to believe; the poet asks the reader to be.

To call poetry different from prose is thus to call light different from the lamp that holds it. Prose may contain poetry, but poetry transcends prose. It is language dreaming of itself — the mother tongue of the soul. It speaks to that part of us that cannot be taught but must be touched. It is both prayer and prophecy, both revelation and rebellion. Poetry is the rebellion of rhythm against rigidity, the revelation of resonance within reason. It does not seek to conform to grammar; it creates grammar anew with each breath of beauty.

And yet, poetry and prose are not enemies — they are eternal companions, complementary as day and night. Prose gives us the ground; poetry gives us the sky. Between them, language lives. Between them, the human heart learns to walk and to fly. The prose writer shows us the world as it is; the poet shows us the world as it could be — luminous, layered, and alive with meaning. If prose is our conversation with others, poetry is our conversation with eternity.

THE POWER OF POETRY: THE PULSE OF THE INVISIBLE

Poetry is not merely written; it is wrought – forged in the furnace of feeling, tempered by thought, and polished by perception until it gleams with the glow of the ineffable. Its power lies not in persuasion, but in presence; not in argument, but in awakening. It does not conquer minds; it kindles souls. Where politics wields power through command, poetry wields power through communion – the silent, sacred bond between word and wonder, between rhythm and revelation. The true poem is a pulse of the invisible – the unseen heartbeat of the universe heard through the human ear.

The power of poetry is alchemy. It turns anguish into art, despair into diamond, sorrow into song. Where others see ruins, the poet sees resurrection. Where the world wounds, poetry weaves. It heals not by hiding pain, but by hallowing it – transforming every tear into a testimony of tenderness. The poet's task is not to escape suffering, but to ennoble it; to distill from despair a drop of divine dew. Poetry redeems what life rejects, reclaims what reason forgets, and restores what time erases. Through it, the fragile becomes eternal, the fleeting becomes infinite. A single stanza can save a soul, for poetry is prayer disguised as sound.

Its power is not measurable in material terms; it is

metaphysical. Poetry can topple tyrants without lifting a sword, because it changes not structures, but souls. Empires fear poets more than armies, for poets plant invisible seeds — ideas that grow underground until they become forests of freedom. Words, once released in rhythm, cannot be repressed. They echo in eternity. When Shelley called poets the "unacknowledged legislators of the world," he meant not that they write laws, but that they reveal laws — moral, emotional, cosmic laws that govern the unseen kingdom of consciousness.

Poetry is the politics of the spirit, the revolution of revelation. It whispers truths that institutions cannot declare and sings sorrows that statistics cannot measure. It dismantles dogma by delight, and it disarms power by beauty. For beauty is a form of resistance — a refusal to accept the ugly as inevitable. Every poem that praises a flower protests against a world that forgets to see. Every poem that names a star defies the darkness that denies wonder. Poetry is rebellion wrapped in rhythm, revolution wearing roses.

But poetry's greatest power is transformation — the turning of the reader into the realized. The moment a poem truly touches us, we are altered. It expands our consciousness, refines our perception, and reawakens our sense of wonder. In its briefest lines, we feel eternity breathing. Poetry trains us to see again — to perceive not with the eye, but with the inward gaze. When Blake wrote, "To see a world in a grain of sand," he wasn't exaggerating; he was describing the very essence of poetic vision — the art of finding infinity in intimacy, universality in the unique. Poetry gives us second sight, the vision beyond visibility.

Poetry is the soul's mirror and magnifier. It reflects who we are while enlarging what we might become. It reminds us that language is not only for communication but for communion — not to say something new, but to feel something eternal. Its power lies in its paradoxes: it is at once fragile and fierce, minute and monumental, personal and planetary. A poem can whisper like a breeze and yet move mountains within minds. It is the quietest form of thunder.

Poetry's power is also cathartic — it cleanses the inner world. When we cannot speak our pain, poetry speaks it for us. It gives shape to the shapeless, sound to the silent, and dignity to despair. In a poem, our grief gains grace, our confusion gains cadence, our chaos gains clarity. It does not erase sorrow, but ennobles it into song. To write a poem is to rescue oneself from the abyss by weaving a bridge of words across it. To read one is to walk that bridge toward one's own becoming.

Poetry's music is medicinal. Its rhythm restores what reality fractures. Every metre is a heartbeat; every rhyme, a pulse. To read poetry aloud is to breathe with the universe — to synchronize one's soul with creation's cadence. That is why chants heal, hymns uplift, and mantras endure: the power of repetition becomes revelation. The poet becomes a priest of the ineffable, officiating the ceremony of sound and silence. For poetry is the sacrament of speech, where words are not merely used, but anointed.

Moreover, the power of poetry is timeless. It survives what civilization forgets. Empires crumble, but a line of verse endures. Cities vanish under sand, but a metaphor migrates across millennia. Homer's heart still beats in every sea song; Kalidasa's clouds still carry love across skies; Shakespeare's syllables still shimmer in the subconscious of speech. Poetry is immortal not because it refuses death, but because it embraces it — turning mortality into meaning.

Every poem is a resurrection: of memory, of moment, of mind.

The poet's power is not in having answers but in asking beautiful questions. Poetry does not instruct; it illumines. It teaches by transforming ignorance into intimacy — by turning confusion into curiosity, and curiosity into communion. It is the philosopher's flame made fragrant; the theologian's truth made tender. When philosophy fails to move the heart, poetry begins to speak. When science measures the world, poetry makes it meaningful. When logic limits, poetry liberates. For logic divides, but poetry unites; logic defines, but poetry divinizes.

In the theatre of thought, prose plays the role of the architect — designing structures of reason; poetry plays the role of the alchemist — transmuting sensation into symbol. It draws its power from paradox: the more personal it becomes, the more universal it feels. A poem about one person's love speaks to every lover; a poem about one's death speaks to every living being. Poetry's particularity is its universality. In describing the smallest thing with sincerity, it describes the whole cosmos. It proves that what is deeply felt is never isolated — it is shared, shining through the collective soul of humanity.

Poetry's power also lies in its brevity. The poem is a concentrated cosmos — an entire universe distilled into a drop of diction. It does in a few lines what prose cannot do in volumes. It carves eternity into syllables. It makes the abstract tactile, the invisible intimate, the ineffable incarnate. That is its secret sorcery — to suggest more than it says, to echo more than it utters, to awaken more than it explains. Poetry does not fill the mind; it fires it. It does not instruct the reader what to think; it invites the reader to feel what thinking cannot reach.

Every civilization that has ever lived has bowed before poetry. For when words lose wonder, worlds lose meaning. The poet is the pulse-keeper of civilization, reminding humanity of its own heartbeat. When the world grows mechanical, poetry restores the mystical; when language decays into noise, poetry revives its nobility. The power of poetry, then, is the power of remembrance — the remembrance of what it means to be human, and more than human. It recalls us to ourselves.

Poetry is the only language where silence speaks louder than sound. Between lines, within pauses, beneath metaphors — the unsaid breathes. And in that breathing, we hear the divine. That is poetry's greatest power: to make the unseen audible, the untouchable tangible, the infinite intimate. To read a poem deeply is to touch eternity with one's thought and to be touched by eternity in return.

Thus, poetry is not a luxury but a lifeline — a luminous thread tying the finite to the infinite, the flesh to the spirit, the word to the Word. It is not decoration but revelation; not a pastime but a path. It does not simply describe life — it redeems it, reminds it, reawakens it. It turns language into light, and that light into life.

THE ASPECTS OF POETRY: THE ANATOMY OF THE SUBLIME

Poetry, like the human soul, has many aspects — each a window into wonder, each a facet of its flaming unity. To speak of the aspects of poetry is not to dissect it, but to discern its divine anatomy — the pulse of rhythm, the breath of imagery, the heartbeat of emotion, the wings of imagination, the mirror of universality, the lantern of symbolism, and the light of spirituality. Each aspect is both independent and interwoven, creating that mysterious totality where language becomes luminous and meaning becomes musical.

Rhythm: The Heartbeat of the Infinite: Rhythm is the first language of existence — the eternal pulse that pervades all creation. The beating of the heart, the falling of rain, the rising of the sun, the whisper of waves — all are rhythm's reflections. Poetry does not invent rhythm; it recognizes it. The poet listens to the universe breathing and then breathes in harmony. In rhythm, poetry becomes music incarnate — a bridge between the seen and the unseen. It binds the listener's heartbeat to the cosmos, fusing flesh with infinity. A poem without rhythm is a body without pulse; a line without cadence is a life without breath. Through rhythm, poetry creates motion within stillness, continuity within chaos. It is rhythm that transforms a string of words into a spell, a sentence into a song, a thought into transcendence.

The rhythm of poetry is the rhythm of revelation — a metrical memory of the universe's own heartbeat.

Imagery: The Eyes of the Imagination: If rhythm is the pulse of poetry, imagery is its perception — the eyes through which the invisible world becomes visible. Imagery is not merely description; it is illumination. It makes the abstract tangible, the eternal intimate. Through imagery, poetry paints with perception itself — it transforms words into windows through which the soul glimpses eternity. A poet does not say "love"; he shows it as a rose trembling under dawn's first dew. He does not say "death"; he shows it as a candle flickering out while stars stand silently watching. Imagery is the art of seeing through symbols — a vision that transcends sight. In every great poem, we do not merely read pictures; we inhabit them. Imagery baptizes thought in color, baptizes emotion in form, baptizes silence in symbol. Through imagery, the inner and outer worlds meet and mirror one another. Thus, poetry becomes the painting of perception — art without canvas, vision without eye, beauty without boundary.

Emotion: The Blood of the Poem: No poetry without passion — for poetry is not the intellect's invention, but the heart's confession. Emotion is the blood that flows through every line, giving it life, warmth, and resonance. Without emotion, poetry becomes architecture without inhabitants. A true poem bleeds; it breathes; it burns. Emotion is not weakness — it is wisdom in its purest form, the soul's syntax. Through emotion, poetry bridges the personal and the universal. What one poet feels, millions recognize — for emotion is the universal tongue of humanity. The tears of Sappho, the rage of Whitman, the melancholy of Baudelaire, the wonder of Tagore — all flow through one invisible river of feeling that nourishes the world's soul. Emotion gives poetry its pulse and its power, its urgency and its eternity. In the trembling of a line, we feel the trembling of life itself. Poetry, then, is the art of feeling finely, of refining raw sentiment into sacred song.

Imagination: The Wings of the Word: If rhythm is the heartbeat and emotion the blood, imagination is the breath of poetry — the divine wind that lifts language beyond the literal into the luminous. It is through imagination that poetry performs its miracles: stones sing, stars speak, shadows shine. The poet does not escape reality; he extends it. Imagination is not illusion, but illumination — it reveals what reality hides. Through imagination, the poet creates what the world forgot to dream. The visionary sees what others see and yet sees more — sees the unseen soul within the seen surface. Blake's angels in trees, Shelley's skylark in the clouds, Keats's Grecian urn — all are embodiments of imagination's infinite reach. Imagination is the faculty of fusion — where opposites coexist and contradictions converse. It is where fire becomes flower, where silence becomes song. Without imagination, poetry is prose in disguise; with it, poetry becomes creation itself continuing.

Universality: The Soul's Symphony: Though every poem springs from a personal heart, the greatest poems transcend personality. They speak for humanity, not for a single human. This is universality — the soul's ability to sing in many voices through one mouth. The poet's "I" becomes the world's "we." In reading Dante, we descend through our own hells; in reading Li Bai, we drink from our own moonlit loneliness; in reading Neruda, we kiss our own unspeakable longing. Poetry proves that the private is public, that the intimate is infinite. Its universality is not the absence of individuality, but its expansion into empathy. The poet is not a solitary singer, but the spokesperson of the species — the one who translates collective feeling into individual form. In the universality of poetry lies its immortality: what speaks to all times never truly dies. Every great poem becomes a mirror in which humanity eternally recognizes itself.

Symbolism: The Soul's Secret Language: Symbolism is the sacred script of poetry — the hidden alphabet of the divine. Through symbols, poetry says the unsayable, reveals the unrevealable. A rose becomes love, a bird becomes freedom, a mirror becomes memory. Symbols are not decorations; they are doors — thresholds through which meaning passes from matter to mystery. They are the soul's shorthand, where infinite truths are written in finite forms. In symbols, poetry becomes mystical mathematics — the geometry of emotion, the algebra of awareness. Through them, the poem ceases to be a message and becomes a mystery. To understand a symbol is not to decode it, but to dwell within it — to let it resonate like a bell in the mind. Every true poem is a temple of symbols where meaning worships its own silence. The poet is both priest and translator — revealing through veils, speaking through silence, shining through shadow.

Spirituality: The Light Beyond Language: At its highest, poetry is spiritual — not in doctrine, but in depth; not in religion, but in revelation. Spirituality is poetry's final and finest aspect — the flame that fuses all others into one. Every poem, consciously or not, is a search for the sacred. The poet yearns to name the nameless, to touch the untouchable, to hear the hush beyond sound. In this sense, poetry is prayer with rhythm, meditation with metaphor, enlightenment written in echo. The spiritual aspect of poetry lies not in preaching divinity, but in perceiving divinity within everything — a dew drop, a dying star, a human tear. Through poetry, the soul speaks to its source. The poem becomes a moment of awakening, where words turn transparent and light looks through them. When language dissolves into luminosity, when thought becomes tenderness, when sound becomes silence — then poetry has fulfilled its final purpose: to return us to wonder.

Thus, in these seven aspects, poetry reveals its anatomy — a living organism of beauty and breath. Rhythm gives it motion; imagery gives it sight; emotion gives it feeling; imagination gives it flight; universality gives it voice; symbolism gives it soul; spirituality gives it light. Together they form the symphonic body of meaning, where matter and mystery dance in eternal embrace. Poetry is not a fragment of art — it is art's full flowering, the embodiment of consciousness becoming self-aware through sound.

THE PROSPECTS OF POETRY: THE FUTURE OF FEELING AND THOUGHT

The prospects of poetry are as boundless as being itself, for poetry is not a product of an era – it is the essence of existence. Civilizations rise and fall, technologies tremble and transform, languages are born and buried, yet poetry persists like a pulse that will not perish. It is older than alphabets and younger than tomorrow's dawn. While prose chronicles the progress of humanity, poetry chronicles the consciousness of humanity – and consciousness never ceases to evolve. Hence, the prospects of poetry are infinite, because it grows not by addition, but by awakening.

In an age obsessed with speed, poetry is slowness sanctified. While the world races toward mechanical immediacy, poetry invites us to pause, to perceive, to ponder. Its very rhythm resists the restlessness of modernity. The future may be filled with artificial intelligence and augmented realities, yet poetry will remain the one thing that is unaugmentable – for it deals not with data but with depth. Machines can mimic language but not longing; they can compute rhythm but not reverence. Poetry will survive technology not by competing with it, but by completing it – by reminding the digital world of its divine origins. When algorithms write, they will write lines; but when souls write, they will write poems.

The prospect of poetry in the digital era is paradoxically luminous. As information multiplies, meaning diminishes — and poetry will arise as the healer of this hollowing. The more we drown in data, the more we thirst for depth. Poetry, in its brevity and brilliance, provides that oasis of distilled meaning amid the deserts of distraction. In the future, when human attention becomes the rarest currency, poetry will be the purest investment — each line a condensation of consciousness, each word a world. The poem will become the antidote to overload, the slow flame in a flickering age.

The prospect of poetry also lies in its adaptability — its chameleon capacity to inhabit every medium. The spoken word, the digital screen, the holographic stage — poetry will evolve, but its essence will remain untouched. It will continue to be the voice of authentic emotion in an age of artificial expression. Even when the medium changes, the message will remain the same: the heart speaking to the heart, the soul singing to the soul. From papyrus to pixels, poetry's pilgrimage continues. The form will transform, but the flame will not falter.

More than any art, poetry prophesies. It foresees what philosophy cannot foretell. The poet stands at the edge of epochs, listening to the winds of the unborn world. Through metaphor, he divines the future in the mirror of the present. The poet is both historian and herald — recording what was, and revealing what will be. The prospects of poetry are thus prophetic — it will continue to guide humanity when science explains too much and understanding too little. When logic builds labyrinths, poetry will build light. The poet's pen will remain a compass pointing not north or south, but inward — toward the sacred center of being.

In a fragmented world, poetry's prospect is unity. It alone possesses the power to reconcile opposites – to weave together what politics divides, what progress forgets. It speaks a language before Babel, a universal tongue of tenderness. As humanity grows more connected technologically yet more disconnected spiritually, poetry will serve as the new spirituality of the secular – a shared sacrament of sound and silence that transcends creed, class, and country. The poem will become a global prayer whispered in a thousand tongues yet meaning the same – the affirmation that all hearts beat to the same rhythm of wonder.

Poetry's future is also ecological – it will emerge as the voice of the voiceless earth. As climate and consciousness collapse into crisis, poetry will rise as nature's own narration. The poet will become the priest of the planet, translating the language of leaves, rivers, and rain into human understanding. In the future, poetry will not only describe landscapes; it will defend them. It will not merely praise the moon; it will protect it. The new poetry will be both elegy and evangel – mourning what we have lost while awakening what we can still save. The poem will become the planet's prayer.

The prospects of poetry also reside in its pedagogical power. As education becomes mechanical, poetry will remain the mystical mentor of the mind. In a world obsessed with answers, poetry will keep asking the eternal questions. It will teach not by information but by initiation – awakening wonder, wisdom, and wholeness in those who listen. Future classrooms will rediscover that to learn a poem by heart is to learn how to have a heart. The prospects of poetry in pedagogy are revolutionary – it can restore imagination where instruction has become imitation.

And what of poetry's place in philosophy? The future thinker will find in poetry the final philosophy — the union of thought and feeling, logic and lyricism, science and spirit. For philosophy seeks truth through reason, but poetry finds truth through reverie. The coming century will not separate them but synthesize them. The philosopher will become a poet of ideas; the poet, a philosopher of emotion. In that union, humanity will discover a new way of knowing — not through division, but through delight.

The prospects of poetry in the social realm are equally profound. As the world becomes louder with slogans, poetry will whisper the truths that slogans cannot contain. As political speech grows more divisive, poetic speech will become the language of reconciliation. The future may be filled with noise, but poetry will remain the music beneath it — reminding us that communication without communion is chaos. Poetry will continue to be the conscience of civilization, calling humanity back from hubris to humility, from profit to purpose, from progress to presence.

Economically, poetry will never be powerful — but existentially, it will always be priceless. Its value cannot be measured in markets, for it deals in meaning, not money. It gives more than it gains, enlightens more than it earns. Its economy is one of grace: a single line can feed generations of souls. In a world that quantifies everything, poetry will remain the last sanctuary of the unquantifiable — proof that not all that matters can be measured, and not all that can be measured matters.

The prospects of poetry also reach inward, into psychology. As machines master memory and mimic emotion, poetry will remind us what it truly means to feel. The poem will be the mirror in which the human psyche sees its own sacred silhouette. It will continue to heal trauma, transform loneliness, and transmute despair into dialogue. Future therapy will rediscover what ancient bards already knew — that healing begins when the heart speaks in rhythm. Poetry will not perish; it will become medicine.

And beyond all these, the ultimate prospect of poetry lies in its immortality. Every age declares poetry dying; every age finds it resurrected, radiant, renewed. Poetry cannot die because it is not a form — it is a force. It is the force that first taught humanity to speak, to sing, to symbolize, to sense the sacred. It will remain long after the last library has turned to dust, because poetry does not live in paper — it lives in people. Wherever a soul feels beauty and cannot explain it, poetry is reborn. Wherever a heart breaks and seeks meaning, poetry returns. Wherever a child sees a star and wonders, poetry begins again.

Thus, the prospects of poetry are as eternal as eternity itself. It will not vanish with vanishing civilizations; it will voyage through them. It is the spirit of expression, the memory of meaning, the light that language carries through darkness. As long as breath exists, poetry exists — for poetry is the breath made visible, the silence made sacred, the finite made infinite.

THE INTROSPECTS OF POETRY: THE SOUL LOOKING AT ITSELF

If the aspects of poetry describe its body, and the prospects of poetry its destiny, then the introspects of poetry reveal its soul — that secret sanctuary where word and wonder merge, where the poem becomes aware of its own divinity. To introspect is to look inward — to gaze into the mirror of meaning until meaning gazes back. Poetry, when introspective, becomes a meditation upon itself: the art aware of its own heartbeat, the song listening to its own silence. The introspects of poetry are its inner mirrors — where rhythm reflects thought, and thought reflects eternity.

At its deepest, poetry is the consciousness of consciousness — the awareness that language can become luminous, that silence can speak through sound. When a poet writes, he does not merely express emotion; he excavates existence. He digs into the strata of self until he strikes the spring of spirit. In that sacred depth, the poem is born not from intellect but from intuition — a whisper from the infinite translated into syllables. The introspective poet becomes both seeker and scripture, both listener and language. Poetry becomes a pilgrimage of perception — from the surface of speech to the sanctum of silence.

To introspect poetry is to realize that every poem is a reflection of the poet's inner weather — storms of sorrow, dawns of delight, eclipses of doubt, and the sudden sunbursts of revelation. The page becomes a sky; the words become clouds drifting through consciousness. Each poem is a climate of the soul — its winds, its rains, its radiant aftermath. Through introspection, the poet does not flee from himself but faces himself. Poetry becomes the mirror of meditation, where the writer sees not only what he feels, but what feeling itself is.

The introspection of poetry begins where explanation ends. It is born from the poet's encounter with the ineffable — that trembling threshold where thought dissolves into transcendence. In that hush, the poet listens not to the noise of the world but to the whisper of the within. This is the sacred solitude where poetry and prayer become indistinguishable. The introspective poet does not invent beauty; he invites it. He becomes a vessel, a voice through which the universe utters its own understanding. The more he empties himself, the more he is filled — with music, with meaning, with the mystery of being.

To introspect poetry is to discover that language is both a ladder and a labyrinth. Each word leads us higher toward revelation, yet also deeper into wonder. The poet climbs and circles, ascends and descends, until he realizes that the goal is not to reach but to realize — that poetry's perfection lies not in completion, but in contemplation. In that moment, the poet becomes aware that poetry is not something he writes but something that writes through him. He is the pen in the hand of the ineffable.

The introspective dimension of poetry reveals its most paradoxical truth — that the poem is not about the world, but about awareness of the world. It does not describe life; it deepens our consciousness of living. Every great poem is a mirror turned inward — reflecting not reality, but the soul perceiving reality. The introspective poet understands that to change one's perception is to change the world itself. Thus, poetry becomes both revelation and revolution — not outwardly, but inwardly. It revolutionizes the reader's relation to reality by making perception sacred again.

The introspection of poetry also awakens the poet to his responsibility — to be honest to the inner voice, to write not for approval but for authenticity. The introspective poet does not seek to please the world; he seeks to pierce it — to penetrate its illusions and reveal its inner light. He knows that every poem is a confession of consciousness, a revelation of what the mind dares to feel and the heart dares to say. Through this inner honesty, poetry becomes purification — a fire that burns away falsity, leaving only essence. In this fire, both poet and poem are refined into truth.

But the introspection of poetry is not solitary; it is shared solitude. When a poet writes sincerely, his inward gaze becomes the mirror for every mind. The reader enters the poet's inner sanctum and finds his own reflection there. The introspective poem thus becomes a communion of consciousness — two souls meeting in silence through sound. This is poetry's miracle: what begins as one person's inward whisper becomes humanity's collective echo. The introspective becomes universal, the personal becomes planetary, and the poet's solitude becomes the reader's sanctuary.

To introspect poetry is also to acknowledge its mystery. The more we understand it, the more it escapes understanding. Like the ocean reflecting the moon, poetry reveals only what light touches, while hiding infinite depths below. The introspective poet accepts this — that the poem's beauty lies in its unexplainability. It is not a riddle to be solved but a radiance to be seen. It does not answer questions; it awakens them. The more we dwell within a poem, the more it dwells within us. We begin to see that poetry is not an act but a state — a mode of being where perception and creation become one.

The introspective power of poetry also lies in its self-awareness of form. Every poet eventually realizes that the poem itself is alive — that it grows, breathes, and resists control. The lines arrange themselves like living organisms, the rhythm reshapes itself as revelation dictates. The introspective poet learns humility before the living word — he does not force meaning but follows it. He listens for where the line wants to go, where the pause wishes to fall, where silence desires to sing. In that surrender, the poet discovers that true creation is collaboration with the cosmos.

And in its deepest introspection, poetry recognizes its divine origin. It realizes that it is not merely human art but cosmic expression — that the universe itself is poetry written in matter and motion. The stars are metaphors; the seas are symbols; the seasons are stanzas in an eternal poem of being. Every leaf is a lyric, every wave a word, every dawn a declaration. The introspective poet reads creation as scripture and writes as its echo. Poetry thus becomes a dialogue between the finite and the infinite — the soul of the universe speaking to itself through human hearts.

The introspective destiny of poetry is silence — not as absence but as arrival. The poem begins in silence, moves through sound, and returns to silence, transformed. It teaches us to listen — not just to language but to life. The poet, after all his words, bows before the unsayable. For beyond rhythm and rhyme, beyond metaphor and metre, there remains that radiant stillness where all poetry originates and all poets disappear. In that silence, the poem ceases to be written and begins to be.

When poetry looks within, it sees eternity looking back. It realizes that its true subject has always been the same: the mystery of existence itself. Every word written in wonder is an offering to that mystery. Every reader who pauses in awe becomes part of that offering. The introspect of poetry, then, is the final fusion — where creation and creator, word and world, silence and song, become one seamless breath.

THE EPILOGUE
THE ETERNAL ECHO

And so, poetry stands — ancient yet unborn, fragile yet fierce, finite yet infinite. It differs from prose as fire from flame, as star from sky, as silence from speech. Its power is transformation, its aspect is beauty, its prospect is immortality, its introspect is divinity. Poetry is not what we read; it is what reads us. It listens through our listening, dreams through our dreaming, and continues long after the final line fades.

For when the last word falls into silence, poetry remains —

as the echo of existence,
the pulse of the invisible,
the light that language leaves behind.

It is not an art — it is the awareness of art. It is not an expression — it is existence expressing itself. Poetry is the mirror in which God beholds Himself through the eyes of man.

Additional Works by the Same Author:

- Aspects of Criticism (Literary Criticism)
- Dispersed Meditation (Literary Criticism)
- Echoes of Emptiness (Poetry)
- The Black Feather (Edited Poetry Anthology)
- The Weighty Words (Edited Poetry Anthology)
- *Ars Abscondita* (Edited Poetry Anthology)
- The Waste Land: An Introspective Commentary (Literary Criticism)
- T.S. Eliot's The Waste Land: A Formal Introduction (Literary Criticism)
- *Eekshyaa-Beekshyaa- Sameekshyaa* (Literary Criticism)
- *Toolee O Tulanaa* (Literary Criticism)
- *Sameekshyaa Saurabha* (Literary Criticism)
- *Sameekshyaa Gauraba* (Literary Criticism)
- *Sameekshyaa Prakaasha* (Literary Criticism)
- *Sameekshyaaa Sanchayana* (Literary Criticism)
- *Sameekshyaa Sandarshana* (Literary Criticism)
- *Chetanaara Chitralipi* (Literary Criticism)
- *Bhaashaa O Saahitya* (Literary Criticism)
- *Bhaasotpati Matabaada* (Literary Criticism)
- *Kaalapurusha* (Literary Criticism)
- *Tulanaatmaka Saahityara Bhitti O Bhaaratee* (Literary Criticism)
- *Abhishapta Pruthibee* (Poetry)

- *Soorjya Uinle Raati* (Poetry)
- *Saandhya Bhramana* (Poetry)
- *Brahmaasmi* (Poetry)
- *Soham* (Poetry)
- *Tathaapi Assiba Pheri* (Poetry)
- *Gopapura O Anyanya Kabitaa* (Poetry)
- *Ghunakeeta* (Free Form)
- *Drusti O Darshana* (Essay)

And few other books.

Black Eagle Books

www.blackeaglebooks.org
info@blackeaglebooks.org

Black Eagle Books, an independent publisher, was founded as a nonprofit organization in April, 2019. It is our mission to connect and engage the Indian diaspora and the world at large with the best of works of world literature published on a collaborative platform, with special emphasis on foregrounding Contemporary Classics and New Writing.